TIP 63

MEDICATIONS F[OR]

Treatment Improvement Protocol 63

For Healthcare and Addiction Professionals, Policymakers, Patients, and Families

This TIP reviews three Food and Drug Administration-approved medications for opioid use disorder treatment—methadone, naltrexone, and buprenorphine—and the other strategies and services needed to support people in recovery.

TIP Navigation

Executive Summary
For healthcare and addiction professionals, policymakers, patients, and families

Part 1: Introduction to Medications for Opioid Use Disorder Treatment
For healthcare and addiction professionals, policymakers, patients, and families

Part 2: Addressing Opioid Use Disorder in General Medical Settings
For healthcare professionals

Part 3: Pharmacotherapy for Opioid Use Disorder
For healthcare professionals

Part 4: Partnering Addiction Treatment Counselors With Clients and Healthcare Professionals
For healthcare and addiction professionals

Part 5: Resources Related to Medications for Opioid Use Disorder
For healthcare and addiction professionals, policymakers, patients, and families

Contents

EXECUTIVE SUMMARY

Foreword .... ES-iii

Introduction ES-1

Overall Key Messages ES-1

Content Overview ES-3

Notes ES-6

TIP Development Participants ES-8

Publication Information ES-12

PART 1: AN INTRODUCTION TO MEDICATIONS FOR THE TREATMENT OF OPIOID USE DISORDER

The Approach to OUD Care 1-1

Overview of Medications for OUD 1-3

Duration of Treatment With OUD Medication 1-8

Treatment Settings 1-9

Challenges to Expanding Access to OUD Medication 1-9

Resources 1-10

Notes 1-11

PART 2: ADDRESSING OPIOID USE DISORDER IN GENERAL MEDICAL SETTINGS

Scope of the Problem 2-1

Screening 2-1

Assessment 2-8

Treatment Planning or Referral 2-17

Resources 2-28

Appendix 2-32

Notes 2-39

PART 3: PHARMACOTHERAPY FOR OPIOID USE DISORDER

Pharmacotherapy for Opioid Use Disorder 3-1

Chapter 3A: Overview of Pharmacotherapy for Opioid Use Disorder 3-5

Chapter 3B: Methadone 3-15

Chapter 3C: Naltrexone 3-35

Chapter 3D: Buprenorphine 3-49

Chapter 3E: Medical Management Strategies for Patients
Taking OUD Medications in Office-Based Settings 3-79

Chapter 3F: Medical Management of Patients Taking OUD
Medications in Hospital Settings 3-99

PART 4: PARTNERING ADDICTION TREATMENT COUNSELORS WITH CLIENTS AND HEALTHCARE PROFESSIONALS

Overview and Context 4-1

Quick Guide to Medications 4-12

Counselor–Prescriber Communications 4-18

Creation of a Supportive Counseling Experience 4-20

Other Common Counseling Concerns 4-34

Notes 4-37

PART 5: RESOURCES RELATED TO MEDICATIONS FOR OPIOID USE DISORDER

General Resources 5-1

Resources for Counselors and Peer Providers 5-10

Resources for Clients and Families 5-11

Provider Tools and Sample Forms 5-17

Glossary of TIP Terminology 5-57

Notes 5-60

This page intentionally left blank.

TIP 63 — MEDICATIONS FOR OPIOID USE DISORDER

Executive Summary
For Healthcare and Addiction Professionals, Policymakers, Patients, and Families

The Executive Summary of this **Treatment Improvement Protocol** provides an overview on the use of the three Food and Drug Administration-approved medications used to treat opioid use disorder—methadone, naltrexone, and buprenorphine—and the other strategies and services needed to support recovery.

TIP Navigation

Executive Summary
For healthcare and addiction professionals, policymakers, patients, and families

Part 1: Introduction to Medications for Opioid Use Disorder Treatment
For healthcare and addiction professionals, policymakers, patients, and families

Part 2: Addressing Opioid Use Disorder in General Medical Settings
For healthcare professionals

Part 3: Pharmacotherapy for Opioid Use Disorder
For healthcare professionals

Part 4: Partnering Addiction Treatment Counselors With Clients and Healthcare Professionals
For healthcare and addiction professionals

Part 5: Resources Related to Medications for Opioid Use Disorder
For healthcare and addiction professionals, policymakers, patients, and families

Substance Abuse and Mental Health Services Administration

SAMHSA

www.samhsa.gov • 1-877-SAMHSA-7 (1-877-726-4727)

TIP 63 MEDICATIONS FOR OPIOID USE DISORDER—Executive Summary

EXECUTIVE SUMMARY

Foreword .... ES-iii
Introduction ES-1
Overall Key Messages ES-1
Content Overview ES-3
Notes ES-6
TIP Development Participants ES-8
Publication Information ES-12

Foreword

The Substance Abuse and Mental Health Services Administration (SAMHSA) is the U.S. Department of Health and Human Services agency that leads public health efforts to advance the behavioral health of the nation. SAMHSA's mission is to reduce the impact of substance abuse and mental illness on America's communities.

The Treatment Improvement Protocol (TIP) series fulfills SAMHSA's mission by providing science-based best-practice guidance to the behavioral health field. TIPs reflect careful consideration of all relevant clinical and health service research, demonstrated experience, and implementation requirements. Select nonfederal clinical researchers, service providers, program administrators, and patient advocates comprising each TIP's consensus panel discuss these factors, offering input on the TIP's specific topic in their areas of expertise to reach consensus on best practices. Field reviewers then assess draft content.

The talent, dedication, and hard work that TIP panelists and reviewers bring to this highly participatory process have helped bridge the gap between the promise of research and the needs of practicing clinicians and administrators to serve, in the most scientifically sound and effective ways, people in need of behavioral health services. We are grateful to all who have joined with us to contribute to advances in the behavioral health field.

Elinore F. McCance-Katz, M.D., Ph.D.
Assistant Secretary for Mental Health and Substance Use
SAMHSA

A. Kathryn Power, M.Ed.
Acting Director
Center for Substance
 Abuse Treatment
SAMHSA

Frances M. Harding
Director
Center for Substance
 Abuse Prevention
SAMHSA

Paolo del Vecchio, M.S.W.
Director
Center for Mental
 Health Services
SAMHSA

Daryl W. Kade, M.A.
Director
Center for Behavioral
 Health Statistics and
 Quality
SAMHSA

This page intentionally left blank.

TIP 63 MEDICATIONS FOR OPIOID USE DISORDER

Executive Summary

The goal of treatment for opioid addiction or opioid use disorder (OUD) is remission of the disorder leading to lasting recovery. Recovery is a process of change through which individuals improve their health and wellness, live self-directed lives, and strive to reach their full potential.[1] This Treatment Improvement Protocol (TIP) reviews the use of the three Food and Drug Administration (FDA)-approved medications used to treat OUD—methadone, naltrexone, and buprenorphine—and the other strategies and services needed to support recovery for people with OUD.

Introduction

Our nation faces a crisis of overdose deaths from opioids, including heroin, illicit fentanyl, and prescription opioids. These deaths represent a mere fraction of the total number of Americans harmed by opioid misuse and addiction. Many Americans now suffer daily from a chronic medical illness called "opioid addiction" or OUD (see the Glossary in Part 5 of this TIP for definitions). Healthcare professionals, treatment providers, and policymakers have a responsibility to expand access to evidence-based, effective care for people with OUD.

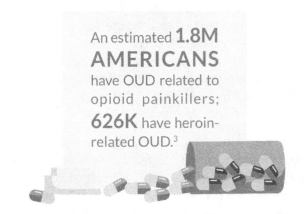

An estimated **1.8M AMERICANS** have OUD related to opioid painkillers; **626K** have heroin-related OUD.[3]

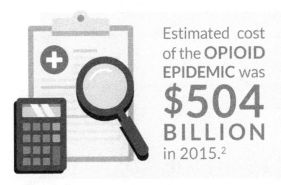

Estimated cost of the **OPIOID EPIDEMIC** was **$504 BILLION** in 2015.[2]

The TIP is divided into parts so that readers can easily find the material they need. Part 1 is a general introduction to providing medications for OUD and issues related to providing that treatment. Some readers may prefer to go directly to those parts most relevant to their areas of interest, but everyone is encouraged to read Part 1 to establish a shared understanding of key facts and issues covered in detail in this TIP.

Following is a summary of the TIP's overall main points and brief summaries of each of the five TIP parts.

Overall Key Messages

Addiction is a chronic, treatable illness. Opioid addiction, which generally corresponds with moderate to severe forms of OUD, often requires continuing care for effective treatment rather than an episodic, acute-care treatment approach.

An expert panel developed the TIP's content based on a review of the literature and on their extensive experience in the field of addiction treatment. Other professionals also generously contributed their time and commitment to this project.

ES-1

Opioid overdose caused **42,249 DEATHS** nationwide in 2016— this exceeded the # caused by motor vehicle crashes.[4,5]

General principles of good care for chronic diseases can guide OUD treatment. Approaching OUD as a chronic illness can help providers deliver care that helps patients stabilize, achieve remission of symptoms, and establish and maintain recovery.

Patient-centered care empowers patients with information that helps them make better treatment decisions with the healthcare professionals involved in their care. Patients should receive information from their healthcare team that will help them understand OUD and the options for treating it, including treatment with FDA-approved medication.

Patients with OUD should have access to mental health services as needed, medical care, and addiction counseling, as well as recovery support services, to supplement treatment with medication.

The words you use to describe OUD and an individual with OUD are powerful. The TIP defines, uses, and encourages providers to adopt terminology that will not reinforce prejudice, negative attitudes, or discrimination.

There is no "one size fits all" approach to OUD treatment. Many people with OUD benefit from treatment with medication for varying lengths of time, including lifelong treatment. Ongoing outpatient medication treatment for OUD is linked to better retention and outcomes than treatment without medication. Even so, some people stop using opioids on their own; others recover through support groups or specialty treatment with or without medication.

The science demonstrating the effectiveness of medication for OUD is strong. For example, methadone, extended-release injectable naltrexone (XR-NTX), and buprenorphine were each found to be more effective in reducing illicit opioid use than no medication in randomized clinical trials, which are the gold standard for demonstrating efficacy in clinical medicine.[6,7,8,9,10] Methadone and buprenorphine treatment have also been associated with reduced risk of overdose death.[11,12,13,14,15]

This doesn't mean that remission and recovery occur only through medication. Some people achieve remission without OUD medication, just as some people can manage type 2 diabetes with exercise and diet alone. But just as it is inadvisable to deny people with diabetes the medication they need to help manage their illness, it is also not sound medical practice to deny people with OUD access to FDA-approved medications for their illness.

Medication for OUD should be successfully integrated with outpatient and residential treatment. Some patients may benefit from different levels of care at different points in their lives, such as outpatient counseling, intensive outpatient treatment, inpatient treatment, or long-term therapeutic communities. Patients treated in these settings should have access to OUD medications.

2.1 MILLION people in the U.S., ages 12 and older, had OUD involving **PRESCRIPTION OPIOIDS, HEROIN,** or both in 2016.[16]

Patients treated with medications for OUD can benefit from individualized psychosocial supports. These can be offered by patients' healthcare providers in the form of medication management and supportive counseling and/or by other providers offering adjunctive addiction counseling, recovery coaching, mental health services, and other services that may be needed by particular patients.

Expanding access to OUD medications is an important public health strategy.[17] The gap between the number of people needing opioid addiction treatment and the capacity to treat them with OUD medication is substantial. In 2012, the gap was estimated at nearly 1 million people, with about 80 percent of opioid treatment programs (OTPs) nationally operating at 80 percent capacity or greater.[18]

Improving access to treatment with OUD medications is crucial to closing the wide gap between treatment need and treatment availability, given the strong evidence of effectiveness for such treatments.[19]

Data indicate that medications for OUD are cost effective and cost beneficial.[20,21]

OPIOID-RELATED **EMERGENCY DEPARTMENT** visits nearly doubled from 2005–2014.[22]

Content Overview

The TIP is divided into parts to make the material more accessible according to the reader's interests.

Part 1: Introduction to Medications for Opioid Use Disorder Treatment

This part lays the groundwork for understanding treatment concepts discussed later in this TIP. The intended audience includes:

- Healthcare professionals (physicians, nurse practitioners, physician assistants, and nurses).
- Professionals who offer addiction counseling or mental health services.
- Peer support specialists.
- People needing treatment and their families.
- People in remission or recovery and their families.
- Hospital administrators.
- Policymakers.

In Part 1, readers will learn that:

- Increasing opioid overdose deaths, illicit opioid use, and prescription opioid misuse constitute a public health crisis.
- OUD medications reduce illicit opioid use, retain people in treatment, and reduce risk of opioid overdose death better than treatment with placebo or no medication.
- Only physicians, nurse practitioners, and physician assistants can prescribe buprenorphine for OUD. They must get a federal waiver to do so.
- Only federally certified, accredited OTPs can dispense methadone to treat OUD. OTPs can administer and dispense buprenorphine without a federal waiver.
- Any prescriber can offer naltrexone.
- OUD medication can be taken on a short- or long-term basis, including as part of medically supervised withdrawal and as maintenance treatment.
- Patients taking medication for OUD are considered to be in recovery.
- Several barriers contribute to the underuse of medication for OUD.

Part 2: Addressing Opioid Use Disorder in General Medical Settings

This part offers guidance on OUD screening, assessment, treatment, and referral. Part 2 is for healthcare professionals working in general medical settings with patients who have or are at risk for OUD.

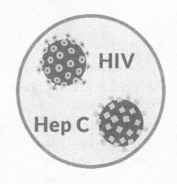

OPIOID ADDICTION is linked with significant MORBIDITY and MORTALITY related to HIV and hepatitis C.[23]

In Part 2, readers will learn that:

- All healthcare practices should screen for alcohol, tobacco, and other substance misuse (including opioid misuse).
- Validated screening tools, symptom surveys, and other resources are readily available; this part lists many of them.
- When patients screen positive for risk of harm from substance use, practitioners should assess them using tools that determine whether substance use meets diagnostic criteria for a substance use disorder (SUD).
- Thorough assessment should address patients' medical, social, SUD, and family histories.
- Laboratory tests can inform treatment planning.
- Practitioners should develop treatment plans or referral strategies (if onsite SUD treatment is unavailable) for patients who need SUD treatment.

Part 3: Pharmacotherapy for Opioid Use Disorder

This part offers information and tools for healthcare professionals who prescribe, administer, or dispense OUD medications or treat other illnesses in patients who take these medications. It provides guidance on the use of buprenorphine, methadone, and naltrexone by healthcare professionals in:

- General medical settings, including hospitals.
- Office-based opioid treatment settings.
- Specialty addiction treatment programs, including OTPs.

In Part 3, readers will learn that:

- OUD medications are safe and effective when used appropriately.
- OUD medications can help patients reduce or stop illicit opioid use and improve their health and functioning.
- Pharmacotherapy should be considered for all patients with OUD. Opioid pharmacotherapies should be reserved for those with moderate-to-severe OUD with physical dependence.
- Patients with OUD should be informed of the risks and benefits of pharmacotherapy, treatment without medication, and no treatment.
- Patients should be advised on where and how to get treatment with OUD medication.

OPIOID-RELATED inpatient hospital stays **INCREASED 64%** nationally from 2005–2014.[24]

- Doses and schedules of pharmacotherapy must be individualized.

Part 4: Partnering Addiction Treatment Counselors With Clients and Healthcare Professionals

This part recommends ways that addiction treatment counselors can collaborate with healthcare professionals to support client-centered, trauma-informed OUD treatment and recovery. It also serves as a quick guide to medications that can treat OUD and presents strategies for clear communication with prescribers, creation of supportive environments for clients who take OUD medication, and ways to address other common counseling concerns when working with this population.

In Part 4, readers will learn that:

- Many patients taking OUD medication benefit from counseling as part of treatment.
- Counselors play the same role for clients with OUD who take medication as for clients with any other SUD.
- Counselors help clients recover by addressing the challenges and consequences of addiction.
- OUD is often a chronic illness requiring ongoing communication among patients and providers to ensure that patients fully benefit from both pharmacotherapy and psychosocial treatment and support.
- OUD medications are safe and effective when prescribed and taken appropriately.
- Medication is integral to recovery for many people with OUD. Medication usually produces better treatment outcomes than outpatient treatment without medication.
- Supportive counseling environments for clients who take OUD medication can promote treatment and help build recovery capital.

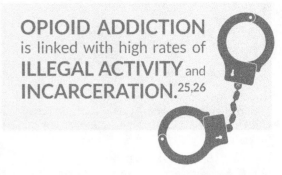

OPIOID ADDICTION is linked with high rates of **ILLEGAL ACTIVITY** and **INCARCERATION.**[25,26]

Part 5: Resources Related to Medications for Opioid Use Disorder

This part has a glossary and audience-segmented resource lists to help medical and behavioral health service providers better understand how to use OUD medications with their patients and to help patients better understand how OUD medications work. It is for all interested readers.

In Part 5, readers will learn that:

- Practice guidelines and decision-making tools can help healthcare professionals with OUD screening, assessment, diagnosis, treatment planning, and referral.
- Patient- and family-oriented resources provide information about opioid addiction in general; the role of medication, behavioral and supportive services, and mutual-help groups in the treatment of OUD; how-tos for identifying recovery support services; and how-tos for locating medical and behavioral health service providers who specialize in treating OUD or other SUDs.

Notes

1. Substance Abuse and Mental Health Services Administration. (2017). Recovery and recovery support [Webpage]. Retrieved November 17, 2017, from www.samhsa.gov/recovery

2. Council of Economic Advisers. (2017, November). *The underestimated cost of the opioid crisis.* Washington, DC: Executive Office of the President of the United States.

3. Center for Behavioral Health Statistics and Quality. (2017). *Key substance use and mental health indicators in the United States: Results from the 2016 National Survey on Drug Use and Health.* Rockville, MD: Substance Abuse and Mental Health Services Administration.

4. Centers for Disease Control and Prevention. (2017). Drug overdose death data [Webpage]. Retrieved January 9, 2018, from www.cdc.gov/drugoverdose/data/statedeaths.html

5. National Safety Council. (2017). *NSC motor vehicle fatality estimates.* Retrieved October 31, 2017, from www.nsc.org/NewsDocuments/2017/12-month-estimates.pdf

6. Johnson, R. E., Chutuape, M. A., Strain, E. C., Walsh, S. L., Stitzer, M. L., & Bigelow, G. E. (2000). A comparison of levomethadyl acetate, buprenorphine, and methadone for opioid dependence. *New England Journal of Medicine, 343*(18), 1290–1297.

7. Krupitsky, E., Nunes, E. V., Ling, W., Illeperuma, A., Gastfriend, D. R., & Silverman, B. L. (2011, April 30). Injectable extended-release naltrexone for opioid dependence: A double-blind, placebo-controlled, multicentre randomised trial. *Lancet, 377*(9776), 1506–1513.

8. Lee, J. D., Friedmann, P. D., Kinlock, T. W., Nunes, E. V., Boney, T. Y., Hoskinson, R. A., Jr., … O'Brien, C. P. (2016). Extended-release naltrexone to prevent opioid relapse in criminal justice offenders. *New England Journal of Medicine, 374*(13), 1232–1242.

9. Mattick, R. P., Breen, C., Kimber, J., & Davoli, M. (2009). Methadone maintenance therapy versus no opioid replacement therapy for opioid dependence. *Cochrane Database of Systematic Reviews, 2009*(3), 1–19.

10. Mattick, R. P., Breen, C., Kimber, J., & Davoli, M. (2014). Buprenorphine maintenance versus placebo or methadone maintenance for opioid dependence. *Cochrane Database of Systematic Reviews, 2014*(2), 1–84.

11. Auriacombe, M., Fatséas, M., Dubernet, J., Daulouède, J. P., & Tignol, J. (2004). French field experience with buprenorphine. *American Journal on Addictions, 13*(Suppl. 1), S17–S28.

12. Degenhardt, L., Randall, D., Hall, W., Law, M., Butler, T., & Burns, L. (2009). Mortality among clients of a state-wide opioid pharmacotherapy program over 20 years: Risk factors and lives saved. *Drug and Alcohol Dependence, 105*(1–2), 9–15.

13. Gibson, A., Degenhardt, L., Mattick, R. P., Ali, R., White, J., & O'Brien, S. (2008). Exposure to opioid maintenance treatment reduces long-term mortality. *Addiction, 103*(3), 462–468.

14. Schwartz, R. P., Gryczynski, J., O'Grady, K. E., Sharfstein, J. M., Warren, G., Olsen, Y., … Jaffe, J. H. (2013). Opioid agonist treatments and heroin overdose deaths in Baltimore, Maryland, 1995–2009. *American Journal of Public Health, 103*(5), 917–922.

15. World Health Organization. (2009). *Guidelines for the psychosocially assisted pharmacological treatment of opioid dependence.* Geneva, Switzerland: WHO Press.

16. Center for Behavioral Health Statistics and Quality. (2017). *Key substance use and mental health indicators in the United States: Results from the 2016 National Survey on Drug Use and Health.* Rockville, MD: Substance Abuse and Mental Health Services Administration.

17. Department of Health and Human Services, Office of the Surgeon General. (2016). *Facing addiction in America: The Surgeon General's report on alcohol, drugs, and health.* Washington, DC: Department of Health and Human Services.

18. Jones, C. M., Campopiano, M., Baldwin, G., & McCance-Katz, E. (2015). National and state treatment need and capacity for opioid agonist medication-assisted treatment. *American Journal of Public Health, 105*(8), e55–e63.

19. Jones, C. M., Campopiano, M., Baldwin, G., & McCance-Katz, E. (2015). National and state treatment need and capacity for opioid agonist medication-assisted treatment. *American Journal of Public Health, 105*(8), e55–e63.

20. Cartwright, W. S. (2000). Cost-benefit analysis of drug treatment services: Review of the literature. *Journal of Mental Health Policy and Economics, 3*(1), 11–26.

21. McCollister, K. E., & French, M. T. (2003). The relative contribution of outcome domains in the total economic benefit of addiction interventions: A review of first findings. *Addiction, 98*(12), 1647–1659.

22. Weiss, A. J., Elixhauser, A., Barrett, M. L., Steiner, C. A., Bailey, M. K., & O'Malley, L. (2017, January). *Opioid-related inpatient stays and emergency department visits by state, 2009–2014.* HCUP Statistical Brief No. 219. Rockville, MD: Agency for Healthcare Research and Quality.

23 Wang, X., Zhang, T., & Ho, W. Z. (2011). Opioids and HIV/HCV infection. *Journal of Neuroimmune Pharmacology, 6*(4), 477–489.

24 Weiss, A. J., Elixhauser, A., Barrett, M. L., Steiner, C. A., Bailey, M. K., & O'Malley, L. (2017, January). *Opioid-related inpatient stays and emergency department visits by state, 2009–2014.* HCUP Statistical Brief No. 219. Rockville, MD: Agency for Healthcare Research and Quality.

25 World Health Organization. (2009). *Guidelines for the psychosocially assisted pharmacological treatment of opioid dependence.* Geneva, Switzerland: WHO Press.

26 Soyka, M., Träder, A., Klotsche, J., Haberthür, A., Bühringer, G., Rehm, J., & Wittchen, H. U. (2012). Criminal behavior in opioid-dependent patients before and during maintenance therapy: 6-year follow-up of a nationally representative cohort sample. *Journal of Forensic Sciences, 57*(6), 1524–1530.

TIP Development Participants

Expert Panelists

Each Treatment Improvement Protocol's (TIP's) expert panel is a group of primarily nonfederal addiction-focused clinical, research, administrative, and recovery support experts with deep knowledge of the TIP's topic. With the Substance Abuse and Mental Health Services Administration's (SAMHSA's) Knowledge Application Program (KAP) team, they develop each TIP via a consensus-driven, collaborative process that blends evidence-based, best, and promising practices with the panel's expertise and combined wealth of experience.

TIP Chair

Robert P. Schwartz, M.D.—TIP Chair
Medical Director/Senior Research Scientist
Friends Research Institute
Baltimore, MD

TIP Expert Panelists

Sarah Church, Ph.D.
Executive Director
Montefiore Medical Center
Wellness Center at Waters Place
Bronx, NY

Diana Coffa, M.D., FM
Associate Professor
University of California School of Medicine
Family Community Medicine
San Francisco, CA

Zwaantje Hamming, M.S.N., FNP-C, CARN-AP
La Familia Medical Center
Santa Fe, NM

Ron Jackson, M.S.W., LICSW
Affiliate Professor
University of Washington School of Social Work
Seattle, WA

Hendree Jones, Ph.D.
Professor and Executive Director
Horizons Program
Chapel Hill, NC

Michelle Lofwall, M.D., DFASAM
Medical Director
University of Kentucky College of Medicine—
 Straus Clinic
Associate Professor of Behavioral Science and
 Psychiatry
Faculty in UK Center on Drug and Alcohol
 Research
Lexington, KY

Shannon C. Miller, M.D., DFASAM, DFAPA (ad hoc panelist)
Director, Addiction Services
Veterans Affairs Medical Center
Cincinnati, OH

Charles Schauberger, M.D.
Obstetrician-Gynecologist
Gundersen Health System
La Crosse, WI

Joycelyn Woods, M.A., CMA
Executive Director
National Alliance for Medication Assisted
 Recovery
New York, NY

SAMHSA's TIP Champion

Melinda Campopiano von Klimo, M.D.
Senior Medical Advisor
Center for Substance Abuse Treatment
SAMHSA
Rockville, MD

Scientific Reviewers

This TIP's scientific reviewers are among the foremost experts on the three medications discussed in this TIP to treat opioid use disorder. Their role in the collaborative TIP development process was to help the KAP team include current, accurate, and comprehensive information and instructions about the use of each of these medications.

Buprenorphine

David A. Fiellin, M.D.
Professor of Investigative Medicine and Public Health
Yale University School of Medicine
New Haven, CT

Naltrexone

Joshua D. Lee, M.D., M.Sc.
Associate Professor
Department of Population Health
Division of General Medicine and Clinical Innovation
NYU Langone Health
New York, NY

Methadone

Andrew J. Saxon, M.D.
Professor
Department of Psychiatry and Behavioral Sciences
University of Washington School of Medicine
Director
Center of Excellence in Substance Abuse Treatment and Education
Veterans Affairs Puget Sound Health Care System
Seattle, WA

Field Reviewers

Field reviewers represent each TIP's intended target audiences. They work in addiction, mental health, primary care, and adjacent fields. Their direct front-line experience related to the TIP's topic allows them to provide valuable input on a TIP's relevance, utility, accuracy, and accessibility.

William Bograkos, M.A., D.O., FACOEP, FACOFP
Adjunct Professor
Center for Excellence in the Neurosciences
University of New England (UNE)
Clinical Professor of Medical Military Science
Family Practice and Emergency Medicine, UNE
Biddeford, ME

Meg Brunner, M.L.I.S.
Librarian, Alcohol and Drug Abuse Institute
University of Washington
Seattle, WA

Kathryn Cates-Wessell
Chief Executive Officer
American Academy of Addiction Psychiatry
East Providence, RI

Mary Catlin, BSN, MPH, CIC
Public Health Nurse
Alcohol and Drug Abuse Institute
University of Washington
Seattle, WA

Kelly J. Clark, M.D., M.B.A., DFASAM
President
American Society of Addiction Medicine
Rockville, MD

Marc Fishman, M.D.
Assistant Professor
Johns Hopkins University School of Medicine, Psychiatry/Behavioral Sciences Expert Team
Baltimore, MD

Katherine Fornili, D.N.P., M.P.H., RN, CARN
Assistant Professor
University of Maryland School of Nursing
Baltimore, MD

Adam Gordon, M.D., M.P.H., FACP, FASAM, CMRO
Associate Professor of Medicine and Advisory Dean
University of Pittsburgh School of Medicine
Pittsburgh, PA

Ellie Grossman, M.D.
Instructor in Medicine
Cambridge Health Alliance
Somerville Hospital Primary Care
Somerville, MA

Kyle Kampman, M.D.
Professor, Department of Psychiatry
Perelman School of Medicine
University of Pennsylvania
Center for Studies of Addiction
Philadelphia, PA

Janice Kauffman, M.P.H., RN, CAS, CADC-1
Vice President of Addiction Treatment Services, North Charles Foundation, Inc.
Director of Addictions Consultation, Department of Psychiatry, Cambridge Health Alliance
Assistant Professor of Psychiatry, Harvard Medical School, the Cambridge Hospital
Cambridge, MA

Jason Kletter, Ph.D.
President, Bay Area Addiction Research and Treatment
President, California Opioid Maintenance Providers
San Francisco, CA

William J. Lorman, J.D., Ph.D., MSN, PMHNP-BC, CARN-AP
Vice President and Chief Clinical Officer
Livengrin Foundation, Inc.
Bensalem, PA

Megan Marx-Varela, M.P.A.
Associate Director
The Joint Commission—Behavioral Health Care Accreditation
Oakbrook Terrace, IL

Alison Newman, MPH
Continuing Education Specialist
Alcohol and Drug Abuse Institute
University of Washington
Seattle, WA

David O'Gurek, M.D., FAAFP
Assistant Professor
Family and Community Medicine, Lewis Katz School of Medicine
Temple University
Philadelphia, PA

Yngvild Olsen, M.D., M.P.H, FASAM
Medical Director
Institutes for Behavior Resources, Inc./Recovery Enhanced by Access to Comprehensive Healthcare (REACH) Health Services
Baltimore, MD

Shawn A. Ryan, M.D., M.B.A., ABEM, FASAM
President & Chief Medical Officer
BrightView
Cincinnati, OH

Paul Stasiewicz, Ph.D.
Senior Research Scientist
Research Institute on Addictions
State University of New York-Buffalo
Buffalo, NY

Kenneth Stoller, M.D.
Director
Broadway Center for Addiction at the Johns Hopkins Hospital
Assistant Professor of Psychiatry and Behavioral Sciences
Johns Hopkins University
Baltimore, MD

Executive Summary

Mishka Terplan, M.D., M.P.H., FACOG
Professor
Department of Obstetrics and Gynecology,
 Division of General Obstetrics and Gynecology
Virginia Commonwealth University
Richmond, VA

Christopher Welsh, M.D.
Associate Professor of Psychiatry
University of Maryland Medical Center
Baltimore, MD

George E. Woody, M.D.
Professor of Psychiatry
Department of Psychiatry Center for Studies of
 Addiction
University of Pennsylvania's Perelman School of
 Medicine
Philadelphia, PA

TIP 63 — MEDICATIONS FOR OPIOID USE DISORDER—Executive Summary

Publication Information

Acknowledgments

This publication was prepared under contract number 270-14-0445 by the Knowledge Application Program (KAP) for the Center for Substance Abuse Treatment, Substance Abuse and Mental Health Services Administration (SAMHSA), U.S. Department of Health and Human Services (HHS). Suzanne Wise served as the Contracting Officer's Representative, and Candi Byrne served as KAP Project Coordinator.

Disclaimer

The views, opinions, and content expressed herein are the views of the consensus panel members and do not necessarily reflect the official position of SAMHSA or HHS. No official support of or endorsement by SAMHSA or HHS for these opinions or for the instruments or resources described is intended or should be inferred. The guidelines presented should not be considered substitutes for individualized client care and treatment decisions.

Public Domain Notice

All materials appearing in this publication except those taken directly from copyrighted sources are in the public domain and may be reproduced or copied without permission from SAMHSA or the authors. Citation of the source is appreciated. However, this publication may not be reproduced or distributed for a fee without the specific, written authorization of the Office of Communications, SAMHSA, HHS.

Electronic Access and Copies of Publication

This publication may be ordered or downloaded from SAMHSA's Publications Ordering webpage at https://store.samhsa.gov. Or, please call SAMHSA at 1-877-SAMHSA-7 (1-877-726-4727) (English and Español).

Recommended Citation

Substance Abuse and Mental Health Services Administration. *Medications for Opioid Use Disorder.* Treatment Improvement Protocol (TIP) Series 63, Full Document. HHS Publication No. (SMA) 18-5063FULLDOC. Rockville, MD: Substance Abuse and Mental Health Services Administration, 2018.

Originating Office

Quality Improvement and Workforce Development Branch, Division of Services Improvement, Center for Substance Abuse Treatment, Substance Abuse and Mental Health Services Administration, 5600 Fishers Lane, Rockville, MD 20857.

Nondiscrimination Notice

SAMHSA complies with applicable federal civil rights laws and does not discriminate on the basis of race, color, national origin, age, disability, or sex. SAMHSA cumple con las leyes federales de derechos civiles aplicables y no discrimina por motivos de raza, color, nacionalidad, edad, discapacidad, o sexo.

HHS Publication No. (SMA) 18-5063FULLDOC
Published 2018

TIP 63

MEDICATIONS FOR OPIOID USE DISORDER

Part 1: Introduction to Medications for Opioid Use Disorder Treatment
For Healthcare and Addiction Professionals, Policymakers, Patients, and Families

Part 1 of this Treatment Improvement Protocol (TIP) will help readers understand key facts and issues related to providing Food and Drug Administration (FDA)-approved medications used to treat opioid use disorder (OUD).

TIP Navigation

Executive Summary
For healthcare and addiction professionals, policymakers, patients, and families

Part 1: Introduction to Medications for Opioid Use Disorder Treatment
For healthcare and addiction professionals, policymakers, patients, and families

Part 2: Addressing Opioid Use Disorder in General Medical Settings
For healthcare professionals

Part 3: Pharmacotherapy for Opioid Use Disorder
For healthcare professionals

Part 4: Partnering Addiction Treatment Counselors With Clients and Healthcare Professionals
For healthcare and addiction professionals

Part 5: Resources Related to Medications for Opioid Use Disorder
For healthcare and addiction professionals, policymakers, patients, and families

KEY MESSAGES

- Increasing opioid overdose deaths, illicit opioid use, and prescription opioid misuse constitute a public health crisis.
- OUD medications reduce illicit opioid use, retain people in treatment, and reduce risk of opioid overdose death better than treatment with placebo or no medication.
- Only physicians, nurse practitioners, and physician assistants can prescribe buprenorphine for OUD. They must get a federal waiver to do so.
- Only federally certified, accredited opioid treatment programs (OTPs) can dispense methadone to treat OUD. OTPs can administer and dispense buprenorphine without a federal waiver.
- Any prescriber can offer naltrexone.
- OUD medication can be taken on a short- or long-term basis, including as part of medically supervised withdrawal and as maintenance treatment.
- Patients taking medication for OUD are considered to be in recovery.
- Several barriers contribute to the underuse of medication for OUD.

Substance Abuse and Mental Health Services Administration
www.samhsa.gov • 1-877-SAMHSA-7 (1-877-726-4727)

PART 1: AN INTRODUCTION TO MEDICATIONS FOR THE TREATMENT OF OPIOID USE DISORDER

The Approach to OUD Care 1-1

Overview of Medications for OUD 1-3

Duration of Treatment With OUD Medication 1-8

Treatment Settings 1-9

Challenges to Expanding Access to OUD Medication 1-9

Resources 1-10

Notes 1-11

TIP 63 — MEDICATIONS FOR OPIOID USE DISORDER

PART 1 of 5
Introduction to Medications for Opioid Use Disorder Treatment

Part 1 of this TIP offers a general introduction to providing medications to address opioid use disorder (OUD). It is for all audiences. Part 1 will help readers understand key facts and issues related to providing FDA-approved medications used to treat OUD. TIP Parts 2 through 5 cover these issues in more detail.

The Approach to OUD Care

According to the Substance Abuse and Mental Health Services Administration (SAMHSA) and the National Institute on Drug Abuse, addiction is a chronic, treatable illness. Opioid addiction, which generally corresponds with moderate to severe forms of OUD (Exhibit 1.1), often requires continuing care for effective treatment rather than an episodic, acute-care treatment approach.

The World Health Organization's (WHO's) principles of good care for chronic diseases can guide OUD care:[1]

- Develop a treatment partnership with patients.
- Focus on patients' concerns and priorities.
- Support patient self-management of illness.
- Use the five A's at every visit (assess, advise, agree, assist, and arrange).
- Organize proactive follow-up.
- Link patients to community resources/support.
- Work as a clinical team.
- Involve "expert patients," peer educators, and support staff in the health facility.
- Ensure continuity of care.

Chronic care management is effective for many long-term medical conditions, such as diabetes and cardiovascular disease, and it can offer

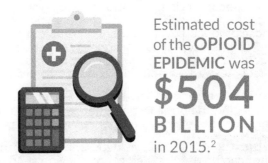

Estimated cost of the OPIOID EPIDEMIC was $504 BILLION in 2015.[2]

similar benefits to patients with substance use disorders (SUDs); for example, it can help them stabilize, achieve remission of symptoms, and establish and maintain recovery. Good continuing care also provides, and links to, other medical, behavioral health, and community and recovery support services.

A noticeable theme in chronic disease management is patient-centered care. Patient-centered care empowers patients with information that helps them make better treatment decisions with the healthcare professionals involved in their care. Patients should receive information from their healthcare team that will help them understand OUD and the options for treating it, including treatment with FDA-approved medications. Healthcare professionals should also make patients aware of available, appropriate recovery support and behavioral health services.

EXHIBIT 1.1. Key Terms

Addiction: As defined by the American Society of Addiction Medicine, "a primary, chronic disease of brain reward, motivation, memory, and related circuitry."[3] It is characterized by inability to consistently abstain, impairment in behavioral control, craving, diminished recognition of significant problems with one's behaviors and interpersonal relationships, and a dysfunctional emotional response. Like other chronic diseases, addiction often involves cycles of **relapse** and **remission.** The *Diagnostic and Statistical Manual of Mental Disorders,* Fifth Edition[4] (DSM-5), does not use the term for diagnostic purposes, but it commonly describes the more severe forms of OUD.

Medically supervised withdrawal (formerly called detoxification): Using an opioid agonist (or an alpha-2 adrenergic agonist if an opioid agonist is not available) in tapering doses or other medications to help a patient discontinue illicit or prescription opioids.

Opioid misuse: The use of prescription opioids in any way other than as directed by a prescriber; the use of any opioid in a manner, situation, amount, or frequency that can cause harm to self or others.[5]

Opioid receptor agonist: A substance that has an affinity for and stimulates physiological activity at cell receptors in the central nervous system (CNS) that are normally stimulated by opioids. Mu-opioid receptor full agonists (e.g., methadone) bind to the mu-opioid receptor and produce actions similar to those produced by the endogenous opioid beta-endorphin. Increasing the dose increases the effect. Mu-opioid receptor partial agonists (e.g., buprenorphine) bind to the mu-opioid receptor. Unlike with full agonists, increasing their dose may not produce additional effects once they have reached their maximal effect. At low doses, partial agonists may produce effects similar to those of full agonists.

Opioid receptor antagonist: A substance that has affinity for opioid receptors in the CNS without producing the physiological effects of opioid agonists. Mu-opioid receptor antagonists (e.g., naltrexone) can block the effects of exogenously administered opioids.

Opioids: All natural, synthetic, and semisynthetic substances that have effects similar to morphine. They can be used as medications having such effects (e.g., methadone, buprenorphine, oxycodone).

Opioid treatment program (OTP): An accredited treatment program with SAMHSA certification and Drug Enforcement Administration registration to administer and dispense opioid agonist medications that are approved by FDA to treat opioid addiction. Currently, these include methadone and buprenorphine products. Other pharmacotherapies, such as naltrexone, may be provided but are not subject to these regulations. OTPs must provide adequate medical, counseling, vocational, educational, and other assessment and treatment services either onsite or by referral to an outside agency or practitioner through a formal agreement.[6]

Opioid use disorder (OUD): Per DSM-5, a disorder characterized by loss of control of opioid use, risky opioid use, impaired social functioning, tolerance, and withdrawal. Tolerance and withdrawal do not count toward the diagnosis in people experiencing these symptoms when using opioids under appropriate medical supervision. OUD covers a range of severity and replaces what DSM-IV termed "opioid abuse" and "opioid dependence." An OUD diagnosis is applicable to a person who uses opioids and experiences at least 2 of the 11 symptoms in a 12-month period. (See Exhibit 2.13 in Part 2 for full DSM-5 diagnostic criteria for OUD.)

Recovery: A process of change through which individuals improve their health and wellness, live self-directed lives, and strive to reach their full potential. Even individuals with severe and chronic SUDs can, with help, overcome their SUDs and regain health and social function. Although abstinence from all substance misuse is a cardinal feature of a recovery lifestyle, it is not the only healthy, prosocial feature. Patients taking FDA-approved medication to treat OUD can be considered in recovery.

Relapse: A process in which a person with OUD who has been in **remission** experiences a return of symptoms or loss of remission. A relapse is different from a **return to opioid use** in that it involves more than a single incident of use. Relapses occur over a period of time and can be interrupted. Relapse need not be long lasting. The TIP uses relapse to describe relapse prevention, a common treatment modality.

Remission: A medical term meaning a disappearance of signs and symptoms of the disease.[7] DSM-5 defines remission as present in people who previously met OUD criteria but no longer meet any OUD criteria (with the possible exception of craving).[8] Remission is an essential element of **recovery.**

Return to opioid use: One or more instances of **opioid misuse** without a return of symptoms of OUD. A return to opioid use may lead to **relapse.**

As is true for patients undergoing treatment for any chronic medical condition, patients with OUD should have access to medical, mental health, addiction counseling, and recovery support services that they may need to supplement treatment with medication. Medical care should include preventive services and disease management. Patients with OUD who have mental disorders should have access to mental health services.

Treatment and support services should reflect each patient's individual needs and preferences. Some patients, particularly those with co-occurring disorders, may require these treatments and services to achieve sustained remission and recovery.

The words you use to describe both OUD and an individual with OUD are powerful and can reinforce prejudice, negative attitudes, and discrimination. Negative attitudes held by the public and healthcare professionals can deter people from seeking treatment, make patients leave treatment prematurely, and contribute to worse treatment outcomes. The TIP expert panel recommends that providers always use medical terms when discussing SUDs (e.g., positive or negative urine sample, not dirty or clean sample) and use person-first language (e.g., a person with an SUD, not a user, alcoholic, or addict). Exhibit 1.1 defines some key terms. A full glossary is in Part 5 of this TIP.

> **RESOURCE ALERT**
>
> **Shared Decision Making**
>
> SAMHSA's shared decision-making tool is helpful for educating patients and their families about OUD. The information this tool provides can help patients make informed decisions about their care (http://archive.samhsa.gov/MAT-Decisions-in-Recovery/Default.aspx).

Overview of Medications for OUD

There is no "one size fits all" approach to OUD treatment. Many people with OUD benefit from treatment with medication for varying lengths of time, including lifelong treatment. Ongoing outpatient medication treatment for OUD is linked to better retention and outcomes than treatment without medication. Even so, some people stop using opioids on their own; others recover through support groups or specialty outpatient or residential treatment with or without medication. Still, FDA-approved medication should be considered and offered to patients with OUD as part of their treatment.

Benefits

The three FDA-approved medications used to treat OUD improve patients' health and wellness by:

- Reducing or eliminating withdrawal symptoms: methadone, buprenorphine.
- Blunting or blocking the effects of illicit opioids: methadone, naltrexone, buprenorphine.
- Reducing or eliminating cravings to use opioids: methadone, naltrexone, buprenorphine.

See Exhibit 1.2 for further comparison between these medications.

Effectiveness

The science demonstrating the effectiveness of medication for OUD is strong. For example, methadone, extended-release injectable naltrexone (XR-NTX), and buprenorphine were each found to be more effective in reducing illicit opioid use than no medication in randomized clinical trials,[9,10,11,12] which are the gold standard for demonstrating efficacy in clinical medicine. Methadone and buprenorphine treatment have also been associated with reduced risk of overdose death.[13,14,15,16,17]

EXHIBIT 1.2. Comparison of Medications for OUD

PRESCRIBING CONSIDERATIONS	METHADONE	NALTREXONE	BUPRENORPHINE
Mechanism of Action at mu-Opioid Receptor	Agonist	Antagonist	Partial agonist
Phase of Treatment	Medically supervised withdrawal, maintenance	Prevention of relapse to opioid dependence, following medically supervised withdrawal	Medically supervised withdrawal, maintenance
Route of Administration	Oral	Oral, intramuscular extended-release	Sublingual, buccal, subdermal implant, subcutaneous extended release
Possible Adverse Effects	Constipation, hyperhidrosis, respiratory depression, sedation, QT prolongation, sexual dysfunction, severe hypotension including orthostatic hypotension and syncope, misuse potential, neonatal abstinence syndrome	Nausea, anxiety, insomnia, precipitated opioid withdrawal, hepatotoxicity, vulnerability to opioid overdose, depression, suicidality, muscle cramps, dizziness or syncope, somnolence or sedation, anorexia, decreased appetite or other appetite disorders **Intramuscular:** Pain, swelling, induration (including some cases requiring surgical intervention)	Constipation, nausea, precipitated opioid withdrawal, excessive sweating, insomnia, pain, peripheral edema, respiratory depression (particularly combined with benzodiazepines or other CNS depressants), misuse potential, neonatal abstinence syndrome **Implant:** Nerve damage during insertion/removal, accidental overdose or misuse if extruded, local migration or protrusion **Subcutaneous:** Injection site itching or pain, death from intravenous injection
Regulations and Availability	Schedule II; only available at federally certified OTPs and the acute inpatient hospital setting for OUD treatment	Not a scheduled medication; not included in OTP regulations; requires prescription; office-based treatment or specialty substance use treatment programs, including OTPs	Schedule III; requires waiver to prescribe outside OTPs **Implant:** Prescribers must be certified in the Probuphine Risk Evaluation and Mitigation Strategy (REMS) Program. Providers who wish to insert/remove implants are required to obtain special training and certification in the REMS Program **Subcutaneous:** Healthcare settings and pharmacies must be certified in the Sublocade REMS Program and only dispense the medication directly to a provider for administration

Adapted with permission.[18] Copyrighted 2017. UBM Medica. 131265:0917SH

This doesn't mean that remission and recovery occur only through medication. Some people achieve remission without OUD medication, just as some people can manage type 2 diabetes with exercise and diet alone. But just as it is inadvisable to deny people with diabetes the medication they need to help manage their illness, it is also not sound medical practice to deny people with OUD access to FDA-approved medications for their illness.

Medication for OUD should be successfully integrated with outpatient and residential treatment. Some patients may benefit from different levels of care during the course of their lives. These different levels include outpatient counseling, intensive outpatient treatment, inpatient treatment, or long-term therapeutic communities. Patients receiving treatment in these settings should have access to FDA-approved medications for OUD.

Patients treated with OUD medications can benefit from individualized psychosocial supports. These can be offered by patients' healthcare providers in the form of medication management and supportive counseling and/or by other providers offering adjunctive addiction counseling, contingency management, recovery coaching, mental health services, and other services (e.g., housing supports) that particular patients may need.

> The TIP expert panel strongly recommends informing all patients with OUD about the risks and benefits of treatment of OUD with all FDA-approved medications. Alternatives to these treatments and their risks and benefits should be discussed. Patients should receive access to such medications if clinically appropriate and desired by the patients.

Expanding access to FDA-approved medications is an important public health strategy.[19] A substantial gap exists between the number of people needing OUD treatment and the capacity to treat those individuals with OUD medication. In 2012, the gap was estimated at nearly 1 million people, with approximately 80 percent of OTPs nationally operating at 80 percent capacity or greater.[20] Blue Cross Blue Shield reported a 493 percent increase in members diagnosed with OUD from 2010 to 2016 but only a 65 percent increase in the use of medication for OUD.[21] **Improving access is crucial to closing the wide gap between the need for treatment with OUD medications and the availability of such treatment,** given the strong evidence of OUD medications' effectiveness.[22]

Methadone

Methadone retains patients in treatment and reduces illicit opioid use more effectively than placebo, medically supervised withdrawal, or no treatment, as numerous clinical trials and meta-analyses of studies conducted in many countries show.[23,24,25] Higher methadone doses are associated with superior outcomes.[26,27] Given the evidence of methadone's effectiveness, WHO lists it as an essential medication.[28]

Methadone treatment has by far the largest, oldest evidence base of all treatment approaches to opioid addiction. Large multisite longitudinal studies from the world over support methadone maintenance's effectiveness.[29,30,31] Longitudinal studies have also found that it is associated with:[32,33,34,35,36,37,38,39,40]

- Reduced risk of overdose-related deaths.
- Reduced risk of HIV and hepatitis C infection.
- Lower rates of cellulitis.
- Lower rates of HIV risk behavior.
- Reduced criminal behavior.

Naltrexone

XR-NTX reduces illicit opioid use and retains patients in treatment more effectively than placebo and no medication, according to findings from randomized controlled trials.[41,42,43]

In a two-group random assignment study of adults who were opioid dependent and involved in the justice system, all participants received brief counseling and community treatment referrals. One group received no medication, and the other group received XR-NTX. During the 6-month follow-up period, compared with the no-medication group, the group that received the medication demonstrated:[44]

- Longer time to return to substance use (10.5 weeks versus 5.0 weeks).
- A lower rate of return to use (43 percent versus 64 percent).
- A higher percentage of negative urine screens (74 percent versus 56 percent).

There are two studies comparing XR-NTX to sublingual buprenorphine. A multisite randomized trial assigned adult residential treatment patients with OUD to either XR-NTX or buprenorphine. Patients randomly assigned to buprenorphine had significantly lower relapse rates during 24 weeks of outpatient treatment than patients assigned to XR-NTX.[45] This finding resulted from challenges in completing XR-NTX induction, such that a significant proportion of patients did not actually receive XR-NTX. However, when comparing only those participants who started their assigned medication, no significant between-group differences in relapse rates were observed. Because dose induction was conducted with inpatients, findings may not be generalizable to dose induction in outpatient settings, where most patients initiate treatment. A 12-week trial among adults with opioid dependence in Norway who were opioid abstinent at the time of random assignment found that XR-NTX was as effective as buprenorphine in retaining patients in treatment and in reducing illicit opioid use.[46]

Oral naltrexone is also available, but it has not been found to be superior to placebo or to no medication in clinical trials.[47] Nonadherence limits its use.

Buprenorphine

Buprenorphine in its sublingual form retains patients in treatment and reduces illicit opioid use more effectively than placebo.[48] It also reduces HIV risk behaviors.[49,50] A multisite randomized trial with individuals addicted to prescription opioids showed that continued buprenorphine was superior to buprenorphine dose taper in reducing illicit opioid use.[51] Another randomized trial showed that continued buprenorphine also improved treatment retention and reduced illicit prescription opioid use compared with buprenorphine dose taper.[52] Long-term studies of buprenorphine show its effectiveness outside of clinical research protocols.[53,54] Naloxone, a short-acting opioid agonist, is also often included in the buprenorphine formulation to help prevent diversion to injected misuse. Because of the evidence of buprenorphine's effectiveness, WHO lists it as an essential medication.[55] Buprenorphine is available in "transmucosal" (i.e., sublingual or buccal) formulations.

Buprenorphine implants can be effective in stable patients. FDA approved implants (Probuphine) after a clinical trial showed them to be as effective as relatively low-dose (i.e., 8 mg or less daily) sublingual buprenorphine/naloxone (Suboxone) for patients who are already clinically stable.[56] More research is needed to establish implants' effectiveness outside of research studies, but findings to date are promising.[57,58]

FDA approved buprenorphine extended-release injection (Sublocade) in November 2017 to treat patients with moderate or severe OUD who have first received treatment with transmucosal buprenorphine for at least 1 week. This buprenorphine formulation is a monthly subcutaneous injection.

Exhibit 1.2 compares medications for OUD.

Cost Effectiveness and Cost Benefits

Cost-effectiveness and cost-benefit analyses can further our understanding of OUD medications' effectiveness.

Data indicate that medications for OUD are cost effective. Cost-effectiveness analyses compare the cost of different treatments with their associated outcomes (e.g., negative opioid urine tests). Such analyses have found that:

- Methadone and buprenorphine are more cost effective than OUD treatment without medication.[59]
- Counseling plus buprenorphine leads to significantly lower healthcare costs than little or no treatment among commercially insured patients with OUD.[60]
- Treatment with any of the three OUD medications this TIP covers led to lower healthcare usage and costs than treatment without medication in a study conducted in a large health plan.[61]

Relatively few cost-benefit analyses have examined addiction treatment with medication separately from addiction treatment in general.[62] Cost-benefit studies compare a treatment's cost with its benefits. The treatment is cost beneficial if its benefits outweigh its cost. These benefits can include:

- Reduced expenditures because of decreased crime.
- Reduced expenditures related to decreases in the use of the justice system.
- Improved quality of life.
- Reduced healthcare spending.
- Greater earned income.

Methadone treatment in OTPs can reduce justice system and healthcare costs.[63,64]

Requirements and Regulations

Following is a summary of regulations and requirements that apply to the three OUD medications. Part 3 of this TIP discusses the pharmacology and dosing of these medications.

Only federally certified and accredited OTPs can dispense methadone for the treatment of OUD. Methadone is typically given orally as a liquid.[65]

OTPs can dispense buprenorphine under OTP regulations without using a federal waiver.

Individual healthcare practitioners can prescribe buprenorphine in any medical setting, as long as they apply for and receive waivers of the special registration requirements defined in the Controlled Substances Act by meeting the requirements of the Drug Addiction Treatment Act of 2000 (DATA 2000) and the revised Comprehensive Addiction and Recovery Act. Physicians can learn how to obtain a waiver online (www.samhsa.gov/medication-assisted-treatment/buprenorphine-waiver-management/qualify-for-physician-waiver), as can nurse practitioners and physician assistants (www.samhsa.gov/medication-assisted-treatment/qualify-nps-pas-waivers).

- Eligible physicians, nurse practitioners, and physician assistants can treat up to 30 patients at one time in the first year of practice.
- They can apply to increase this number to 100 patients in the second year.
- After a year at the 100-patient limit, **only** physicians may apply to increase to up to 275 patients (with additional practice and reporting requirements).

Prescribing buprenorphine implants requires Probuphine REMS Program certification. Providers who wish to insert or remove implants must obtain live training and certification in the REMS Program.

Healthcare settings and pharmacies must get Sublocade REMS Program certification to dispense this medication and can only dispense it directly to healthcare providers for subcutaneous administration.

Naltrexone has no regulations beyond those that apply to any prescription pharmaceutical. Any healthcare provider with prescribing authority, including those practicing in OTPs, can prescribe its oral formulation and administer its long-acting injectable formulation.

The Controlled Substances Act contains a few exceptions from the requirement to provide methadone through an OTP or buprenorphine through an OTP or a waivered practitioner. These include (1) administering (not prescribing) an opioid for no more than 3 days to a patient in acute opioid withdrawal while preparations are made for ongoing care and (2) administering opioid medications in a hospital to maintain or detoxify a patient as an "incidental adjunct to medical or surgical treatment of conditions other than addiction."[66]

Duration of Treatment With OUD Medication

Patients can take medication for OUD on a short-term or long-term basis. However, patients who discontinue OUD medication generally return to illicit opioid use. Why is this so, even when discontinuation occurs slowly and carefully? Because the more severe form of OUD (i.e., addiction) is more than physical dependence. Addiction changes the reward circuitry of the brain, affecting cognition, emotions, and behavior. Providers and their patients should base decisions about discontinuing OUD medication on knowledge of the evidence base for the use of these medications, individualized assessments, and an individualized treatment plan they collaboratively develop and agree upon. Arbitrary time limits on the duration of treatment with OUD medication are inadvisable.

Maintenance Treatment

The best results occur when a patient receives medication for as long as it provides a benefit. This approach is often called "maintenance treatment."[67,68] Once stabilized on OUD medication, many patients stop using illicit opioids completely. Others continue to use for some time, but less frequently and in smaller amounts, which reduces their risk of morbidity and overdose death.

OUD medication gives people the time and ability to make necessary life changes associated with long-term remission and recovery (e.g., changing the people, places, and things connected with their drug use), and to do so more safely. Maintenance treatment also minimizes cravings and withdrawal symptoms. And it lets people better manage other aspects of their life, such as parenting, attending school, or working.

Medication Taper

After some time, patients may want to stop opioid agonist therapy for OUD through gradually tapering doses of the medication. Their outcomes will vary based on factors such as the length of their treatment, abstinence from illicit drugs, financial and social stability, and motivation to discontinue medication.[69] Longitudinal studies show that most patients who try to stop methadone treatment relapse during or after completing the taper.[70,71] For example, in a large, population-based retrospective study, only 13 percent of patients who tapered

---

RESOURCE ALERT

OUD Medication Treatment Limits and Reporting Requirements

The following websites provide information about (1) the Department of Health and Human Services final rule to increase patient access to medication for OUD and (2) associated reporting requirements:

www.federalregister.gov/documents/2016/07/08/2016-16120/medication-assisted-treatment-for-opioid-use-disorders

www.samhsa.gov/sites/default/files/programs_campaigns/medication_assisted/understanding-patient-limit275.pdf

from methadone had successful outcomes (no treatment reentry, death, or opioid-related hospitalization within 18 months after taper).[72] A clinical trial of XR-NTX versus treatment without medication also found increased risk of returning to illicit opioid use after discontinuing medication.[73]

Adding psychosocial treatments to taper regimens may not significantly improve outcomes compared with remaining on medication. One study randomly assigned participants to methadone maintenance or to 6 months of methadone treatment with a dose taper plus intensive psychosocial treatment. The maintenance group had more days in treatment and lower rates of heroin use and HIV risk behavior at 12-month follow-up.[74] Patients wishing to taper their opioid agonist medication should be offered psychosocial and recovery support services. They should be monitored during and after dose taper, offered XR-NTX, and encouraged to resume treatment with medication quickly if they return to opioid use.

Medically Supervised Withdrawal

Medically supervised withdrawal is a process in which providers offer methadone or buprenorphine on a short-term basis to reduce physical withdrawal signs and symptoms. Formerly called detoxification, this process gradually decreases the dose until the medication is discontinued, typically over a period of days or weeks. Studies show that most patients with OUD who undergo medically supervised withdrawal will start using opioids again and won't continue in recommended care.[75,76,77,78,79,80,81,82,83] Psychosocial treatment strategies, such as contingency management, can reduce dropout from medically supervised withdrawal, opioid use during withdrawal, and opioid use following completion of withdrawal.[84] Medically supervised withdrawal is necessary for patients starting naltrexone, which requires at least 7 days without short-acting opioids and 10 to 14 days without long-acting opioids.

Patients who complete medically supervised withdrawal are at risk of opioid overdose.

> Primary care physicians are on the front lines of providing office-based treatment with medication for OUD.

Treatment Settings

Almost all healthcare settings are appropriate for screening and assessing for OUD and offering medication onsite or by referral. Settings that offer OUD treatment have expanded from specialty sites (certified OTPs, residential facilities, outpatient addiction treatment programs, and addiction specialist physicians' offices) to general primary care practices, health centers, emergency departments, inpatient medical and psychiatric units, jails and prisons, and other settings.

OUD medications should be available to patients across all settings and at all levels of care—as a tool for remission and recovery. Because of the strength of the science, a 2016 report from the Surgeon General[85] urged adoption of medication for OUD along with recovery supports and other behavioral health services throughout the healthcare system.

Challenges to Expanding Access to OUD Medication

Despite the urgent need for treatment throughout the United States, only about 21.5 percent of people with OUD received treatment from 2009 to 2013.[86] The Centers for Disease Control and Prevention lists more than 200 U.S. counties as at risk for an HIV or a hepatitis C virus outbreak related to injection drug use.[87]

> Sustained public health efforts are essential to address the urgent need for OUD treatment and the risk of related overdose, HIV, and hepatitis C virus epidemics. These efforts must remove barriers and increase access to OUD medication.

Resources

Patient success stories are inspirational. They highlight the power of OUD medication to help people achieve remission and recovery. See the "Patient Success Stories" section in Part 5 of this TIP.

Part 5 of this TIP also contains community resources and advocacy resources. The community resources are for OTP, addiction treatment, and office-based providers The advocacy resources can help patients and others advocate for OUD medication for themselves and in their communities.

Notes

1. World Health Organization. (2009). *Guidelines for the psychosocially assisted pharmacological treatment of opioid dependence.* Geneva, Switzerland: WHO Press.

2. Council of Economic Advisers. (2017). *The underestimated cost of the opioid crisis.* Washington, DC: Executive Office of the President of the United States.

3. American Society of Addiction Medicine. (2011). *Definition of addiction.* Retrieved January 9, 2018, from www.asam.org/resources/definition-of-addiction

4. American Psychiatric Association. (2013). *Diagnostic and statistical manual of mental disorders* (5th ed.). Arlington, VA: American Psychiatric Publishing.

5. Department of Health and Human Services, Office of the Surgeon General. (2016). *Facing addiction in America: The Surgeon General's report on alcohol, drugs, and health.* Washington, DC: Department of Health and Human Services.

6. Substance Abuse and Mental Health Services Administration. (2015). *Federal guidelines for opioid treatment programs.* HHS Publication No. (SMA) PEP15-FEDGUIDEOTP. Rockville, MD: Substance Abuse and Mental Health Services Administration.

7. National Cancer Institute. (n.d.). Remission. In *NCI dictionary of cancer terms.* Retrieved November, 22, 2017, from www.cancer.gov/publications/dictionaries/cancer-terms?cdrid=45867

8. American Psychiatric Association. (2013). *Diagnostic and statistical manual of mental disorders* (5th ed.). Arlington, VA: American Psychiatric Publishing.

9. Krupitsky, E., Nunes, E. V., Ling, W., Illeperuma, A., Gastfriend, D. R., & Silverman, B. L. (2011, April 30). Injectable extended-release naltrexone for opioid dependence: A double-blind, placebo-controlled, multicentre randomised trial. *Lancet, 377*(9776), 1506–1513.

10. Lee, J. D., Friedmann, P. D., Kinlock, T. W., Nunes, E. V., Boney, T. Y., Hoskinson, R. A., Jr., … O'Brien, C. P. (2016). Extended-release naltrexone to prevent opioid relapse in criminal justice offenders. *New England Journal of Medicine, 374*(13), 1232–1242.

11. Mattick, R. P., Breen, C., Kimber, J., & Davoli, M. (2009). Methadone maintenance therapy versus no opioid replacement therapy for opioid dependence. *Cochrane Database of Systematic Reviews, 2009*(3), 1–19.

12. Mattick, R. P., Breen, C., Kimber, J., & Davoli, M. (2014). Buprenorphine maintenance versus placebo or methadone maintenance for opioid dependence. *Cochrane Database of Systematic Reviews, 2014*(2), 1–84.

13. Auriacombe, M., Fatséas, M., Dubernet, J., Daulouède, J. P., & Tignol, J. (2004). French field experience with buprenorphine. *American Journal on Addictions, 13*(Suppl. 1), S17–S28.

14. Degenhardt, L., Randall, D., Hall, W., Law, M., Butler, T., & Burns, L. (2009). Mortality among clients of a state-wide opioid pharmacotherapy program over 20 years: Risk factors and lives saved. *Drug and Alcohol Dependence, 105*(1–2), 9–15.

15. Gibson, A., Degenhardt, L., Mattick, R. P., Ali, R., White, J., & O'Brien, S. (2008). Exposure to opioid maintenance treatment reduces long-term mortality. *Addiction, 103*(3), 462–468.

16. Schwartz, R. P., Gryczynski, J., O'Grady, K. E., Sharfstein, J. M., Warren, G., Olsen, Y., … Jaffe, J. H. (2013). Opioid agonist treatments and heroin overdose deaths in Baltimore, Maryland, 1995–2009. *American Journal of Public Health, 103*(5), 917–922.

17. World Health Organization. (2009). *Guidelines for the psychosocially assisted pharmacological treatment of opioid dependence.* Geneva, Switzerland: WHO Press.

18. Brezing, C., & Bisaga, A. (2015, April 30). Opioid use disorder: Update on diagnosis and treatment. *Psychiatric Times, 32*(4) 1–4.

19. Department of Health and Human Services, Office of the Surgeon General. (2016). *Facing addiction in America: The Surgeon General's report on alcohol, drugs, and health.* Washington, DC: Department of Health and Human Services.

20. Jones, C. M., Campopiano, M., Baldwin, G., & McCance-Katz, E. (2015). National and state treatment need and capacity for opioid agonist medication-assisted treatment. *American Journal of Public Health, 105*(8), e55–e63.

21. Blue Cross Blue Shield. (2017). *America's opioid epidemic and its effect on the nation's commercially insured population.* Washington, DC: Blue Cross Blue Shield Association.

22. Jones, C. M., Campopiano, M., Baldwin, G., & McCance-Katz, E. (2015). National and state treatment need and capacity for opioid agonist medication-assisted treatment. *American Journal of Public Health, 105*(8), e55–e63.

23. Mattick, R. P., Breen, C., Kimber, J., & Davoli, M. (2014). Buprenorphine maintenance versus placebo or methadone maintenance for opioid dependence. *Cochrane Database of Systematic Reviews, 2014*(2), 1–84.

24. Sees, K. L., Delucchi, K. L., Masson, C., Rosen, A., Clark, H. W., Robillard, H., … Hall, S. M. (2000). Methadone maintenance vs 180-day psychosocially enriched detoxification for treatment of opioid dependence: A randomized controlled trial. *JAMA, 283*(10), 1303–1310.

25. Nielsen, S., Larance, B., Degenhardt, L., Gowing, L., Kehler, C., & Lintzeris, N. (2016). Opioid agonist treatment for pharmaceutical opioid dependent people. *Cochrane Database of Systematic Reviews, 2016*(5), 1–61.

26. Amato, L., Davoli, M., Perucci, C. A., Ferri, M., Faggiano, F., & Mattick, R. P. (2005). An overview of systematic reviews of the effectiveness of opiate maintenance therapies: Available evidence to inform clinical practice and research. *Journal of Substance Abuse Treatment, 28*(4), 321–329.

27. Faggiano, F., Vigna-Taglianti, F., Versino, E., & Lemma, P. (2003). Methadone maintenance at different dosages for opioid dependence. *Cochrane Database of Systematic Reviews, 2003*(3), 1–45.

28. Herget, G. (2005). Methadone and buprenorphine added to the WHO list of essential medicines. *HIV/AIDS Policy and Law Review, 10*(3), 23–24.

29. Gossop, M., Marsden, J., Stewart, D., & Kidd, T. (2003). The National Treatment Outcome Research Study (NTORS): 4–5 year follow-up results. *Addiction, 98*(3), 291–303.

30. Lawrinson, P., Ali, R., Buavirat, A., Chiamwongpaet, S., Dvoryak, S., Habrat, B., ... Zhao, C. (2008). Key findings from the WHO collaborative study on substitution therapy for opioid dependence and HIV/AIDS. *Addiction, 103*(9), 1484–1492.

31. Teesson, M., Ross, J., Darke, S., Lynskey, M., Ali, R., Ritter, A., & Cooke, R. (2006). One year outcomes for heroin dependence: Findings from the Australian Treatment Outcome Study (ATOS). *Drug and Alcohol Dependence, 83*(2), 174–180.

32. Bruce, R. D. (2010). Methadone as HIV prevention: High volume methadone sites to decrease HIV incidence rates in resource limited settings. *International Journal on Drug Policy, 21*(2), 122–124.

33. Fullerton, C. A., Kim, M., Thomas, C. P., Lyman, D. R., Montejano, L. B., Dougherty, R. H., ... Delphin-Rittmon, M. E. (2014). Medication-assisted treatment with methadone: Assessing the evidence. *Psychiatric Services, 65*(2), 146–157.

34. Gowing, L., Farrell, M. F., Bornemann, R., Sullivan, L. E., & Ali, R. (2011). Oral substitution treatment of injecting opioid users for prevention of HIV infection. *Cochrane Database of Systematic Reviews, 2011*(8), 1–117.

35. MacArthur, G. J., Minozzi, S., Martin, N., Vickerman, P., Deren, S., Bruneau, J., ... Hickman, M. (2012). Opiate substitution treatment and HIV transmission in people who inject drugs: Systematic review and meta-analysis. *BMJ, 345*, e5945.

36. Mattick, R. P., Breen, C., Kimber, J., & Davoli, M. (2009). Methadone maintenance therapy versus no opioid replacement therapy for opioid dependence. *Cochrane Database of Systematic Reviews, 2009*(3), 1–19.

37. Metzger, D. S., & Zhang, Y. (2010). Drug treatment as HIV prevention: Expanding treatment options. *Current HIV/AIDS Reports, 7*(4), 220–225.

38. Woody, G. E., Bruce, D., Korthuis, P. T., Chhatre, S., Poole, S., Hillhouse, M., ... Ling, W. (2014). HIV risk reduction with buprenorphine-naloxone or methadone: Findings from a randomized trial. *Journal of Acquired Immune Deficiency Syndromes, 66*(3), 288–293.

39. Fullerton, C. A., Kim, M., Thomas, C. P., Lyman, D. R., Montejano, L. B., Dougherty, R. H., ... Delphin-Rittmon, M. E. (2014). Medication-assisted treatment with methadone: Assessing the evidence. *Psychiatric Services, 65*(2), 146–157.

40. Schwartz, R. P., Jaffe, J. H., O'Grady, K. E., Kinlock, T. W., Gordon, M. S., Kelly, S. M., ... Ahmed, A. (2009). Interim methadone treatment: Impact on arrests. *Drug and Alcohol Dependence, 103*(3), 148–154.

41. Lee, J. D., Friedmann, P. D., Kinlock, T. W., Nunes, E. V., Boney, T. Y., Hoskinson, R. A., Jr., ... O'Brien, C. P. (2016). Extended-release naltrexone to prevent opioid relapse in criminal justice offenders. *New England Journal of Medicine, 374*(13), 1232–1242.

42. Comer, S. D., Sullivan, M. A., Yu, E., Rothenberg, J. L., Kleber, H. D., Kampman, K., ... O'Brien, C. P. (2006). Injectable, sustained-release naltrexone for the treatment of opioid dependence: A randomized, placebo-controlled trial. *Archives of General Psychiatry, 63*(2), 210–218.

43. Krupitsky, E., Nunes, E. V., Ling, W., Illeperuma, A., Gastfriend, D. R., & Silverman, B. L. (2011, April 30). Injectable extended-release naltrexone for opioid dependence: A double-blind, placebo-controlled, multicentre randomised trial. *Lancet, 377*(9776), 1506–1513.

44. Lee, J. D., Friedmann, P. D., Kinlock, T. W., Nunes, E. V., Boney, T. Y., Hoskinson, R. A., Jr., ... O'Brien, C. P. (2016). Extended-release naltrexone to prevent opioid relapse in criminal justice offenders. *New England Journal of Medicine, 374*(13), 1232–1242.

45. Lee, J. D., Nunes, E. V., Jr., Novo, P., Bachrach, K., Bailey, G. L., Bhatt, S., ... Rotrosen, J. (2018). Comparative effectiveness of extended-release naltrexone versus buprenorphine-naloxone for opioid relapse prevention (X:BOT): A multicentre, open-label, randomised controlled trial. *Lancet, 391*(10118), 309–318.

46. Tanum, L., Solli, K. K., Latif, Z. E., Benth, J. Š., Opheim, A., Sharma-Haase, K., ... Kunøe, N. (2017). Effectiveness of injectable extended-release naltrexone vs daily buprenorphine-naloxone for opioid dependence: A randomized clinical noninferiority trial. *JAMA Psychiatry, 74*(12), 1197–1205.

47. Minozzi, S., Amato, L., Vecchi, S., Davoli, M., Kirchmayer, U., & Verster, A. (2011). Oral naltrexone maintenance treatment for opioid dependence. *Cochrane Database of Systematic Reviews, 2011*(2), 1–45.

48. Mattick, R. P., Breen, C., Kimber, J., & Davoli, M. (2014). Buprenorphine maintenance versus placebo or methadone maintenance for opioid dependence. *Cochrane Database of Systematic Reviews, 2014*(2), 1–84.

49. Edelman, E. J., Chantarat, T., Caffrey, S., Chaudhry, A., O'Connor, P. G., Weiss, L., … Fiellin, L. E. (2014). The impact of buprenorphine/naloxone treatment on HIV risk behaviors among HIV-infected, opioid-dependent patients. *Drug and Alcohol Dependence, 139*, 79–85.

50. Sullivan, L. E., Moore, B. A., Chawarski, M. C., Pantalon, M. V., Barry, D., O'Connor, P. G., … Fiellin, D. A. (2008). Buprenorphine/naloxone treatment in primary care is associated with decreased human immunodeficiency virus risk behaviors. *Journal of Substance Abuse Treatment, 35*(1), 87–92.

51. Weiss, R. D., Potter, J. S., Fiellin, D. A., Byrne, M., Connery, H. S., Dickinson, W., … Ling, W. (2011). Adjunctive counseling during brief and extended buprenorphine-naloxone treatment for prescription opioid dependence: A 2-phase randomized controlled trial. *Archives of General Psychiatry, 68*(12), 1238–1246.

52. Fiellin, D. A., Schottenfeld, R. S., Cutter, C. J., Moore, B. A., Barry, D. T., & O'Connor, P. G. (2014). Primary care-based buprenorphine taper vs maintenance therapy for prescription opioid dependence: A randomized clinical trial. *JAMA Internal Medicine, 174*(12), 1947–1954.

53. Fiellin, D. A., Moore, B. A., Sullivan, L. E., Becker, W. C., Pantalon, M. V., Chawarski, M. C., … Schottenfeld, R. S. (2008). Long-term treatment with buprenorphine/naloxone in primary care: Results at 2–5 years. *American Journal on Addictions, 17*(2), 116–120.

54. Soeffing, J. M., Martin, L. D., Fingerhood, M. I., Jasinski, D. R., & Rastegar, D. A. (2009). Buprenorphine maintenance treatment in a primary care setting: Outcomes at 1 year. *Journal of Substance Abuse Treatment, 37*(4), 426–430.

55. Herget, G. (2005). Methadone and buprenorphine added to the WHO list of essential medicines. *HIV/AIDS Policy and Law Review, 10*(3), 23–24.

56. Rosenthal, R. N., Lofwall, M. R., Kim, S., Chen, M., Beebe, K. L., Vocci, F. J., & PRO-814 Study Group. (2016). Effect of buprenorphine implants on illicit opioid use among abstinent adults with opioid dependence treated with sublingual buprenorphine: A randomized clinical trial. *Journal of the American Medical Association, 316*(3), 282–290.

57. Rosenthal, R. N., Lofwall, M. R., Kim, S., Chen, M., Beebe, K. L., & Vocci, F. J. (2016). Effect of buprenorphine implants on illicit opioid use among abstinent adults with opioid dependence treated with sublingual buprenorphine: A randomized clinical trial. *JAMA, 316*(3), 282–290.

58. Barnwal, P., Das, S., Mondal, S., Ramasamy, A., Maiti, T., & Saha, A. (2017). Probuphine® (buprenorphine implant): Promising candidate in opioid dependence. *Therapeutic Advances in Psychopharmacology, 7*(3), 119–134.

59. Connock, M., Juarez-Garcia, A., Jowett, S., Frew, E., Liu, Z., Taylor, R. J., … Taylor, R. S. (2007, March). Methadone and buprenorphine for the management of opioid dependence: A systematic review and economic evaluation. *Health Technology Assessment, 11*(9), 1–171, iii–iv.

60. Lynch, F. L., McCarty, D., Mertens, J., Perrin, N. A., Green, C. A., Parthasarathy, S., … Pating, D. (2014). Costs of care for persons with opioid dependence in commercial integrated health systems. *Addiction Science and Clinical Practice, 9*, 16.

61. Baser, O., Chalk, M., Fiellin, D. A., & Gastfriend, D. R. (2011). Cost and utilization outcomes of opioid-dependence treatments. *American Journal of Managed Care, 17*(Suppl. 8), S235–S248.

62. Schwartz, R. P., Alexandre, P. K., Kelly, S. M., O'Grady, K. E., Gryczynski, J., & Jaffe, J. H. (2014). Interim versus standard methadone treatment: A benefit-cost analysis. *Journal of Substance Abuse Treatment, 46*(3), 306–314.

63. Cartwright, W. S. (2000). Cost-benefit analysis of drug treatment services: Review of the literature. *Journal of Mental Health Policy and Economics, 3*(1), 11–26.

64. McCollister, K. E., & French, M. T. (2003). The relative contribution of outcome domains in the total economic benefit of addiction interventions: A review of first findings. *Addiction, 98*(12), 1647–1659.

65. Substance Abuse and Mental Health Services Administration. (2015). *Federal guidelines for opioid treatment programs.* HHS Publication No. (SMA) PEP15-FEDGUIDEOTP. Rockville, MD: Substance Abuse and Mental Health Services Administration.

66. Drug Enforcement Administration. (n.d.). Title 21 Code of Federal Regulations. Part 1306—Prescriptions. §1306.07 Administering or dispensing of narcotic drugs. Retrieved November 22, 2017, from www.deadiversion.usdoj.gov/21cfr/cfr/1306/1306_07.htm

67. Mattick, R. P., Breen, C., Kimber, J., & Davoli, M. (2009). Methadone maintenance therapy versus no opioid replacement therapy for opioid dependence. *Cochrane Database of Systematic Reviews, 2009*(3), 1–19.

68. Mattick, R. P., Breen, C., Kimber, J., & Davoli, M. (2014). Buprenorphine maintenance versus placebo or methadone maintenance for opioid dependence. *Cochrane Database of Systematic Reviews, 2014*(2), 1–84.

69 Calsyn, D. A., Malcy, J. A., & Saxon, A. J. (2006). Slow tapering from methadone maintenance in a program encouraging indefinite maintenance. *Journal of Substance Abuse Treatment, 30*, 159–163.

70 Stimmel, B., Goldberg, J., Rotkopf, E., & Cohen, M. (1977). Ability to remain abstinent after methadone detoxification. *JAMA, 237*, 1216–1220.

71 Cushman, P. (1978). Abstinence following detoxification and methadone maintenance treatment. *American Journal of Medicine, 65*, 46–52.

72 Nosyk, B., Sun, H., Evans, E., Marsh, D. C., Anglin, M. D., Hser, Y. I., & Anis, A. H. (2012). Defining dosing pattern characteristics of successful tapers following methadone maintenance treatment: Results from a population-based retrospective cohort study. *Addiction, 107*(9), 1621–1629.

73 Lee, J. D., Friedmann, P. D., Kinlock, T. W., Nunes, E. V., Boney, T. Y., Hoskinson, R. A., Jr., … O'Brien, C. P. (2016). Extended-release naltrexone to prevent opioid relapse in criminal justice offenders. *New England Journal of Medicine, 374*(13), 1232–1242.

74 Sees, K. L., Delucchi, K. L., Masson, C., Rosen, A., Clark, H. W., Robillard, H., … Hall, S. M. (2000). Methadone maintenance vs 180-day psychosocially enriched detoxification for treatment of opioid dependence: A randomized controlled trial. *JAMA, 283*(10), 1303–1310.

75 Wines, J. D., Jr., Saitz, R., Horton, N. J., Lloyd-Travaglini, C., & Samet, J. H. (2007). Overdose after detoxification: A prospective study. *Drug and Alcohol Dependence, 89*(2–3), 161–169.

76 Strang, J., McCambridge, J., Best, D., Beswick, T., Bearn, J., Rees, S., & Gossop, M. (2003). Loss of tolerance and overdose mortality after inpatient opiate detoxification: Follow up study. *British Medical Journal, 326*(7396), 959–960.

77 Weiss, R. D., Potter, J. S., Fiellin, D. A., Byrne, M., Connery, H. S., Dickinson, W., … Ling, W. (2011). Adjunctive counseling during brief and extended buprenorphine-naloxone treatment for prescription opioid dependence: A 2-phase randomized controlled trial. *Archives of General Psychiatry, 68*(12), 1238–1246.

78 Ling, W., Amass, L., Shoptaw, S., Annon, J. J., Hillhouse, M., Babcock, D., … Ziedonis, D. (2005). A multi-center randomized trial of buprenorphine-naloxone versus clonidine for opioid detoxification: Findings from the National Institute on Drug Abuse Clinical Trials Network. *Addiction, 100*(8), 1090–1100.

79 McCusker, J., Bigelow, C., Luippold, R., Zorn, M., & Lewis, B. F. (1995). Outcomes of a 21-day drug detoxification program: Retention, transfer to further treatment, and HIV risk reduction. *American Journal of Drug and Alcohol Abuse, 21*(1), 1–16.

80 Fiellin, D., Schottenfeld, R., Cutter, C., Moore, A., Barry, D., & O'Connor, P. (2014). Primary care based buprenorphine taper vs maintenance therapy for prescription opioid dependence: A randomized clinical trial. *JAMA Internal Medicine, 174*(12), 1947–1954.

81 Gruber, V., Delucchi, K., Kielstein, A., & Batki, S. (2008). A randomized trial of six-month methadone maintenance with standard or minimal counseling versus 21-day methadone detoxification. *Drug and Alcohol Dependence, 94*, 199.

82 Ling, W., Hillhouse, M., Domier, C., Doraimani, G., Hunter, J., Thomas, C., … Bilangi, R. (2009). Buprenorphine tapering schedule and illicit opioid use. *Addiction, 104*(2), 256–265.

83 Smyth, B. P., Barry, J., Keenan, E., & Ducray, K. (2010). Lapse and relapse following inpatient treatment of opiate dependence. *Irish Medical Journal, 103*(6), 176–179.

84 Amato, L., Minozzi, S., Davoli, M., & Vecchi, S. (2011). Psychosocial and pharmacological treatments versus pharmacological treatments for opioid detoxification. *Cochrane Database of Systematic Reviews, 2011*(9), 1–55.

85 Department of Health and Human Services, Office of the Surgeon General. (2016). *Facing addiction in America: The Surgeon General's report on alcohol, drugs, and health*. Washington, DC: Department of Health and Human Services.

86 Saloner, B., & Karthikeyan, S. (2015). Changes in substance abuse treatment use among individuals with opioid use disorders in the United States, 2004–2013. *JAMA, 314*(14), 1515–1517.

87 Van Handel, M. M., Rose, C. E., Hallisey, E. J., Kolling, J. L., Zibbell, J. E., Lewis, B., … Brooks, J. T. (2016). County-level vulnerability assessment for rapid dissemination of HIV or HCV infections among persons who inject drugs, United States. *Journal of Acquired Immune Deficiency Syndromes, 73*(3), 323–331.

TIP 63 — MEDICATIONS FOR OPIOID USE DISORDER

Part 2: Addressing Opioid Use Disorder in General Medical Settings
For Healthcare Professionals

Part 2 of this **Treatment Improvement Protocol (TIP)** will guide practitioners' efforts to identify, assess, and treat or refer patients with opioid use disorder (OUD) in general medical settings.

TIP Navigation

Executive Summary
For healthcare and addiction professionals, policymakers, patients, and families

Part 1: Introduction to Medications for Opioid Use Disorder Treatment
For healthcare and addiction professionals, policymakers, patients, and families

Part 2: Addressing Opioid Use Disorder in General Medical Settings
For healthcare professionals

Part 3: Pharmacotherapy for Opioid Use Disorder
For healthcare professionals

Part 4: Partnering Addiction Treatment Counselors With Clients and Healthcare Professionals
For healthcare and addiction professionals

Part 5: Resources Related to Medication for Opioid Use Disorder
For healthcare and addiction professionals, policymakers, patients, and families

KEY MESSAGES

- All healthcare practices should screen for alcohol, tobacco, and other substance misuse (including opioid misuse).
- Validated screening tools, symptom surveys, and other resources are readily available; this part lists many of them.
- When patients screen positive for risk of harm from substance use, practitioners should assess them using tools that determine whether substance use meets diagnostic criteria for a substance use disorder (SUD).
- Thorough assessment should address patients' medical, social, SUD, and family histories.
- Laboratory tests can inform treatment planning.
- Practitioners should develop treatment plans or referral strategies (if onsite SUD treatment is unavailable) for patients who need SUD treatment.

Substance Abuse and Mental Health Services Administration
www.samhsa.gov • 1-877-SAMHSA-7 (1-877-726-4727)

PART 2: ADDRESSING OPIOID USE DISORDER IN GENERAL MEDICAL SETTINGS

Scope of the Problem 2-1

Screening 2-1

Assessment 2-8

Treatment Planning or Referral 2-17

Resources 2-28

Appendix 2-32

Notes 2-39

TIP 63  MEDICATIONS FOR OPIOID USE DISORDER

PART 2 of 5
Addressing Opioid Use Disorder in General Medical Settings

Part 2 of this TIP is for healthcare professionals who work in general medical settings* and care for patients who misuse opioids or have OUD. Healthcare professionals in such settings address most personal healthcare needs, develop sustained partnerships with patients, and practice in the context of family and community. Thus, they have a good basis from which to understand patients' needs related to OUD screening, assessment, and treatment (or referral to specialty treatment.

Scope of the Problem

The number of patients presenting with OUD in medical clinics, community health centers, and private practices is increasing. Healthcare professionals in these general settings are in an important position to identify, assess, and treat OUD or to refer patients for treatment. Moreover, patients who are medically and mentally stable can benefit from receiving OUD medications in integrated care settings, where they often have already established therapeutic relationships with their healthcare providers.

Exhibit 2.1 defines key terms in Part 2. For more definitions, see the glossary in Part 5 of this TIP.

Screening

Screening can identify patients who may have diseases or conditions related to their substance use. Health care in general medical settings routinely includes screening for common, treatable conditions such as cancer that are associated with significant morbidity and mortality. Screening for SUDs is important, as misuse of alcohol, tobacco, and other substances is common among patients in medical settings (Exhibit 2.2).[1]

An estimated **1.9M AMERICANS** have OUD related to opioid painkillers; **589K,** related to heroin.[2]

Screening can identify substance misuse in patients who wouldn't otherwise discuss it or connect it with the negative consequences they're experiencing. Some patients may spontaneously reveal their substance use and ask for help. This is more likely when they're experiencing harmful consequences of substance use. However, screening may identify unhealthy substance use (e.g., binge drinking) and SUDs

The TIP expert panel recommends that healthcare professionals screen patients for alcohol, tobacco, prescription drug, and illicit drug use at least annually.

---

*In this TIP, the term "general medical setting" includes medical clinics, community health centers, and private practices.

EXHIBIT 2.1. Key Terms

Addiction: As defined by the American Society of Addiction Medicine (ASAM),[3] "a primary, chronic disease of brain reward, motivation, memory, and related circuitry." It is characterized by inability to consistently abstain, impairment in behavioral control, craving, diminished recognition of significant problems with one's behaviors and interpersonal relationships, and a dysfunctional emotional response. Like other chronic diseases, addiction often involves cycles of **relapse** and **remission.** The *Diagnostic and Statistical Manual of Mental Disorders,* Fifth Edition[4] (DSM-5), does not use the term for diagnostic purposes, but it commonly describes the more severe forms of OUD.

Healthcare professionals: Physicians, nurse practitioners (NPs), physician assistants (PAs), and other medical service professionals who are eligible to prescribe medications for and treat patients with OUD. The term "**prescribers**" also refers to these healthcare professionals.

Maintenance treatment: Providing medications to achieve and sustain clinical remission of signs and symptoms of OUD and support the individual process of recovery without a specific endpoint (as with the typical standard of care in medical and psychiatric treatment of other chronic illnesses).

Medically supervised withdrawal (formerly called detoxification): Using an opioid agonist (or an alpha-2 adrenergic agonist if an opioid agonist is not available) in tapering doses or other medications to help a patient discontinue illicit or prescription opioids.

Medical management: Process whereby healthcare professionals provide medication, basic brief supportive counseling, monitoring of drug use and medication adherence, and referrals, when necessary, to addiction counseling and other services to address the patient's medical, mental health, comorbid addiction, and psychosocial needs.

Office-based opioid treatment (OBOT): Providing medication for OUD in outpatient settings other than certified opioid treatment programs (OTPs).

Opioid misuse: The use of prescription opioids in any way other than as directed by a prescriber; the use of any opioid in a manner, situation, amount, or frequency that can cause harm to self or others.[5]

Opioid receptor agonist: A substance that has an affinity for and stimulates physiological activity at cell receptors in the central nervous system that are normally stimulated by opioids. **Mu-opioid receptor full agonists** (e.g., methadone) bind to the mu-opioid receptor and produce actions similar to those produced by the endogenous opioid beta-endorphin. Increasing the dose increases the effect. **Mu-opioid receptor partial agonists** (e.g., buprenorphine) bind to the mu-opioid receptor. Unlike with full agonists, increasing their dose may not produce additional effects once they have reached their maximal effect. At low doses, partial agonists may produce effects similar to those of full agonists.

Opioid receptor antagonist: A substance that has an affinity for opioid receptors in the central nervous system without producing the physiological effects of opioid agonists. Mu-opioid receptor antagonists (e.g., naltrexone) can block the effects of exogenously administered opioids.

Opioid treatment program (OTP): An accredited treatment program with Substance Abuse and Mental Health Services Administration (SAMHSA) certification and Drug Enforcement Administration (DEA) registration to administer and dispense opioid agonist medications that are approved by the Food and Drug Administration (FDA) to treat opioid addiction. Currently, these include methadone and buprenorphine products. Other pharmacotherapies, such as naltrexone, may be provided but are not subject to these regulations. OTPs must provide adequate medical, counseling, vocational, educational, and other assessment and treatment services either onsite or by referral to an outside agency or practitioner through a formal agreement.[6]

Continued on next page

EXHIBIT 2.1. Key Terms (continued)

Opioid use disorder (OUD): Per DSM-5,[7] a disorder characterized by loss of control of opioid use, risky opioid use, impaired social functioning, tolerance, and withdrawal. Tolerance and withdrawal do not count toward the diagnosis in people experiencing these symptoms when using opioids under appropriate medical supervision. OUD covers a range of severity and replaces what the *Diagnostic and Statistical Manual of Mental Disorders,* Fourth Edition, termed "opioid abuse" and "opioid dependence." An OUD diagnosis is applicable to a person who uses opioids and experiences at least 2 of the 11 symptoms in a 12-month period. (See Exhibit 2.13 and the Appendix in Part 2 for full DSM-5 diagnostic criteria for OUD.)

Recovery: A process of change through which individuals improve their health and wellness, live a self-directed life, and strive to reach their full potential. Even individuals with severe and chronic SUDs can, with help, overcome their SUDs and regain health and social function. Although abstinence from all substance misuse is a cardinal feature of a recovery lifestyle, it is not the only healthy, prosocial feature. Patients taking FDA-approved medication to treat OUD can be considered in recovery.

Relapse: A process in which a person with OUD who has been in **remission** experiences a return of symptoms or loss of remission. A relapse is different from a **return to opioid use** in that it involves more than a single incident of use. Relapses occur over a period of time and can be interrupted. Relapse need not be long lasting. The TIP uses relapse to describe relapse prevention, a common treatment modality.

Remission: A medical term meaning a disappearance of signs and symptoms of the disease.[8] DSM-5 defines remission as present in people who previously met OUD criteria but no longer meet any OUD criteria (with the possible exception of craving).[9] Remission is an essential element of **recovery**.

Return to opioid use: One or more instances of **opioid misuse** without a return of symptoms of OUD. A return to opioid use may lead to **relapse**.

Tolerance: Alteration of the body's responsiveness to alcohol or other drugs (including opioids) such that higher doses are required to produce the same effect achieved during initial use. See also **medically supervised withdrawal**.

---

before patients connect their substance use with their presenting complaint. Screening is also helpful when patients feel ashamed or afraid to reveal their concerns spontaneously.

Every medical practice should determine which screening tools to use and when, how, and by whom they will be administered. Each practice should also identify steps to take when a patient screens positive. One efficient workflow strategy is to have clinical assistants or nurses administer the screening instrument in an interview or provide patients with a paper or computer tablet version for self-administration. (Self-administration is generally as reliable as interviewer administration.)[10] Providers should be nonjudgmental and rely on established rapport when discussing screening results with patients.

The following sections summarize reliable screening tools. (See Part 5 for more resources.)

Alcohol Screening

Screening for alcohol misuse can identify patients at increased risk for opioid use. When screening patients for opioid misuse, providers should also screen for alcohol misuse and alcohol use disorder (AUD), which cause considerable morbidity and mortality.[11] Providers should warn patients who use opioids that alcohol may increase opioid overdose risk.[12] The U.S. Preventive Services Task Force (USPSTF) recommends screening adults for alcohol misuse, including risky drinking and AUD. USPSTF also recommends brief counseling for patients with risky drinking.[13,14]

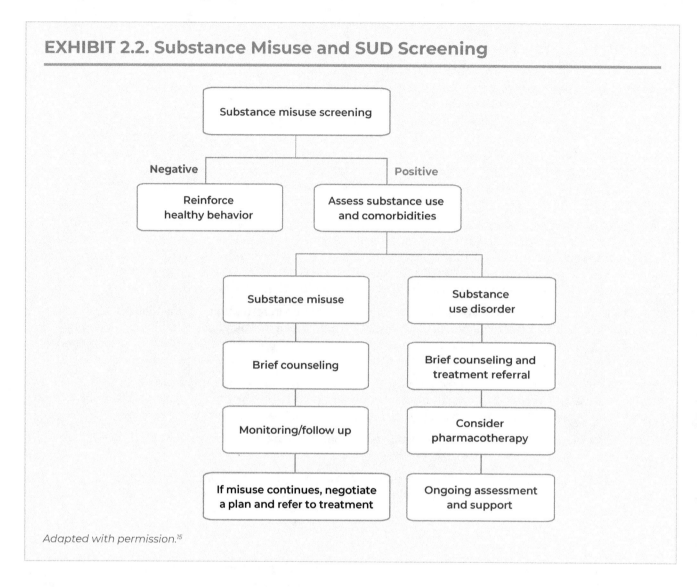

Adapted with permission.[15]

USPSTF recommends the following alcohol screeners:

- **The single-item National Institute on Alcohol Abuse and Alcoholism (NIAAA) Screener** is the briefest tool available (Exhibit 2.3). It can help distinguish at-risk patients who require further screening from those not at risk for AUD. Encourage patients in the latter category to maintain healthy behavior.
- **The Alcohol Use Disorders Identification Test (AUDIT)[16] or its briefer version, the AUDIT-Consumption,[17]** can elicit more information from patients who screen positive on the single-item screener. The full AUDIT tool (Exhibit 2.4) and its briefer version have demonstrated acceptable reliability in AUD screening.[18] Assess patients with positive screens for AUD.

Practitioners should consider pharmacotherapy and referral for counseling for people with AUD. The three FDA-approved medications to treat AUD—acamprosate, disulfiram, and naltrexone (oral and extended-release injectable naltrexone [XR-NTX])—can be prescribed in general medical and specialty SUD treatment settings. (For more information on AUD treatment, see the SAMHSA/NIAAA publication *Medication for the Treatment of Alcohol Use Disorder: A Brief Guide*.)[19]

EXHIBIT 2.3. NIAAA Single-Item Screener

How many times in the past year have you had five or more drinks in a day (four drinks for women and all adults older than age 65)?

One or more times constitutes a positive screen. Patients who screen positive should have an assessment for AUD.

Adapted with permission.[20]

Tobacco Screening

More than 80 percent of patients who are opioid dependent smoke cigarettes.[21] Understanding of the major health consequences and risks associated with tobacco use has grown significantly over the past 50 years. Among preventable causes of premature death, smoking remains most prevalent, with more than 480,000 deaths per year in the United States.[22] In addition, more than 40 percent of all people who smoke are mentally ill or have SUDs.[23,24]

USPSTF recommends that primary care providers screen for tobacco use, advise patients to quit, and provide counseling and FDA-approved medications for tobacco cessation.[25] The six-item Fagerström Test for Nicotine Dependence[26] assesses cigarette use and nicotine dependence. The maximum score is 10; the higher the total score, the more severe the patient's nicotine dependence. The two-item Heaviness of Smoking Index (Exhibit 2.5) is also useful.[27]

Drug Screening

Screening for illicit drug use and prescription medication misuse is clinically advantageous. USPSTF's position as of this writing is that insufficient evidence exists to recommend for or against routine screening for illicit drug use in primary care.[28] However, there are clinical reasons to screen for prescription medication misuse and use of illicit substances. Identifying misuse of prescription or illegal drugs can prevent harmful drug interactions, lead to adjustments in prescribing practices, improve medical care adherence, and increase the odds of patients getting needed interventions or treatment.[29]

Brief screening instruments for drug use can determine which patients need further assessment. Providers should reinforce healthy behaviors among patients who report "no use" and direct those who report "some use" for further screening and assessment to obtain a diagnosis.

Several brief screening instruments for drug use can help primary care practitioners identify patients who use drugs.[30,31] For example, a single-item screen is available for the general public (Exhibit 2.6).[32] A two-item valid screener is available for use with U.S. veterans (Exhibit 2.7).[33]

Brief drug screens don't indicate specific types of drugs used (nor does the longer Drug Abuse Screening Test; see the Part 2 Appendix).[34] If providers use nonspecific screens, they need to assess further which substances patients use and to what degree.

The TIP expert panel recommends universal OUD screening. Given the high prevalence of SUDs in patients visiting primary care settings and the effectiveness of medications to treat OUD specifically, the TIP expert panel recommends screening all patients for opioid misuse.

EXHIBIT 2.4. AUDIT Screener

1. How often do you have a drink containing alcohol?

    (0) Never [Skip to Questions 9–10]
    (1) Monthly or less
    (2) 2 to 4 times a month
    (3) 2 to 3 times a week
    (4) 4 or more times a week

2. How many drinks containing alcohol do you have on a typical day when you are drinking?

    (0) 1 or 2
    (1) 3 or 4
    (2) 5 or 6
    (3) 7, 8, or 9
    (4) 10 or more

3. How often do you have six or more drinks on one occasion?

    (0) Never
    (1) Less than monthly
    (2) Monthly
    (3) Weekly
    (4) Daily or almost daily

    Skip to Questions 9 and 10 if total score for Questions 2 and 3 = 0

4. How often during the last year have you found that you were not able to stop drinking once you had started?

    (0) Never
    (1) Less than monthly
    (2) Monthly
    (3) Weekly
    (4) Daily or almost daily

5. How often during the last year have you failed to do what was normally expected from you because of drinking?

    (0) Never
    (1) Less than monthly
    (2) Monthly
    (3) Weekly
    (4) Daily or almost daily

6. How often during the last year have you needed an alcoholic drink first thing in the morning to get yourself going after a night of heavy drinking?

    (0) Never
    (1) Less than monthly
    (2) Monthly
    (3) Weekly
    (4) Daily or almost daily

7. How often during the last year have you had a feeling of guilt or remorse after drinking?

    (0) Never
    (1) Less than monthly
    (2) Monthly
    (3) Weekly
    (4) Daily or almost daily

8. How often during the last year have you been unable to remember what happened the night before because you had been drinking?

    (0) Never
    (1) Less than monthly
    (2) Monthly
    (3) Weekly
    (4) Daily or almost daily

9. Have you or someone else been injured as a result of your drinking?

    (0) No
    (2) Yes, but not in the last year
    (4) Yes, during the last year

10. Has a relative, friend, doctor, or another health professional expressed concern about your drinking or suggested you cut down?

    (0) No
    (2) Yes, but not in the last year
    (4) Yes, during the last year

Note: Add up the points associated with answers. A score of 8 or more is considered a positive test for unhealthy drinking. Adapted from material in the public domain.[35] Available online (http://auditscreen.org).

EXHIBIT 2.5. Heaviness of Smoking Index

Ask these two questions of current or recent smokers:

1. How soon after waking do you smoke your first cigarette?
   - Within 5 minutes (3 points)
   - 5–30 minutes (2 points)
   - 31–60 minutes (1 point)
   - 61 or more minutes (no points)

2. How many cigarettes a day do you smoke?
   - 10 or less (no points)
   - 11–20 (1 point)
   - 21–30 (2 points)
   - 31 or more (3 points)

Total score:
1–2 points = very low dependence
3 points = low to moderate dependence
4 points = moderate dependence
5 or more points = high dependence

Adapted with permission.[36]

EXHIBIT 2.6. Single-Item Drug Screener

How many times in the past year have you used an illegal drug or a prescription medication for nonmedical reasons?

(A positive screen is 1 or more days.)

Reprinted with permission.[39]

EXHIBIT 2.7. Two-Item Drug Use Disorder Screener for Primary Care Clinics Serving U.S. Veterans

Question 1: How many days in the past 12 months have you used drugs other than alcohol? (A positive screen is 7 or more days.) If fewer than 7, proceed with Question 2.

Question 2: How many days in the past 12 months have you used drugs more than you meant to? (A positive screen is 2 or more days.)

Adapted with permission.[40]

The Alcohol, Smoking, and Substance Involvement Screening Test (ASSIST) screens patients for all categories of substance misuse, including alcohol and tobacco. This World Health Organization (WHO) screener also assesses substance-specific risk. The ASSIST's length and rather complex scoring system have hindered its adoption, but a computerized version and a briefer hard copy version (ASSIST-lite) make its use more efficient.[37,38] (See the "Screening, Assessment, and Drug Testing Resources" section for a link to a modified version of the ASSIST.)

The TIP expert panel does not recommend routine universal drug testing with urine, blood, or oral fluids in primary care. Still, drug testing can confirm recent drug use in patients receiving diagnostic workups for changes in mental status, seizures, or other disorders. Conduct drug testing before patients start OUD medication and during treatment for monitoring.

Follow up any positive one-question screen with a brief assessment. An example of a two-step screening and brief assessment is the Tobacco, Alcohol, Prescription Medications, and Other Substance Use (TAPS Tool; see Part 2 Appendix), developed and tested in primary care settings.[41] This tool is based on the National Institute on Drug Abuse (NIDA) Quick Screen V1.0[42,43] and a modified WHO ASSIST-lite.[44]

The TAPS Tool screens for clinically relevant heroin and prescription opioid misuse (meeting one or more DSM-5 SUD criteria) and misuse of an array of other substances in primary care patients. However, it may also detect SUDs only for the most often-used substances (i.e., alcohol, tobacco, and marijuana). Patients with positive screens for heroin or prescription opioid misuse need more indepth assessment.[45]

Assessment

Determine the Need for and Extent of Assessment

Assess patients for OUD if:

- They screen positive for opioid misuse.
- They disclose opioid misuse.
- Signs or symptoms of opioid misuse are present.

The extent of assessment depends on a provider's ability to treat patients directly.

If a provider does not offer pharmacotherapy, the focus should be on medical assessment, making a diagnosis of OUD, and patient safety. This allows the provider to refer patients to the appropriate level of treatment. The provider can also conduct:

- Assessment and treatment for co-occurring medical conditions or mental disorders.
- Motivational brief interventions to promote safer behavior and foster effective treatment engagement.
- Overdose prevention education and provide a naloxone prescription.
- Education for patients who inject drugs on how to access sterile injecting equipment.
- An in-person follow-up, regardless of referral to specialty treatment.

If the provider offers pharmacotherapy, the patient needs more comprehensive assessment, including:

- A review of the prescription drug monitoring program (PDMP).
- A history, including a review of systems.
- A targeted physical exam for signs of opioid withdrawal, intoxication, injection, and other medical consequences of misuse.
- Determination of OUD diagnosis and severity.
- Appropriate laboratory tests (e.g., urine or oral fluid drug tests, liver function tests, hepatitis B and C tests, HIV tests).[46]

OPIOID ADDICTION is linked with significant **MORBIDITY** and **MORTALITY** related to HIV and hepatitis C.[47]

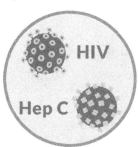

A comprehensive assessment is intended to:

- Establish the diagnosis of OUD.
- Determine the severity of OUD.
- Identify contraindicated medications.
- Indicate other medical conditions to address during treatment.
- Identify mental and social issues to address.

Set the Stage for Successful Assessment

The medical setting should create a welcoming environment that is nonjudgmental, respectful, and empathetic. Many patients with OUD are reluctant to discuss their opioid use in medical settings.[48] A welcoming environment can help patients feel safe disclosing facts they may find embarrassing.[49] Motivational interviewing strategies, such as asking open-ended questions, foster successful assessment.[50] (Refer to TIP 34, *Brief Interventions and Brief Therapies for Substance Abuse*, for more specific examples of interview questions and responses.)[51]

Staff should explore patients' ambivalence and highlight problem areas to help them find motivations for change. Almost all patients have some ambivalence about their opioid use. They will find some aspects pleasant and

Open-ended, thought-provoking questions encourage patients to explore their own experiences. Ask questions like "In what ways has oxycodone affected your life?" or "What could you do to prevent infections like this in the future?" Closed-ended questions with yes/no answers—like "Has oxycodone caused your family trouble?"—can seem judgmental to patients who already feel ashamed and defensive. Closed-ended questions don't help patients become aware of and express their own circumstances and motivations, nor do they encourage patients to identify what they see as the consequences of their substance use.

beneficial, but others problematic, painful, or destructive. By exploring that ambivalence and highlighting problem areas, providers can help patients discover their own motivations for change. *Motivational Interviewing: Helping People Change*[52] discusses specific applications of motivational interviewing in health care.

Take a Complete History

Staff should prioritize medical, mental health, substance use, and SUD treatment histories. When obtaining patient histories, staff should address these domains before starting treatment. As providers and staff build trust over future visits, they can get into more detailed elements of the assessment.

Medical history

Taking a complete medical history of patients with OUD is critical, as it is for patients with any other medical condition treatable with pharmacotherapy. Asking about patients' medical/surgical history can:

- Reveal medical effects of substance use (e.g., endocarditis, soft tissue infection, hepatitis B or C, HIV infection) that may need treatment.
- Highlight consequences that motivate change.
- Identify medical issues (e.g., severe liver disease) that contraindicate or alter dosing approaches for OUD pharmacotherapies.
- Reveal chronic pain issues.
- Help providers consider interactions among various medications and other substances.

Exhibit 2.8 lists medical problems associated with opioid misuse.

Mental health history

Assessing for comorbid mental illness is critical. Mental illness is prevalent among people with SUDs; it can complicate their treatment and worsen their prognosis. In one study, nearly 20 percent of primary care patients with OUD had major depression.[53] SUDs can also mimic or induce depression and anxiety disorders. Although substance-induced depression and anxiety disorders may improve with abstinence, they may still require treatment in their own right after a period of careful observation.[54] Take a history of the relationship between a patient's psychiatric symptoms and periods of substance use and abstinence. Treatment for mental disorders and SUDs can occur concurrently.

Substance use history

Substance use histories can help gauge OUD severity, inform treatment planning, clarify potential drug interactions, and highlight the negative consequences of patients' opioid use.

To help determine the severity of patients' substance use, explore historical features of their use, like:

- Age at first use.
- Routes of ingestion (e.g., injection).
- History of tolerance, withdrawal, drug mixing, and overdose.

Histories should also explore current patterns of use,[55] which inform treatment planning and include:

- Which drugs patients use.

EXHIBIT 2.8. Medical Problems Associated With Opioid Misuse[56]

CATEGORY	POSSIBLE COMPLICATIONS
Cancer	**Injection drug use:** Hepatocellular carcinoma related to hepatitis C
Cardiovascular	**Injection drug use:** Endocarditis, septic thrombophlebitis
Endocrine/metabolic	**Opioids:** Osteopenia, hypogonadism, erectile dysfunction, decreased sperm motility, menstrual irregularity including amenorrhea, infertility
Hematologic	**Injection drug use/sharing intranasal use equipment:** Hematologic consequences of liver disease from hepatitis C, hepatitis C-related cryoglobulinemia and purpura
Hepatic	**Injection drug use/sharing intranasal use equipment:** Hepatitis B, C, D; infectious and toxic hepatitis
Infectious	**Opioids:** Aspiration pneumonia, sexually transmitted infections **Injection drug use:** Endocarditis, cellulitis, necrotizing fasciitis, pneumonia, septic thrombophlebitis, mycotic aneurysm, septic arthritis (unusual joints, such as sternoclavicular), osteomyelitis (including vertebral), epidural and brain abscess, abscesses and soft tissue infections, mediastinitis, malaria, tetanus, hepatitis B, hepatitis C, hepatitis D, HIV, botulism
Neurologic	**Opioids:** Seizure (overdose and hypoxia), compression neuropathy (following overdose), sleep disturbances
Nutritional	**Opioids:** Protein malnutrition
Other gastrointestinal	**Opioids:** Constipation, ileus, intestinal pseudo-obstruction, sphincter of Oddi spasm, nausea
Pulmonary	**Opioids:** Respiratory depression/failure, bronchospasm, exacerbation of sleep apnea, noncardiogenic pulmonary edema, bullae **Injection drug use:** Pulmonary hypertension, talc granulomatosis, septic pulmonary embolism, pneumothorax, emphysema, needle embolization
Renal	**Opioids:** Rhabdomyolysis, acute renal failure (not direct toxic effect of opioids but secondary to central nervous system depression and resulting complications), factitious hematuria **Injection drug use:** Focal glomerular sclerosis (HIV, heroin), glomerulonephritis from hepatitis or endocarditis, chronic renal failure, amyloidosis, nephrotic syndrome (hepatitis C)

- Comorbid alcohol and tobacco use.
- Frequency, recency, and intensity of use.

To diagnose an SUD, assess patients' negative consequences of use, which can affect:

- Physical health.
- Mental health.
- Family relationships.
- Work/career status.
- Legal involvement.
- Housing status.

Buprenorphine and methadone can cause complications for patients who misuse or have

SUDs involving alcohol or benzodiazepines. Providers should take specific histories on the use of these substances.

SUD treatment history

Information about a patient's past efforts to get treatment or quit independently can inform treatment planning. The same is true for details about the events and behaviors that led to a patient's return to substance use after periods of abstinence and remission of SUD. Similarly, identifying the features of successful quit attempts can help guide treatment plan decisions. Such features may involve:

- Specific treatment settings.
- Use of support groups.
- Previous responses to OUD medications.

Social history

Information about a patient's social environments and relationships can aid treatment planning. Social factors that may influence treatment engagement and retention, guide treatment planning, and affect prognosis include:

- Transportation and child care needs.
- Adequacy and stability of housing.
- Criminal justice involvement.
- Employment status and quality of work environment.
- Close/ongoing relationships with people with SUDs.
- Details about drug use from people the patient lives or spends time with (obtained with patient's consent).
- Sexual orientation, identity, and history, including risk factors for HIV/sexually transmitted infections.
- Safety of the home environment. Substance misuse substantially increases the risk of intimate partner violence; screen all women presenting for treatment for domestic violence.[57]

Family history

Learn the substance use histories of patients' parents, siblings, partners, and children. One

Understanding patients' motivations for change can be more useful than assessing "readiness" for change. Patients coerced into treatment—such as through parole and probation or drug courts—are as likely to succeed in treatment as patients engaging voluntarily. Readiness fluctuates and depends on context. Helping patients explore why they want to change their drug use can motivate them and prepare their providers to support them during assessment and treatment.

of the strongest risk factors for developing SUDs is having a parent with an SUD. Genetic factors, exposure to substance use in the household during childhood, or both can contribute to the development of SUDs.[58]

Conduct a Physical Examination

Perform a physical exam as soon as possible if recent exam records aren't accessible. Assess for:

- Opioid intoxication or withdrawal.
- Physical signs of opioid use.
- Medical consequences of opioid use.

Exhibit 2.9 provides an overview of physical and mental status findings for opioid intoxication.

EXHIBIT 2.9. Signs of Opioid Intoxication

Physical findings
Drowsy but arousable
Sleeping intermittently ("nodding off")
Constricted pupils

Mental status findings
Slurred speech
Impaired memory or concentration
Normal to euphoric mood

PATIENT TESTIMONY
Opioid Withdrawal

"Severe opioid withdrawal isn't something I'd wish on my worst enemy. The last time I went cold turkey, I was determined to come off all the way. The physical symptoms were just the tip of the iceberg. My mind was a nightmare that I thought I would never wake up from. There were times when I was almost convinced that dying would be better than what I was feeling. I did not experience a moment of ease for the first 3 months, and it was 6 months until I started to feel normal."

Opioid withdrawal

Opioid withdrawal can be extremely uncomfortable. Symptoms are similar to experiencing gastroenteritis, severe influenza, anxiety, and dysphoria concurrently.

Severity of withdrawal can indicate a patient's level of physical dependence and can inform medication choices and dosing decisions. The duration of withdrawal depends on the specific opioid from which the patient is withdrawing and can last 1 to 4 weeks. After the initial withdrawal phase is complete, many patients experience a prolonged phase of dysphoria, craving, insomnia, and hyperalgesia that can last for weeks or months.

Assess opioid withdrawal in the physical exam by noting physical signs and symptoms (Exhibit 2.10). Structured measures (e.g., Clinical Opiate Withdrawal Scale [COWS]; Clinical Institute Narcotic Assessment Scale for Withdrawal Symptoms) can help standardize documentation of signs and symptoms to support diagnosis, initial management, and treatment planning. See the "Resources" section for links to standardized scales. Part 3 of this TIP covers withdrawal symptom documentation for pharmacotherapy initiation.

EXHIBIT 2.10. Physical Signs of Opioid Withdrawal and Time to Onset

STAGE	GRADE	PHYSICAL SIGNS/SYMPTOMS
Early withdrawal Short-acting opioids: 8–24 hours after last use Long-acting opioids: Up to 36 hours after last use	Grade 1	Lacrimation, rhinorrhea, or both Diaphoresis Yawning Restlessness Insomnia
Early withdrawal Short-acting opioids: 8–24 hours after last use Long-acting opioids: Up to 36 hours after last use	Grade 2	Dilated pupils Piloerection Muscle twitching Myalgia Arthralgia Abdominal pain
Fully developed withdrawal Short-acting opioids: 1–3 days after last use Long-acting opioids: 72–96 hours after last use	Grade 3	Tachycardia Hypertension Tachypnea Fever Anorexia or nausea Extreme restlessness
Fully developed withdrawal Short-acting opioids: 1–3 days after last use Long-acting opioids: 72–96 hours after last use	Grade 4	Diarrhea, vomiting, or both Dehydration Hyperglycemia Hypotension Curled-up position

Total duration of withdrawal:
- Short-acting opioids: 7–10 days
- Long-acting opioids: 14 days or more

The physical signs of opioid misuse vary depending on the route of ingestion:

- Patients who primarily smoke or sniff ("snort") opioids or take them orally often have few physical signs of use other than signs of intoxication and withdrawal. However, snorting can cause congestion and damage nasal mucosa.
- Patients who inject opioids may develop:
  - Sclerosis or scarring of the veins and needle marks, or "track marks," in the arms, legs, hands, neck, or feet (intravenous use).
  - Edema in the foot, hand, or both (common in injection use, but may occur in oral use).
  - Abscesses or cellulitis.
  - Jaundice, caput medusa, palmar erythema, spider angiomata, or an enlarged or hardened liver secondary to liver disease.
  - Heart murmur secondary to endocarditis.

Obtain Appropriate Laboratory Tests

Urine or oral fluid drug testing

Urine or oral fluid drug testing is useful before initiating OUD pharmacotherapy. Testing establishes a baseline of substances the patient has used so that the provider can monitor the patient's response to treatment over time. Testing for a range of commonly used substances helps confirm patient histories, facilitates discussion of recent drug use and symptoms, and aids in diagnosing and determining severity of SUDs. Drug testing is an important tool in the diagnosis and treatment of addiction. A national guideline on the use of drug testing is available from ASAM.[59] Exhibit 2.11 provides guidance on talking with patients about drug testing.

> **During ongoing pharmacotherapy with buprenorphine or methadone, drug testing can confirm medication adherence.**

EXHIBIT 2.11. Patient–Provider Dialog: Talking About Drug Testing

Frame drug testing in a clinical, nonpunitive way. For example, before obtaining a drug test, ask the patient, "What do you think we'll find on this test?" The patient's response is often quite informative and may make the patient less defensive than confrontation with a positive test result.

SCENARIO: A provider discusses urine drug testing with a patient being assessed for OUD treatment with medication.

Provider: When we assess patients for medication for opioid addiction, we always check urine samples for drugs.

Patient: I'll tell you if I used. You don't need to test me.

Provider: Thank you, I really appreciate that. The more we can talk about what's going on with you, the more I can help. I'm not checking the urine to catch you or because I don't trust you. I trust you. I can see how motivated you are. But I don't trust the addiction because I know how powerful addiction can be, too. To monitor your safety on medication and help determine what other services you may need, it's important for us to test you periodically and discuss the results. Does that sound okay?

Patient: Yeah, that makes sense.

To assess and manage patients with OUD properly, providers must know which tests to order and how to interpret results. There are many drug testing panels; cutoffs for positive results vary by laboratory. One widely used panel, the NIDA-5, tests for cannabinoids, cocaine, amphetamines, opiates, and phencyclidine. Additional testing for benzodiazepines, the broader category of opioids, and specific drugs commonly used in the patient's locality may be warranted. The typical opioid immunoassay will only detect morphine, which is a metabolite of heroin, codeine, and some other opioids. The typical screen will not detect methadone, buprenorphine, or fentanyl and may not detect hydrocodone, hydromorphone, or oxycodone. Specific testing is needed to identify these substances.

Co-occurring SUDs require separate, specific treatment plans.

Testing for substances that can complicate OUD pharmacotherapy is essential. Testing for cocaine, benzodiazepines, and methamphetamine is clinically important because these and other substances (and related SUDs, which may require treatment in their own right), especially benzodiazepines, can complicate pharmacotherapy for OUD. Benzodiazepine and other sedative misuse can increase the risk of overdose among patients treated with opioid agonists. When assessing benzodiazepine use, note that typical benzodiazepine urine immunoassays will detect diazepam but perhaps not lorazepam or clonazepam. Providers must specifically request testing for these two benzodiazepines. Exhibit 2.12 shows urine drug testing windows of detection.

EXHIBIT 2.12. Urine Drug Testing Window of Detection[60,61]

DRUG	POSITIVE TEST	WINDOW OF DETECTION*	COMMENTS
Amphetamine; methamphetamine; 3,4-methylenedioxy-methamphetamine	Amphetamine	1–2 days	False positives with bupropion, chlorpromazine, desipramine, fluoxetine, labetalol, promethazine, ranitidine, pseudoephedrine, trazadone, and other common medications. Confirm unexpected positive results with the laboratory.
Barbiturates	Barbiturates	Up to 6 weeks	N/A
Benzodiazepines	Benzodiazepines	1–3 days; up to 6 weeks with heavy use of long-acting benzodiazepines	Immunoassays may not be sensitive to therapeutic doses, and most immunoassays have low sensitivity to clonazepam and lorazepam. Check with your laboratory regarding sensitivity and cutoffs. False positives with sertraline or oxaprozin.

*Detection time may vary depending on the cutoff.

Continued on next page

EXHIBIT 2.12. Urine Drug Testing Window of Detection (continued)

DRUG	POSITIVE TEST	WINDOW OF DETECTION*	COMMENTS
Buprenorphine	Buprenorphine	3–4 days	Will screen negative on opiate screen. Tramadol can cause false positives. Can be tested for specifically.
Cocaine	Cocaine, benzoylecgonine	2–4 days; 10–22 days with heavy use	N/A
Codeine	Morphine, codeine, high-dose hydrocodone	1–2 days	Will screen positive on opiate immunoassay.
Fentanyl	Fentanyl	1–2 days	Will screen negative on opiate screen. Can be tested for specifically. May not detect all fentanyl-like substances.[62]
Heroin	Morphine, codeine	1–2 days	Will screen positive on opiate immunoassay. 6-monoacetylmorphine, a unique metabolite of heroin, is present in urine for about 6 hours. Can be tested for specifically to distinguish morphine from heroin, but this is rarely clinically useful.
Hydrocodone	Hydrocodone, hydromorphone	2 days	May screen negative on opiate immunoassay. Can be tested for specifically.
Hydromorphone	May not be detected	1–2 days	May screen negative on opiate immunoassay. Can be tested for specifically.
Marijuana	Tetrahydrocannabinol	Infrequent use of 1–3 days; chronic use of up to 30 days	False positives possible with efavirenz, ibuprofen, and pantoprazole.
Methadone	Methadone	2–11 days	Will screen negative on opiate screen. Can be tested for specifically.
Morphine	Morphine, hydromorphone	1–2 days	Will screen positive on opiate immunoassay. Ingestion of poppy plant/seed may screen positive.
Oxycodone	Oxymorphone	1–1.5 days	Typically screens negative on opiate immunoassay. Can be tested for specifically.

*Detection time may vary depending on the cutoff.

Positive opioid tests can confirm recent use. Document recent use before starting patients on buprenorphine or methadone. Positive methadone or buprenorphine tests are expected for patients receiving these treatments. **Positive opioid tests contraindicate starting naltrexone.**

Negative opioid test results require careful interpretation. A patient may test negative for opioids despite presenting with opioid withdrawal symptoms if he or she hasn't used opioids for several days. A negative opioid test in the absence of symptoms of opioid withdrawal likely indicates that the patient has little or no opioid tolerance, which is important information for assessment and treatment planning. Consider that the opioid the patient reports using may not be detected on the particular immunoassay.

Screening tests are not definitive; false positive and false negative test results are possible. Confirmatory testing should follow all unexpected positive screens. Urine drug testing will detect metabolites from many prescription opioids but miss others, so it is easy to misinterpret results in patients taking these medications.[63] False positives are also common in amphetamine testing.[64]

Point-of-service testing provides the opportunity to discuss results with patients immediately. However, cutoffs for positive screens are not standardized across point-of-service tests. Know the specifications of the screens used.[65]

Other laboratory tests

Patients with OUD, particularly those who inject drugs, are at risk for liver disease and blood-borne viral infections. Pregnancy is another important consideration in determining treatment course. **Recommended laboratory tests for patients with OUD include:**

Pregnancy testing, which is important because:

- It is not advisable for patients to start naltrexone during pregnancy.
- Pregnant women treated for active OUD typically receive buprenorphine or methadone.

- The American College of Obstetricians and Gynecologists and a recent SAMHSA-convened expert panel on the treatment of OUD in pregnancy[66] recommend that pregnant women with OUD receive opioid receptor agonist pharmacotherapy.[67]
- Providers should refer pregnant women to prenatal care or, if qualified, provide it themselves.

Liver function tests (e.g., aspartate aminotransferase, alanine aminotransferase, bilirubin), which can:

- Guide medication selection and dosing.
- Rule out severe liver disease, which may contraindicate OUD medication (see Part 3 of this TIP).

Hepatitis B and C serology, which can indicate:

- Patients with positive tests (evaluate for hepatitis treatment).
- The need to administer hepatitis A and B and tetanus vaccines, if appropriate.

HIV serology, which can help identify:

- Patients who are HIV positive (evaluate for antiretroviral treatment).
- Patients who are HIV negative (evaluate for preexposure prophylaxis and targeted education).

Review the PDMP

Before initiating OUD medication, providers should check their states' PDMPs to determine whether their patients receive prescriptions for controlled substances from other healthcare professionals. Using the PDMP improves the ability to manage the risks of controlled substances and to identify potentially harmful drug interactions.[68] Although OTPs are not permitted to report methadone treatment to PDMPs, pharmacies that dispense buprenorphine and other controlled substances do report to PDMPs. Medications that need monitoring and required frequency of updates vary by state (for more information about state PDMPs, visit www.pdmpassist.org/content/state-profiles).

Determine Diagnosis and Severity of OUD

Use DSM-5 criteria to make an OUD diagnosis (Exhibit 2.13).[69] Patients who meet two or three criteria have mild OUD. Those meeting four or five criteria have moderate OUD, and those meeting six or more criteria have severe OUD.[70] A printable checklist of DSM-5[71] criteria is available in the Part 2 Appendix.

Treatment Planning or Referral

Making Decisions About Treatment

Start by sharing the diagnosis with patients and hearing their feedback. Patients with OUD need to make several important treatment decisions:

- Whether to begin medication to treat OUD.
- What type of OUD medication to take.

RESOURCE ALERT

Shared Decision-Making Tool for Patients and Family Members

SAMHSA's online shared decision-making tool for patients is a good information source for patients to review before their visit or in the office (http://brsstacs.com/Default.aspx). In addition, providers can suggest that family, friends, and other potential recovery supports (e.g., 12-Step program sponsors, employers, clergy) read educational material tailored for them. See *Medication-Assisted Treatment for Opioid Addiction: Facts for Families and Friends* (http://mha.ohio.gov/Portals/0/assets/Initiatives/GCOAT/SMA14-4443.pdf).

EXHIBIT 2.13. DSM-5 Criteria for OUD[72]

A problematic pattern of opioid use leading to clinically significant impairment or distress, as manifested by at least two of the following, occurring within a 12-month period:

1. Opioids are often taken in larger amounts or over a longer period of time than was intended.
2. There is a persistent desire or unsuccessful efforts to cut down or control opioid use.
3. A great deal of time is spent in activities to obtain the opioid, use the opioid, or recover from its effects.
4. Craving, or a strong desire or urge to use opioids.
5. Recurrent opioid use resulting in a failure to fulfill major role obligations at work, school, or home.
6. Continued opioid use despite having persistent or recurrent social or interpersonal problems caused by or exacerbated by the effects of opioids.
7. Important social, occupational, or recreational activities are given up or reduced because of opioid use.
8. Recurrent opioid use in situations in which it is physically hazardous.
9. Continued opioid use despite knowledge of having a persistent or recurrent physical or psychological problem that's likely to have been caused or exacerbated by the substance.
10. Tolerance,* as defined by either of the following:
    a. A need for markedly increased amounts of opioids to achieve intoxication or desired effect
    b. A markedly diminished effect with continued use of the same amount of an opioid
11. Withdrawal,* as manifested by either of the following:
    a. The characteristic opioid withdrawal syndrome
    b. The same—or a closely related—substance is taken to relieve or avoid withdrawal symptoms

*This criterion is not met for individuals taking opioids solely under appropriate medical supervision.
Severity: mild = 2–3 symptoms; moderate = 4–5 symptoms; severe = 6 or more symptoms

- Where and how to access desired treatment.
- Whether to access potentially beneficial mental health, recovery support, and other ancillary services, whether or not they choose pharmacotherapy.

Offer information to patients about the various treatments for OUD and collaborate with them to make decisions about treatment plans or referrals (Exhibit 2.14). Consider discussing:

- Indications, risks, and benefits of medications and alternatives to pharmacotherapy.
- Types of settings that deliver medications (including healthcare professionals' own practice locations, if applicable).
- Availability of and accessibility to treatment (i.e., transportation).
- Alternative treatments without medication (e.g., residential treatment, which often offers medically supervised opioid withdrawal).
- Costs of treatment with OUD medication, including insurance coverage and affordability.

Give patients' expressed preferences significant weight when making decisions. Patient characteristics can't reliably predict greater likelihood of success with one approved medication or another. For detailed information on medications to treat OUD, refer to Part 3 of this TIP.

Strategies to engage patients in shared decision making include:

- Indicating to patients a desire to collaborate with them to find the best medication and treatment setting for them.
- Including family members in the treatment planning process, if possible (and only with patients' consent).
- Exploring what patients already know about treatment options and dispelling misconceptions.
- Offering information on medications and their side effects, benefits, and risks (Exhibit 2.14; Part 3).

> **Part 1 of this TIP gives an overview of the three FDA-approved medications used to treat OUD. Part 3 covers the details of their use.**

- Informing patients of the requirements of the various treatment options (e.g., admission criteria to an OTP; frequency of visits to an OBOT or OTP).
- Offering options, giving recommendations after deliberation, and supporting patients' informed decisions.

Understanding Treatment Settings and Services

Support patient preferences for treatment settings and services. Some patients prefer to receive OUD medication via physicians' offices. Others choose outpatient treatment programs that provide opioid receptor agonist treatment for medically supervised withdrawal (with or without naltrexone) or for ongoing opioid receptor agonist maintenance treatment. Still others may want OUD treatment in a residential program with or without pharmacotherapy (Exhibit 2.15).

Many patients initially form a preference for a certain treatment without knowing all the risks, benefits, and alternatives. Providers should ensure that patients understand the risks and benefits of all options. Without this understanding, patients can't give truly informed consent.

Outpatient OUD Treatment Settings

Refer patients who prefer treatment with methadone or buprenorphine via an OTP and explain that:

- They will have to visit the program from 6 to 7 times per week at first.
- Additional methadone take-home doses are possible at every 90 days of demonstrated progress in treatment.
- Buprenorphine take-home doses are not bound by the same limits as methadone.

EXHIBIT 2.14. Comparison of OUD Medications To Guide Shared Decision Making

CATEGORY	BUPRENORPHINE	METHADONE	NALTREXONE
Appropriate patients	Typically for patients with OUD who are physiologically dependent on opioids	Typically for patients with OUD who are physiologically dependent on opioids and who meet federal criteria for OTP admission	Typically for patients with OUD who are abstinent from short-acting opioids for 7 days and long-acting opioids for 10–14 days
Outcome: Retention in treatment	Higher than treatment without medication and treatment with placebo[73]	Higher than treatment without OUD medication and treatment with placebo[74]	Treatment retention with oral naltrexone is no better than with placebo or no medication;[75] for XR-NTX, treatment retention is higher than for treatment without OUD medication and treatment with placebo;[76,77] treatment retention is lower than with opioid receptor agonist treatment
Outcome: Suppression of illicit opioid use	Effective	Effective	Effective
Outcome: Overdose mortality	Lower for people in treatment than for those not in it	Lower for people in treatment than for those not in it	Unknown
Location/ frequency of office visits	**Office/clinic:** Begins daily to weekly, then tailored to patient's needs **OTP:** Can treat with buprenorphine 6–7 days/week initially; take-homes are allowed without the time-in-treatment requirements of methadone	**OTP only:** 6–7 days/week initially; take-homes are allowed based on time in treatment and patient progress	**Office/clinic:** Varies from weekly to monthly
Who can prescribe/order?	Physicians, NPs,* and PAs* possessing federal waiver can prescribe and dispense; can be dispensed by a community pharmacy or an OTP	OTP physicians order the medication; nurses and pharmacists administer and dispense it	Physicians, NPs,* and PAs*

*NPs and PAs should check with their state to determine whether prescribing buprenorphine, naltrexone, or both is within their allowable scope of practice.

Continued on next page

EXHIBIT 2.14. Comparison of OUD Medications To Guide Shared Decision Making (continued)

CATEGORY	BUPRENORPHINE	METHADONE	NALTREXONE
Administration	Sublingual/buccal; implant by specially trained provider, and only for stabilized patients	Oral	Oral or intramuscular (Note: Oral naltrexone is less effective than the other OUD medications.)
Misuse/diversion potential	Low in OTPs or other settings with observed dose administration; moderate for take-home doses; risk can be mitigated by providing take-homes to stable patients and a diversion control plan	Low in OTPs with directly observed therapy; moderate for take-home doses; risk can be mitigated by a diversion control plan	None
Sedation	Low unless concurrent substances are present (e.g., alcohol, benzodiazepines)	Low unless dose titration is too quick or dose is not adjusted for the presence of concurrent substances (e.g., alcohol, benzodiazepines)	None
Risk of medication-induced respiratory depression	Very rare; lower than methadone	Rare, although higher than buprenorphine; may be elevated during the first 2 weeks of treatment or in combination with other sedating substances	None
Risk of precipitated withdrawal when starting medication	Can occur if started too prematurely after recent use of other opioids	None	Severe withdrawal is possible if period of abstinence is inadequate before starting medication
Withdrawal symptoms on discontinuation	Present; lower than methadone if abruptly discontinued	Present; higher than buprenorphine if abruptly discontinued	None
Most common side effects	Constipation, vomiting, headache, sweating, insomnia, blurred vision	Constipation, vomiting, sweating, dizziness, sedation	Difficulty sleeping, anxiety, nausea, vomiting, low energy, joint and muscle pain, headache, liver enzyme elevation XR-NTX: Injection site pain, nasopharyngitis, insomnia, toothache

D. Coffa, December 2017 (personal communication). Adapted with permission.

EXHIBIT 2.15. Treatment Setting Based on Patient's Choice of OUD Medication

MEDICATION	POSSIBLE TREATMENT SETTING
Buprenorphine	Office-based treatment, outpatient or residential SUD treatment programs (prescriber must have a federal waiver), OTP
Methadone	OTP
Naltrexone	Office-based treatment, outpatient or residential SUD treatment programs, OTP

- Counseling and drug testing are required parts of OTP treatment.
- Some programs also offer case management, peer support, medical services, mental disorder treatment, and other services.

Try to arrange OTP intake appointments for patients before they leave the office. If no immediate openings are available, consider starting buprenorphine as a bridge or alternative to the OTP.

Gauge the appropriate intensity level for patients seeking non-OTP outpatient treatment for OUD. These programs range from low intensity (individual or group counseling once to a few times a week) to high intensity (2 or more hours a day of individual and group counseling several days a week). Appropriate treatment intensity depends on each patient's:[78]

- Social circumstances.
- Severity of addiction.
- Personal preferences.
- Psychiatric/psychological needs.
- Ability to afford treatment at a given intensity.

Outpatient medical settings

Healthcare professionals cannot provide methadone in their clinics. Only those with a buprenorphine waiver can provide buprenorphine. Any healthcare professional with a license can provide naltrexone.

Once providers obtain the necessary waiver, they should offer buprenorphine treatment to all patients who present with OUD if such treatment is available and appropriate. Referring them to treatment elsewhere will likely result in delay or lack of patient access to care. Develop a treatment plan to determine where patients will receive continuing care (see the "Treatment Planning" section). Continue to provide naltrexone for patients who were already receiving it from some other setting (e.g., a prison, a specialty addiction treatment program) or for patients who meet opioid abstinence requirements and wish to take a medication for relapse prevention.

Residential drug treatment settings

Patients who have OUD, concurrent other substance use problems, unstable living situations, or a combination of the three may be appropriate candidates for residential treatment, which can last from a week to several weeks or more. Inform patients about the services and requirements typical of this treatment setting.

Some patients taking buprenorphine (or methadone) who have other SUDs, such as AUD or cocaine use disorder, can benefit from residential treatment. If such treatment is indicated, determine whether the residential program allows patients to continue their opioid receptor agonist medication while in treatment. Some residential programs require patients to discontinue these medications to receive residential treatment, which could destabilize patients and result in opioid overdose.

Residential treatment programs typically provide:

- Room and board.
- Recovery support.
- Counseling.
- Case management.
- Medically supervised withdrawal (in some programs).
- Starting buprenorphine or naltrexone (in some programs).
- Onsite mental health services (in some cases).
- Buprenorphine or methadone continuation for patients already enrolled in treatment prior to admission if their healthcare professionals have waivers or their OTP permits.

Transitioning out of residential settings requires careful planning. During a patient's stay in residential treatment, plan for his or her transition out of the program. A good transition plan maximizes the likelihood of continuity of care after discharge. Plans should also address overdose risk. Patients who are no longer opioid tolerant are at heightened risk of opioid overdose if they don't get OUD medication at discharge. Providing XR-NTX, buprenorphine, or methadone during treatment and continuing the medication after discharge can help prevent return to opioid use after discharge. Providing a naloxone prescription and overdose prevention information is appropriate.

> **RESOURCE ALERT**
>
> **Treatment and Provider Locator**
>
> SAMHSA's Behavioral Health Treatment Services Locator (https://findtreatment.samhsa.gov) provides information on drug and alcohol treatment programs across states. Another SAMHSA tool identifies the locations of buprenorphine providers (www.samhsa.gov/medication-assisted-treatment/physician-program-data/treatment-physician-locator).

> **RESOURCE ALERT**
>
> **Maintaining Confidentiality**
>
> **Providers who treat patients with addiction must know substance use-related disclosure rules and confidentiality requirements. SAMHSA's webpage lists frequently asked questions on substance use confidentiality and summarizes federal regulations about disclosure and patient records that federal programs maintain on addiction treatment** (https://www.samhsa.gov/about-us/who-we-are/laws-regulations/confidentiality-regulations-faqs). Key points include:
>
> - Confidentiality regulations prohibit specialty SUD treatment programs from sharing information with healthcare professionals about patients' SUD treatment without specific consent from patients.
> - Referrals to other behavioral health services require consent for sharing information on treatment progress.
> - Healthcare professionals should discuss confidentiality and consent with patients during the referral process.
> - OUD pharmacotherapy prescribers may consider requiring patient consent for communicating with treatment programs as a condition of receiving OUD treatment.
>
> Treatment program staff members can help identify returns to substance use, or risk of such, before the prescriber and can work with the prescriber to stabilize patients.

Determining OUD Service Intensity and Ensuring Follow-Through

Use ASAM placement criteria for guidance on selecting the right level of OUD treatment. ASAM criteria define the level of care and key features that may make a given level (e.g., residential, intensive outpatient, standard outpatient) appropriate for a patient[79] (see the "Treatment Planning" section). To help patients select programs, note that some focus on specific populations (e.g., gender-specific programs; parents with children; lesbian, gay, bisexual, transgender, and questioning populations).

Make an appointment with the referral program during the patient's visit rather than giving the patient a phone number to call. Follow up with the patient later to determine whether he or she kept the appointment. Doing so increases the chances of a successful referral.

Referring patients to behavioral health and support services

Discuss patients' potential need for behavioral health, peer support, and other ancillary services, like:

- Drug and alcohol counseling.
- Mental health services.
- Case management.
- Mutual-help groups.
- Peer recovery support services.

Offer referrals to counseling and tailored psychosocial support to patients receiving OUD medication (Exhibit 2.16).

Drug Addiction Treatment Act of 2000 legislation requires that buprenorphine prescribers be able to refer patients to counseling, but making referrals is not mandatory.[80] Many patients benefit from referral to mental health services or specialized addiction counseling and recovery support services. However, four randomized trials found no extra benefit to adding adjunctive counseling to well-conducted medical management visits delivered by the buprenorphine prescriber. There is evidence of benefits to adding contingency management to pharmacotherapy.[81,82,83,84,85]

> ### RESOURCE ALERT
> **Mutual-Support Groups**
>
> For an introduction to mutual-support groups, see SAMHSA's *Substance Abuse in Brief*, "An Introduction to Mutual Support Groups for Alcohol and Drug Abuse" (https://store.samhsa.gov/shin/content/SMA08-4336/SMA08-4336.pdf).

Make referrals to mutual-help groups. Patients may wish to participate in mutual-help groups (e.g., Alcoholics Anonymous, Narcotics Anonymous, Methadone Anonymous, Medication-Assisted Recovery Services, SMART Recovery) in addition to or instead of specialized treatment. These programs can be highly supportive, but they may pressure patients to stop taking OUD medication. If possible, refer patients to groups that welcome patients who take OUD medication.

Make referrals to medical and mental health services. Respectful, consistent medical care can support patients' efforts to recover from OUD and all other SUDs. As for any patient, providers should make appropriate referrals for patients with OUD to receive medical or mental health services beyond the providers' own scope of practice.

Patients with depression, anxiety disorders, and other mental disorders may be more likely to succeed in addiction treatment if those conditions are managed.[86] If the severity or type of a patient's psychiatric comorbidity is beyond a provider's scope of practice, the provider should refer the patient to mental health services as appropriate.

Make referrals to ancillary services. Besides medical care and mental health services, OUD patients, like patients with other illnesses, may

EXHIBIT 2.16. Referring Patients Who Receive OUD Pharmacotherapy to Behavioral Health Therapies

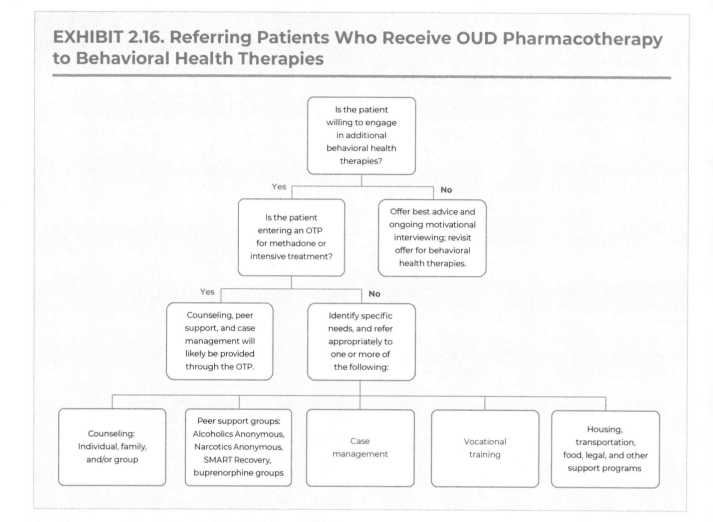

RESOURCE ALERT

Guidance on Providing Integrated Care

Fragmented healthcare services are less likely to meet all patient needs. Integrated medical and behavioral healthcare delivery can effectively provide patient-focused, comprehensive treatments that address the full range of symptoms and service needs patients with OUD often have.[87] The key components of integration should be in place to make sure that SUD treatment in a primary care setting works. For more information about how to provide integrated services for individuals taking medication for OUD, see:

- **The Agency for Healthcare Research and Quality's** report *Medication-Assisted Treatment Models of Care for Opioid Use Disorder in Primary Care Settings.* (www.ncbi.nlm.nih.gov/books/NBK402352).

- **The Agency for Healthcare Research and Quality's Academy for Integrating Behavioral Mental Health and Primary Care.** (https://integrationacademy.ahrq.gov).

- **SAMHSA's Center for Integrated Health Solutions' Resource Library for providing integrated care.** (www.samhsa.gov/integrated-health-solutions/resource-library?combine=substance+abuse&=Apply%20or%20https://www.samhsa.gov/integrated-health-solutions).

OPPORTUNITY ALERT

Becoming an OUD Medication Treatment Provider

SAMHSA strongly urges physicians, NPs, and PAs to obtain waivers that will qualify them to offer buprenorphine pharmacotherapy. They can become qualified to use buprenorphine to taper appropriate patients with OUD off illicit or prescription opioids or to provide long-term OUD treatment.

Only healthcare professionals with a federal waiver may prescribe buprenorphine for the treatment of OUD. To get waivers, providers must meet set criteria, complete buprenorphine training (online or in person), and apply for a waiver from SAMHSA. Waivered prescribers are assigned an additional DEA registration number (usually their existing number with an added "X").

NPs and PAs need to meet additional criteria for waivers.[88] Check with the state licensing board about restrictions and requirements at the state level before applying for a waiver.

Waiver training: ASAM, the American Academy of Addiction Psychiatry, the American Psychiatric Association, and the American Osteopathic Academy of Addiction Medicine all provide the waiver training courses for physicians. Providers' Clinical Support System for Medication Assisted Treatment (PCSS-MAT) provides the required 8-hour OUD medication waiver course for physicians and 24-hour waiver course for NPs and PAs for free (https://pcssmat.org/education-training/mat-waiver-training). ASAM and others also provide NP and PA courses.

New prescribers can benefit from mentorship from experienced providers in their practice or community. Mentorship is available for free from PCSS-MAT (http://pcssmat.org/mentoring).

For detailed information on prescribing OUD medications, review Part 3 of this TIP.

---

need more support in some areas, including ancillary services such as:

- Case management.
- Food access.
- Vocational training.
- Housing.
- Transportation.
- Legal assistance.

Helping patients who are not ready to engage in OUD treatment

Help reluctant patients be safer and approach readiness. Patients may seem unwilling to discuss their drug use if they're ashamed or fear being judged. Accepting, nonjudgmental attitudes help patients overcome shame and discuss concerns honestly while also instilling hope.

Every visit is a chance to help patients begin healthy changes and move toward treatment and recovery. Patients may not be ready to change right away. Successfully quitting drug use can take many attempts. Returns to substance use, even after periods of remission, are expected parts of the recovery process.

Patients with OUD are much more likely to die than their peers,[89,90] and HIV, hepatitis C, and skin and soft tissue infections are common among this population. **Help reduce these OUD-related risks by educating patients** about:

- Using new syringes.
- Avoiding syringe sharing.
- Avoiding sharing other supplies during the injection process.
- Preventing opioid overdose (see the "Preventing Opioid-Related Overdose" section).

- Obtaining overdose prevention information (e.g., *SAMHSA Opioid Overdose Prevention Toolkit* [https://store.samhsa.gov/product/SAMHSA-Opioid-Overdose-Prevention-Toolkit/SMA16-4742]).
- Obtaining naloxone and instructions for its use.

Refer patients to syringe exchange sites. The North American Syringe Exchange Network provides options (see the "Syringe Exchange" section).

Preventing Opioid-Related Overdose

Every patient who misuses opioids or has OUD should receive opioid overdose prevention education and a naloxone prescription.[91] Healthcare professionals should educate patients and their families about overdose risk, prevention, identification, and response (Exhibit 2.17). FDA has approved an autoinjectable naloxone device (Evzio) and a naloxone nasal spray (Narcan) for use by patients and others. For information about all forms of naloxone,

---

EXHIBIT 2.17. Opioid Overdose: Risk, Prevention, Identification, and Response

Overdose risk
- Using heroin (possibly mixed with illicitly manufactured fentanyl or fentanyl analogs)
- Using prescription opioids that were not prescribed
- Using prescription opioids more frequently or at higher doses than prescribed
- Using opioids after a period of abstinence or reduced use (e.g., after medically supervised withdrawal or incarceration)
- Using opioids with alcohol, benzodiazepines, or both

Overdose prevention
- Don't use opioids that were not prescribed.
- Take medications only as prescribed.
- Don't use drugs when you are alone.
- Don't use multiple substances at once.
- Have naloxone available and make sure others know where it is and how to use it.
- Use a small "test dose" if returning to opioid use after a period of abstinence, if the substance appears altered, or if it has been acquired from an unfamiliar source. Beware: This doesn't guarantee safety; illicitly manufactured fentanyl or other substances may be present in the drug, and **any use may be fatal.**

Overdose identification
- Fingernails or lips are blue or purple.
- Breathing or heartbeat is slow or stopped.
- The person is vomiting or making gurgling noises.
- The person can't be awakened or is unable to speak.

Overdose response
- Call 9-1-1.
- Administer naloxone (more than one dose may be needed to restore adequate spontaneous breathing).
- Perform rescue breathing. If certified to provide cardiopulmonary resuscitation, perform chest compressions if there is no pulse.
- Put the person in the "recovery position," on his or her side and with the mouth facing to the side to prevent aspiration of vomit, if he or she is breathing independently.
- Stay with the person until emergency services arrive. Naloxone's duration of action is 30–90 minutes. The person should be observed after this time for a return of opioid overdose symptoms.

Adapted from material in the public domain.[92]

The United States is experiencing a death epidemic related to opioid overdose. Opioids (including prescription opioids and heroin) killed more than 33,000 people in 2015, more than in any prior year. Almost half of opioid overdose deaths involve prescription opioids. Since 2010, heroin overdose deaths have more than quadrupled.[93,94] Overdose deaths from illicit fentanyl have risen sharply.[95]

prescribing, and patient and community education, see the *SAMHSA Opioid Overdose Prevention Toolkit* (https://store.samhsa.gov/product/SAMHSA-Opioid-Overdose-Prevention-Toolkit/SMA16-4742).

Municipalities with community-based naloxone distribution programs have seen substantial decreases in opioid overdose death rates.[96,97] Many syringe exchange programs also dispense naloxone. For information and resources on prescribing naloxone for overdose prevention, including educational patient handouts and videos, see the "Opioid-Related Overdose Prevention" section.

Resources

The following selected resources address key content presented in Part 2. Part 5 of this TIP includes comprehensive resources on topics pertaining to substance misuse and medications to treat OUD.

Alcohol and Drug Use Screening

- **American Academy of Addiction Psychiatry:** Provides Performance in Practice Clinical Modules for screening of tobacco use and AUD. www.aaap.org/education-training/cme-opportunities
- **NIAAA, Professional Education Materials:** Provides links to screening, treatment planning, and general information for clinicians in outpatient programs. www.niaaa.nih.gov/publications/clinical-guides-and-manuals
- **NIDA, Medical and Health Professionals:** Provides resources for providers to increase awareness of the impact of substance use on patients' health and help identify drug use early and prevent it from escalating to misuse or addiction. www.drugabuse.gov/nidamed-medical-health-professionals

Tobacco Screening

- **American Psychiatric Nursing Association, Tobacco & Nicotine Use Screening Tools and Assessments:** Provides the Fagerström screening tools for nicotine dependence and smokeless tobacco and a screening checklist for tobacco use. www.apna.org/i4a/pages/index.cfm?pageID=6150
- **U.S. Department of Health and Human Services' Be Tobacco Free:** Provides information for individuals struggling with nicotine addiction and links for clinicians that provide guidance on caring for patients with nicotine addiction. https://betobaccofree.hhs.gov/health-effects/nicotine-health
- **U.S. Department of Health and Human Services' Million Hearts Initiative:** Provides templates for developing and guidance on implementing tobacco cessation programs and guidance on implementing them as part of clinical care. https://millionhearts.hhs.gov/tools-protocols/protocols.html
- **Centers for Disease Control and Prevention (CDC):** Offers resources and information for patients and clinicians; includes a webpage with resource links for clinicians on treating tobacco dependence. www.cdc.gov/tobacco/index.htm and www.cdc.gov/tobacco/basic_information/related_links/index.htm

Buprenorphine Treatment Locator

- **SAMHSA, Buprenorphine Treatment Practitioner Locator:** Provides a state-by-state list of providers who offer buprenorphine. www.samhsa.gov/medication-assisted-treatment/physician-program-data/treatment-physician-locator

Buprenorphine Training, Mentorship, and Waivers

- **SAMHSA, Buprenorphine Waiver Management:** Provides information on buprenorphine waivers with links to waiver applications; explains waiver processes, requirements, and recordkeeping. www.samhsa.gov/medication-assisted-treatment/buprenorphine-waiver-management
- **SAMHSA, Buprenorphine Training for Physicians:** Provides links to organizations that train physicians on buprenorphine treatment. www.samhsa.gov/medication-assisted-treatment/training-resources/buprenorphine-physician-training
- **SAMHSA, Qualify for NPs and PAs Waiver:** Provides information for NPs and PAs about the buprenorphine waiver training, with links to trainings and the application process. www.samhsa.gov/medication-assisted-treatment/qualify-nps-pas-waivers

- **PCSS-MAT:** Provides buprenorphine waiver training and mentorship for healthcare professionals (physicians, NPs, and PAs); includes updates and other resources about medication for OUD. http://pcssmat.org

Medication Treatment for OUD

- **SAMHSA, *Medication-Assisted Treatment of Opioid Use Disorder*:** Provides a clinical pocket guide for medication treatment for OUD. https://store.samhsa.gov/shin/content/SMA16-4892PG/SMA16-4892PG.pdf
- **SAMHSA, MATx Mobile App to Support Medication-Assisted Treatment of OUD:** Provides a mobile app to support healthcare professionals providing medication treatment for OUD. https://store.samhsa.gov/apps/mat
- **SAMHSA, *Advisory*, Sublingual and Transmucosal Buprenorphine for Opioid Use Disorder: Review and Update:** Summarizes information on the use of buprenorphine to treat OUD. https://store.samhsa.gov/product/Advisory-Sublingual-and-Transmucosal-Buprenorphine-for-Opioid-Use-Disorder-Review-and-Update/SMA16-4938
- **SAMHSA, *Clinical Use of Extended-Release Injectable Naltrexone in the Treatment of Opioid Use Disorder: A Brief Guide*:** Provides a brief review of the use of XR-NTX. https://store.samhsa.gov/product/Clinical-Use-of-Extended-Release-Injectable-Naltrexone-in-the-Treatment-of-Opioid-Use-Disorder-A-Brief-Guide/SMA14-4892R
- **ASAM, *The ASAM National Practice Guideline for the Use of Medications in the Treatment of Addiction Involving Opioid Use*:** Provides national practice guidelines for the use of medications to treat OUD. www.asam.org/docs/default-source/practice-support/guidelines-and-consensus-docs/asam-national-practice-guideline-supplement.pdf
- **Department of Veterans Affairs/ Department of Defense, *VA/DoD Clinical Practice Guideline for the Management of Substance Use Disorders*:** Provides substance use disorder practice guidelines. www.healthquality.va.gov/guidelines/MH/sud/VADoDSUDCPGRevised22216.pdf
- **PCSS-MAT:** Provides training and mentorship for healthcare professionals (physicians, NPs, and PAs) on medications for OUD treatment including buprenorphine, naltrexone, and methadone. https://pcssmat.org

Syringe Exchange

- **North American Syringe Exchange Network:** Provides a national directory of syringe exchange programs in the United States. https://nasen.org/directory

Opioid-Related Overdose Prevention

- **Prescribe To Prevent:** Provides information about naloxone prescribing for overdose prevention, including educational patient handouts and videos. http://prescribetoprevent.org
- ***SAMHSA Opioid Overdose Prevention Toolkit*:** Provides healthcare professionals, communities, and local governments with material to develop practices and policies to help prevent opioid-related overdoses and deaths. It addresses issues for healthcare professionals, first responders, treatment providers, and those recovering from opioid overdose as well as their families. https://store.samhsa.gov/product/SAMHSA-Opioid-Overdose-Prevention-Toolkit/SMA16-4742
- **CDC—Injury Prevention and Overdose:** Provides links and tools for clinicians to help prevent opioid overdose deaths. https://www.cdc.gov/drugoverdose/prevention/index.html

- **NIDA, Opioid Overdose Reversal with Naloxone (Narcan, Evzio):** Provides naloxone information for providers. www.drugabuse.gov/related-topics/opioid-overdose-reversal-naloxone-narcan-evzio

Opioid Withdrawal Scales

- ***WHO Guidelines for the Psychosocially Assisted Pharmacological Treatment of Opioid Dependence: Annex 10:*** Provides COWS and other opioid withdrawal scales. www.ncbi.nlm.nih.gov/books/NBK143183
- **The Clinical Institute Narcotic Assessment Scale for Withdrawal Symptoms:** Provides a scale that measures signs and symptoms observed in patients during withdrawal. www.ncpoep.org/wp-content/uploads/2015/02/Appendix_7_Clinical_Institute_Narcotic_Assessment_CINA_Scale_for_Withdrawal_Symptoms.pdf

Patient and Family Education on Medications To Treat OUD

- **SAMHSA Store:** Provides patient and family educational resources about OUD and medication treatment for OUD; some resources are available in multiple languages, including Spanish. https://store.samhsa.gov
  - Buprenorphine. https://store.samhsa.gov/product/The-Facts-about-Buprenorphine-for-Treatment-of-Opioid-Addiction/SMA15-4442
  - Methadone. https://store.samhsa.gov/product/What-Every-Individual-Needs-to-Know-About-Methadone-Maintenance/SMA06-4123
- **ASAM Resources:** Provides patient and family education tools about addiction in general and OUD specifically.
  - Patient Resources. www.asam.org/resources/patientresources
  - *Opioid Addiction Treatment: A Guide for Patients, Families, and Friends.* https://www.asam.org/docs/default-source/publications/asam-opioid-patient-piece_-5bopt2-5d_3d.pdf

Referral and Treatment Locators

- **SAMHSA, OTP Directory:** Provides a state-by-state directory of methadone OTPs. https://dpt2.samhsa.gov/treatment/directory.aspx
- **SAMHSA, Behavioral Health Treatment Services Locator:** Provides a directory of treatment facilities. https://findtreatment.samhsa.gov
- **SAMHSA, Behavioral Health Treatment Services Locator—Self-Help, Peer Support, and Consumer Groups:** Provides a directory for mutual-help groups. https://findtreatment.samhsa.gov/locator/link-focSelfGP

Screening, Assessment, and Drug Testing Resources

- **NIDA, Screening, Assessment, and Drug Testing Resources:** Provides an evidence-based screening tool chart for adolescents and adults, drug use screening tool support materials, and a clinician resource and quick reference guide for drug screening in general medical settings, including a brief version of the ASSIST-lite. www.drugabuse.gov/nidamed-medical-health-professionals/tool-resources-your-practice/additional-screening-resources
- **ASAM, *The ASAM Appropriate Use of Drug Testing in Clinical Addiction Medicine:*** Discusses appropriate use of drug testing in identifying, diagnosing, and treating people with or at risk for SUDs. www.asam.org/quality-practice/guidelines-and-consensus-documents/drug-testing

Treatment Planning

- ***The ASAM Criteria:*** Provides criteria and a comprehensive set of guidelines for placement, continued stay, and transfer/discharge of patients with addiction and co-occurring conditions. The ASAM six-dimensional assessment tool is designed to guide treatment planning and offers a template to organize assessments and to determine level of care.[98] www.asam.org/quality-practice/guidelines-and-consensus-documents/the-asam-criteria

- **SAMHSA, Decisions in Recovery—Treatment for Opioid Use Disorder:** Provides an online interactive tool to support people with OUD in making informed decisions about their care. https://archive.samhsa.gov/MAT-Decisions-in-Recovery An accompanying handbook is also available. https://store.samhsa.gov/product/Decisions-in-Recovery-Treatment-for-Opioid-Use-Disorders/SMA16-4993

- **SAMHSA, TIP 42, *Substance Abuse Treatment for Persons With Co-Occurring Disorders:*** Provides comprehensive treatment guidance for individuals with co-occurring mental and substance use disorders. https://store.samhsa.gov/shin/content//SMA13-3992/SMA13-3992.pdf

Appendix

Stable Resource Toolkit

Audit-C – Overview
The AUDIT-C is a 3-item alcohol screen that can help identify persons who are hazardous drinkers or have active alcohol use disorders (including alcohol abuse or dependence). The AUDIT-C is a modified version of the 10 question AUDIT instrument.

Clinical Utility
The AUDIT-C is a brief alcohol screen that reliably identifies patients who are hazardous drinkers or have active alcohol use disorders.

Scoring
The AUDIT-C is scored on a scale of 0-12.

Each AUDIT-C question has 5 answer choices. Points allotted are:
a = 0 points, **b** = 1 point, **c** = 2 points, **d** = 3 points, **e** = 4 points

- **In men,** a score of 4 or more is considered positive, optimal for identifying hazardous drinking or active alcohol use disorders.
- **In women,** a score of 3 or more is considered positive (same as above).
- However, when the points are all from Question #1 alone (#2 & #3 are zero), it can be assumed that the patient is drinking below recommended limits and it is suggested that the provider review the patient's alcohol intake over the past few months to confirm accuracy.[3]
- Generally, the higher the score, the more likely it is that the patient's drinking is affecting his or her safety.

Psychometric Properties
For identifying patients with heavy/hazardous drinking and/or Active-DSM alcohol abuse or dependence

	MEN[1]	WOMEN[2]
≥3	Sens: 0.95 / Spec. 0.60	Sens: 0.66 / Spec. 0.94
≥4	Sens: 0.86 / Spec. 0.72	Sens: 0.48 / Spec. 0.99

For identifying patients with active alcohol abuse or dependence

	MEN[1]	WOMEN[2]
≥3	Sens: 0.90 / Spec. 0.45	Sens: 0.80 / Spec. 0.87
≥4	Sens: 0.79 / Spec. 0.56	Sens: 0.67 / Spec. 0.94

1. Bush K, Kivlahan DR, McDonell MB, et al. The AUDIT Alcohol Consumption Questions (AUDIT-C): An effective brief screening test for problem drinking. *Arch Internal Med.* 1998 (3): 1789-1795.
2. Bradley KA, Bush KR, Epler AJ, et al. Two brief alcohol-screening tests from the Alcohol Use Disorders Identification Test (AUDIT): Validation in a female veterans affairs patient population. *Arch Internal Med Vol 165,* April 2003: 821-829.
3. Frequently Asked Questions guide to using the AUDIT-C can be found via the website:
   https://www.queri.research.va.gov/tools/alcohol-misuse/alcohol-faqs-print.cfm

Continued on next page

AUDIT-C Questionnaire

Patient Name: _____   Dates of Visit: _____

1. How often do you have a drink containing alcohol?
   - ☐ a. Never
   - ☐ b. Monthly or less
   - ☐ c. 2-4 times a month
   - ☐ d. 2-3 times a week
   - ☐ e. 4 or more times a week

2. How many standard drinks containing alcohol do you have on a typical day?
   - ☐ a. 1 or 2
   - ☐ b. 3 or 4
   - ☐ c. 5 or 6
   - ☐ d. 7 to 9
   - ☐ e. 10 or more

3. How often do you have six or more drinks on one occasion?
   - ☐ a. Never
   - ☐ b. Less than monthly
   - ☐ c. Monthly
   - ☐ d. Weekly
   - ☐ e. Daily or almost daily

AUDIT-C is available for use in the public domain.

Reprinted from material in the public domain.[99] Available online (https://www.integration.samhsa.gov/images/res/tool_auditc.pdf).

Drug Abuse Screening Test (DAST-10)

General Instructions

"Drug use" refers to (1) the use of prescribed or over-the-counter drugs in excess of the directions, and (2) any nonmedical use of drugs. The various classes of drugs may include cannabis (i.e., marijuana, hashish), solvents (e.g., paint thinner), tranquilizers (e.g., Valium), barbiturates, cocaine, stimulants (e.g., speed), hallucinogens (e.g., LSD), or narcotics (e.g., heroin). The questions do not include alcoholic beverages.

Please answer every question. If you have trouble with a question, then choose the response that is mostly right.

Segment: _____   Visit Number: _____   Date of Assessment: ____/____/_____

These questions refer to drug use in the past 12 months. Please answer No or Yes.

1. Have you used drugs other than those required for medical reasons? ☐ No ☐ Yes
2. Do you use more than one drug at a time? ☐ No ☐ Yes
3. Are you always able to stop using drugs when you want to? ☐ No ☐ Yes
4. Have you had "blackouts" or "flashbacks" as a result of drug use? ☐ No ☐ Yes
5. Do you ever feel bad or guilty about your drug use? ☐ No ☐ Yes
6. Does your spouse (or parents) ever complain about your involvement with drugs? ☐ No ☐ Yes
7. Have you neglected your family because of your use of drugs? ☐ No ☐ Yes
8. Have you engaged in illegal activities to obtain drugs? ☐ No ☐ Yes
9. Have you ever experienced withdrawal symptoms (i.e., felt sick) when you stopped taking drugs? ☐ No ☐ Yes
10. Have you had medical problems as a result of your drug use (e.g., memory loss, hepatitis, convulsions, bleeding)? ☐ No ☐ Yes

Comments:

Scoring
Score 1 point for each "Yes," except for question 3, for which a "No" receives 1 point.

DAST Score: _____

Interpretation of Score:

Score	Degree of Problems Related to Drug Abuse	Suggested Action
0	No problems reported	None at this time
1–2	Low level	Monitor, reassess at a later date
3–5	Moderate level	Further investigation
6–8	Substantial level	Intensive assessment
9–10	Severe level	Intensive assessment

Adapted with permission.[100,101]

Part 2 of 5—Addressing Opioid Use Disorder in General Medical Settings **TIP 63**

DSM-5 Opioid Use Disorder Checklist[102]

Patient's Name: _____   Date of Birth: _____

Worksheet for DSM-5 Criteria for Diagnosis of Opioid Use Disorder

DIAGNOSTIC CRITERIA (Opioid use disorder requires that at least 2 criteria be met within a 12-month period.)	MEETS CRITERIA? Yes OR No	NOTES/SUPPORTING INFORMATION
1. Opioids are often taken in larger amounts or over a longer period of time than intended.		
2. There is a persistent desire or unsuccessful efforts to cut down or control opioid use.		
3. A lot of time is spent in activities necessary to obtain the opioid, use the opioid, or recover from its effects.		
4. Craving, or a strong desire to use opioids.		
5. Recurrent opioid use resulting in failure to fulfill major role obligations at work, school, or home.		
6. Continued opioid use despite having persistent or recurrent social or interpersonal problems caused or exacerbated by the effects of opioids.		
7. Important social, occupational, or recreational activities are given up or reduced because of opioid use.		
8. Recurrent opioid use in situations in which it is physically hazardous.		
9. Continued use despite knowledge of having a persistent or recurrent physical or psychological problem that is likely to have been caused or exacerbated by opioids.		
10. Tolerance,* as defined by either of the following: (a) a need for markedly increased amounts of opioids to achieve intoxication or desired effect (b) markedly diminished effect with continued use of the same amount of an opioid		
11. Withdrawal,* as manifested by either of the following: (a) the characteristic opioid withdrawal syndrome (b) the same (or a closely related) substance is taken to relieve or avoid withdrawal symptoms		

*This criterion is not met for individuals taking opioids solely under appropriate medical supervision.

Severity: mild = 2–3 symptoms; moderate = 4–5 symptoms; severe = 6 or more symptoms

Signed: _____   Date: _____

TAPS Tool Part I

Directions: The TAPS Tool Part 1 is a 4-item screening for tobacco use, alcohol use, prescription medication misuse, and illicit substance use in the PAST YEAR. Question 2 should be answered by males, and Question 3 should be answered by females. Each of the four multiple-choice items has five possible responses to choose from. Check the box to select your answer.

In the PAST 12 MONTHS:

1. How often have you used any tobacco product (for example, cigarettes, ecigarettes, cigars, pipes, or smokeless tobacco)?

   ☐ Never ☐ Less than monthly ☐ Monthly ☐ Weekly ☐ Daily or almost daily

2. How often have you had 5 or more drinks containing alcohol in 1 day? One standard drink is about 1 small glass of wine (5 oz), 1 beer (12 oz), or 1 single shot of liquor. *(Note: This question should only be answered by males.)*

   ☐ Never ☐ Less than monthly ☐ Monthly ☐ Weekly ☐ Daily or almost daily

3. How often have you had 4 or more drinks containing alcohol in 1 day? One standard drink is about 1 small glass of wine (5 oz), 1 beer (12 oz), or 1 single shot of liquor. *(Note: This question should only be answered by females.)*

   ☐ Never ☐ Less than monthly ☐ Monthly ☐ Weekly ☐ Daily or almost daily

4. How often have you used any drugs including marijuana, cocaine or crack, heroin, methamphetamine (crystal meth), hallucinogens, or ecstasy/MDMA?

   ☐ Never ☐ Less than monthly ☐ Monthly ☐ Weekly ☐ Daily or almost daily

5. How often have you used any prescription medications just for the feeling, more than prescribed, or that were not prescribed for you? Prescription medications that may be used this way include opiate pain relievers (for example, OxyContin, Vicodin, Percocet, or methadone), medications for anxiety or sleeping (for example, Xanax, Ativan, or Klonopin), or medications for ADHD (for example, Adderall or Ritalin).

   ☐ Never ☐ Less than monthly ☐ Monthly ☐ Weekly ☐ Daily or almost daily

TAPS Tool Part 2

Directions: The TAPS Tool Part 2 is a brief assessment for tobacco use, alcohol use, illicit substance use, and prescription medication misuse in the PAST 3 MONTHS ONLY. Each of the following questions and subquestions has two possible answers, yes or no. Check the box to select your answer.

In the PAST 3 MONTHS:

1. **Did you smoke a cigarette containing tobacco?** ☐ Yes ☐ No

   If "Yes," answer the following questions:
   - Did you usually smoke more than 10 cigarettes each day? ☐ Yes ☐ No
   - Did you usually smoke within 30 minutes after waking? ☐ Yes ☐ No

2. **Did you have a drink containing alcohol?** ☐ Yes ☐ No

   If "Yes," answer the following questions:
   - Did you have 4 or more drinks containing alcohol in a day?* ☐ Yes ☐ No
     (Note: This question should only be answered by females.)
   - Did you have 5 or more drinks containing alcohol in a day?* ☐ Yes ☐ No
     (Note: This question should only be answered by males.)
   - Have you tried and failed to control, cut down, or stop drinking? ☐ Yes ☐ No
   - Has anyone expressed concern about your drinking? ☐ Yes ☐ No

3. **Did you use marijuana (hash, weed)?** ☐ Yes ☐ No

   If "Yes," answer the following questions:
   - Have you had a strong desire or urge to use marijuana at least once a week or more often? ☐ Yes ☐ No
   - Has anyone expressed concern about your use of marijuana? ☐ Yes ☐ No

4. **Did you use cocaine, crack, or methamphetamine (crystal meth)?** ☐ Yes ☐ No

   If "Yes," answer the following questions:
   - Did you use cocaine, crack, or methamphetamine (crystal meth) at least once a week or more often? ☐ Yes ☐ No
   - Has anyone expressed concern about your use of cocaine, crack, or methamphetamine (crystal meth)? ☐ Yes ☐ No

5. **Did you use heroin?** ☐ Yes ☐ No

   If "Yes," answer the following questions:
   - Have you tried and failed to control, cut down, or stop using heroin? ☐ Yes ☐ No
   - Has anyone expressed concern about your use of heroin? ☐ Yes ☐ No

6. **Did you use a prescription opiate pain reliever (for example, Percocet or Vicodin) not as prescribed or that was not prescribed for you?** ☐ Yes ☐ No

   If "Yes," answer the following questions:
   - Have you tried and failed to control, cut down, or stop using an opiate pain reliever? ☐ Yes ☐ No
   - Has anyone expressed concern about your use of an opiate pain reliever? ☐ Yes ☐ No

*One standard drink is about 1 small glass of wine (5 oz), 1 beer (12 oz), or 1 single shot of liquor.

Continued on next page

TAPS Tool Part 2 (continued)

7. **Did you use medication for anxiety or sleep (for example, Xanax, Ativan, or Klonopin) not as prescribed or that was not prescribed for you?** ☐ Yes ☐ No

   If "Yes," answer the following questions:
   - Have you had a strong desire or urge to use medications for anxiety or sleep at least once a week or more often? ☐ Yes ☐ No
   - Has anyone expressed concern about your use of medication for anxiety or sleep? ☐ Yes ☐ No

8. **Did you use medication for ADHD (for example, Adderall or Ritalin) not as prescribed or that was not prescribed for you?** ☐ Yes ☐ No

   If "Yes," answer the following questions:
   - Did you use a medication for ADHD (for example, Adderall or Ritalin) at least once a week or more often? ☐ Yes ☐ No
   - Has anyone expressed concern about your use of medication for ADHD (for example, Adderall or Ritalin)? ☐ Yes ☐ No

9. **Did you use any other illegal or recreational drugs (for example, ecstasy, molly, GHB, poppers, LSD, mushrooms, special K, bath salts, synthetic marijuana ["spice"], or whip-its)?** ☐ Yes ☐ No

   If "Yes," answer the following question:
   - What were the other drug(s) you used? (write in response)

The complete tool is available online (https://cde.drugabuse.gov/instrument/29b23e2e-e266-f095-e050-bb89ad43472f). *Adapted from material in the public domain.*[103]

Notes

1. Shapiro, B., Coffa, D., & McCance-Katz, E. F. (2013). A primary care approach to substance misuse. *American Family Physician, 88*(2), 113–121.

2. Center for Behavioral Health Statistics and Quality. (2017). *Key substance use and mental health indicators in the United States: Results from the 2016 National Survey on Drug Use and Health.* Rockville, MD: Substance Abuse and Mental Health Services Administration.

3. American Society of Addiction Medicine. (2011). Definition of addiction. Retrieved October 30, 2017, from www.asam.org/resources/definition-of-addiction

4. American Psychiatric Association. (2013). *Diagnostic and statistical manual of mental disorders* (5th ed.). Arlington, VA: American Psychiatric Publishing.

5. Department of Health and Human Services, Office of the Surgeon General. (2016). *Facing addiction in America: The Surgeon General's report on alcohol, drugs, and health.* Washington, DC: Department of Health and Human Services.

6. Substance Abuse and Mental Health Services Administration. (2015). *Federal guidelines for opioid treatment programs.* HHS Publication No. (SMA) PEP15-FEDGUIDEOTP. Rockville, MD: Substance Abuse and Mental Health Services Administration.

7. American Psychiatric Association. (2013). *Diagnostic and statistical manual of mental disorders* (5th ed.). Arlington, VA: American Psychiatric Publishing.

8. National Cancer Institute. (n.d.). Remission. In *NCI dictionary of cancer terms.* Retrieved November 22, 2017, from www.cancer.gov/publications/dictionaries/cancer-terms?cdrid=45867

9. American Psychiatric Association. (2013). *Diagnostic and statistical manual of mental disorders* (5th ed.). Arlington, VA: American Psychiatric Publishing.

10. McNeely, J., Wu, L. T., Subramaniam, G., Sharma, G., Cathers, L. A., Svikis, D., ... Schwartz, R. P. (2016). Performance of the Tobacco, Alcohol, Prescription Medication, and Other Substance Use (TAPS) Tool for substance use screening in primary care patients. *Annals of Internal Medicine, 165*(10), 690–699.

11. Centers for Disease Control and Prevention. (2013). *Alcohol and public health: Alcohol-Related Disease Impact (ARDI). Average for United States 2006-2010 alcohol-attributable deaths due to excessive alcohol use.* Retrieved October 12, 2017, from https://nccd.cdc.gov/DPH_ARDI/Default/Report.aspx?T=AAM&P=f6d7eda7-036e-4553-9968-9b17ffad620e&R=d7a9b303-48e9-4440-bf47-070a4827e1fd&M=8E1C5233-5640-4EE8-9247-1ECA7DA325B9&F=&D=

12. Warner-Smith, M., Darke, S., Lynskey, M., & Hall, W. (2001). Heroin overdose: Causes and consequences. *Addiction, 96*(8), 1113–1125.

13. Moyer, V. A. (2013). Screening and behavioral counseling interventions in primary care to reduce alcohol misuse: U.S. Preventive Services Task Force recommendation statement. *Annals of Internal Medicine, 159*(3), 210–218.

14. U.S. Preventive Services Task Force. (2013). *Final recommendation statement: Alcohol misuse: Screening and behavioral counseling interventions in primary care.* Retrieved October 12, 2017, from www.uspreventiveservicestaskforce.org/Page/Document/RecommendationStatementFinal/alcohol-misuse-screening-and-behavioral-counseling-interventions-in-primary-care

15. Shapiro, B., Coffa, D., & McCance-Katz, E. F. (2013). A primary care approach to substance misuse. *American Family Physician, 88*(2), 113–121.

16. Babor, T. F., Higgins-Biddle, J. C., Saunders, J. B., & Monteiro, M. G. (2001). *The Alcohol Use Disorders Identification Test: Guidelines for use in primary care* (2nd ed.). Geneva, Switzerland: World Health Organization.

17. Bush, K., Kivlahan, D. R., McDonell, M. B., Fihn, S. D., & Bradley, K. A. (1998). The AUDIT alcohol consumption questions (AUDIT-C): An effective brief screening test for problem drinking. Ambulatory Care Quality Improvement Project (ACQUIP). Alcohol Use Disorders Identification Test. *Archives of Internal Medicine, 158*(16), 1789–1795.

18. Dawson, D. A., Smith, S. M., Saha, T. D., Rubinsky, A. D., & Grant, B. F. (2012). Comparative performance of the AUDIT-C in screening for DSM-IV and DSM-5 alcohol use disorders. *Drug and Alcohol Dependence, 126*(3), 384–388.

19. Substance Abuse and Mental Health Services Administration, & National Institute on Alcohol Abuse and Alcoholism. (2015). *Medication for the treatment of alcohol use disorder: A brief guide.* HHS Publication No. (SMA) 15-4907. Rockville, MD: Substance Abuse and Mental Health Services Administration.

20. Smith, P. C., Schmidt, S. M., Allensworth-Davies, D., & Saitz, R. (2009). Primary care validation of a single-question alcohol screening test. *Journal of General Internal Medicine, 24*(7), 783–788.

21. Kalman, D., Morissette, S. B., & George, T. P. (2005). Co-morbidity of smoking in patients with psychiatric and substance use disorders. *American Journal of Addictions, 14*, 106–123.

22 Department of Health and Human Services. (2014). *The health consequences of smoking—50 years of progress: A report of the Surgeon General*. Atlanta, GA: Department of Health and Human Services, Centers for Disease Control and Prevention, National Center for Chronic Disease Prevention and Health Promotion, Office on Smoking and Health.

23 Lasser, K., Boyd, J. W., Woolhandler, S., Himmelstein, D. U., McCormick, D., & Bor, D. H. (2000). Smoking and mental illness: A population-based prevalence study. *JAMA, 284*, 2606–2610.

24 Ong, M. O., Zhou, Q., & Sung, H. (2011). Primary care providers advising smokers to quit: Comparing effectiveness between those with and without alcohol, drug, or mental disorders. *Nicotine and Tobacco Research, 13*(12), 1193–1201.

25 U.S. Preventive Services Task Force. (2015). Tobacco smoking cessation in adults, including pregnant women: Behavioral and pharmacotherapy interventions. Retrieved October 12, 2017, from www.uspreventiveservicestaskforce.org/Page/Document/UpdateSummaryFinal/tobacco-use-in-adults-and-pregnant-women-counseling-and-interventions1

26 Heatherton, T. F., Kozlowski, L. T., Frecker, R. C., & Fagerström, K. O. (1991). The Fagerström Test for Nicotine Dependence: A revision of the Fagerström Tolerance Questionnaire. *British Journal of Addiction, 86*(9), 1119–1127.

27 John, U., Meyer, C., Schumann, A., Hapke, U., Rumpf, H. J., Adam, C., ... Lüdemann, J. (2004). A short form of the Fagerström Test for Nicotine Dependence and the Heaviness of Smoking Index in two adult population samples. *Addictive Behaviors, 29*(6), 1207–1212.

28 U.S. Preventive Services Task Force. (2008). Drug use, illicit: Screening. Retrieved November 22, 2017, from www.uspreventiveservicestaskforce.org/Page/Document/UpdateSummaryFinal/drug-use-illicit-screening

29 Shapiro, B., Coffa, D., & McCance-Katz, E. F. (2013). A primary care approach to substance misuse. *American Family Physician, 88*(2), 113–121.

30 McNeely, J., Cleland, C. M., Strauss, S. M., Palamar, J. J., Rotrosen, J., & Saitz, R. (2015). Validation of self-administered single-item screening questions (SISQs) for unhealthy alcohol and drug use in primary care patients. *Journal of General Internal Medicine, 30*(12), 1757–1764.

31 McNeely, J., Wu, L. T., Subramaniam, G., Sharma, G., Cathers, L. A., Svikis, D., ... Schwartz, R. P. (2016). Performance of the Tobacco, Alcohol, Prescription Medication, and Other Substance Use (TAPS) Tool for substance use screening in primary care patients. *Annals of Internal Medicine, 165*(10), 690–699.

32 Smith, P. C., Schmidt, S. M., Allensworth-Davies, D., & Saitz, R. (2010). A single-question screening test for drug use in primary care. *Archives of Internal Medicine, 170*(13), 1155–1160.

33 Tiet, Q. Q., Leyva, Y. E., Moos, R. H., Frayne, S. M., Osterberg, L., & Smith, B. (2015). Screen of drug use: Diagnostic accuracy of a new brief tool for primary care. *JAMA Internal Medicine, 175*(8), 1371–1377.

34 Skinner, H. A. (1982). The Drug Abuse Screening Test. *Addictive Behaviors, 7*(4), 363–371.

35 Babor, T. F., Higgins-Biddle, J. C., Saunders, J. B., & Monteiro, M. G. (2001). *The Alcohol Use Disorders Identification Test: Guidelines for use in primary care* (2nd ed.). Geneva, Switzerland: World Health Organization.

36 Heatherton, T. F., Kozlowski, L. T., Frecker, R. C., & Fagerström, K. O. (1991). The Fagerström Test for Nicotine Dependence: A revision of the Fagerström Tolerance Questionnaire. *British Journal of Addiction, 86*(9), 1119–1127.

37 McNeely, J., Strauss, S. M., Rotrosen, J., Ramautar, A., & Gourevitch, M. N. (2016). Validation of an audio computer-assisted self-interview (ACASI) version of the Alcohol, Smoking and Substance Involvement Screening Test (ASSIST) in primary care patients. *Addiction, 111*(2), 233–244.

38 Ali, R., Meena, S., Eastwood, B., Richards, I., & Marsden, J. (2013). Ultra-rapid screening for substance-use disorders: The Alcohol, Smoking and Substance Involvement Screening Test (ASSIST-Lite). *Drug and Alcohol Dependence, 132*(1–2), 352–361.

39 Smith, P. C., Schmidt, S. M., Allensworth-Davies, D., & Saitz, R. (2010). A single-question screening test for drug use in primary care. *Archives of Internal Medicine, 170*(13), 1155–1160.

40 Tiet, Q. Q., Leyva, Y. E., Moos, R. H., Frayne, S. M., Osterberg, L., & Smith, B. (2015). Screen of drug use: Diagnostic accuracy of a new brief tool for primary care. *JAMA Internal Medicine, 175*(8), 1371–1377.

41 McNeely, J., Wu, L. T., Subramaniam, G., Sharma, G., Cathers, L. A., Svikis, D., ... Schwartz, R. P. (2016). Performance of the Tobacco, Alcohol, Prescription Medication, and Other Substance Use (TAPS) Tool for substance use screening in primary care patients. *Annals of Internal Medicine, 165*(10), 690–699.

42 National Institute on Drug Abuse. (2012). *Resource guide: Screening for drug use in general medical settings*. Rockville, MD: Author.

43 National Institute on Drug Abuse. (n.d.). NIDA Quick Screen V1. Retrieved October 16, 2017, from www.drugabuse.gov/sites/default/files/pdf/nmassist.pdf

44 Ali, R., Meena, S., Eastwood, B., Richards, I., & Marsden, J. (2013). Ultra-rapid screening for substance-use disorders: The Alcohol, Smoking and Substance Involvement Screening Test (ASSIST-Lite). *Drug and Alcohol Dependence, 132*(1–2), 352–361.

45 Schwartz, R. P., McNeely, J., Wu, L. T., Sharma, G., Wahle, A., Cushing, C., … Subramaniam, G. (2017). Identifying substance misuse in primary care: TAPS Tool compared to the WHO ASSIST. *Journal of Substance Abuse Treatment, 76*, 69–76.

46 Wang, X., Zhang, T., & Ho, W. Z. (2011). Opioids and HIV/HCV infection. *Journal of Neuroimmune Pharmacology, 6*(4), 477–489.

47 Wang, X., Zhang, T., & Ho, W. Z. (2011). Opioids and HIV/HCV infection. *Journal of Neuroimmune Pharmacology, 6*(4), 477–489.

48 Merrill, J. O., Rhodes, L. A., Deyo, R. A., Marlatt, G. A., & Bradley, K. A. (2002). Mutual mistrust in the medical care of drug users: The keys to the "narc" cabinet. *Journal of General Internal Medicine, 17*(5), 327–333.

49 Shapiro, B., Coffa, D., & McCance-Katz, E. F. (2013). A primary care approach to substance misuse. *American Family Physician, 88*(2), 113–121.

50 Miller, W. R., & Rollnick, S. (2013). *Motivational interviewing: Helping people change* (3rd ed.). New York, NY: Guilford Press.

51 Center for Substance Abuse Treatment. (1999). *Brief interventions and brief therapies for substance abuse.* Treatment Improvement Protocol (TIP) Series. 34. HHS Publication No. (SMA) 12-3952. Rockville, MD: Substance Abuse and Mental Health Services Administration.

52 Miller, W. R., & Rollnick, S. (2013). *Motivational interviewing: Helping people change* (3rd ed.). New York, NY: Guilford Press.

53 Savant, J. D., Barry, D. T., Cutter, C. J., Joy, M. T., Dinh, A., Schottenfeld, R. S., & Fiellin, D. A. (2013). Prevalence of mood and substance use disorders among patients seeking primary care office-based buprenorphine/naloxone treatment. *Drug and Alcohol Dependence, 127*(1–3), 243–247.

54 Hassan, A. N., Howe, A. S., Samokhvalov, A. V., Le Foll, B., & George, T. P. (2017). Management of mood and anxiety disorders in patients receiving opioid agonist therapy: Review and meta-analysis. *American Journal on Addictions, 26*(6), 551–563.

55 Hall, W. D., & Strang, J. (2017). Alcohol problems need more attention in patients receiving long-term opioid substitution therapy. *Lancet Psychiatry, 4*(4), 265–266.

56 Saitz, R. (2014). Medical and surgical complications of addiction. In R. K. Ries, D. A. Fiellin, S. C. Miller, & R. Saitz (Eds.), *The ASAM principles of addiction medicine* (5th ed.). Philadelphia, PA: Wolters Kluwer.

57 Soper, R. G. (2014, October 6). Intimate partner violence and co-occurring substance abuse/addiction. *ASAM Magazine.* Retrieved October 16, 2017, from www.asam.org/magazine/read/article/2014/10/06/intimate-partner-violence-and-co-occurring-substance-abuse-addiction

58 Stone, A. L., Becker, L. G., Huber, A. M., & Catalano, R. F. (2012). Review of risk and protective factors of substance use and problem use in emerging adulthood. *Addictive Behaviors, 37*(7), 747–775.

59 American Society of Addiction Medicine. (2017). *The ASAM appropriate use of drug testing in clinical addiction medicine.* Rockville, MD: ASAM. Retrieved October 30, 2017, through www.asam.org/resources/guidelines-and-consensus-documents/drug-testing

60 Lynch, K. (2014). *San Francisco General Hospital laboratory protocol.* San Francisco, CA: San Francisco General Hospital.

61 Warner, E., & Lorch, E. (2014). Laboratory diagnosis. In R. K. Ries, D. A. Fiellin, S. C. Miller, & R. Saitz (Eds.), *Principles of addiction medicine* (5th ed., pp. 332–343). Philadelphia, PA: Wolters Kluwer.

62 Milone, M. C. (2012). Laboratory testing for prescription opioids. *Journal of Medical Toxicology, 8*(4), 408–416.

63 Reisfield, G. M., Bertholf, R., Barkin, R. L., Webb, F., & Wilson, G. (2007). Urine drug test interpretation: What do physicians know? *Journal of Opioid Management, 3*(2), 80–86.

64 Standridge, J. B., Adams, S. M., & Zotos, A. P. (2010). Urine drug screening: A valuable office procedure. *American Family Physician, 81*(5), 635–640.

65 Warner, E., & Lorch, E. (2014). Laboratory diagnosis. In R. K. Ries, D. A. Fiellin, S. C. Miller, & R. Saitz (Eds.), *Principles of addiction medicine* (5th ed., pp. 332–343). Philadelphia, PA: Wolters Kluwer.

66 Substance Abuse and Mental Health Services Administration. (2018). *Clinical guidance for treating pregnant and parenting women with opioid use disorder and their infants.* HHS Publication No. (SMA) 18-5054. Rockville, MD: Substance Abuse and Mental Health Services Administration.

67 American College of Obstetricians and Gynecologists. (2017, August). Opioid use and opioid use disorder in pregnancy. Retrieved October 30, 2017, from www.acog.org/-/media/Committee-Opinions/Committee-on-Obstetric-Practice/co711.pdf?dmc=1&ts=20170929T1541517316

68 Ali, M. M., Dowd, N., Classen, T., Mutter, R., & Scott, P. (2017). Prescription drugs monitoring program, nonmedical use of prescription drug and heroin use: Evidence from the National Survey of Drug Use and Health. *Addictive Behaviors, 69*, 65–77.

69 American Psychiatric Association. (2013). *Diagnostic and statistical manual of mental disorders* (5th ed.). Arlington, VA: American Psychiatric Publishing.

70 American Psychiatric Association. (2013). *Diagnostic and statistical manual of mental disorders* (5th ed.). Arlington, VA: American Psychiatric Publishing.

71 Clinical Tools. (n.d.). DSM 5 opioid use disorder checklist. Retrieved October 16, 2017, from www.buppractice.com/printpdf/19556

72 American Psychiatric Association. (2013). *Diagnostic and statistical manual of mental disorders* (5th ed.). Arlington, VA: American Psychiatric Publishing.

73 Mattick, R. P., Breen, C., Kimber, J., & Davoli, M. (2014). Buprenorphine maintenance versus placebo or methadone maintenance for opioid dependence. *Cochrane Database of Systematic Reviews, 2014*(2), 1–84.

74 Mattick, R. P., Breen, C., Kimber, J., & Davoli, M. (2009). Methadone maintenance therapy versus no opioid replacement therapy for opioid dependence. *Cochrane Database of Systematic Reviews, 2009*(3), 1–19.

75 Minozzi, S., Amato, L., Vecchi, S., Davoli, M., Kirchmayer, U., & Verster, A. (2011). Oral naltrexone maintenance treatment for opioid dependence. *Cochrane Database of Systematic Reviews, 4*, CD001333.

76 Krupitsky, E., Zvartau, E., Blokhina, E., Verbitskaya, E., Wahlgren, V., Tsoy-Podosenin, M., ... Woody, G. E. (2012). Randomized trial of long-acting sustained-release naltrexone implant vs oral naltrexone or placebo for preventing relapse to opioid dependence. *Archives of General Psychiatry, 69*(9), 973–981.

77 Lee, J. D., Friedmann, P. D., Kinlock, T. W., Nunes, E. V., Boney, T. Y., Hoskinson, R. A., Jr., ... O'Brien, C. P. (2016). Extended-release naltrexone to prevent opioid relapse in criminal justice offenders. *New England Journal of Medicine, 374*(13), 1232–1242.

78 McCarty, D., Braude, L., Lyman, D. R., Dougherty, R. H., Daniels, A. S., Ghose, S. S., & Delphin-Rittmon, M. E. (2014). Substance abuse intensive outpatient programs: Assessing the evidence. *Psychiatric Services, 65*(6), 718–726.

79 Mee-Lee, D., Shulman, G. D., Fishman, M. J., Gastfriend, D. R., & Miller, M. M. (Eds.). (2013). *The ASAM criteria: Treatment criteria for addictive, substance-related, and co-occurring conditions* (3rd ed.). Carson City, NV: The Change Companies.

80 Drug Enforcement Administration. (n.d.). Informational documents. Retrieved November 21, 2017, from www.deadiversion.usdoj.gov/pubs/docs/index.html

81 Carroll, K. M., & Weiss, R. D. (2016). The role of behavioral interventions in buprenorphine maintenance treatment: A review. *American Journal of Psychiatry, 174*(8), 738–774.

82 Fiellin, D. A., Barry, D. T., Sullivan, L. E., Cutter, C. J., Moore, B. A., O'Connor, P. G., & Schottenfeld, R. S. (2013). A randomized trial of cognitive behavioral therapy in primary care-based buprenorphine. *American Journal of Medicine, 126*(1), 74.e11–74.e77.

83 Fiellin, D. A., Pantalon, M. V., Chawarski, M. C., Moore, B. A., Sullivan, L. E., O'Connor, P. G., & Schottenfeld, R. S. (2006). Counseling plus buprenorphine-naloxone maintenance therapy for opioid dependence. *New England Journal of Medicine, 355*(4), 365–374.

84 Ling, W., Hillhouse, M., Ang, A., Jenkins, J., & Fahey, J. (2013). Comparison of behavioral treatment conditions in buprenorphine maintenance. *Addiction, 108*(10), 1788–1798.

85 Weiss, R. D., Potter, J. S., Fiellin, D. A., Byrne, M., Connery, H. S., Dickinson, W., ... Ling, W. (2011). Adjunctive counseling during brief and extended buprenorphine-naloxone treatment for prescription opioid dependence: A 2-phase randomized controlled trial. *Archives of General Psychiatry, 68*(12), 1238–1246.

86 Pettinati, H. M., O'Brien, C. P., & Dundon, W. D. (2013). Current status of co-occurring mood and substance use disorders: A new therapeutic target. *American Journal of Psychiatry, 170*(1), 23–30.

87 Chou, R., Korthuis, P. T., Weimer, M., Bougatsos, C., Blazina, I., Zakher, B., ... McCarty, D. (2016). *Medication-assisted treatment models of care for opioid use disorder in primary care settings.* Technical Brief No. 28. Rockville, MD: Agency for Healthcare Research and Quality.

88 American Society of Addiction Medicine. (n.d.). *Nurse practitioners and physician assistants prescribing buprenorphine*. Retrieved October 16, 2017, from www.asam.org/quality-practice/practice-resources/nurse-practitioners-and-physician-assistants-prescribing-buprenorphine

89 Bogdanowicz, K. M., Stewart, R., Broadbent, M., Hatch, S. L., Hotopf, M., Strang, J., & Hayes, R. D. (2015). Double trouble: Psychiatric comorbidity and opioid addiction—All-cause and cause-specific mortality. *Drug and Alcohol Dependence, 148*, 85–92.

90 Bogdanowicz, K. M., Stewart, R., Chang, C. K., Downs, J., Khondoker, M., Shetty, H., ... Hayes, R. D. (2016). Identifying mortality risks in patients with opioid use disorder using brief screening assessment: Secondary mental health clinical records analysis. *Drug and Alcohol Dependence, 164*, 82–88.

91 Department of Health and Human Services. (2016). *The opioid epidemic: By the numbers*. Washington, DC: Department of Health and Human Services.

92 Substance Abuse and Mental Health Services Administration. (2016). *SAMHSA opioid overdose prevention toolkit*. HHS Publication No. (SMA) 16-4742. Rockville, MD: Author.

93 Centers for Disease Control and Prevention. (2017). Opioid overdose. Retrieved October 16, 2017, from www.cdc.gov/drugoverdose

94 Centers for Disease Control and Prevention. (2017). Heroin overdose data. Retrieved November 20, 2017, from www.cdc.gov/drugoverdose/data/heroin.html

95 Centers for Disease Control and Prevention. (2016). Increases in drug and opioid-involved overdose deaths—United States, 2010–2015. *Morbidity and Mortality Weekly Report, 65*(50–51), 1445–1452.

96 Albert, S., Brason, F. W., II, Sanford, C. K., Dasgupta, N., Graham, J., & Lovette, B. (2011). Project Lazarus: Community-based overdose prevention in rural North Carolina. *Pain Medicine, 12*(Suppl. 2), S77–S85.

97 Walley, A. Y., Xuan, Z., Hackman, H. H., Quinn, E., Doe-Simkins, M., Sorensen-Alawad, A., ... Ozonoff, A. (2013). Opioid overdose rates and implementation of overdose education and nasal naloxone distribution in Massachusetts: Interrupted time series analysis. *British Medical Journal, 346*, f174.

98 Mee-Lee, D. (2013, November–December). How to really use the new edition of *The ASAM Criteria*: What to do and what not to do. *Counselor, 14*(6), 34–40.

99 Bush, K., Kivlahan, D. R., McDonell, M. B., Fihn, S. D., & Bradley, K. A. (1998). The AUDIT alcohol consumption questions (AUDIT-C): An effective brief screening test for problem drinking. Ambulatory Care Quality Improvement Project (ACQUIP). Alcohol Use Disorders Identification Test. *Archives of Internal Medicine, 158*(16), 1789–1795.

100 Skinner, H. A. (1982). The Drug Abuse Screening Test. *Addictive Behavior, 7*(4), 363–371.

101 Yudko, E., Lozhkina, O., & Fouts, A. (2007). A comprehensive review of the psychometric properties of the Drug Abuse Screening Test. *Journal of Substance Abuse Treatment, 32*, 189–198.

102 American Psychiatric Association. (2013). *Diagnostic and statistical manual of mental disorders* (5th ed., p. 541). Arlington, VA: American Psychiatric Publishing.

103 McNeely, J., Wu, L. T., Subramaniam, G., Sharma, G., Cathers, L. A., Svikis, D., ... Schwartz, R. P. (2016). Performance of the Tobacco, Alcohol, Prescription Medication, and Other Substance Use (TAPS) Tool for substance use screening in primary care patients. *Annals of Internal Medicine, 165*(10), 690–699.

This page intentionally left blank.

TIP 63

MEDICATIONS FOR OPIOID USE DISORDER

Part 3: Pharmacotherapy for Opioid Use Disorder
For Healthcare Professionals

Part 3 of this **Treatment Improvement Protocol (TIP)** describes general principles of opioid use disorder (OUD) pharmacotherapy and discusses medication formulations, indications, and dosing for the three medications used to treat OUD—methadone, naltrexone, and buprenorphine.

TIP Navigation

Executive Summary
For healthcare and addiction professionals, policymakers, patients, and families

Part 1: Introduction to Medications for Opioid Use Disorder Treatment
For healthcare and addiction professionals, policymakers, patients, and families

Part 2: Addressing Opioid Use Disorder in General Medical Settings
For healthcare professionals

Part 3: Pharmacotherapy for Opioid Use Disorder
For healthcare professionals

Part 4: Partnering Addiction Treatment Counselors With Clients and Healthcare Professionals
For healthcare and addiction professionals

Part 5: Resources Related to Medications for Opioid Use Disorder
For healthcare and addiction professionals, policymakers, patients, and families

KEY MESSAGES

- OUD medications are safe and effective when used appropriately.
- OUD medications can help patients reduce or stop illicit opioid use and improve their health and functioning.
- Pharmacotherapy should be considered for all patients with OUD. Reserve opioid pharmacotherapies for those with moderate-to-severe OUD with physical dependence.
- Patients with OUD should be informed of the risks and benefits of pharmacotherapy, treatment without medication, and no treatment.
- Patients should be advised on where and how to get treatment with OUD medication.
- Doses and schedules of pharmacotherapy must be individualized.

Substance Abuse and Mental Health Services Administration

www.samhsa.gov • 1-877-SAMHSA-7 (1-877-726-4727)

PART 3: PHARMACOTHERAPY FOR OPIOID USE DISORDER

Pharmacotherapy for Opioid Use Disorder 3-1

Chapter 3A: Overview of Pharmacotherapy for Opioid Use Disorder 3-5

Chapter 3B: Methadone 3-15

Chapter 3C: Naltrexone 3-35

Chapter 3D: Buprenorphine 3-49

Chapter 3E: Medical Management Strategies for Patients Taking OUD Medications in Office-Based Settings 3-79

Chapter 3F: Medical Management of Patients Taking OUD Medications in Hospital Settings 3-99

PART 3 of 5
Pharmacotherapy for Opioid Use Disorder

Part 3 of this TIP describes general principles of OUD pharmacotherapy and discusses medication formulations, indications, and dosing for the three Food and Drug Administration (FDA)-approved medications used to treat OUD—methadone, naltrexone, and buprenorphine. Part 3 also discusses patient management and monitoring in outpatient settings other than opioid treatment programs (OTPs) as well as medical management of patients with OUD in hospital settings.

Scope of the Problem

The United States is experiencing an opioid addiction epidemic.[1] In 2016, an estimated 2.1 million Americans had OUD.[2] Illicit opioid use contributes to the development of OUD, the spread of HIV and hepatitis infections, and increasing numbers of overdose deaths.

OUD is a set of cognitive, behavioral, and physiological symptoms marked by an inability to stop opioid use despite negative consequences.[3] When severe, it can present as a chronic, recurring condition with compulsive opioid use that is often termed "addiction." It can cause serious physical and mental health, employment, legal, and family problems.

Each FDA-approved medication used to treat OUD can help patients achieve remission and

OPIOID-RELATED **EMERGENCY DEPARTMENT** visits nearly doubled from 2005–2014.[4]

begin or maintain recovery. Pharmacotherapy for OUD should be accompanied by individually tailored medical management and psychosocial and recovery support services as needed and wanted by patients to support their remission and recovery.

Medication supports the efforts of the individual to achieve lasting recovery.

Exhibit 3.1 defines key terms in Part 3. For more definitions, see the glossary in Part 5 of this TIP.

NOTE TO HEALTHCARE PROFESSIONALS

This TIP cannot replace sound clinical judgment and shared decision making based on careful patient assessment. Providers should familiarize themselves with FDA labeling of all OUD medications and current practices standards described here and in other resources such as the Providers' Clinical Support System (https://pcssmat.org).

EXHIBIT 3.1. Key Terms

Addiction: As defined by the American Society of Addiction Medicine,[5] "a primary, chronic disease of brain reward, motivation, memory, and related circuitry." It is characterized by inability to consistently abstain, impairment in behavioral control, craving, diminished recognition of significant problems with one's behaviors and interpersonal relationships, and a dysfunctional emotional response. Like other chronic diseases, addiction often involves cycles of **relapse** and **remission.** The *Diagnostic and Statistical Manual of Mental Disorders,* Fifth Edition,[6] does not use the term for diagnostic purposes, but it commonly describes the more severe forms of OUD.

Induction: Process of initial dosing with medication for OUD treatment until the patient reaches a state of stability; also called initiation.

Maintenance treatment: Providing medications to achieve and sustain clinical remission of signs and symptoms of OUD and support the individual process of recovery without a specific endpoint (as is the typical standard of care in medical and psychiatric treatment of other chronic illnesses).

Medically supervised withdrawal (formerly called detoxification): Using an opioid agonist (or an alpha-2 adrenergic agonist if opioid agonist is not available) in tapering doses or other medications to help a patient discontinue illicit or prescription opioids.

Medical management: Process whereby healthcare professionals provide medication, basic brief supportive counseling, monitoring of drug use and medication adherence, and referrals, when necessary, to addiction counseling and other services to address the patient's medical, mental health, comorbid addiction, and psychosocial needs.

Office-based opioid treatment: Providing medication for OUD in outpatient settings other than certified OTPs.

Opioid treatment program (OTP): An accredited treatment program with Substance Abuse and Mental Health Services Administration certification and Drug Enforcement Administration registration to administer and dispense opioid agonist medications that are approved by FDA to treat opioid addiction. Currently, these include methadone and buprenorphine products. Other pharmacotherapies, such as naltrexone, may be provided but are not subject to these regulations. OTPs must provide adequate medical, counseling, vocational, educational, and other assessment and treatment services either onsite or by referral to an outside agency or practitioner through a formal agreement.[7]

Key Terms Related to OUD Medication Pharmacology

Abuse liability: The likelihood that a medication with central nervous system activity will cause desirable psychological effects, such as euphoria or mood changes, that promote the medication's misuse.

Bioavailability: Proportion of medication administered that reaches the bloodstream.

Cross-tolerance: Potential for people tolerant to one opioid (e.g., heroin) to be tolerant to another (e.g., methadone).

Dissociation: Rate at which a drug uncouples from the receptor. A drug with a longer dissociation rate will have a longer duration of action than a drug with a shorter dissociation rate.

Half-life: Rate of removal of a drug from the body. One half-life removes 50 percent from the plasma. After a drug is stopped, it takes five half-lives to remove about 95 percent from the plasma. If a drug is continued at the same dose, its plasma level will continue to rise until it reaches steady-state concentrations after about five half-lives.

EXHIBIT 3.1. Key Terms (continued)

Intrinsic activity: The degree of receptor activation attributable to drug binding. **Full agonist, partial agonist,** and **antagonist** are terms that describe the intrinsic activity of a drug.

Opiates: A subclass of opioids derived from opium (e.g., morphine, codeine, thebaine).

Opioid blockade: Blunting or blocking of the euphoric effects of an opioid through opioid receptor occupancy by an opioid agonist (e.g., methadone, buprenorphine) or antagonist (e.g., naltrexone).

Opioid receptor agonist: A substance that has an affinity for and stimulates physiological activity at cell receptors in the nervous system that are normally stimulated by opioids. **Mu-opioid receptor full agonists** (e.g., methadone) bind to the mu-opioid receptor and produce actions similar to those produced by the endogenous opioid beta-endorphin. Increasing the dose increases the effect. **Mu-opioid receptor partial agonists** (e.g., buprenorphine) bind to the mu-opioid receptor. Unlike with full agonists, increasing their dose in an opioid-tolerant individual may not produce additional effects once they have reached their maximal effect. At low doses, partial agonists may produce effects similar to those of full agonists. Methadone and buprenorphine can blunt or block the effects of exogenously administered opioids.

Opioid receptor antagonist: A substance that has an affinity for opioid receptors in the central nervous system without producing the physiological effects of opioid agonists. Mu-opioid receptor antagonists (e.g., naltrexone) can block the effects of exogenously administered opioids.

Opioids: All natural, synthetic, and semisynthetic substances that have effects similar to morphine. They can be used as medications having such effects (e.g., methadone, buprenorphine, oxycodone).

Receptor affinity: Strength of the bond between a medication and its receptor. A medication with high mu-opioid receptor affinity requires lower concentrations to occupy the same number of mu-opioid receptors as a drug with lower mu-opioid receptor affinity. Drugs with high mu-opioid receptor affinity may displace drugs with lower affinity.

This page intentionally left blank.

Chapter 3A: Overview of Pharmacotherapy for Opioid Use Disorder

Chapter 3A describes general principles of OUD pharmacotherapy and summarizes formulations, indications, and dosing for the three FDA-approved OUD medications.

There are three FDA-approved medications used to treat OUD, including the mu-opioid receptor partial agonist buprenorphine, the mu-opioid receptor full agonist methadone, and the mu-opioid receptor antagonist naltrexone. Extended-release naltrexone (XR-NTX) is FDA approved to prevent relapse in patients who have remained opioid abstinent for sufficient time.

Discussing medications that can treat OUD with patients who have this disorder is the clinical standard of care and should cover at least:

- The proven effectiveness of methadone, naltrexone, and buprenorphine compared with placebo and with outpatient counseling without medication.
- Risks and benefits of pharmacotherapy with all three types of medication, treatment without medication, and no treatment.
- Safety and effectiveness of the medications when used appropriately.
- Pharmacologic properties, routes of administration, and where and how to access treatment with each medication (Exhibit 3A.1).

EXHIBIT 3A.1. OUD Medications: An Overview[8,9]

CATEGORY	BUPRENORPHINE*	METHADONE	XR-NTX**
Appropriate patients	Typically for patients with OUD who are physiologically dependent on opioids.	Typically for patients with OUD who are physiologically dependent on opioids and who meet federal criteria for OTP admission.	Typically for patients with OUD who have abstained from short-acting opioids for at least 7–10 days and long-acting opioids for at least 10–14 days.
Pharmacology	Opioid receptor partial agonist Reduces opioid withdrawal and craving; blunts or blocks euphoric effects of self-administered illicit opioids through cross-tolerance and opioid receptor occupancy.	Opioid receptor agonist Reduces opioid withdrawal and craving; blunts or blocks euphoric effects of self-administered illicit opioids through cross-tolerance and opioid receptor occupancy.	Opioid receptor antagonist Blocks euphoric effects of self-administered illicit opioids through opioid receptor occupancy. Causes no opioid effects.

*Long-acting buprenorphine implants (every 6 months) for patients on a stable dose of buprenorphine are also available through implanters and prescribers with additional training and certification through the Probuphine Risk Evaluation and Mitigation Strategy (REMS) Program. Extended-release buprenorphine monthly subcutaneous injections are available only through prescribers and pharmacies registered with the Sublocade REMS Program.

**Naltrexone hydrochloride tablets (50 mg each) are also available for daily oral dosing but have not been shown to be more effective than treatment without medication or placebo because of poor patient adherence.

Continued on next page

EXHIBIT 3A.1. OUD Medications: An Overview (continued)

CATEGORY	BUPRENORPHINE*	METHADONE	XR-NTX**
Patient education	Tell patients: • That they will need to be in opioid withdrawal to receive their first dose to avoid buprenorphine-precipitated opioid withdrawal. • About the risk of overdose with concurrent benzodiazepine or alcohol use, with injecting buprenorphine, and after stopping the medication.	Tell patients: • That their dose will start low and build up slowly to avoid oversedation; it takes several days for a given dose to have its full effect. • About overdose risk in the first 2 weeks of treatment, especially with concurrent benzodiazepine or alcohol use, and after stopping the medication.	Tell patients: • That they will need to be opioid free for at least 7–10 days for short-acting opioids and at least 10–14 days for long-acting opioids before their first dose to avoid XR-NTX-precipitated opioid withdrawal (which may require hospitalization). • About the risk of overdose after stopping the medication.
Administration	Daily (or off-label less-than-daily dosing regimens) administration of sublingual or buccal tablet or film. Subdermal implants every 6 months, for up to 1 year, for stable patients. Monthly subcutaneous injection of extended-release formulation in abdominal region for patients treated with transmucosal buprenorphine for at least 1 week.	Daily oral administration as liquid concentrate, tablet, or oral solution from dispersible tablet or powder (unless patients can take some home).	Every 4 weeks or once-per-month intramuscular injection.
Prescribing	Physicians, nurse practitioners (NPs), and physician assistants (PAs) need a waiver to prescribe. Any pharmacy can fill a prescription for sublingual or buccal formulations. OTPs can administer/dispense by OTP physician order without a waiver.	SAMHSA-certified OTPs can provide methadone for daily onsite administration or at-home self-administration for stable patients.	Physicians, NPs, or PAs prescribe or order administration by qualified healthcare professionals.

*Long-acting buprenorphine implants (every 6 months) for patients on a stable dose of buprenorphine are also available through implanters and prescribers with additional training and certification through the Probuphine Risk Evaluation and Mitigation Strategy (REMS) Program. Extended-release buprenorphine monthly subcutaneous injections are available only through prescribers and pharmacies registered with the Sublocade REMS Program.

**Naltrexone hydrochloride tablets (50 mg each) are also available for daily oral dosing but have not been shown to be more effective than treatment without medication or placebo because of poor patient adherence.

Introduction to Medications That Address OUD

Methadone

Methadone is the most used and most studied OUD medication in the world.[10,11] The World Health Organization (WHO) considers it an essential medication.[12] Many clinical trials and meta-analyses have shown that **it effectively reduces illicit opioid use, treats OUD, and retains patients in treatment** better than placebo or no medication.[13,14,15] (Part 1 of this Treatment Improvement Protocol [TIP] further covers methadone's efficacy.)

In the United States, roughly 1,500 federally certified opioid treatment programs (OTPs) offer methadone for OUD. Increasingly, they also offer buprenorphine, and some provide XR-NTX. Core OTP services include medical oversight of treatment, direct observation of dose administration, take-home dose dispensing under certain conditions, counseling, and drug testing.

Some OTPs provide other services, including mental health and primary care, HIV and hepatitis C virus care, and recovery support. Even so, significant demand remains for better integration and coordination of care among OTPs, primary care services, and mental health services to treat the range of needs common in people with OUD.[16] Coordination is especially important for people with co-occurring medical, mental, and substance use disorders, who need multiple services and face challenges in treatment access and adherence.

> Although only OTPs can administer or dispense methadone for OUD, **all healthcare professionals and addiction and mental health counselors should be familiar with methadone.** Their patients may be enrolled in or need referral to OTPs.

> **RESOURCE ALERT**
>
> **Substance Abuse and Mental Health Services Administration (SAMHSA) Federal Guidelines for OTPs**
>
> *Federal Guidelines for Opioid Treatment Programs* offers guidance on how to satisfy federal OTP regulations (https://store.samhsa.gov/shin/content//PEP15-FEDGUIDEOTP/PEP15-FEDGUIDEOTP.pdf).

Naltrexone

XR-NTX has demonstrated efficacy in reducing return to illicit opioid use, increasing treatment retention, and reducing opioid craving compared with placebo or no medication in randomized controlled trials.[17,18,19] (See Part 1 for more information on naltrexone's efficacy in OUD treatment.) Because the injectable form was approved more recently by FDA than methadone and buprenorphine, XR-NTX has been less studied than those medications. Physicians, NPs, and PAs may prescribe or order XR-NTX for administration by qualified staff members without additional waiver requirements.

XR-NTX initiated prior to release from controlled environments (e.g., jails, prisons, residential rehabilitation programs) **may be useful in preventing return to opioid use after release.**[20] These settings are typically associated with extended periods of opioid abstinence, so maintaining abstinence for sufficient time to start naltrexone is less challenging than initiating it among outpatients in the community. Short-term pilot studies show that offering naltrexone under these circumstances can increase treatment engagement after release.[21,22]

The oral formulation of naltrexone is not widely used to treat OUD because of low rates of patient acceptance and high rates of

> **RESOURCE ALERT**
>
> **SAMHSA Brief Guide on the Use of XR-NTX**
>
> SAMHSA's *Clinical Use of Extended-Release Injectable Naltrexone in the Treatment of Opioid Use Disorder: A Brief Guide* offers guidance on the use of XR-NTX and is available online (https://store.samhsa.gov/product/Clinical-Use-of-Extended-Release-Injectable-Naltrexone-in-the-Treatment-of-Opioid-Use-Disorder-A-Brief-Guide/SMA14-4892R).

nonadherence leading to a lack of efficacy.[23] However, consideration should be given to its use in situations where adherence can be ensured, such as with observed daily dosing. Naltrexone is also FDA approved for the treatment of alcohol use disorder and therefore may be useful for patients with both OUD and alcohol use disorder.

Buprenorphine

Buprenorphine is effective in retaining patients in treatment and reducing illicit opioid use, as demonstrated by many clinical trials comparing buprenorphine with placebo or no medication.[24] Buprenorphine treatment is available throughout the world. WHO includes it in its list of essential medicines.[25] (See Part 1 for more information on buprenorphine's efficacy in OUD treatment.)

Buprenorphine is a partial agonist with a ceiling effect on opioid activity. Hence, it is less likely than methadone and other full agonists to cause respiratory depression in an accidental overdose. This property contributed to the decision permitting buprenorphine to be prescribed to treat opioid dependence outside OTPs.[26] That being said, lethal overdose with buprenorphine is possible in opioid-naïve individuals or when it is taken in combination with central nervous system depressants such as benzodiazepines or alcohol.

Transmucosal buprenorphine is available by prescription through pharmacies, because the Drug Addiction Treatment Act of 2000 (DATA 2000) created an exception to the Controlled Substances Act to permit FDA schedule III, IV, and V medications approved to treat opioid dependence to be prescribed for that purpose outside OTPs. Buprenorphine, in various formulations, is the only medication to which DATA 2000 currently applies.

Qualifying physicians, NPs, and PAs can prescribe buprenorphine if they receive special training, obtain a SAMHSA waiver under DATA 2000, and get a unique Drug Enforcement Administration registration number. This has greatly increased the number and type of settings where medication for OUD is available and the number of patients in treatment. New settings include non-OTP outpatient addiction treatment programs, as well as general medical and mental health practices or clinics (office-based opioid treatment). OTPs can also provide buprenorphine.

In 2016, FDA approved buprenorphine implants (Probuphine) that last about 6 months for patients stabilized on sublingual or buccal formulations. Implants have been found to be more effective than placebo in reducing illicit opioid use among opioid-dependent patients receiving counseling.[27] Implants are available in the same settings as other buprenorphine formulations but require waivered providers to receive specific training from the manufacturer on insertion and removal per the FDA-approved REMS (www.accessdata.fda.gov/scripts/cder/rems/index.cfm?event=IndvRemsDetails.page&REMS=356).

In 2017, FDA approved a monthly extended-release buprenorphine injectable formulation (Sublocade) for patients with moderate-to-

> DATA 2000 restrictions currently apply only to buprenorphine used to treat OUD. They do not apply to pain treatment using buprenorphine formulations approved to treat pain.

Part 3 of 5—Pharmacotherapy for Opioid Use Disorder

> **RESOURCE ALERT**
>
> **How To Obtain a Waiver To Prescribe Buprenorphine**
>
> - Learn how to qualify for a DATA 2000 physician waiver: www.samhsa.gov/medication-assisted-treatment/buprenorphine-waiver-management/qualify-for-physician-waiver
> - Learn how to qualify for an NP or PA waiver: www.samhsa.gov/medication-assisted-treatment/qualify-nps-pas-waivers
> - Learn how waivered physicians can increase their patient limit from 30 to 100, and then to 275 patients: www.samhsa.gov/sites/default/files/programs_campaigns/medication_assisted/understanding-patient-limit275.pdf

severe OUD who had been initiated and treated with transmucosal buprenorphine for at least 7 days. The medication is for subcutaneous abdominal injection by a healthcare provider and is intended to be available for ordering and dispensing (not by prescription to patients) in healthcare settings that receive special certification, pursuant to the FDA-approved REMS (www.accessdata.fda.gov/scripts/cder/rems/index.cfm?event=IndvRemsDetails.page&REMS=376).

Choosing an OUD Medication

Currently, no empirical data indicate which patients will respond better to which OUD medications. All patients considering treatment should be educated about the effectiveness, risks, and benefits of each of the three OUD medications, treatment without medication, and no treatment. Emphasize that OUD medications are safe and effective when used appropriately, and point out that these medications can help patients reduce or stop illicit opioid use and improve their health and functioning.

Tailor decisions to patients' medical, psychiatric, and substance use histories; to their preferences; and to treatment availability when deciding which medication and treatment to provide. Consider:

- Patients' prior response to a medication.
- The medication's side effect profile.
- The strength of the published data on safety and effectiveness.
- Patients' use of other substances (e.g., naltrexone is also approved for the treatment of alcohol dependence).
- Patients' occupation. For patients in safety-sensitive occupations, consider naltrexone.
- Patients' pregnancy status.*
- Patients' physical dependence on opioids. Patients not currently physically dependent on opioids who are returning to the community from a residential treatment program or incarceration should have the option of XR-NTX,[28] methadone, or buprenorphine based on which best suits their needs and circumstances (see below for special safety dosing considerations for methadone and buprenorphine in nontolerant patients).[29,30,31,32]
- Patients' preferences. Respect patients' preferences for agonist versus antagonist medication. (See Part 2 of this TIP for an indepth discussion of treatment planning.)

---

*Methadone or buprenorphine maintenance is recommended for OUD treatment during pregnancy,[33] as these medications have better maternal and infant outcomes than no treatment or medically supervised withdrawal.[34,35,36] Methadone and buprenorphine are not associated with birth defects and have minimal long-term neurodevelopmental impact on infants.[37] However, neonatal abstinence syndrome can occur, which requires hospitalization.[38] The American College of Obstetricians and Gynecologists notes that limited data exist on the safety and effectiveness of naltrexone in pregnancy.[39] Starting naltrexone rather than opioid agonist treatment in pregnancy is not recommended, given the risk of precipitated withdrawal. An expert panel did not agree on whether women already receiving treatment with naltrexone at the onset of pregnancy should remain on that medication during pregnancy.[40] Patients who were taking naltrexone before their pregnancy should weigh with their providers the risks regarding unknown potential harm to the developing fetus versus the potential benefits of continuing this medication during pregnancy.[41] Pregnant patients who discontinue naltrexone and return to opioid use should be considered for methadone or buprenorphine treatment.[42]

Comparative Effectiveness

A Cochrane review of 5 randomized clinical trials with 788 participants found that, when provided at flexible doses on an outpatient basis, methadone retained patients in treatment longer than buprenorphine.[43] That same review found that methadone and buprenorphine equally reduced illicit opioid use based on 8 studies with urine drug testing data from 1,027 participants and 4 studies with self-reported drug use from 501 participants.

There is not yet a Cochrane review on the comparative effectiveness of XR-NTX and buprenorphine. However, in 2017, two randomized trials comparing buprenorphine to XR-NTX were published. A multisite study with 570 participants in the United States compared initiating buprenorphine versus XR-NTX at 8 inpatient treatment programs.[44] That study found that patients randomly assigned to start buprenorphine had significantly lower return-to-use rates during 24 weeks of outpatient treatment compared with those patients assigned to start XR-NTX. This finding was due to the known difficulty in successfully completing induction in the XR-NTX group. However, comparing only the subgroups of those participants who did start their assigned medication, there were no significant between-group differences in return-to-use rates. In a 12-week trial in Norway with 159 participants who were opioid abstinent at the time of random assignment, XR-NTX was found to be noninferior to buprenorphine in terms of treatment retention and illicit opioid use.[45] There is no extant literature evaluating the comparative effectiveness of methadone, XR-NTX, buprenorphine implant, or extended-release buprenorphine injection to one another.

Duration of Medication

Continued treatment with buprenorphine or methadone is associated with better outcomes than medically supervised withdrawal.[46,47,48] Continued treatment with XR-NTX is associated with better outcomes than discontinuing XR-NTX.[49] Patients should be informed of the risks and benefits of discontinuing medication. Buprenorphine or methadone can be used for medically supervised withdrawal over a period of days to weeks (Exhibit 3A.2) for patients who prefer it to ongoing opioid agonist treatment. When opioid agonist medications are unavailable, the alpha$_2$-adrenergic agonist clonidine can relieve some withdrawal symptoms, although clinical trials found it less effective.[50] Pair medically supervised withdrawal with the chance to begin XR-NTX. Discontinuing medication increases risk of return to substance use and overdose death.[51] Stable patients can continue on their selected OUD medication indefinitely as long as it is beneficial.[52,53,54,55]

> The TIP expert panel recommends offering maintenance therapy with medication, not short-term medically supervised withdrawal. The TIP expert panel also supports maintaining patients on OUD medication for years, decades, and even a lifetime if patients are benefiting.

During medically supervised withdrawal, ancillary medications can treat some of the withdrawal symptoms (Exhibit 3A.3).

Principles of OUD Pharmacotherapy

Basic Function

Several factors underlie the development of addiction involving opioids and the difficulty people have in achieving and maintaining abstinence from them. These factors include:[56,57]

- Short-term direct and indirect mu-opioid receptor agonist effects.
- Neuroplastic changes in the brain.
- Genetic, developmental, and environmental factors (e.g., exposure to high-risk environments, effect of stress on the hypothalamic–pituitary–adrenal axis).

EXHIBIT 3A.2. Medically Supervised Withdrawal Using Buprenorphine or Methadone

Medically supervised withdrawal using buprenorphine or methadone is appropriate when patients:
- Prefer it to treatment without medications, after they have been told the risks and benefits of this approach compared with treatment with medications.
- Wish to start XR-NTX, which is also FDA approved for the treatment of alcohol dependence.
- Are entering a controlled environment or workplace that disallows opioid agonists.

Data conflict on the ideal duration of medically supervised withdrawal.[58,59,60] Even so, shorter term dose reductions alone (formerly, "detoxification") are rarely effective.[61,62,63]

The TIP expert panel does not recommend short-term medically supervised withdrawal alone because of its high rates of return to illicit opioid use.[64,65,66] If patients prefer this approach, it should be provided with psychosocial treatment.[67] XR-NTX treatment should always be considered to reduce the likelihood of return to use after medically supervised withdrawal is completed and an adequate period of abstinence achieved,[68] as well as to reduce the likelihood of overdose death upon a return to opioid use.

If withdrawal is appropriate for the patient, the TIP expert panel recommends the following strategies:
- Individualize supervised withdrawal duration per patient preference and response to lower medication doses.
- Note that patients may benefit from nonopioid medication (e.g., clonidine, ondansetron, loperamide) or nonsteroidal anti-inflammatory medications to manage withdrawal symptoms near the end of the taper.
- Consider discontinuing dose reduction and increasing the dose if the patient begins to use illicit opioids.
- Encourage patients to continue receiving counseling, monitoring, and other psychosocial support after medication discontinuation.
- Urge patients to reenter treatment promptly if they return or think they may return to illicit opioid use.

EXHIBIT 3A.3. Medications for Management of Opioid Withdrawal Symptoms

SYMPTOM	MEDICATION
Nausea	Ondansetron, metoclopramide (avoid promethazine; it potentiates opioids)
Diarrhea	Loperamide
Anxiety, irritability, sweating	Clonidine
Insomnia	Diphenhydramine, trazodone
Pain	Nonsteroidal anti-inflammatory drugs

Methadone, buprenorphine, and naltrexone bind to the mu-opioid receptors in the central and peripheral nervous systems, gastrointestinal tract, and vascular system. In the brain, these receptors mediate opioids' analgesic and other effects (e.g., euphoria, respiratory depression, meiosis).[69,70,71] Through modulation of mu-opioid receptor activity in the brain, these medications exert therapeutic efficacy in treating OUD.

Intrinsic Activity

Intrinsic activity at the mu-opioid receptor varies based on whether the medication is a full agonist, partial agonist, or antagonist (Exhibit 3A.4). The amount of intrinsic activity corresponds to the amount of opioid receptor agonist effects. **A full agonist exerts maximal effects at increasing doses. A partial agonist has a ceiling effect.** Its opioid effects increase as the dose increases, but only up to a certain point. **An antagonist binds to the opioid receptor but does not stimulate the receptor at all.** Thus, it has no intrinsic activity regardless of its dose.

Overview of Medication Indications and Dosing

Healthcare professionals should consider pharmacotherapy for all patients with OUD. Prescribers must read FDA labels (i.e., package inserts) for the medications they prescribe. They must also evaluate patients clinically to determine the safety and effectiveness of the medication and dose. Exhibit 3A.5 summarizes OUD medication formulations, indications, and dosing.

The dosing guidance in subsequent chapters for methadone (Chapter 3B), naltrexone (Chapter 3C), and buprenorphine (Chapter 3D) is for healthcare professionals in general medical and addiction treatment settings. This guidance is based on:

- A review of the literature.
- A review of national and international organizations' guidelines.
- FDA-approved medication labels.
- The TIP expert panel's recommendations.

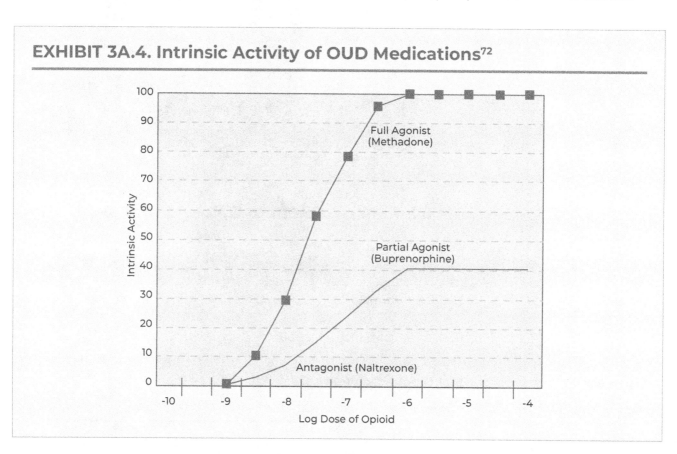

EXHIBIT 3A.4. Intrinsic Activity of OUD Medications[72]

EXHIBIT 3A.5. OUD Medications: Formulations[73,74]

GENERIC/ TRADE NAME	FORMULATIONS	ACTION AT THE RECEPTOR	FDA INDICATIONS	DOSING REGIMEN
Methadone (Methadose, Dolophine)	Orally as liquid concentrate, tablet, or oral solution of powder or dispersible tablet	Mu-opioid receptor full agonist	Medically supervised withdrawal and maintenance treatment of opioid dependence; additional formulations FDA approved for pain are not a focus of this TIP	Once daily (also off-label dosing regimens if appropriate, such as split dose twice daily)
Generic buprenorphine monoproduct	Sublingual tablet	Mu-opioid receptor partial agonist	Treatment of opioid dependence; additional formulations FDA approved for pain are not a focus of this TIP	Once daily (also alternative off-label regimens)
Generic buprenorphine/ naloxone combination product	Sublingual tablet	Mu-opioid receptor partial agonist combined with mu-opioid receptor antagonist; the latter is not absorbed sublingually	Treatment of opioid dependence	Once daily (also alternative off-label regimens)
Buprenorphine/ naloxone (Zubsolv)	Sublingual tablet	Mu-opioid receptor partial agonist combined with mu-opioid receptor antagonist; the latter is not absorbed sublingually	Treatment of opioid dependence	Once daily (also alternative off-label regimens)
Buprenorphine/ naloxone (Bunavail)	Buccal film	Mu-opioid receptor partial agonist combined with mu-opioid receptor antagonist; the latter is not absorbed sublingually	Treatment of opioid dependence	Once daily (also alternative off-label regimens)
Buprenorphine/ naloxone (Suboxone)	Sublingual film; may also be administered buccally	Mu-opioid receptor partial agonist combined with mu-opioid receptor antagonist; the latter is not absorbed sublingually	Treatment of opioid dependence	Once daily (also alternative off-label regimens)

Continued on next page

EXHIBIT 3A.5. OUD Medications: Formulations (continued)

GENERIC/ TRADE NAME	FORMULATIONS	ACTION AT THE RECEPTOR	FDA INDICATIONS	DOSING REGIMEN
Buprenorphine (Probuphine)	Implants	Mu-opioid receptor partial agonist	Maintenance treatment of opioid dependence in clinically stable patients taking 8 mg/day or less of Suboxone equivalents	Implants last for 6 months and are then removed, after which a second set can be inserted
Extended-release injection buprenorphine (Sublocade)	Subcutaneous injection in the abdominal region	Mu-opioid receptor partial agonist	Treatment of moderate-to-severe OUD among patients initiated and taking transmucosal buprenorphine for at least 7 days	Monthly
Oral naltrexone (Revia)	Oral tablet	Mu-opioid receptor antagonist	Block the effects of administered opioid agonists	Once daily (also alternative off-label regimens)
XR-NTX (Vivitrol)	Intramuscular injection	Mu-opioid receptor antagonist	Prevent return to opioid dependence after medically supervised opioid withdrawal	Once monthly by injection

Chapter 3B: Methadone

Chapter 3B provides an overview of methadone pharmacology and discussion of key methadone dosing considerations for healthcare professionals working in opioid treatment programs (OTPs).

Methadone is the most studied pharmacotherapy for opioid use disorder (OUD). Of all OUD pharmacotherapies, it is used to treat the most people throughout the world and has by far the longest track record (nearly 50 years).[75,76] Numerous clinical trials and meta-analyses have shown that methadone treatment is associated with significantly higher rates of treatment retention and lower rates of illicit opioid use compared with placebo and with no treatment.[77] Other research associates methadone treatment with reduced mortality, criminal behavior, and HIV seroconversion.[78,79,80] A Cochrane meta-analysis found that, at flexible doses, methadone compared with buprenorphine retains patients in treatment significantly longer and equally reduces illicit opioid use.[81]

In the United States, OTPs can offer methadone to treat OUD, but all providers who may care for patients with OUD should be familiar with this treatment.

Formulations

There are several formulations of methadone:

- Liquid concentrate, which is the formulation most commonly used in treatment programs.
- Powder, which is dissolved in water and administered as a liquid.
- Dispersible tablets, which are scored tablets that are dissolved in water.
- Tablets, which are most commonly used outside of OTPs for analgesia.

Pharmacology

Methadone, a long-acting mu-opioid receptor full agonist, is a schedule II controlled medication. It is highly plasma–protein bound and binds to proteins within tissues throughout the body.[82] Through mu-opioid receptor binding and opioid cross-tolerance to other mu-opioid agonists, at adequate doses, **methadone reduces opioid craving and withdrawal and blunts or blocks the effects of illicit opioids.**

There is wide individual variability in methadone pharmacokinetics. The half-life of methadone can vary from 8 to 59 hours[83] depending on the patient. The average is 24 hours.[84]

Methadone has no ceiling effect. As a full agonist, increasing doses of methadone produce maximal physiological effects at the opioid receptors. Plasma levels reach steady state in about 5 days (i.e., five half-lives). Before achievement of steady state, release from tissue reservoirs can lead to increasing serum plasma levels and toxicity, even if the daily methadone dose is not changed.

Methadone induction, thus, should begin at a low dose and increase gradually with daily monitoring over days or weeks. At stable daily doses, serum levels peak 2 to 4 hours after dosing, then slowly decrease, providing 24 hours without overmedication or withdrawal.[85]

Bioavailability

Methadone is approximately 70 to 80 percent bioavailable when patients take it orally for OUD. There is notable individual variability in bioavailability, ranging from 36 to 100 percent.[86,87]

The liver's CYP450 3A4 enzyme is primarily responsible for metabolizing methadone,[88] although CYP2B6 and CYP2D6 enzymes are also involved.[89] At the start of methadone treatment, methadone can increase CYP3A4 activity and accelerate its own metabolism in some individuals.[90]

Dosing must be individualized because methadone's bioavailability, clearance, and half-life can vary considerably among patients.

Providers should check for potential drug–drug interactions and monitor patients receiving concomitant medications. Some medications (e.g., benzodiazepines, anticonvulsants, antibiotics, antiretroviral agents, some antidepressants) can induce or inhibit CYP450 enzymes, resulting in potential changes in methadone serum concentration, effectiveness, and side effect profile.

Dosing Considerations

Methadone is indicated for people meeting OTP admission criteria, which for people 18 and older are:

- Being currently "opioid-addicted"—the term the Substance Abuse and Mental Health Services Administration (SAMHSA) OTP regulations use (e.g., meeting *Diagnostic and Statistical Manual of Mental Disorders,* Fifth Edition,[91] criteria for OUD). Not all patients meeting OUD criteria, particularly those with mild OUD, are appropriate candidates for methadone. This is discussed in detail in Part 2 of this Treatment Improvement Protocol (TIP).
- Having a history of at least 1 year of opioid addiction before admission.
- Providing voluntary, written informed consent.

OTP physicians can waive the history requirement per Code of Federal Regulations (42 CFR 8.12)[92] for:

- Women who are pregnant.
- Former patients (up to 2 years after discharge).
- Patients within 6 months of release from incarceration.

For patients younger than 18, admission criteria are different. They include two documented, unsuccessful, medically supervised withdrawals or treatments without OUD medication (e.g., methadone) in a 12-month period. The parent or legal guardian must provide written informed consent.

Contraindications

Contraindications to treatment with methadone include an allergy to methadone and other instances in which opioids are contraindicated, such as acute asthma, in patients with abnormally high carbon dioxide blood levels (e.g., from pulmonary disease or sleep apnea), or paralytic ileus.

Precautions and Warnings

Respiratory depression

Methadone can cause respiratory depression, particularly during initial dosing and dose titration. The goal of methadone dosing in the first weeks of treatment (i.e., induction) is to relieve withdrawal but avoid oversedation and respiratory depression. Patients who are older or cachectic or who have chronic obstructive pulmonary disease are more susceptible to respiratory depression and should be treated cautiously with lower doses.

> A standard formula for dose induction for all patients, without careful monitoring of response to treatment, and individualized dose adjustment is inadvisable. This can lead to methadone intoxication and overdose death.

Individualize dosing decisions through daily monitoring of patients' responses to treatment. Opioid tolerance cannot be accurately gauged based on patient self-reports of the type, amount, or purity of the opioids they've used or of the severity of their opioid withdrawal symptoms.

The best approach to dosing is to start low and go slow. Methadone has a relatively long half-life (24–36 hours or longer). Steady-state serum levels are generally not reached until about five half-lives. **This means that patients will not feel the full effect of the initial dose for 4 or more days** even if the daily dose is the same. Slow release of methadone from tissues causes serum levels to continue to increase until reaching steady state. Initially a dose may seem appropriate, but the third or fourth day of the same dose can lead to oversedation and even respiratory depression and death.[93]

Use a lower-than-usual starting dose in individuals with no or low opioid tolerance (5 mg to 10 mg). Increase doses slowly and with careful monitoring for patients who:

- Have not used opioids for 5 or more days (e.g., after leaving a controlled environment).
- Do not use opioids daily.
- Use weaker opioids (e.g., codeine).

Do not determine doses by analgesic equivalence dose conversion tables for patients using high doses of prescription opioids, whether by prescription or illicitly. This can lead to death owing to incomplete cross-tolerance[94] and the unique pharmacology of methadone.

Concurrent substance use disorders (SUDs) involving benzodiazepines or alcohol

Concurrent misuse of alcohol or benzodiazepines with methadone (or buprenorphine) increases respiratory depression risk. Use of alcohol and benzodiazepines (illicit and prescription) is common in patients with OUD. Managing OUD with methadone for patients with alcohol or benzodiazepine use disorder is challenging and should be undertaken with care. A 2017 Food and Drug Administration (FDA) Drug Safety Communication noted that although concomitant use of buprenorphine or methadone with benzodiazepines increases the risk of an adverse reaction, including overdose death, opioid agonist treatment should not be denied to patients solely on the basis of their taking benzodiazepines, because untreated OUD can pose a greater risk of morbidity and mortality.[95] FDA advises that careful medication management by healthcare professionals can reduce risk (see www.fda.gov/downloads/Drugs/DrugSafety/UCM576377.pdf for more information).

Strategies to manage patients with concurrent alcohol or benzodiazepine use disorders include the following (see also Exhibit 3B.1):

- **Obtain permission to communicate with the benzodiazepine prescriber** to confirm the reason for use, adherence to treatment, and prescriber awareness of the patient's OUD. It can also help to speak (with permission) with close family members or friends to assess the extent and impact of any alcohol or benzodiazepine misuse.
- **Ensure that patients understand the risk** of potential respiratory depression and unintentional overdose death when combining methadone with alcohol, benzodiazepines, or other central nervous system (CNS) depressants.
- **Determine whether patients require medically supervised withdrawal or tapering from alcohol or benzodiazepines.** Patients at risk for serious alcohol or benzodiazepine withdrawal syndrome (including seizures and delirium tremens) may need inpatient medically supervised withdrawal.
- **Attempt gradual outpatient medically supervised withdrawal for benzodiazepines when indicated.** Some OTPs have the staffing and capacity to provide a supervised

Strategies for Managing Benzodiazepine Use by [Patients in MAT Treatment]

- [Assess] the patient's benzodiazepine [use], including:
  - [Ext]ent of use.
  - Source (check the state's prescription drug monitoring program [PDMP]).
  - Amount and route of use.
  - Binge use.
  - Prior overdoses.
  - Harms (e.g., car crashes, criminal acts, sleep trouble).
  - Co-use with other substances that further increase risk for respiratory depression and overdose.
  - Withdrawal history (e.g., seizures, delirium).
- **Also assess for:**
  - Psychiatric and medical comorbidity.
  - Motivation for change.
  - Psychosocial support system (obtain history from a significant other if the patient permits).
- **Gauge level of care and setting needed** (e.g., residential, outpatient). Inpatient treatment may be best for patients with poor motivation, limited psychosocial support, serious or complicated comorbidity, or injection or binge use.
- **Coordinate with other prescribers.** Some patients may have taken appropriately prescribed benzodiazepines for years with limited or no evidence of misuse. For such patients, tapering benzodiazepines may be contraindicated and unrealistic.
- **Address comorbid mental disorders** (e.g., anxiety, depression) with other medications or psychosocial treatments, when feasible.
- **Provide medically supervised withdrawal** from benzodiazepines or refer to specialty care for same.
- **Create a treatment plan with built-in conditions** (e.g., urine testing, more frequent visits, short medication supply).
- **Frequently review patient progress and objective outcomes,** such as:
  - Urine drug testing.
  - PDMP reports.
  - Psychosocial functioning.
  - Reports from significant others.
- **Revise treatment plans** as needed, and document the rationale for treatment decisions.

Adapted with permission.[96]

---

outpatient taper from benzodiazepines. This usually requires use of a long-acting benzodiazepine, management of anxiety and sleeplessness, and careful monitoring with observed dosing and toxicology screening. It may also require lower-than-usual methadone doses. Engage in outpatient medically supervised withdrawal only with patients who are physically dependent on benzodiazepines but do not inject or binge. This may only be successful in a minority of patients. Attempt the taper while continuing treatment with methadone, subject to certain conditions that promote safety and reduce risk.

- **Consider increasing counseling frequency as appropriate.**

For more information on managing benzodiazepine use, see *Management of Benzodiazepines in Medication-Assisted Treatment* (http://ireta.org/wp-content/uploads/2014/12/BP_Guidelines_for_Benzodiazepines.pdf).

QTc prolongation and cardiac arrhythmia

Methadone treatment has been associated with QTc prolongation, which often occurs without clinical consequences.[97,98] Since 2006, methadone has had an FDA black box warning on QTc prolongation and Torsades de Pointes. QTc intervals above 500 milliseconds can increase risk for this rare ventricular arrhythmia, which can be lethal.[99,100] The prevalence of QTc prolongation among methadone patients is

QTc prolongation is an abnormally long time in electrocardiogram (ECG) tracing between the start of a Q wave and the end of a T wave. Various cutoffs define prolonged QTc interval, including greater than 450 milliseconds for men, greater than 460 to 470 milliseconds for women, or greater than 450 milliseconds for either gender.[101] However, the faster the heart rate, the shorter the QTc interval. Hence, correct the QTc interval for heart rate; divide the QTc interval in milliseconds by the square root of the R-R interval in seconds.[102]

not known with certainty. It has been estimated that about 2 percent of patients in methadone treatment have QTc intervals greater than 500 milliseconds.[103] According to methadone's FDA label, most Torsades de Pointes cases occur in patients receiving methadone for pain treatment, although some cases have occurred among those in methadone maintenance.[104] High methadone doses may be associated with prolonged QTc intervals.[105] Other risk factors include:[106]

- Some medications (e.g., antidepressants, antibiotics, antifungals).
- Congenital prolonged QTc interval.
- Hypokalemia.
- Bradycardia.

There is considerable controversy about how best to screen for QTc prolongation without creating barriers to methadone treatment entry.[107] Indeed, a Cochrane review of the literature was unable to draw any conclusions about the effectiveness of QTc screening strategies in preventing cardiac morbidity or mortality among methadone patients.[108] Notwithstanding the uncertainty about the best approach, OTPs can take steps to identify patients who may be at risk for cardiac arrhythmia. **The TIP expert panel concurs with the recommendations of other expert panels (which included cardiologists) that OTPs develop a cardiac risk management plan,**[109,110] **to the extent possible. OTPs should consider the following elements in crafting a cardiac risk management plan:**

- **An intake assessment of risk factors, which can include:**
  - Family history of sudden cardiac death, arrhythmia, myocardial infarction, heart failure, prolonged QTc interval, or unexplained syncope.
  - Patient history of arrhythmia, myocardial infarction, heart failure, prolonged QTc interval, unexplained syncope, palpitations, or seizures.
  - Current use of medications that may increase QTc interval (for a complete list, see www.crediblemeds.org/pdftemp/pdf/CompositeList.pdf; register for free for the most current list).
  - Patient history of use of cocaine and methamphetamines (which can prolong the QTc interval).
  - Electrolyte assessment (for hypokalemia or hypomagnesemia).

- **A risk stratification plan, which can include the following:**
  - **Conduct an ECG for patients with significant risk factors** at admission; repeat within 30 days. Repeat once a year and if the patient is treated with more than 120 mg of methadone per day.
  - Discuss risks and benefits of methadone with patients with QTc intervals between 450 and 500 milliseconds. Adjust modifiable risk factors to reduce their risk.
  - **Do not start methadone treatment for patients with known QTc intervals above 500 milliseconds.** If such an interval is discovered during treatment, have a risk/benefit discussion. Strongly consider lowering the methadone dose, changing concurrent medications that prolong the

QTc interval, eliminating other risk factors, and, if necessary, switching to buprenorphine. Include follow-up ECG monitoring.
- Consider providing routine universal ECG screening if feasible, although there is insufficient evidence to formally recommend doing so.[111]

Accidental ingestion
Inform patients that accidental ingestion can be fatal for opioid-naïve individuals, particularly children. Patients should safeguard take-home methadone in a lockbox out of the reach of children.

Neonatal abstinence syndrome (NAS)
Ensure awareness among pregnant patients or patients who may become pregnant that NAS can occur in newborns of mothers treated with methadone. Women receiving methadone treatment while pregnant should talk with their healthcare provider about NAS and how to reduce it. Research has shown that the dose of opioid agonist medication is not reliably related to the severity of NAS.[112,113,114] Thus, each woman should receive the dose of medication that best manages her illness.

Misuse and diversion
Alert patients to the potential for misuse and diversion of methadone.

Physical dependence
Inform patients that they will develop physical dependence on methadone and will experience opioid withdrawal if they stop taking it.

Sedation
Caution patients that methadone may affect cognition and psychomotor performance and can have sedating effects. Urge patients to be cautious in using heavy machinery and driving until they are sure that their abilities are not compromised.

Adrenal insufficiency
Adrenal insufficiency has been reported in patients treated with opioids. Ask patients to alert healthcare providers of nausea, vomiting, loss of appetite, fatigue, weakness, dizziness, or low blood pressure.[115]

Drug Interactions
Methadone has more clinically significant drug–drug interaction than buprenorphine.[116] Carefully monitor each patient's response to treatment if they are prescribed or stop taking a CYP450 34A inducer or inhibitor. Methadone dosages may need to be adjusted up or down depending on the medication and whether treatment is starting or stopping. Exhibit 3B.2 lists common interactions between methadone and other medications.

Medications that induce CYP450 activity can increase methadone metabolism. Patients may experience craving or opioid withdrawal symptoms between doses if they begin these medications or become sedated if they discontinue them:

- Some antibiotics (e.g., rifampin).
- Antiretrovirals (e.g., efavirenz, nevirapine, ritonavir).
- Anticonvulsants (carbamazepine, phenobarbital, phenytoin).

Other medications can inhibit CYP450 activity and decrease methadone metabolism, causing symptoms of overmedication (e.g., sedation) when the medication is started and possibly withdrawal or cravings when it is stopped. Among such medications are:[117]

- Some antibiotics (ciprofloxacin, erythromycin).
- Antacids (cimetidine).
- Antifungals (fluconazole).
- Antidepressants (e.g., fluvoxamine, paroxetine, sertraline).

Methadone can affect the metabolism of other medications. For example, zidovudine levels are reported to increase significantly during

EXHIBIT 3B.2. Common Potential Methadone Drug–Drug Interactions

Antiretrovirals

CLASS OR SPECIFIC DRUG	INTERACTION	PUTATIVE MECHANISM	NOTES
Efavirenz, lopinavir, nevirapine	Reduction in serum methadone levels	Induction of CYP450 enzymes	Clinically significant opioid withdrawal symptoms likely
Abacavir, etravirine, nelfinavir, ritonavir, saquinavir, tipranavir	May reduce serum methadone levels	Induction of CYP450 enzymes	Clinically pertinent opioid withdrawal symptoms unlikely
Didanosine	Reduction in didanosine plasma concentrations	Decreased bioavailability	Possible decreased efficacy of didanosine
Zidovudine	Increase in zidovudine plasma concentration	Unknown	Risk of zidovudine toxicity

Antidepressants

CLASS OR SPECIFIC DRUG	INTERACTION	PUTATIVE MECHANISM	NOTES
Tricyclic: Amitriptyline, clomipramine, desipramine, doxepin, imipramine, nortriptyline, protriptyline, trimipramine	Increased risk for constipation, sedation, QTc prolongation, and arrhythmia	Anticholinergic effects; blockade of human ether-a-go-go-related gene (hERG) channel	Clinical experience with combination indicates it is generally safe with careful clinical monitoring
Serotonin reuptake inhibitors: citalopram, escitalopram, fluvoxamine, fluoxetine, paroxetine, sertraline	May increase serum methadone levels; increased risk for serotonin syndrome	Inhibition of CYP enzymes; blockade of serotonin transporter	Clinical experience with combination indicates it is generally safe with careful clinical monitoring
Monoamine oxidase inhibitors: Isocarboxazid, phenelzine, selegiline, tranylcypromine	Increased risk for serotonin syndrome	Inhibition of serotonin metabolism	Avoid or use with extreme caution and careful clinical monitoring
Serotonin/norepinephrine reuptake inhibitors: Duloxetine, desvenlafaxine, venlafaxine	Increased risk for serotonin syndrome; increased risk for QTc prolongation and arrhythmia (venlafaxine)	Blockade of serotonin transporter; blockade of hERG channel (venlafaxine)	Clinical experience with combination indicates it is generally safe with careful clinical monitoring

Continued on next page

EXHIBIT 3B.2. Common Potential Methadone Drug–Drug Interactions (continued)

Antibiotics

CLASS OR SPECIFIC DRUG	INTERACTION	PUTATIVE MECHANISM	NOTES
Ciprofloxacin, clarithromycin, erythromycin, azithromycin	May increase methadone serum levels; increased risk for QTc prolongation and arrhythmia	Inhibition of CYP enzymes; blockade of hERG channel	One case report of sedation (ciprofloxacin); clinical monitoring required
Rifampin	Reduction in serum methadone levels	Induction of CYP enzymes	Severe opioid withdrawal can occur; need increased methadone dose

Antifungals

CLASS OR SPECIFIC DRUG	INTERACTION	PUTATIVE MECHANISM	NOTES
Ketoconazole, fluconazole	May increase methadone serum levels	Inhibition of CYP enzymes	Little evidence for important clinical effects

Anticonvulsants

CLASS OR SPECIFIC DRUG	INTERACTION	PUTATIVE MECHANISM	NOTES
Carbamazepine, phenytoin, phenobarbital	Reduction in serum methadone levels	Induction of CYP enzymes	Severe opioid withdrawal can occur; will need increased methadone dose

Antiarrhythmics

CLASS OR SPECIFIC DRUG	INTERACTION	PUTATIVE MECHANISM	NOTES
Procainamide, quinidine	Increases risk for QTc prolongation and arrhythmia	Blockade of hERG channel	Careful clinical monitoring required
Amiodarone	May increase methadone serum levels; increased risk for QTc prolongation and arrhythmia	Inhibition of CYP enzymes; blockade of hERG channel	Careful clinical monitoring required

Continued on next page

EXHIBIT 3B.2. Common Potential Methadone Drug–Drug Interactions (continued)

Other Drugs and Specific Classes

CLASS OR SPECIFIC DRUG	INTERACTION	PUTATIVE MECHANISM	NOTES
Benzodiazepines	Additive CNS and respiratory depressant effects	Increased GABA activity	Careful clinical monitoring required
Barbiturates	Additive CNS and respiratory depressant effects	Increased GABA activity	Careful clinical monitoring required
Cimetidine	May increase serum methadone levels	Inhibition of CYP enzymes	No evidence of major clinical effect
Naltrexone	Precipitated opioid withdrawal	Displaces methadone from mu-opioid receptors	Contraindicated

Adapted with permission.[118]

methadone treatment. Monitoring for zidovudine side effects during treatment is warranted.[119] Check drug–drug interactions online (www.drugs.com/drug_interactions.php).

Side Effects

Possible side effects of methadone include the following (methadone FDA labels list all potential side effects and are available at https://dailymed.nlm.nih.gov/dailymed/search.cfm?labeltype=all&query=METHADONE:

- Constipation
- Nausea
- Sweating
- Sexual dysfunction or decreased libido
- Drowsiness
- Amenorrhea
- Weight gain
- Edema

Assessment

A thorough assessment will help decide whether a patient is appropriate for admission and meets federal and any state regulatory requirements for methadone treatment. (See Part 2 of this TIP for detailed discussion of screening and assessment.) **Before ordering methadone:**

- **Check the state PDMP** for opioid or benzodiazepine prescriptions from other providers (see www.nascsa.org/stateprofiles.htm for links to state PDMPs). Note that methadone for OUD treatment will not appear in the PDMP because of confidentiality regulations regarding substance use treatment records. Obtain the patient's consent to release information and speak with treating providers to coordinate care for patient safety.

- **Take the patient's history.**
  - Conduct a medical, psychiatric, substance use, and substance use treatment history.

- Assess recent opioid use, including frequency, quantity, type, route, and recency (last day of use and use in the past 30 days).
- Establish OUD diagnosis.
- Assess for other SUDs, including those that involve alcohol, benzodiazepines, or stimulants.

- **Conduct a physical exam.**
    - **Assess for signs and symptoms of intoxication.** Do not give patients who are sedated or intoxicated their first dose. Instead, assess and treat them appropriately:
        - Identify causes of sedation or intoxication.
        - Ensure the patient's immediate safety.
        - Reassess methadone induction appropriateness.
        - Develop a plan to reattempt induction or follow a different course of treatment as appropriate.
    - **Assess for signs and symptoms of opioid withdrawal and physiological dependence.** One approach to documenting withdrawal symptoms is to use a scale such as the Clinical Opioid Withdrawal Scale (COWS) or the Clinical Institute Narcotic Assessment (CINA) Scale for Withdrawal Symptoms (see "Resource Alert: Opioid Withdrawal Scales"). Before the first dose of methadone, confirm signs of opioid withdrawal to provide some confidence that the patient is opioid tolerant and can begin dose induction. The Naloxone Challenge should not be routinely used to determine physiologic withdrawal because withdrawal symptoms will be visible, if present, on physical exam if enough time has passed since last opioid use.[120]

- **Obtain laboratory tests.**
    - **Conduct drug and alcohol tests.** Use reliable urine tests for drugs, including opioids (e.g., morphine, methadone, buprenorphine, oxycodone), benzodiazepines, cocaine, and other drugs that may be commonly used in the area (e.g., methamphetamine). Obtain an opioid urine or oral fluid test before initiating treatment. A negative opioid test in the absence of clear opioid withdrawal symptoms indicates that the patient is likely no longer opioid tolerant; diagnosis should be reconfirmed. If such patients are to start taking methadone (rather than naltrexone for relapse prevention), use caution in initiating treatment (see the subsection "First dose for patients without current opioid tolerance" in the section "Initiating Methadone Treatment"). Use an alcohol breathalyzer to estimate the patient's blood alcohol content. Do not provide methadone until the alcohol reading is considerably below the legal level of alcohol intoxication.

> **RESOURCE ALERT**
>
> **Opioid Withdrawal Scales**
>
> The COWS and other opioid withdrawal scales from Annex 10 of the World Health Organization's *Guidelines for the Psychosocially Assisted Pharmacological Treatment of Opioid Dependence* can be downloaded from the National Center for Biotechnology Information website (www.ncbi.nlm.nih.gov/books/NBK143183).
>
> The CINA Scale for Withdrawal Symptoms also is available online (www.ncbi.nlm.nih.gov/books/NBK64244/table/A72912).

- **Conduct a pregnancy test.** Pregnant patients with OUD should be treated with methadone or transmucosal buprenorphine.[121,122] Discuss risks and benefits of treatment with methadone and alternative approaches for each patient and fetus versus the risks of continued illicit opioid use. Refer pregnant patients to prenatal care. Women should be advised that their menstrual cycle may return to normal once they are stabilized on medication, and hence they should use birth control if they wish to avoid pregnancy.
- **Conduct liver function tests.** If possible, assess liver function tests. It is not necessary to wait for the results of these tests to begin treatment, because the risk of not starting methadone outweighs the benefits of having the test results. Patients with suspected cirrhosis based on history and clinical exam should be started at a lower methadone dose than typical patients, with more cautious titration. Patients who have chronic hepatitis can be treated with methadone. Have a risk/benefit discussion with patients whose liver enzymes are at or greater than five times the normal level and monitor their liver function during treatment.
- **Conduct hepatitis and HIV testing.** Hepatitis B and C are common among patients who enter methadone treatment. HIV infection is also prevalent. If possible, test patients for these infections and refer them to treatment as appropriate. The Centers for Disease Control and Prevention recommends hepatitis B vaccination for people seeking treatment for SUDs.[123]

Patient Selection

No evidence clearly predicts which patients will respond best to methadone treatment versus alternative pharmacotherapies. Inform patients of all options and the settings in which they're available, as appropriate. (See "Treatment Planning or Referral" in Part 2 of this TIP for more on shared decision making.)

Patients who responded well to methadone in the past should be considered for this treatment.

Unsuccessful treatment experiences with methadone in the past do not necessarily indicate that methadone will be ineffective again. Motivation and circumstances change over time. Also, treatment varies by OTP, as it does for other medical illnesses. Records from previous providers can contextualize the extent of past treatment.

Pregnant women should be considered for methadone treatment.

Methadone (or buprenorphine) treatment through OTPs may be best for patients who need a higher level of outpatient structure or supervision of medication adherence. Tailor medication decisions to patients' medical and substance use histories, patient preferences, and treatment availability.

Informed Consent

Inform all patients of:

- Their OUD diagnosis and the nature of the disorder.
- Risks and benefits of methadone and other OUD medications.
- Risks and benefits of nonmedication treatments.

Patients should sign consent forms before starting treatment. The Chapter 3B Appendix provides a sample consent form for treatment in an OTP.

Educate patients about what to expect when receiving methadone treatment (Exhibit 3B.3). Caution them against using alcohol and drugs

> Use language and written materials appropriate to each patient's comprehension level to ensure that he or she understands the options and can make informed decisions.

EXHIBIT 3B.3. Key Points of Patient Education for Methadone

Before starting OUD treatment with methadone, patients should:

- Be told that the methadone dose is started low and increased slowly over days and weeks with monitoring, because it takes 4 or more days for the body to adjust to a dose change. This is necessary to avoid the risk of overdose.
- Understand that the goal of the first weeks of treatment is to improve withdrawal symptoms without oversedation. Patients should inform providers if they feel sedated or "high" within the first 4 hours after their dose.
- Learn the symptoms of methadone intoxication and how to seek emergency care. The first 2 weeks of treatment have the highest risk of overdose.
- Be aware that rescue naloxone does not last very long, so they should remain in emergency care for observation if they are treated for opioid overdose.
- Know that concurrent alcohol, benzodiazepine, or other sedative use with methadone increases the risk of overdose and death.
- Inform OTP nursing/medical staff about prescribed and over-the-counter medications and herbs (e.g., St. John's wort) they are taking, stopping, or changing doses of to allow assessment of potential drug–drug interactions.
- Inform other treating healthcare professionals that they are receiving methadone treatment.
- Plan to avoid driving or operating heavy machinery until their dose is stabilized.
- Learn about other possible side effects of methadone, including dizziness, nausea, vomiting, sweating, constipation, edema, and sexual dysfunction.
- Agree to keep take-home doses locked up and out of the reach of others. Understand that giving methadone, even small amounts, to others may be fatal.
- Inform providers if they become pregnant.
- Understand that stopping methadone increases their risk of overdose death if they return to illicit opioid use.

during methadone treatment. Warn them of the increased risk of overdose during the first 2 weeks of treatment. Also warn them that discontinuing treatment and returning to opioid use will increase their risk of overdose. Document patient education in the medical record.

Educate patients about the importance of safe storage of take-home methadone doses. Discuss with patients where they will store their take-home medication. Advise them against storing medication in common areas of the home where visitors or children would have access, such as kitchens and bathrooms. Take-home doses should be kept in their original childproof packaging in a lockbox. The key should not be left in the box. Inform patients that any portion of a dose taken by another person, a child, or pet can be deadly. If this occurs, call 9-1-1 immediately.

> **RESOURCE ALERT**
>
> **Patient and Family Member Educational Resources**
>
> *Decisions in Recovery: Treatment for Opioid Use Disorder* offers information for patients on the use of medications for OUD (https://store.samhsa.gov/product/SMA16-4993)
>
> *Medication-Assisted Treatment for Opioid Addiction: Facts for Families and Friends* offers information for family members and friends (www.ct.gov/dmhas/lib/dmhas/publications/MAT-InfoFamilyFriends.pdf)

Initiating Methadone Treatment

Observing patients directly when they take doses early in treatment is not just required; it's beneficial. It maximizes adherence, provides a daily opportunity to assess response to the medication, and minimizes the likelihood of medication diversion. Federal OTP regulations permit patients to receive one take-home dose per week, given routine clinic closure on weekends. Patients who demonstrate progress can earn one additional take-home dose per week for the first 90 days of treatment at the OTP medical director's discretion. All other doses are directly observed at the clinic in the first 90 days.

The goal of initiating methadone treatment is to increase the patient's methadone dose gradually and safely, stabilizing the patient and reducing his or her opioid use while recognizing that the risk of dropout or overdose from illicit opioid use may increase if induction is too slow.

Day 1

The first dose should reduce opioid withdrawal symptoms. Perform induction cautiously; it's impossible to judge a patient's level of tolerance with certainty. For patients addicted to prescription opioids, opioid conversion tables should not be relied on to determine methadone dosage.

First dose for patients with opioid tolerance

The first dose for patients tolerant to opioids is generally between 10 mg and 30 mg (30 mg is the maximum first dose per federal OTP regulations). After the first dose, patients should remain for observation for 2 to 4 hours if possible to see whether the dose is sedating or relieves withdrawal signs.

- If withdrawal symptoms lessen, the patient should return the next day to be reassessed and to continue the dose induction process.
- If sedation or intoxication occurs after the first dose, the patient should stay under observation at the clinic until symptoms resolve. In this case, the patient should be reassessed the following day, and the subsequent day's dose should be substantially reduced. Extremely rarely, the patient will need to be treated for overdose with naloxone. If necessary, begin rescue breathing and call 9-1-1.
- If the patient shows neither sedation nor reduction of objective signs of opioid withdrawal during the 2- to 4-hour waiting period, administer another 5 mg dose. A final 5 mg dose after another waiting period of 2 to 4 hours can be administered if necessary. The maximum total methadone dose on the first day of treatment should not exceed 40 mg.[124] However, caution dictates against exceeding a total first day's dose of 30 mg except in rare cases. In such cases, the patient should be carefully monitored on subsequent days to rule out oversedation.
- Patients transferring from another OTP whose methadone dose and last date of medication administration can be confirmed by the medical staff and documented in the medical record can be continued on the same methadone dose administered in the original OTP, even if the dose exceeds the maximum permitted 40 mg.

For some patients, the lower range of initial doses is best. Dose with 10 mg to 20 mg in patients who:

- Are ages 60 and older.
- May have lower levels of opioid tolerance based on their recent history.
- Use sedating medications, such as benzodiazepines, antipsychotics, or antidepressants.
- Engage in problem drinking or have alcohol use disorder.
- Take medications that can increase methadone serum levels or are stopping medications that decrease methadone serum levels.[125]
- Have medical disorders that may cause hypoxia, hypercapnia, or cardiac arrhythmias. These include:
  - Asthma, chronic obstructive pulmonary disease, and kyphoscoliosis.
  - Obesity.

- Sleep apnea.
- QTc prolongation.
- A family history of cardiac arrhythmias, fainting or dizziness, or sudden death.
- Cor pulmonale.
- Electrolyte abnormalities, such as hypokalemia or hypomagnesemia.

First dose for patients without current opioid dependence

In some circumstances, patients who are not currently dependent on opioids may be admitted to an OTP (e.g., individuals with a history of OUD who are returning from controlled environments).[126] In these instances, consider treatment with extended-release naltrexone (XR-NTX) to avoid establishing new physiological opioid dependence. Instead of starting methadone, consider starting with a low dose of buprenorphine because of buprenorphine's superior safety threshold.[127] In one such study, 1 mg of buprenorphine was the starting dose, which was increased slowly[128] (see Chapter 3D of this TIP). If XR-NTX and buprenorphine are not available, or the patient prefers methadone treatment, consider starting methadone at a 5 mg daily dose (as was done in one study[129]) after discussing risks and benefits with the patient.

Titrate the dose much more slowly than for patients who are opioid tolerant. Increase initially by 5 mg about every week, based on patient response. Doses can be increased somewhat more rapidly after careful assessment of response if the patient begins to use illicit opioids. As with other methadone dosing, induction in these cases should not be based on a standing order.

Dose Titration (Weeks 1 to 2)

The goals of early dose titration for patients with current opioid dependence starting on Day 2 of the first week of treatment through stabilization are to avoid sedation at peak serum levels and to gradually extend time without opioid withdrawal symptoms and craving. When patients attend the program, before dose administration, nursing and/or medical staff members should ask patients whether they felt sedation, opioid intoxication effects, or opioid withdrawal symptoms 2 to 4 hours after their methadone administration the prior day (Exhibit 3B.4). Doses should be decreased for reports of symptoms of opioid intoxication or oversedation. **Dosing must be individualized based on careful patient assessment and generally should not be increased every day, because plasma methadone levels do not reach steady state until about five methadone half-lives (Exhibit 3B.5).**

Even when holding the methadone dose constant over several days, the patient's methadone serum level will rise each day until it reaches steady state (Exhibit 3B.5). For example, if the patient remains on 20 mg per day for the first few days of induction, the serum level on Day 2 would reflect the 20 mg second day's dose plus 10 mg that remained in the body from the first day's dose (for the equivalent single dose total of 30 mg). The third day would reflect the 20 mg third day's dose, plus 10 mg remaining in the body from the second day's dose, and 5 mg remaining from the first day's dose (for the equivalent single dose total of 35 mg), and so on. **Patients who report relief from withdrawal 4 to 12 hours after their last dose may benefit from staying at that same dose for a few days** so that their serum level can stabilize.[130]

An American Society of Addiction Medicine expert panel recommended increasing the methadone dose in this phase by 5 mg or less every 5 or more days.[131] Other expert recommendations suggest somewhat faster dose increases,[132] including increases of 5 mg to 10 mg no sooner than every 3 to 4 days.[133,134] The most important principle is to individualize dose induction based on careful assessment of the patient's response to the medication.

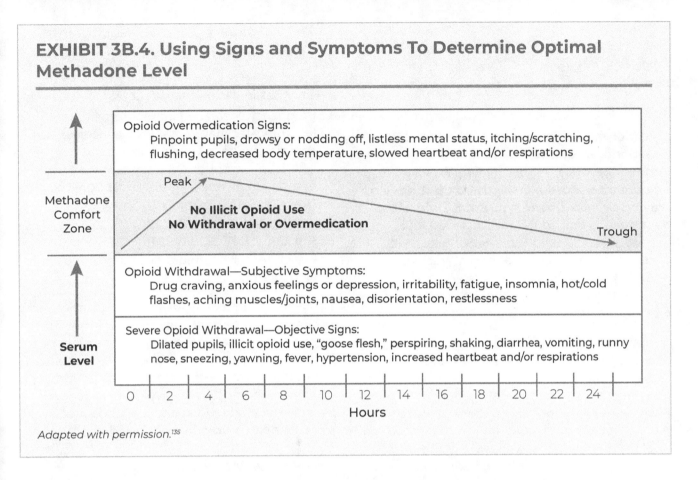

EXHIBIT 3B.4. Using Signs and Symptoms To Determine Optimal Methadone Level

Adapted with permission.[135]

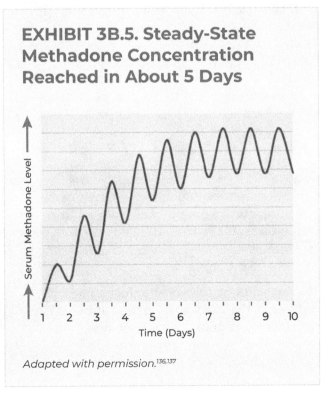

EXHIBIT 3B.5. Steady-State Methadone Concentration Reached in About 5 Days

Adapted with permission.[136,137]

Dose Titration (Weeks 3 to 4)

Methadone doses can be increased further in 5 mg increments about every 3 to 5 days based on the patient's symptoms of opioid withdrawal or sedation.[138] Patients who miss more than four doses must be reassessed. Their next methadone dose should be decreased substantially and built back up gradually. It may be necessary to restart the dose induction process from Day 1. Be aware of any specific state requirements regarding missed doses.

Serum Levels

Dosing must be individualized because methadone's bioavailability, clearance, and half-life vary among patients, affecting their clinical responses and requiring doses to be changed. Many factors can affect serum levels and clinical responses to treatment. Along with age and diet, these factors include:

- Other medications and herbs (e.g., St. John's wort).
- Genetic differences in metabolizing enzymes.
- Pregnancy.
- Changes in urinary pH.[139]

Consider measuring serum methadone levels in patients who, after being on a stable methadone dose, report feeling drowsy 2 to 4 hours after dose administration but develop craving or withdrawal symptoms before the next dose is due to be administered. This may occur in the third trimester of pregnancy, when concomitant medications interact with methadone, or when patients rapidly metabolize opioids. In such cases, consider dividing the daily methadone dose into twice-daily dosing.[140]

To assess serum methadone levels, draw peak and trough blood specimens at about 3 hours and 24 hours, respectively, after dose administration. Serum methadone levels generally correlate with methadone dose,[141] but there is no defined therapeutic window based on serum methadone level because response varies widely among patients. Minimum trough methadone levels of 300 ng/mL to 400 ng/mL may be associated with reduced likelihood of heroin use,[142] but determining the therapeutic dose should depend on the overall patient response, not the serum plasma levels. Peak:trough ratios above 2:1 may indicate rapid metabolism.[143]

Dose Stabilization (Week 5 and Beyond)

Once the patient achieves an adequate dose, extended continuation is possible without dose adjustment. Continuing treatment goals are to avoid sedation, eliminate withdrawal and craving, and blunt or block euphoric effects of illicit opioids.

There may be reasons to further adjust the dose, including:

- Changes in health that can affect medications (e.g., acute hepatitis, exacerbation of pulmonary disease, sleep apnea).

> The TIP expert panel advises against arbitrary methadone dosage caps.

- Changes in patient medications.
- Pregnancy. Increased metabolism in the last trimester may warrant dose increase or split dosing.[144,145] This may require a SAMHSA exception for daily take-home half-doses via an SMA-168 Exception Request (www.samhsa.gov/medication-assisted-treatment/opioid-treatment-programs/submit-exception-request).
- Concurrent illicit opioid or other drug or alcohol use.

As illicit opioid use stops and stabilization is achieved, the patient may wish to lower the dose to reduce any unpleasant side effects. Typical stabilization doses of at least 60 mg are associated with greater treatment retention; 80 mg to 120 mg[146] is the typical daily range.[147] However, there is wide variation, and some patients benefit from higher daily doses.

Take-Home Medication

OTPs can provide gradually increasing numbers of take-home doses to patients who discontinue illicit drug use and begin achieving treatment goals, commensurate with their tenure in the program. This provides a powerful incentive for patients to achieve treatment goals.[148] It also furthers patients' recovery goals by allowing them to attend work, school, or other activities without daily OTP visits.

Federal OTP regulations describe the conditions under which take-home doses are permitted. Some states have additional regulations. OTPs should be familiar with these regulations and have written procedures to address take-home dosing.

The benefits of take-home doses must outweigh the risks and further patients' rehabilitation goals. When deciding whether patients can handle the responsibility of take-home doses of methadone or buprenorphine, OTP medical directors should consider whether patients demonstrate:

- No recent misuse of substances.
- Regular clinic attendance.
- No serious behavioral problems at the clinic.
- No recent criminal activity (e.g., selling drugs).
- Stability at home and in social relationships.
- Sufficient time in treatment.
- Ability and intent to store take-home medication safely.
- Rehabilitative benefits from decreasing the frequency of clinic attendance that outweigh the potential risks of diversion.

Federal regulations based on patients' time in treatment determine eligibility to be considered for receiving take-home doses of methadone (but buprenorphine is not bound by these limits):

- One earned dose/week (beyond a weekly clinic closure day or federal holiday, when clinics typically close) in the first 90 days of treatment
- Two doses during the second 90 days
- Three doses during the third 90 days
- Up to 6 doses during the last 90 days
- Up to 2 weeks of doses after 1 year
- Up to 1 month of doses after 2 years

Assessing responsible handling of take-home doses

Methadone diversion is a risk. People with OUD who are not in treatment more frequently use illicit methadone to self-medicate withdrawal symptoms than to achieve euphoria.[149,150] Still, diversion is a public health risk; people who self-medicate may not know what dose they are taking. Moreover, opioid-naïve people (including children) who ingest methadone can die of methadone intoxication.

OTPs must assess patients' adherence to responsible take-home-dose handling and have a diversion control plan. The plan may require that the OTP:

- **Remain open 7 days per week or arrange dosing at another clinic on days the clinic is closed** for certain patients to avoid providing take-home doses to new or unstable patients.
- **Contact patients randomly and request that they return their take-home containers** within a day or two to see whether they still have the medication in their possession or have altered the medication in any way.
- **Establish an appropriate drug testing program** with policies to prevent falsification of specimens and to respond to tests that are negative for methadone.
- **Require patients to store their take-home medication in a lockbox** to prevent theft or accidental use by children or others.

Duration of Methadone Treatment

Longer lengths of stay in methadone treatment are associated with superior treatment outcomes.[151] Leaving methadone treatment is associated with increased risk of death from overdose and other causes.[152,153] Patients should continue as long as they benefit, want to, and develop no contraindications.

RESOURCE ALERT

Guidance on Federal Take-Home Methadone Dose Regulations

For more information on federal take-home dose regulations for OTPs, see SAMHSA's *Federal Guidelines for Opioid Treatment Programs* (https://store.samhsa.gov/shin/content/PEP15-FEDGUIDEOTP/PEP15-FEDGUIDEOTP.pdf).

The TIP expert panel considers arbitrary time limits on OUD treatment with methadone to be medically unwarranted and inappropriate. They pose a risk to patients and the public.

Dose Tapering and Methadone Discontinuation

Discuss risks and benefits with patients who wish to discontinue treatment. Explore their reasons for wanting to discontinue and solutions for potential barriers to treatment, which may include:

- **Logistics (e.g., travel, scheduling).** Transportation services, including publicly funded ride services, ride sharing, or peer support workers, may be available. If not, transferring patients to a closer OTP or to one with more suitable hours of operation may resolve the problem.
- **Costs.** Providers can help patients explore publicly supported treatment options or apply for insurance.
- **Side effects.** Changing the dose or treating side effects may resolve the problem.
- **Opinions of friends or family.** When external pressure from family or friends drives the decision, a discussion with the patient and those individuals may help.
- **A desire to switch to buprenorphine or XR-NTX treatment.** These options should be discussed.

Caution patients who are not yet stable against discontinuing treatment, because of high rates of return to illicit opioid use and increased chance of overdose death.[154] Discuss the alternative of switching to a different OUD medication. Give patients who stop treatment information about overdose prevention and encourage them to return to treatment. Prescribe naloxone to use in case of overdose.

Create a plan collaboratively with stable patients who wish to discontinue treatment that addresses:

- Gradually tapering their dose.
- Increasing psychosocial and recovery supports.
- Discontinuing dose reduction if necessary.
- Returning to medication treatment after discontinuation if they return to illicit opioid use.
- Increasing dosage if destabilization occurs.

Individualize the pace of methadone dose reduction to the patient's response. One approach is to decrease the methadone dose gradually by 5 to 10 percent every 1 to 2 weeks. Once patients reach a relatively low dose, often between 20 mg and 40 mg, they may begin to feel more craving. Some patients may choose to switch to buprenorphine for a period to complete the dose reduction. They may also wish to begin XR-NTX after an appropriate period of opioid abstinence.

Encourage patients to use techniques for preventing return to use, such as participating in recovery support groups and gaining support from counseling and family. Doing so can help patients succeed in tapering off their medication.

RESOURCE ALERT

Guidance on Opioid Overdose Prevention

For more information on preventing opioid overdose, see the *SAMHSA Opioid Overdose Prevention Toolkit* (https://store.samhsa.gov/shin/content//SMA16-4742/SMA16-4742.pdf).

Methadone Dosing Summary

The initial goal is to reduce opioid withdrawal and craving safely.

- Use the "start low and go slow" approach but increase dose at a rate that minimizes chances of continued illicit drug use, while monitoring for side effects.
- Increase doses gradually over several weeks.
- Assess for sedation at peak serum concentration (2–4 hours after the dose).

The eventual target is an adequate dose that:

- Stops withdrawal symptoms for 24 hours.
- Reduces or eliminates craving.
- Blunts or blocks euphoria from self-administered illicit opioids.

In general, after induction is complete, higher doses are more effective than lower doses.

Enhancing Access to OUD Medication in OTPs

Individuals on waiting lists for OTPs should receive interim methadone maintenance treatment. People on waiting lists typically continue to use illicit opioids. Many never gain admission through the waiting list process. Federal OTP regulations permit use of interim methadone maintenance to address this problem by providing methadone treatment for up to 120 days to someone on an OTP waiting list. Routine counseling and treatment planning are not required during this period.

Interim methadone maintenance has been shown to be more effective than a waiting list to facilitate entry into comprehensive methadone treatment and to reduce illicit opioid use, according to two randomized trials.[155,156] Interim methadone *requires* approval by SAMHSA and the state opioid treatment authority. For more detailed information on interim methadone maintenance, see SAMHSA's *Federal Guidelines for Opioid Treatment Programs* (https://store.samhsa.gov/shin/content/PEP15-FEDGUIDEOTP/PEP15-FEDGUIDEOTP.pdf).

OTPs can overcome geographic barriers by opening a medication unit of the parent OTP site. Under the aegis of a certified OTP, a medication unit may provide methadone or buprenorphine administration, dispensing capacity, and urine drug testing, but not counseling. The parent clinic must provide counseling and other required services. Such arrangements can lessen the amount of time required to drive to a parent OTP location in large states with rural populations.

SAMHSA's *Federal Guidelines for Opioid Treatment Programs* offers more information on medication units and other OTP regulations (https://store.samhsa.gov/shin/content/PEP15-FEDGUIDEOTP/PEP15-FEDGUIDEOTP.pdf)

Chapter 3B Appendix

Sample Standard Consent to Opioid Maintenance Treatment Form for OTPs

---

CONSENT TO PARTICIPATE IN METHADONE OR BUPRENORPHINE TREATMENT

Patient's Name: _____ **Date:** _____

I authorize and give voluntary consent to _____ [insert name of program] to dispense and administer medications—including methadone or buprenorphine—to treat my opioid use disorder. Treatment procedures have been explained to me, and I understand that I should take my medication at the schedule determined by the program physician, or his/her designee, in accordance with federal and state regulations.

I understand that, like all other medications, methadone or buprenorphine can be harmful if not taken as prescribed. It has been explained to me that I must safeguard these medications and not share them with anyone because they can be fatal to children and adults if taken without medical supervision.

I also understand that methadone and buprenorphine produce physical opioid dependence.

Like all medications, they may have side effects. Possible side effects, as well as alternative treatments and their risks and benefits, have been explained to me.

I understand that it is important for me to inform any medical and psychiatric provider who may treat me that I am enrolled in an opioid treatment program. In this way, the provider will be aware of all the medications I am taking, can provide the best possible care, and can avoid prescribing medications that might affect my treatment with methadone or buprenorphine or my recovery.

I understand that I may withdraw voluntarily from this treatment program and discontinue the use of these medications at any time. If I choose this option, I understand I will be offered medically supervised withdrawal.

For women of childbearing age: Pregnant women treated with methadone or sublingual or buccal buprenorphine have better outcomes than pregnant women not in treatment who continue to use opioid drugs. Newborns of mothers who are receiving methadone or buprenorphine treatment may have opioid withdrawal symptoms (i.e., neonatal abstinence syndrome). The delivery hospital may require babies who are exposed to opioids before birth to spend a number of days in the hospital for monitoring of withdrawal symptoms. Some babies may also need medication to stop withdrawal. If I am or become pregnant, I understand that I should tell the medical staff of the OTP right away so I can receive or be referred to prenatal care. I understand that there are ways to maximize the healthy course of my pregnancy while I am taking methadone or buprenorphine.

Signature of Patient: _____ **Date of Birth:** _____

Date: _____ **Witness:** _____

Adapted from material in the public domain[157]

Chapter 3C: Naltrexone

Chapter 3C gives an overview of naltrexone pharmacology and specific guidance on dosing for oral and injectable naltrexone.

The opioid receptor antagonist naltrexone was synthesized in the 1960s to block the euphoric effects of morphine.[158] Oral naltrexone was approved by the Food and Drug Administration (FDA) in 1984 for the blockade of the effects of exogenously administered opioids. Long-acting, sustained-release opioid agonist preparations have been investigated since the 1970s to improve adherence over oral medications. In 2010, FDA approved injectable extended-release naltrexone (XR-NTX) for preventing return to opioid dependence after medically supervised withdrawal.

Despite its potential advantages (e.g., no abuse liability, no special regulatory requirements), oral naltrexone is not widely used to treat opioid use disorder (OUD) because of low rates of patient acceptance, difficulty in achieving abstinence for the necessary time before initiation of treatment, and high rates of medication nonadherence.[159]

Before initiating either formulation of naltrexone, patients must be opioid abstinent for an adequate period of time after completing opioid withdrawal. Medically supervised opioid withdrawal can be conducted on an outpatient or inpatient basis. The latter is often reserved for patients with co-occurring substance use disorders (SUDs) or medical or psychiatric illness.

There are several pharmacological approaches to medically supervised withdrawal. Methadone can be used for this purpose in opioid treatment programs (OTPs) and hospital settings. Patients in opioid withdrawal typically receive an individualized dose between 20 mg and 30 mg per day, gradually reduced over 6 days or more. Buprenorphine can be used in an adequate dose to lessen withdrawal symptoms and then reduced gradually over several days or more. If an opioid agonist is used for medically supervised withdrawal, an adequate interval of time following the last dose must occur before naltrexone induction. When it is not possible to use opioid agonists, alpha-2 adrenergic agonists such as clonidine can be used off label at doses from 0.1 mg to 0.3 mg every 6 to 8 hours to treat symptoms.[160]

Formulations

Oral: Oral naltrexone is a 50 mg tablet of naltrexone hydrochloride. It was approved by FDA in 1984 for blockade of the effects of exogenously administered opioids and in 1994 for alcohol dependence treatment. A Cochrane review examined 13 randomized trials among 1,158 patients who were opioid dependent and provided counseling. They were treated with or without oral naltrexone. The review concluded that **oral naltrexone was not superior to placebo or to no medication in treatment retention or illicit opioid use reduction.**[161]

XR-NTX: In 2006, FDA approved XR-NTX as an intramuscular (IM) injection every 4 weeks or once a month for the treatment of alcohol dependence. In 2010, FDA approved XR-NTX for the prevention of return to opioid dependence following medically supervised withdrawal. XR-NTX is a suspension of 380 mg naltrexone embedded in microspheres made from a biodegradable copolymer that undergoes hydrolysis as it absorbs water. XR-NTX requires refrigeration and is supplied as a vial of dry powder along with a separate vial of an aqueous diluent, which providers combine just before use.[162]

XR-NTX is more effective than placebo[163] or no medication[164] in reducing risk of return to opioid use.[165] A multisite randomized trial in the United States started in residential treatment programs found that buprenorphine treatment was associated with lower rates of return to use during 24 weeks of postdischarge outpatient treatment compared with XR-NTX,[166] given the significant proportion of patients who did not actually receive XR-NTX because of challenges related to XR-NTX induction. The same study found no significant between-group differences in rates of return to use when data were analyzed based solely on patients who did begin assigned medications. Study findings may not generalize to outpatient settings, where naltrexone induction may be more difficult than in residential treatment settings.

One additional study merits mention. A 12-week trial was conducted in Norway with 159 participants who, at the time of random assignment to XR-NTX or buprenorphine, had completed medically supervised withdrawal or were already opioid abstinent. XR-NTX was found to be noninferior to buprenorphine in terms of treatment retention or reduction in illicit opioid use.[167]

Pharmacology

Naltrexone is a competitive mu-opioid receptor antagonist with strong receptor affinity. **Naltrexone does not activate the mu-opioid receptor and exerts no opioid effects.** Unlike opioid agonists, naltrexone will not alleviate withdrawal symptoms, will not cause withdrawal when stopped, and cannot be diverted.

If patients maintained on naltrexone use opioid agonists, naltrexone can block their effects—a key feature of its therapeutic efficacy. However, because the interaction at the receptor is competitive, the **blockade can potentially be overridden with high doses of opioids.**

Taking naltrexone after recent use of opioids can precipitate opioid withdrawal. Given its strong affinity, naltrexone can displace other opioids from the receptor. Patients must typically wait 7 to 10 days after their last use of short-acting opioids and 10 to 14 days after their last use of long-acting opioids before taking their first dose of naltrexone.

Bioavailability

Oral: The gastrointestinal tract readily absorbs oral naltrexone. Peak concentrations occur in 1 to 2 hours.[168]

XR-NTX: IM injection causes a transient peak blood concentration 2 hours after injection and another at 2 to 3 days after injection.[169] About 14 days after injection, concentrations gradually diminish, with measurable blood levels for more than 1 month.

Both formulations are extensively metabolized by the kidneys and liver, but without CYP450 enzyme system involvement. Unlike methadone and buprenorphine, **naltrexone has limited potential drug–drug interactions.** Its major metabolite, 6-beta naltrexol, is also a mu-opioid receptor antagonist. It is eliminated primarily by the kidneys in the urine.[170]

Orally administered naltrexone has a half-life of approximately 4 hours. Its primary metabolite, 6-beta-naltrexol, is a weak mu-opioid receptor antagonist with a half-life of approximately 12 hours.[171]

XR-NTX, or "depot naltrexone," is encapsulated in biodegradable polymer microspheres. **It provides opioid blockade by delivering steady naltrexone concentrations for about 1 month.**[172] Elimination half-life is 5 to 10 days. Repeated administration causes no accumulation of naltrexone or its metabolites.

Dosing Considerations

XR-NTX

XR-NTX is indicated for the prevention of return to opioid dependence following medically supervised opioid withdrawal. Appropriate patients should have an adequate period of abstinence with no signs of opioid withdrawal before XR-NTX administration. Patients must be willing to receive monthly IM injections. Become acquainted with the FDA label for XR-NTX, which is available online (https://dailymed.nlm.nih.gov/dailymed/drugInfo.cfm?setid=cd11c435-b0f0-4bb9-ae78-60f101f3703f).

Contraindications

Contraindications to receiving XR-NTX (as well as to receiving oral naltrexone, with the exception of hypersensitivity to the XR-NTX suspension and diluent) include:[173]

- Current pain treatment with opioid analgesics.
- Current physiological opioid dependence.
- Current acute opioid withdrawal.
- Severe hepatic impairment.
- Naloxone challenge (Exhibit 3C.1) or oral naltrexone dose causing opioid withdrawal symptoms.
- Positive urine opioid screen for morphine, methadone, buprenorphine, oxycodone, fentanyl, or other opioids.
- History of hypersensitivity to naltrexone, polylactide-co-glycolide, carboxymethylcellulose, or any other components of the diluent.

Precautions and warnings

- **Discuss the risks and benefits of continuing naltrexone with patients who become pregnant while receiving naltrexone treatment and whose OUD is in remission.** Unlike methadone and buprenorphine, naltrexone has been little researched in pregnant populations.[174,175]
- **Patients are vulnerable to opioid overdose death** after completing the every-4-weeks or once-monthly dosing period, missing a dose, or stopping treatment. Trying to override opioid blockade with high opioid doses may cause overdose.
- **Patients may experience injection site reactions** including pain, tenderness, induration, swelling, erythema, bruising, or pruritus. Severe injection site reactions may occur (e.g., cellulitis, hematoma, abscess, sterile abscess, necrosis). Some cases may require surgical intervention and may result in significant scarring. (See the Chapter 3C Appendix for techniques to reduce injection site reactions). As with any IM injection, use caution in patients with thrombocytopenia or a coagulation disorder.
- **Precipitated opioid withdrawal can occur in patients who used illicit opioids recently or switched from an opioid agonist medication.** Symptoms may be severe enough for hospitalization. To avoid precipitated withdrawal from either formulation, patients should typically stop use of short-acting opioid agonists for 7 to 10 days and long-acting agonists for 10 to 14 days.[176] There is active research on approaches to initiate XR-NTX more quickly for patients physically dependent on opioid agonists.[177]
- **Hepatitis has been associated with XR-NTX,** often in the presence of other potential causes of hepatic toxicity (e.g., alcohol liver disease, viral hepatitis). Monitor liver function tests during treatment. Stop naltrexone in the presence of acute hepatitis and severe liver disease.[178] Initiate or refer patients to treatment for hepatitis.
- **Use cautiously in patients with moderate-to-severe renal impairment,** because the medication is eliminated primarily through the kidneys.
- **Hypersensitivity reactions** can occur, including rash, urticaria, angioedema, and anaphylaxis.
- **Monitor patients with OUD for depression and suicidal ideation.** Naltrexone use has been occasionally associated with dysphoria,[179] although it's unclear whether this is a side effect of the medication or a manifestation of underlying depression or depressed mood related to OUD.[180] Monitor patients for depression, which is common with OUD.
- **If a patient needs emergency pain treatment,** regional anesthesia or nonopioid analgesics are alternatives to opioid analgesics. A patient who must have opioids for pain treatment or anesthesia requires continuous monitoring in an anesthesia care setting.

EXHIBIT 3C.1. Naloxone Challenge

Use the naloxone challenge to assess lack of physical opioid dependence. Naloxone can be administered via intravenous, subcutaneous, or IM routes to patients who report an adequate period of opioid abstinence and have a negative opioid urine test (including morphine, methadone, buprenorphine, and oxycodone). **A negative naloxone challenge does not guarantee that the patient will not experience precipitated opioid withdrawal upon naltrexone administration.**[181]

Intravenous Administration

1. Draw 0.8 mg naloxone into a sterile syringe.
2. Inject 0.2 mg naloxone intravenously.
3. Wait 30 seconds for signs and symptoms of withdrawal. If withdrawal signs/symptoms are present, stop the naloxone challenge and treat symptomatically.
4. If no withdrawal signs and symptoms are present and vital signs are stable, inject remaining naloxone (0.6 mg) and observe for 20 minutes. Check the patient's vital signs and monitor for withdrawal.
5. If withdrawal signs and symptoms are present, stop the naloxone challenge and treat symptomatically. The test can be repeated in 24 hours or the patient can be considered for opioid agonist treatment.
6. If no withdrawal signs and symptoms are present* and **oral naltrexone is the desired treatment course,** give the patient two tablets of 25 mg naltrexone (take one tablet on each of the next 2 days) and a sufficient number of 50 mg naltrexone tablets (take one 50 mg tablet daily starting on the third day) until they are able to fill their prescription for oral naltrexone. Skip to Step 8.
7. If no withdrawal signs and symptoms are present** and **XR-NTX is the desired treatment course,** administer XR-NTX in the upper outer quadrant of the buttock, following package insert directions (summarized below).
8. Instruct the patient about the risk of overdose and death if they use opioids to override the blockade.

Subcutaneous Administration

1. Inject 0.8 mg naloxone subcutaneously.
2. Wait 20 minutes while checking vital signs and observing for signs and symptoms of opioid withdrawal.
3. If withdrawal signs and symptom are present, stop the naloxone challenge and treat symptomatically. The test can be repeated in 24 hours or the patient can be considered for opioid agonist treatment.
4. If no withdrawal signs and symptoms are present, follow Step 6 (for oral naltrexone treatment) or Step 7 (for XR-NTX treatment) above.

* **Optional:** If withdrawal signs and symptoms are absent, administer 25 mg oral naltrexone and observe for 2 hours. If the patient develops opioid withdrawal, treat symptomatically. If no withdrawal signs or symptoms are present following the 25 mg naltrexone dose and oral naltrexone is the desired treatment course, give the patient one tablet of 25 mg naltrexone to take the next day and 50 mg naltrexone tablets to take daily starting the day after.

** **Optional:** If withdrawal signs and symptoms are absent, administer 25 mg oral naltrexone and observe for 2 hours. If the patient develops opioid withdrawal, treat symptomatically and do not administer XR-NTX. This step is recommended to minimize the likelihood of longer lasting precipitated withdrawal in patients given XR-NTX who took buprenorphine recently (naloxone may not displace it from opioid receptors). This step can help identify a naltrexone allergy before providing XR-NTX. If no withdrawal symptoms are present following the 25 mg naltrexone dose and XR-NTX is the desired course, administer XR-NTX as described above.

Adapted from material in the public domain.[182]

Side effects

Possible side effects of XR-NTX include (see the FDA label for a complete list https://dailymed.nlm.nih.gov/dailymed/drugInfo.cfm?setid=cd11c435-b0f0-4bb9-ae78-60f101f3703f):[183]

- Insomnia.
- Injection site pain.
- Hepatic enzyme abnormalities.
- Nasopharyngitis.

Assessment

Thorough assessment helps determine whether naltrexone treatment is appropriate for a patient. (Part 2 of this Treatment Improvement Protocol [TIP] covers screening and assessment in more detail.)

Patients who have been abstinent from short-acting opioids (including tramadol) for 7 to 10 days or long-acting opioids (e.g., methadone, buprenorphine) for 10 to 14 days can initiate naltrexone following assessment that includes:

- **Checking the state prescription drug monitoring program database.**
- **Taking the patient's history.**
  - Conduct a medical, psychiatric, substance use, and substance use treatment history.
  - **Assess recent opioid use,** including frequency, quantity, type, route, and last day of use. Confirm an adequate opioid abstinence period.
  - Establish OUD diagnosis.
  - Assess for other SUDs, including those that involve alcohol, benzodiazepines, or stimulants.
- **Conducting a physical exam.**
  - **Assess for signs and symptoms of intoxication.** Do not give a first dose to a patient who is sedated or intoxicated. Assess and treat him or her appropriately.
  - **Assess for evidence of opioid withdrawal and physiological dependence.** The Clinical Opioid Withdrawal Scale (COWS) or the Clinical Institute Narcotic Assessment (CINA) Scale for Withdrawal Symptoms can be used to assess withdrawal signs (see "Resource Alert: Opioid Withdrawal Scales"). The patient should not exhibit any signs of opioid withdrawal before taking the first dose of naltrexone, to avoid precipitated withdrawal.
- **Obtaining laboratory tests.**
  - **Conduct drug and alcohol tests.** Use reliable urine tests for opioids (including morphine, methadone, buprenorphine, and oxycodone), benzodiazepines, cocaine, and other drugs commonly used in the area. Use a breathalyzer to estimate the patient's blood alcohol content.
  - **Conduct a pregnancy test.** Naltrexone is not recommended for OUD treatment in pregnancy. Refer pregnant patients to prenatal care.[184]
  - **Assess liver function.** Obtain liver function tests followed by periodic monitoring at 6- or 12-month intervals during treatment.[185]
  - **Obtain kidney function tests** (e.g., creatinine) for people who inject drugs.

RESOURCE ALERT

Opioid Withdrawal Scales

The COWS and other opioid withdrawal scales from Annex 10 of the World Health Organization's *Guidelines for the Psychosocially Assisted Pharmacological Treatment of Opioid Dependence* can be downloaded from the National Center for Biotechnology Information website (www.ncbi.nlm.nih.gov/books/NBK143183).

The CINA Scale for Withdrawal Symptoms is also available online (www.ncpoep.org/wp-content/uploads/2015/02/Appendix_7_Clinical_Institute_Narcotic_Assessment_CINA_Scale_for_Withdrawal_Symptoms.pdf).

- **Conduct hepatitis and HIV tests.** Hepatitis B and C are common among patients entering naltrexone treatment. HIV infection is also prevalent. If possible, test the patient for these infections and refer to treatment as appropriate. The Centers for Disease Control and Prevention recommends hepatitis B vaccine for individuals seeking treatment for SUDs.[186]

During assessment, discuss with patients the risks and benefits of naltrexone and alternative treatment approaches. Explore patients' motivation to initiate medication treatment and to adhere to the dosing regimen. Start naltrexone if the patient:

- Meets *Diagnostic and Statistical Manual of Mental Disorders*, Fifth Edition, criteria for OUD.
- Understands risks and benefits.
- Reports opioid abstinence for 7 to 10 days (short acting) or 10 to 14 days (long acting).
- Reports no allergies to naltrexone or the components of the XR-NTX preparation.
- Does not have a coagulation disorder.
- Will not soon require opioid analgesia.
- Has a negative pregnancy test.
- Has a negative urine opioid screen for morphine, methadone, buprenorphine, oxycodone, and other opioids.
- Is free of current opioid withdrawal signs and symptoms (Exhibit 3C.2).
- Has liver function test results that do not indicate acute hepatitis or liver failure.
- Has a negative naloxone challenge result (Exhibit 3C.1).

Patient selection

No evidence clearly predicts which patients are best treated with XR-NTX versus other OUD medications. A secondary analysis of the data from a randomized trial of XR-NTX versus placebo conducted in Russia found no significant baseline predictors of successes among the 25 variables examined, including demographics, clinical severity, level of functioning, craving, and HIV serostatus.[187]

Inform patients of all their treatment options and the settings in which they are available. OTPs may be best for patients needing more structure. Tailor decisions about which medication to use to patients' medical and substance use histories, patient preferences, and treatment availability.

Pregnant women are not appropriate candidates for XR-NTX treatment.

Consider for XR-NTX treatment patients who:[188]

- **Do not wish to take opioid agonists.**
- **Have been opioid abstinent for at least 1 week,** have recently been or will soon be released from controlled environments (e.g., incarceration, residential addiction treatment), and do not wish to initiate (or are not able to access) opioid agonist treatment. For patients requesting opioid agonist treatment, methadone or buprenorphine must be started at much lower doses and increased much more slowly than for opioid-tolerant patients (see sections on methadone and buprenorphine dosing).

EXHIBIT 3C.2. Signs and Symptoms of Opioid Withdrawal

Signs	Symptoms
Runny nose	Skin crawling
Tearing	Abdominal cramps
Yawning	Temperature changes
Sweating	Nausea
Tremor	Vomiting
Vomiting	Diarrhea
Piloerection	Bone or muscle pain
Pupillary dilation	Dysphoria
	Craving for opioids

- **Have not responded well to prior adequate treatment** with opioid agonist therapy.[189]
- **Are part of an overall program with external monitoring** and significant, immediate external consequences for lack of adherence. These patients (e.g., healthcare professionals, pilots, probationers, parolees) may show higher rates of retention with XR-NTX because of required external monitoring.[190]
- **Have home locations or work schedules making daily or almost-daily OTP visits impossible or risky** (e.g., job loss).

Informed consent

Inform all patients of the following basic information:

- Their OUD diagnosis and the nature of the disorder
- Risks and benefits of XR-NTX and other OUD medications
- Risks and benefits of nonmedication treatments

Consider asking patients to sign a treatment agreement form before starting treatment. (See Appendix 3C for a sample treatment agreement.) Document informed consent discussions in the medical record.

Educate patients and their families about what to expect from naltrexone treatment (Exhibit 3C.3). A naltrexone medication guide should be dispensed to patients with each injection. Caution them about increased risk of overdose if they stop treatment and return to illicit opioid use or attempt to override the receptor blockade of XR-NTX. Document education in the medical record. Chapter 3C Appendix has a patient education counseling tool for XR-NTX.

> Use language and written materials appropriate to each patient's comprehension level to ensure that he or she understands the options and can make informed decisions.

Initiating XR-NTX treatment

Storage and preparation

A pharmacy will send XR-NTX and its diluent in a refrigerated package with two sets of administration needles (1.5 and 2 inches), a 1-inch preparation needle, and a needle protection device.

The XR-NTX microspheres are temperature sensitive. When the carton arrives from the pharmacy, store it in a refrigerator at 36 to 46 degrees Fahrenheit (2 to 8 degrees Celsius). The refrigerator should have a working thermometer; check the temperature regularly.

Do not freeze the carton or expose it to temperatures above 77 degrees Fahrenheit (25 degrees Celsius). XR-NTX can be stored unrefrigerated for up to 7 days before administration.

Before preparing XR-NTX for administration, keep it at room temperature for about 45 minutes. Examine the microspheres and diluent to ensure that no particulate matter or discoloration are present. Mix following FDA-approved package insert directions, using the 1-inch preparation needle. Resulting suspension should be milky white, without clumps, and able to move freely down the wall of the vial.

Two sets of needles of two different lengths are shipped with the medication in case the first needle clogs before injection. **Use the 1.5-inch needle for lean patients and the 2-inch needle for patients with more subcutaneous tissue** overlying the gluteal muscle. The longer needle helps ensure that the injection reaches the muscle. Inject patients with average body habitus with either needle.

Administration

Administer XR-NTX every 4 weeks or once a month as a 380 mg IM gluteal injection. Alternate buttocks for each 4-week injection. Given the risk of severe injection site reactions, FDA requires a risk evaluation and mitigation strategy (www.vivitrolrems.com) for XR-NTX including a patient counseling tool, a patient medication guide, and a visual aid to reinforce proper XR-NTX injection technique.

EXHIBIT 3C.3. Key Points of Patient Education for Naltrexone

- Do not use any opioids in the 7 to 10 days (for short acting) or 10 to 14 days (for long acting) before starting XR-NTX, to avoid potentially serious opioid withdrawal symptoms. Opioids include:
  - Heroin.
  - Prescription opioid analgesics (including tramadol).
  - Cough, diarrhea, or other medications that contain codeine or other opioids.
  - Methadone.
  - Buprenorphine.
- Seek immediate medical help if symptoms of allergic reaction or anaphylaxis occur, such as:
  - Itching.
  - Swelling.
  - Hives.
  - Shortness of breath.
  - Throat tightness.
- Do not try to override the opioid blockade with large amounts of opioids, which could result in overdose.
- Understand the risk of overdose from using opioids near the time of the next injection, after missing a dose, or after stopping medications.
- Report injection site reactions including:
  - Pain.
  - Hardening.
  - Lumps.
  - Blisters.
  - Blackening.
  - Scabs.
  - An open wound.

  Some of these reactions could require surgery to repair (rarely).
- Report signs and symptoms of hepatitis (e.g., fatigue, abdominal pain, yellowing skin or eyes, dark urine).
- Report depression or suicidal thoughts. Seek immediate medical attention if these symptoms appear.
- Seek medical help if symptoms of pneumonia appear (e.g., shortness of breath, fever).
- Inform providers of naltrexone treatment, as treatment differs for various types of pneumonia.
- Inform all healthcare professionals of XR-NTX treatment.
- Report pregnancy.
- Inform providers of any upcoming medical procedures that may require pain medication.
- Understand that taking naltrexone may result in difficulty achieving adequate pain control if acute medical illness or trauma causes severe acute pain.
- Wear medical alert jewelry and carry a medical alert card indicating you are taking XR-NTX. A patient wallet card or medical alert bracelet can be ordered at 1-800-848-4876.

Follow-up care after first dose

Examine patients within a week of administering their first XR-NTX dose. It can be clinically beneficial to maintain weekly contact in the first month to:

- Provide supportive counseling.
- Assess ongoing drug or alcohol use.
- Monitor side effects.
- Obtain drug testing.
- Follow up on status of referrals to counseling or other services.

Patients who test the opioid blockade of XR-NTX may discontinue use because of the blocking of the euphoric effects of illicit opioids.[191] Patients who miss a dose can restart medication (use procedures outlined earlier in this section) after an adequate period of opioid abstinence (7 to 14 days).

> The TIP expert panel cautions that, based on current data, arbitrary time limits on XR-NTX are inappropriate.

See Chapter 3E for information on the management of patients taking naltrexone in office-based treatment settings.

Duration of treatment

Barring contraindications, patients should continue taking XR-NTX as long as they benefit from it and want to continue. Data are limited on the long-term effectiveness of XR-NTX compared with methadone or buprenorphine.

Treatment discontinuation

When patients wish to discontinue naltrexone, engage in shared decision making and explore:

- Their reasons for wanting to discontinue.
- The risks and benefits of discontinuing.
- Problem-solving strategies that can help them make an informed choice.
- Their appropriateness for buprenorphine or methadone treatment.

Discourage patients who are not yet stable from discontinuing treatment, because of the high rate of return to illicit opioid use and the increased chance of overdose death.

Signs that a patient may be ready to discontinue medication include:[192]

- Sustaining illicit drug abstinence over time.
- Having stable housing and income.
- Having no legal problems.
- Having substantially reduced craving.
- Attending counseling or mutual-help groups.

Patients who discontinue should have a recovery plan that may include monitoring as well as adjunctive counseling and recovery support. If they return to opioid use, encourage them to return for assessment and reentry into treatment.

Given the high risk of return to illicit opioid use, **offer patients information about opioid overdose prevention and a naloxone prescription they can use in case of overdose.** When patients stop using naltrexone, they will have no tolerance for opioids. Their risk of overdose is very high if they use again. For more information, see the *SAMHSA Opioid Overdose Prevention Toolkit* (https://store.samhsa.gov/shin/content//SMA16-4742/SMA16-4742.pdf).

Rapid naltrexone induction

Patients with OUD need to discontinue opioids and wait 7 to 14 days after last opioid use (including any given for withdrawal treatment) before receiving XR-NTX. As described above, they can do so through medically supervised withdrawal in a controlled environment, such as an inpatient unit, residential addiction treatment program, correctional facility, or hospital, or on an outpatient basis.

Financial issues and managed care constraints may influence patients' access to controlled treatment environments. The alternative—**abstaining long enough after outpatient medically supervised withdrawal—is challenging.** Thus, various approaches to rapid naltrexone induction have been developed[193] and more recently refined in research settings.[194,195,196]

Consider rapid induction in specialty addiction treatment programs, not general medical settings. It may be hard for providers in general medical settings to start XR-NTX successfully with patients who need medically supervised opioid withdrawal. Rapid induction approaches are likely beyond the scope of general outpatient

> **RESOURCE ALERT**
>
> ### Patient and Family Educational Resources
>
> *Decisions in Recovery: Treatment for Opioid Use Disorder* offers information for patients on the use of medications for OUD (https://store.samhsa.gov/product/SMA16-4993)
>
> *Medication-Assisted Treatment for Opioid Addiction: Facts for Families and Friends* offers information for family and friends (www.ct.gov/dmhas/lib/dmhas/publications/MAT-InfoFamilyFriends.pdf)

settings. However, patients can successfully initiate XR-NTX in a general outpatient medical setting if they:

- Have been abstinent for sufficient time and pass the naloxone challenge.
- Started taking XR-NTX elsewhere and are due for the next injection.

One randomized trial compared two approaches to starting XR-NTX on an outpatient basis. This study assigned adults dependent on opioids to either a standard 14-day buprenorphine-assisted opioid withdrawal or more rapid 7-day oral naltrexone-assisted opioid withdrawal.[197] Naltrexone-assisted withdrawal was conducted over 7 days. It included 1 day of buprenorphine administration; 1 day with ancillary medications including clonidine and clonazepam but no buprenorphine; followed by 4 days of ancillary medications and increasing daily doses of oral naltrexone (starting with 1 mg, 3 mg, 12 mg, and 25 mg); and concluding on day 7 with XR-NTX administration. Buprenorphine-assisted withdrawal consisted of a 7-day buprenorphine taper followed by the recommended 7 days without opioids. The naltrexone-assisted withdrawal group was significantly more likely to begin XR-NTX compared with the buprenorphine-assisted withdrawal group (56.1 percent versus 32.7 percent, respectively). This type of approach, which must be conducted with careful daily monitoring, is used in some residential programs and may prove to be a useful approach to outpatient XR-NTX induction in specialty programs. More discussion on rapid induction approaches is available in *Implementing Antagonist-Based Relapse Prevention Treatment for Buprenorphine-Treated Individuals*,[198] available online (http://pcssmat.org/wp-content/uploads/2015/02/PCSSMAT-Implementing-Antagonist-with-Case.Bisaga.CME_.pdf).

Oral Naltrexone

The effectiveness of oral naltrexone is limited, given poor adherence and the requirement of 7 to 14 days of opioid abstinence before initiation. During this waiting period, patients may drop out of care. One study found significantly lower patient retention in treatment after incarceration for patients treated with oral naltrexone compared with methadone.[199]

Oral naltrexone blocks opioid-induced euphoria for only a day or two. When patients stop taking it, risks of return to opioid use and overdose increase.

The TIP expert panel doesn't recommend using oral naltrexone except in the limited circumstances described in the following sections. This view is in keeping with expert reviews for the United Kingdom's National Health Service,[200] a clinical practice guideline published by the Department of Veterans Affairs and Department of Defense,[201] and a Cochrane review.[202]

Indications and contraindications, precautions and warnings, side effects, and assessment.
All are similar to those for XR-NTX, save issues specific to suspension/diluent contents and the injection itself.

Patient Selection

In limited circumstances, oral naltrexone may be considered after the risks and benefits, as well as alternative treatments, are discussed with the patient. Examples include:

- **Patients who cannot afford XR-NTX** but wish to take an opioid receptor antagonist.
- **Patients with high levels of monitoring and negative consequences for nonadherence,** such as healthcare professionals who may not be permitted to have opioid agonist treatment.[203,204]

The TIP expert panel does not recommend that payers require patients to fail oral naltrexone before providing access to XR-NTX, given the risk of unintentional overdose death if the patient returns to illicit opioid use.

- **Patients leaving controlled environments** (e.g., prisons, hospitals, inpatient addiction rehabilitation) who may benefit from medication to prevent return to illicit drug use but cannot or will not take XR-NTX and do not wish to be treated with (or do not have access to) opioid agonists.

Patients who have taken methadone or extensively used heroin are especially poor oral naltrexone candidates.[205]

Dosing

Following a negative naloxone challenge, the first oral dose of naltrexone can be 25 mg (half of the usual daily naltrexone maintenance dose). This reduces risk of a more severe precipitated opioid withdrawal than could occur with a full 50 mg dose. This lower dose may also reduce nausea associated with the first naltrexone dose. The dose can be increased to 50 mg daily on the second day.

To increase adherence, arrange for directly observed administration of oral naltrexone. This is more feasible if patients who tolerate a daily dose of 50 mg are switched to a 3-days-per-week regimen for a total weekly dose of 350 mg (e.g., administer 100 mg on Monday and Wednesday and 150 mg on Friday). A member of the patient's social network (e.g., spouse) may also directly observe therapy.

Duration of treatment

The optimal length of treatment with oral naltrexone is not known. In general, the longer patients take an effective medication, the better their outcomes.

Use of illicit opioids during treatment with oral naltrexone is a cause of concern and may be a precursor to treatment discontinuation.[206] Some patients will initially test the opioid blockade with illicit opioids and then discontinue opioid use. However, others will continue using illicit opioids.[207]

If patients continue to test the blockade, immediately discuss alternative treatment plans that include:
- Increased counseling.
- Switching to XR-NTX.
- Closer monitoring.
- Directly observed oral naltrexone therapy.
- Residential treatment.
- Assessment for the appropriateness of buprenorphine or methadone.

Naltrexone Dosing Summary

XR-NTX
- Before administering XR-NTX, keep it at room temperature for about 45 minutes.
- Use the correct needle length to ensure the injection is in the gluteal muscle.
  - Use the 2-inch needle for patients with more subcutaneous tissue and the 1.5-inch needle for patients with less adipose tissue.
  - Use either length in patients with normal body habitus.
- Use proper aseptic technique.
- Use proper gluteal IM injection technique.
- Never inject intravenously or subcutaneously.
- Repeat the injection every 4 weeks or once per month.

Oral Naltrexone
- Use in limited circumstances after discussing risks and benefits, as well as alternative treatment options, with the patient.
- Do the naloxone challenge.
- The first oral naltrexone dose should be 25 mg.
- The dose can be increased on the second day to 50 mg daily if necessary.
- If desired, switch patients who tolerate a daily dose of 50 mg to a 3-days-per-week regimen for a total weekly dose of 350 mg.

Chapter 3C Appendix

Sample XR-NTX Treatment Agreement

This form is for educational/informational purposes only. It doesn't establish a legal or medical standard of care. Healthcare professionals should use their judgment in interpreting this form and applying it in the circumstances of their individual patients and practice arrangements. The information provided in this form is provided "as is" with no guarantee as to its accuracy or completeness.

TREATMENT AGREEMENT

I agree to accept the following treatment agreement for extended-release injectable naltrexone office-based opioid use disorder treatment:

1. The risks and benefits of extended-release injectable naltrexone treatment have been explained to me.
2. The risks and benefits of other treatment for opioid use disorder (including methadone, buprenorphine, and nonmedication treatments) have been explained to me.
3. I will be on time to my appointments and respectful to the office staff and other patients.
4. I will keep my healthcare provider informed of all my medications (including herbs and vitamins) and medical problems.
5. I agree not to obtain or take prescription opioid medications prescribed by any other healthcare provider without consultation from my naltrexone prescriber.
6. If I am going to have a medical procedure that will cause pain, I will let my healthcare provider know in advance so that my pain will be adequately treated.
7. If I miss a scheduled appointment for my next extended-release naltrexone injection, I understand that I should reschedule the appointment as soon as possible because it is important to receive the medication on time to reduce the risk of opioid overdose should I return to use.
8. If I come to the office intoxicated, I understand that my healthcare provider will not see me.
9. Violence, threatening language or behavior, or participation in any illegal activity at the office will result in treatment termination from the clinic.
10. I understand that random urine drug testing is a treatment requirement. If I do not provide a urine sample, it will count as a positive drug test.
11. I understand that initially I will have weekly office visits until my condition is stable.
12. I can be seen every 2 weeks in the office starting the second month of treatment if I have two negative urine drug tests in a row.
13. I may be seen less than every 2 weeks based on goals made by my healthcare provider and me.
14. I understand that people have died trying to overcome the naltrexone opioid blockade by taking large amounts of opioids.
15. I understand that treatment of opioid use disorder involves more than just taking medication. I agree to follow my healthcare provider's recommendations for additional counseling and/or for help with other problems.
16. I understand that there is no fixed time for being on naltrexone and that the goal of treatment is for me to stop using all illicit drugs and become successful in all aspects of my life.
17. I understand that my risk of overdose increases if I go back to using opioids after stopping naltrexone.
18. I have been educated about the other two FDA-approved medications used to treat opioid use disorder, methadone and buprenorphine, and I prefer to receive treatment with naltrexone.
19. I have been educated about the increased chance of pregnancy when stopping illicit opioid use and starting naltrexone treatment and have been informed about methods for preventing pregnancy.
20. I have been informed that if I become pregnant during naltrexone treatment, I should inform my provider and have a discussion about the risks and benefits of continuing to take naltrexone.

Other specific items unique to my treatment include:

Patient's Name (print): _____

Patient's Signature: _____ Date: _____

This form is adapted from the American Society of Addiction Medicine's Sample Treatment Agreement, which is updated periodically; the most current version of the agreement is available online (www.asam.org/docs/default-source/advocacy/sample-treatment-agreement30fa159472bc604ca5b7ff000030b21a.pdf?sfvrsn=0).

Adapted with permission.[208]

Part 3 of 5—Pharmacotherapy for Opioid Use Disorder

TIP 63

Patient Counseling Tool for XR-NTX

Patient Counseling Tool
VIVITROL® (naltrexone for extended-release injectable suspension)

Risk of sudden opioid withdrawal during initiation and re-initiation of VIVITROL
Using any type of opioid including street drugs, prescription pain medicines, cough, cold or diarrhea medicines that contain opioids, or opioid dependence treatments buprenorphine or methadone, in the 7 to 14 days before starting VIVITROL may cause severe and potentially dangerous sudden opioid withdrawal.

Risk of opioid overdose
Patients may be more sensitive to the effects of lower amounts of opioids:

- After stopping opioids (detoxification)
- When the next VIVITROL dose is due
- If a dose of VIVITROL is missed
- After VIVITROL treatment stops

Patients should tell their family and people close to them about the increased sensitivity to opioids and the risk of overdose even when using lower doses of opioids or amounts that they used before treatment. Using large amounts of opioids, such as prescription pain pills or heroin, to overcome effects of VIVITROL can lead to serious injury, coma, and death.

Risk of severe reactions at the injection site
Remind patients of these **possible** symptoms at the **injection site:**

- Intense pain
- The area feels hard
- Large areas of swelling
- Lumps
- Blisters
- Open wound
- Dark scab

Some of these injection site reactions have required surgery.
Tell your patients to contact a healthcare provider if they have any reactions at the injection site.

Risk of liver injury, including liver damage or hepatitis
Remind patients of the possible symptoms of liver damage or hepatitis.

- Stomach area pain lasting more than a few days
- Dark urine
- Yellowing of the whites of eyes
- Tiredness

Patients may not feel the therapeutic effects of opioid-containing medicines for pain, cough or cold, or diarrhea while taking VIVITROL.

Patients should carry written information with them at all times to alert healthcare providers that they are taking VIVITROL, so they can be treated properly in an emergency.

A Patient Wallet Card or Medical Alert Bracelet can be ordered from: 1-800-848-4876, Option #1.

PLEASE SEE PRESCRIBING INFORMATION AND MEDICATION GUIDE.

Alkermes® and VIVITROL® are registered trademarks of Alkermes, Inc.
©2013 Alkermes, Inc.
All rights reserved VIV-001317 Printed in U.S.A
www.vivitrol.com

(naltrexone for extended-release injectable suspension)

Available online (www.vivitrolrems.com/content/pdf/patinfo-counseling-tool.pdf).
Reprinted with permission.[209]

Key Techniques for Reducing Injection Site Reactions[210]

To reduce severe injection site reactions when administering XR-NTX via intramuscular injection, use the following techniques:

- **Use one of the administration needles provided with the XR-NTX kit to ensure that the injection reaches the gluteal muscle.** Use the 2-inch needle for patients who have more subcutaneous adipose tissue. Use the 1.5-inch needle for patients with less subcutaneous adipose tissue. Either needle is appropriate for use with patients who have average amounts of subcutaneous adipose tissue.
- **Use aseptic technique when administering intramuscularly.** Using a circular motion, clean the injection site with an alcohol swab. Let the area dry before administering the injection. Do not touch this area again before administration.
- **Use proper deep intramuscular injection technique into the gluteal muscle.** XR-NTX must not be injected intravenously, subcutaneously, or into adipose tissue. Accidental subcutaneous injection may increase the risk of severe injection site reactions.
  - **Administer the suspension by deep intramuscular injection into the upper outer quadrant of gluteal muscle,** alternating buttocks per monthly injection.
  - **Remember to aspirate for blood before injection.** If blood aspirates or the needle clogs, do not inject. Change to the spare needle provided in the package and administer into an adjacent site in the same gluteal region, again aspirating for blood before injection.
  - **Inject the suspension in a smooth, continuous motion.**

A patient counseling tool is available to help you counsel your patients before administration about the serious risks associated with XR-NTX.

The above information is a selection of key safety information about the XR-NTX injection. For complete safety information, refer to the directions for use and the prescribing information provided in the medication kit. You can also obtain this information online (www.vivitrolrems.com) or by calling 1-800-VIVITROL.

Available online (www.vivitrolrems.com/content/pdf/patinfo-injection-poster.pdf).

Chapter 3D: Buprenorphine

Chapter 3D is an overview of buprenorphine pharmacology and specific dosing guidance for sublingual and buccal formulations and buprenorphine implants.

Buprenorphine and buprenorphine/naloxone formulations are effective treatments for opioid use disorder (OUD). Numerous clinical studies and randomized clinical trials have demonstrated buprenorphine's efficacy in retaining patients in treatment and reducing illicit opioid use compared with treatment without medication and medically supervised withdrawal.[211,212,213] Other research has associated it with reduction in HIV risk behavior and risk of overdose death, and its effectiveness has been shown in primary care settings.[214,215,216,217,218] Buprenorphine is on the World Health Organization (WHO) list of essential medications.[219]

The Treatment Improvement Protocol (TIP) expert panel recommends offering the option of Food and Drug Administration (FDA)-approved buprenorphine formulations to appropriate patients with OUD, considering patient preferences for and experience with other medications or no medication. These recommendations align with recent Department of Veterans Affairs guidelines.[220]

Formulations

History of Approvals

FDA originally approved buprenorphine for analgesia. Formulations for OUD treatment were approved in:

- 2002: Sublingual buprenorphine/naloxone sublingual tablets (Suboxone); sublingual buprenorphine tablets (Subutex). The manufacturer discontinued the tablet dosage of the latter from the U.S. market after the film's approval, but generic tablet formulations are still available (Exhibit 3A.5, Chapter 3A).
- 2010: Buprenorphine/naloxone sublingual films.
- 2013: Buprenorphine/naloxone sublingual tablets (Zubsolv).[221]
- 2014: Buprenorphine/naloxone buccal films (Bunavail).[222]
- 2016: Buprenorphine implants (Probuphine).
- 2017: Buprenorphine extended-release injection (Sublocade).

FDA approved generic buprenorphine and buprenorphine/naloxone formulations based on evidence that they produce similar (within 90 percent confidence intervals) bioequivalence on pharmacokinetic measures, such as peak serum concentration, compared with the original sublingual buprenorphine/naloxone product.

The 2013 and 2014 branded formulations have greater bioavailability than Suboxone, meaning they deliver more buprenorphine to the bloodstream, thus achieving the same effect as the original product with lower doses. For example, 5.7 mg/1.4 mg of Zubsolv and 4.2 mg/0.7 mg of Bunavail provide the same buprenorphine exposure as 8 mg/2 mg of Suboxone.

Opioid treatment programs (OTPs) may administer or dispense buprenorphine, but only providers with Substance Abuse and Mental Health Services Administration (SAMHSA) waivers can prescribe buprenorphine for OUD. See "Resource Alert: How To Obtain a Waiver To Prescribe Buprenorphine" in Chapter 3A of this TIP.

Exhibit 3D.1 lists product strengths and recommended once-daily maintenance doses. For simplicity, dosing information here refers to sublingual Suboxone equivalents. An 8 mg/2 mg tablet of sublingual Suboxone is equivalent to 5.7 mg/1.4 mg of sublingual Zubsolv and 4.2 mg/0.7 mg of buccal Bunavail.

Patients who switch formulations may experience clinically significant plasma concentration changes that may require dose adjustments; bioavailability is similar, but not identical, between formulations.

Implants

In 2016, FDA approved buprenorphine implants for OUD maintenance treatment in patients who have achieved sustained clinical stability (e.g., periods of abstinence, minimal or no desire to use illicit opioids, stable housing, social support) while taking no more than 8 mg of daily Subutex (buprenorphine monoproduct) or Suboxone (buprenorphine/naloxone) equivalents. The implants are a set of four rods, each 2.5 mm in diameter and 26 mm in length. Each rod contains the equivalent of 80 mg of

EXHIBIT 3D.1. Buprenorphine Transmucosal Products for OUD Treatment

PRODUCT NAME/ ACTIVE INGREDIENT	ROUTE OF ADMINISTRATION/ FORM	AVAILABLE STRENGTHS	RECOMMENDED ONCE-DAILY MAINTENANCE DOSE
Bunavail[223] • Buprenorphine hydrochloride • Naloxone hydrochloride	Buccal film	2.1 mg/0.3 mg 4.2 mg/0.7 mg 6.3 mg/1 mg	**Target:** 8.4 mg/1.4 mg **Range:** 2.1 mg/0.3 mg to 12.6 mg/2.1 mg
Generic combination product[224,225] • Buprenorphine hydrochloride • Naloxone hydrochloride	Sublingual tablet	2 mg/0.5 mg 8 mg/2 mg	**Target:** 16 mg/4 mg **Range:** 4 mg/1 mg to 24 mg/6 mg*
Generic monoproduct[226,227] • Buprenorphine hydrochloride	Sublingual tablet	2 mg 8 mg	**Target:** 16 mg **Range:** 4 mg to 24 mg*
Suboxone[228,229] • Buprenorphine hydrochloride • Naloxone hydrochloride	Sublingual film	2 mg/0.5 mg 4 mg/1 mg 8 mg/2 mg 12 mg/3 mg	**Target:** 16 mg/4 mg **Range:** 4 mg/1 mg to 24 mg/6 mg*
Zubsolv[230,231] • Buprenorphine hydrochloride • Naloxone hydrochloride	Sublingual tablet	0.7 mg/0.18 mg 1.4 mg/0.36 mg 2.9 mg/0.71 mg 5.7 mg/1.4 mg 8.6 mg/2.1 mg 11.4 mg/2.9 mg	**Target:** 11.4 mg/2.9 mg **Range:** 2.9 mg/0.71 mg to 17.2 mg/4.2 mg

*Dosages above 24 mg buprenorphine or 24 mg/6 mg buprenorphine/naloxone per day have shown no clinical advantage.[232,233]

Adapted from material in the public domain.[234]

buprenorphine hydrochloride. The implants are for subdermal insertion on the inside of the upper arm and provide 6 months of buprenorphine. The implants must be removed after 6 months.

Peak buprenorphine plasma concentrations occur 12 hours after implant insertion, slowly decrease, and reach steady-state concentrations in about 4 weeks. Steady-state concentrations are comparable to trough buprenorphine plasma levels produced by daily sublingual buprenorphine doses of 8 mg or less. Implant effectiveness lasts up to 6 months.

Injectables

In November 2017, FDA approved extended-release (monthly) subcutaneous injectable buprenorphine for moderate-to-severe OUD treatment among patients who initiated treatment with transmucosal buprenorphine, followed by at least 7 days of dose adjustment. It is available in two doses, 300 mg/1.5 mL and 100 mg/0.5 mL. Both are stored refrigerated in prefilled syringes with safety needles and administered by subcutaneous injection in the abdomen. The first two monthly doses recommended are 300 mg each followed by a 100 mg monthly maintenance dose. Peak buprenorphine concentrations occur about 24 hours after the injection. Steady state is achieved after 4 to 6 months. After discontinuation, patients may have detectable plasma levels of buprenorphine for 12 months or longer. Duration of detection in urine is not known.[235]

Pharmacology

Buprenorphine, an opioid receptor partial agonist, is a schedule III controlled medication derived from the opium alkaloid thebaine. Through cross-tolerance and mu-opioid receptor occupancy, **at adequate doses, buprenorphine reduces opioid withdrawal and craving and blunts the effects of illicit opioids.**

Buprenorphine binds tightly to the mu-opioid receptor because of its particularly high receptor affinity. This prevents other opioids with lower affinity (e.g., heroin) from binding. The net result is a blunting or blocking of the euphoria, respiratory depression, and other effects of these opioids.

Buprenorphine has less potential to cause respiratory depression, given its ceiling effect. As a partial agonist, buprenorphine's maximum effect on respiratory depression is more limited than full agonists. Once reaching a moderate dose, its effects no longer increase if the dose is increased.[236,237,238]

There is wide individual variability in buprenorphine pharmacokinetics. For example, the mean time to maximum plasma buprenorphine concentration after a single sublingual dose ranges from 40 minutes to 3.5 hours.[239] Thus, after providing the first dose of buprenorphine, wait at least 2 hours to decide whether a second dose is necessary.

Buprenorphine has a long elimination half-life, which varies from 24 to 69 hours[240] with a mean half-life of 24 to 42 hours.[241] It dissociates slowly from the receptor.

Buprenorphine can be safely dosed (even at double the *stabilized* dose) less than daily.[242] For example, a patient *stabilized* on 12 mg of buprenorphine/naloxone daily can be treated with 24 mg every other day or 24 mg on Monday/Wednesday and 36 mg on Friday. Such schedules reduce travel burden for patients who need or want supervised dosing at an OTP or a clinic. Such schedules may also be useful for patients who must spend weekends in jails that disallow buprenorphine dosing.

Bioavailability

Buprenorphine has poor oral bioavailability compared with sublingual and buccal bioavailability. Naloxone, a short-acting mu-opioid receptor antagonist, has very poor oral, sublingual, and buccal bioavailability but is absorbed when injected or snorted. The addition of naloxone decreases buprenorphine's potential for misuse. In the Suboxone formulation of buprenorphine/naloxone, the ratio of buprenorphine to naloxone is 4:1. The ratio of buprenorphine to naloxone varies across products, as the absorption of both active ingredients is different for buccal versus sublingual films versus tablets.

Buprenorphine/naloxone transmucosal products are abuse-deterrent formulations, although they can still be misused. When a patient takes these formulations as prescribed, he or she absorbs buprenorphine but only a biologically negligible amount of naloxone. But if crushed or dissolved for intranasal or intravenous (IV) misuse, both medications are bioavailable. Naloxone then blunts the immediate opioid agonist effects of buprenorphine. It also induces opioid withdrawal in people who are physically dependent on opioids. This reduces misuse liability compared with transmucosal formulations with buprenorphine alone.[243,244]

Subdermal buprenorphine implants release buprenorphine in steady concentrations over 6 months. These concentrations are approximately equivalent to 8 mg or less of the buprenorphine sublingual formulations. Once implanted, these rods are unlikely to be diverted.

Extended-release buprenorphine for subcutaneous injection releases buprenorphine over at least a 1-month period. After injection, an initial buprenorphine plasma level peaks around 24 hours and then slowly declines to a plateau. With monthly injections, steady state is reached at 4 to 6 months.[245]

Metabolism and Excretion

Buprenorphine:[246,247]

- Is highly plasma bound.
- Crosses the blood–brain barrier readily because of its high lipid solubility.
- Is excreted in urine and feces.
- Has only one known pharmacologically active metabolite: norbuprenorphine.

Be aware of potential CYP450 3A4 inducers,[248] substrates, and inhibitors while monitoring for potential drug–drug interactions (see the "Drug Interactions" section below). Buprenorphine undergoes metabolism in the liver primarily by cytochrome P450 (CYP450) 3A4 enzymes. Coadministration of other medications metabolized along this pathway can affect the rate of buprenorphine metabolism.

Buprenorphine has fewer clinically relevant drug interactions than methadone in general. For detailed explanations of metabolism and excretion, see the package inserts for each buprenorphine product.

Dosing Considerations

Buprenorphine is used for the treatment of OUD. Formulations are available as sublingual tablets and film, buccal film, implants, and extended-release injection (Exhibit 3A.5 in Chapter 3A of this TIP).

Contraindications

Buprenorphine is contraindicated in patients who are allergic to it. Patients with true allergic reactions to naloxone should not be treated with the combination buprenorphine/naloxone product. Allergy to naloxone is infrequent. Some patients may falsely or mistakenly claim an allergy to naloxone and request buprenorphine monoproduct. Carefully assess such claims and explain the differences between an allergic reaction and symptoms of opioid withdrawal precipitated by buprenorphine or naloxone; the monoproduct has more abuse liability than buprenorphine/naloxone.[249]

Precautions and Warnings

- **Respiratory depression and overdoses are uncommon in adults, but they do happen.**[250] Most fatal overdoses involve IV buprenorphine misuse or concurrent central nervous system depressant use, including high doses of benzodiazepines, alcohol, or other sedatives.[251,252] However, fatal overdoses have been reported in opioid-naïve patients treated with 2 mg buprenorphine for pain.[253] Exhibit 3D.2 summarizes the management of patients with preexisting respiratory impairment.

- **Unintentional pediatric exposure can be life threatening or fatal.**[254] Thus, emphasize safe storage of medication, and teach patients to remove any buprenorphine found in a child's mouth immediately (even if it was only a partial tablet or film). Call 9-1-1 so the child can go to the nearest emergency department for immediate medical attention.

- **Cases of hepatitis and liver failure exist but often involve predisposing hepatic risk factors,** such as preexisting liver enzyme abnormalities, hepatitis B or C infections, and use of other potentially hepatotoxic drugs or IV drugs. A multisite randomized trial of hepatic effects in patients taking methadone or buprenorphine found no evidence of liver damage in the first 6 months of treatment. The authors concluded that prescribing these medications should not cause major concern for liver injury.[255] Exhibit 3D.2 summarizes management of patients with hepatic impairment.

EXHIBIT 3D.2. Medication Management for Patients With Respiratory or Hepatic Impairment

CONTRAINDICATION/CAUTION	MANAGEMENT
Compromised respiratory function For example, chronic obstructive pulmonary disease, decreased respiratory reserve, hypoxia, hypercapnia (abnormally elevated blood levels of carbon dioxide), preexisting respiratory depression.	• Prescribe with caution; monitor closely. • Warn patients about the risk of using benzodiazepines or other depressants while taking buprenorphine.[256] • Support patients in their attempts to discontinue tobacco use.
Hepatic impairment Buprenorphine and naloxone are extensively metabolized by the liver. Moderate-to-severe impairment results in decreased clearance, increased overall exposure to both medications, and higher risk of buprenorphine toxicity and precipitated withdrawal from naloxone. These effects have not been observed in patients with mild hepatic impairment.[257,258]	• Mild impairment (Child-Pugh score of 5–6):[259] No dose adjustment needed. • Moderate impairment (Child-Pugh score of 7–9):[260] Combination products are not recommended; they may precipitate withdrawal. *Use combination products cautiously for maintenance treatment in patients who've been inducted with a monoproduct;[261,262] monitor for signs and symptoms of buprenorphine toxicity or overdose.[263] Naloxone may interfere with buprenorphine's efficacy.[264,265] • Severe impairment (Child-Pugh score of 10–15):[266] Do not use the combination product.[267] For monoproduct, consider halving the starting and titration doses used in patients with normal liver function; monitor for signs and symptoms of toxicity or overdose caused by increased buprenorphine levels.[268]

*Moderate-to-severe impairment results in much more reduced clearance of naloxone than of buprenorphine. Nasser et al.[269] found that moderate impairment doubled or tripled exposure (compared with subjects with no or mild impairment) for both medications. In subjects with severe impairment, buprenorphine exposure was also two to three times higher; naloxone exposure increased more than tenfold.

Adapted from material in the public domain.[270]

- **Potential for misuse and diversion exists.** People can misuse buprenorphine via intranasal or IV routes or divert it for others to misuse. Do not give early or multiple refills without careful assessment and monitoring suited to the patient's level of stability.[271,272]
- Discourage misuse and diversion by:
  - Requiring frequent office visits until patients are stable.
  - Testing urine for buprenorphine and norbuprenorphine or buprenorphine glucuronide (both metabolites of buprenorphine).
  - Using other methods to ensure adequate adherence to the medication as prescribed, such as developing and adopting a diversion control plan (see Chapter 3E: Medical Management Strategies).
- **Adrenal insufficiency has been reported** with opioid use, most often after more than 1 month of buprenorphine maintenance.[273]
- **Patients will develop physical dependence on buprenorphine.** Alert patients that they'll experience opioid withdrawal if they stop buprenorphine.
- **Buprenorphine may affect cognition and psychomotor performance and can have sedating effects** in some people (particularly those who've lost tolerance after a period of abstinence from opioids). Concurrent use of illicit drugs, other prescribed medications, or medical or psychiatric comorbidity can affect cognition and psychomotor performance. Urge patients to exercise caution in using heavy machinery and driving until they're sure that their abilities are not compromised.[274]
- **Allergic reactions** have occurred in patients treated with buprenorphine, including rash, urticaria, angioedema, and anaphylaxis.
- **Buprenorphine can cause precipitated opioid withdrawal.** It has weaker opioid agonist effects and stronger receptor affinity than full agonists (e.g., heroin, methadone). It can displace full agonists from receptors, precipitating opioid withdrawal.[275] Factors affecting this possibility include:
  - Current level of opioid physical dependence. The higher the level of physical dependence, the higher the likelihood of precipitating withdrawal.[276] Ensuring that patients are in opioid withdrawal when initiating buprenorphine decreases this risk.
  - Time since the last mu-opioid receptor full agonist dose. The longer the time since the last dose, the lower the likelihood of precipitated withdrawal.[277]
  - Dose of buprenorphine administered. The smaller the dose of buprenorphine, the less likely it is to precipitate withdrawal.[278,279]
- **Neonatal abstinence syndrome (NAS) may occur in newborns of pregnant women who take buprenorphine.** Women receiving opioid agonist therapy while pregnant should talk with their healthcare provider about NAS and how to reduce it. Not all babies born to women treated with opioid agonists require treatment for NAS. Research has shown that the dose of opioid agonist medication is not reliably related to the severity of NAS.[280,281,282] Thus, each woman should receive the dose of medication that best manages her illness.

REDUCING NAS SEVERITY

Offer the following advice to pregnant women receiving treatment with an opioid agonist:

- Avoid smoking during pregnancy.
- Avoid benzodiazepines.
- Meet with the neonatologist and/or pediatrician to learn how the hospital assesses and treats NAS and what they suggest you can do as a parent to help soothe a baby with NAS.
- Request rooming-in with the child.
- Talk with the healthcare professional providing obstetric care about breastfeeding, as this may help make NAS less severe.
- In the first week after birth, keeping lights low, speaking softly, avoiding too much stimulation, and providing frequent skin-to-skin contact can help prevent or limit symptoms of NAS.

Drug Interactions

Buprenorphine has fewer documented clinically significant drug interactions than methadone,[283] but monitoring is still needed for patients who are starting or stopping medications that are CYP450 3A4 enzyme inhibitors or inducers for overdosing/underdosing of buprenorphine or coadministered medication. Exhibit 3D.3 lists these medications, including some anticonvulsants, antibiotics, and

EXHIBIT 3D.3. Partial List of Medications Metabolized by Cytochrome P450 3A4

Inhibitors (Potentially Increase Blood Levels of Buprenorphine)

Amiodarone	Fluoxetine	Miconazole	Ritonavir
Atazanavir	Fluvoxamine	Nefazodone	Saquinavir
Atazanavir/ritonavir	Grapefruit juice	Nelfinavir	Sertraline
Clarithromycin	Indinavir	Nicardipine	Verapamil
Delavirdine	Itraconazole	Norfloxacin	Zafirlukast
Erythromycin	Ketoconazole	Omeprazol	Zileuton
Fluconazole	Metronidazole	Paroxetine	

Substrates

Alprazolam	Disopyramide	Loratadine	Prednisone
Amlodipine	Doxorubicin	Losartan	Progestins
Astemizole	Erythromycin	Lovastatin	Quinidine
Atorvastatin	Estrogens	Miconazole	Rifampin
Carbamazepine	Etoposide	Midazolam	Ritonavir
Cisapride	Felodipine	Navelbine	R-Warfarin
Clindamycin	Fentanyl	Nefazodone	Saquinavir
Clonazepam	Fexofenadine	Nelfinavir	Sertraline
Cyclobenzaprine	Glyburide	Nicardipine	Simvastatin
Cyclosporine	Ifosfamide	Nifedipine	Tacrolimus
Dapsone	Indinavir	Nimodipine	Tamoxifen
Delavirdine	Ketoconazole	Ondansetron	Verapamil
Dexamethasone	Lansoprazole	Oral contraceptives	Vinblastine
Diazepam	Lidocaine	Paclitaxel	Zileuton
Diltiazem			

Inducers (Potentially Decrease Blood Levels of Buprenorphine)

Carbamazepine	Ethosuximide	Phenobarbital	Primidone
Dexamethasone	Nevirapine	Phenytoin	Rifampin
Efavirenz			

Note: Consult a point-of-service medical reference application for the most up-to-date drug–drug interactions before making medication management decisions.

Adapted from material in the public domain.[284]

HIV medications, and Exhibit 3D.4 lists more HIV medications. More information on drug–drug interactions is available online (www.drugs.com/drug-interactions/buprenorphine-index.html?filter=3&generic_only=).

Monitor responses to buprenorphine in patients taking nonnucleoside reverse transcriptase inhibitors. Changes in buprenorphine concentrations can be clinically significant.[285]

Combination antiretroviral therapy (atazanavir/ritonavir) increases buprenorphine and norbuprenorphine serum concentrations.[286] Case reports have demonstrated signs of buprenorphine excess (sedation). Decreasing buprenorphine can improve this symptom.[287] Other research has demonstrated no need to adjust the buprenorphine dose among patients taking atazanavir.[288]

For tuberculosis treatment, rifampin but not rifabutin may decrease buprenorphine concentrations. Rifampin produced opioid withdrawal in 50 percent of research volunteers with opioid dependence.[289]

FDA warns of increased serotonin syndrome risk with prescription opioids, including buprenorphine. Serotonin syndrome can include:

- Changes in mental status.
- Fever.
- Tremor.
- Sweating.
- Dilated pupils.

EXHIBIT 3D.4. Potential Interactions Between Buprenorphine and HIV Medications

MEDICATION	TYPE	POTENTIAL INTERACTION
Atazanavir	Protease inhibitor	Increased buprenorphine concentrations. May cause cognitive impairment[290,291] or oversedation.[292,293] Slower titration or dose reduction of buprenorphine may be warranted.[294, 295]
Darunavir-ritonavir	Protease inhibitor	Some pharmacokinetic (PK) effect; dose adjustments unlikely to be needed, but clinical monitoring is recommended.[296]
Delavirdine	Nonnucleoside reverse transcriptase inhibitor	Increased buprenorphine concentrations, but no clinically significant effect. Dose adjustments unlikely to be needed. However, use with caution, as long-term effects (more than 7 days) are unknown.[297,298]
Efavirenz	Nonnucleoside reverse transcriptase inhibitor	Some PK effect; dose adjustments unlikely to be needed.[299]
Elvitegravir (with cobicistat)	Integrase inhibitor	Some PK effect; no dose adjustments needed.[300]
Nevirapine	Nonnucleoside reverse transcriptase inhibitor	Some PK effect; no dose adjustments needed.[301]
Ritonavir	Protease inhibitor	Some PK effect; no dose adjustments needed.[302]
Tipranavir	Protease inhibitor	Some PK effect; no dose adjustments needed.[303]

Adapted from material in the public domain.[304]

Serotonin syndrome can occur with simultaneous opioid and antidepressant treatment. There are only a few case reports of serotonin syndrome with buprenorphine,[305] but be aware of this possibility given the frequent treatment of mood disorders in patients with OUD.

Side Effects

Buprenorphine's side effects may be less intense than those of full agonists. Otherwise, they resemble those of other mu-opioid agonists. Possible side effects include the following (buprenorphine FDA labels list all potential side effects https://dailymed.nlm.nih.gov/dailymed/drugInfo.cfm?setid=8a5edcf9-828c-4f97-b671-268ab13a8ecd):

- Oral hypoesthesia (oral numbness)
- Constipation
- Glossodynia (tongue pain)
- Oral mucosal erythema
- Vomiting
- Intoxication
- Disturbance in attention
- Palpitations
- Insomnia
- Opioid withdrawal syndrome
- Excessive sweating
- Blurred vision

Serious implant-related adverse events are uncommon but possible according to the FDA label (www.accessdata.fda.gov/drugsatfda_docs/label/2016/204442Orig1s000lbl.pdf). Still, more than 10 percent of patients experience implant site pain, itching, or swelling. Migration beyond the local insertion site is rare but possible, as is nerve damage. Buprenorphine may be extruded from implants for potential misuse. Insert implants only in stable patients, for whom FDA has approved this formulation.

Implants may extrude and potentially come out (e.g., from incomplete insertion or infection). Tell patients to call the implanting physician if an implant looks like it is extruding or comes out. If the implant comes out, patients should safely store and dispose of it (following local and federal regulations) to protect others from unintended exposure.

Serious injection site adverse events for the extended-release formulation are uncommon but possible. The most common injection site adverse reactions were pain (7.2 percent), pruritus (6.6 percent), and erythema (4.7 percent) in phase three trials. Two cases of surgical removal of the monthly depot were reported in premarketing clinical studies. Surgical excision under local anesthesia within 14 days of injection is possible. It is recommended that, before treatment, baseline liver function tests be assessed with monthly monitoring during treatment, particularly with the 300 mg dose. There are limited data regarding use of the extended-release injection formulation in pregnant women with OUD. In animal reproductive studies with Sublocade's excipient, N-Methyl-2-pyrrolidone, there were reported fetal adverse reactions. Women should be advised that the use of Sublocade during pregnancy should be considered only if the benefits outweigh the risks (see FDA package insert for full details www.accessdata.fda.gov/drugsatfda_docs/label/2017/209819s000lbl.pdf).

Assessment

No evidence clearly predicts which patients are best matched to buprenorphine versus other OUD medications. Thorough assessment helps determine whether buprenorphine treatment is appropriate for a patient. (Part 2 of this TIP covers screening and assessment in more detail.) **Before prescribing buprenorphine:**

- **Check the state prescription drug monitoring program database.**
- **Assess the patient's history.**
  - Conduct a medical, psychiatric, substance use, and substance use treatment history.
  - Assess recent opioid use, including frequency, quantity, type, route, and last day of use.

- Establish OUD diagnosis.
- Assess for other substance use disorders (SUDs), including those involving alcohol, benzodiazepines, or stimulants.
- **Conduct a focused physical examination,** refer for a physical exam, or get a record of a recent one.
  - **Assess for signs and symptoms of intoxication.** Do not give a first dose to a patient who is sedated or intoxicated. Assess and treat him or her appropriately.
  - **Assess for evidence of opioid withdrawal and physiological dependence.** The Clinical Opioid Withdrawal Scale (COWS) or the Clinical Institute Narcotic Assessment (CINA) Scale for Withdrawal Symptoms can be used to assess withdrawal signs (see "Resource Alert: Opioid Withdrawal Scales"). The patient should exhibit signs of opioid withdrawal before taking the first dose of buprenorphine to avoid precipitated withdrawal. For example, the Risk Evaluation and Mitigation Strategy (REMS) for buprenorphine indicates that a COWS score of 12 or higher is typically adequate for a first dose. Confirming opioid withdrawal suggests that the patient is physically dependent on opioids and can begin induction with a typical 2 mg/0.5 mg or 4 mg/1 mg buprenorphine/naloxone dose.
- **Obtain laboratory tests.**
  - **Conduct drug and alcohol tests.** Use reliable urine tests for opioids (including morphine, methadone, buprenorphine, and oxycodone), benzodiazepines, cocaine, and other drugs commonly used in the area. Use a breathalyzer to estimate the patient's blood alcohol content. Do not provide buprenorphine until the alcohol reading is considerably below the legal level of alcohol intoxication.
  - **Conduct a pregnancy test.** Transmucosal buprenorphine or methadone maintenance treatment is recommended for OUD in pregnancy.[306] There are limited data regarding use in pregnant women with OUD with the buprenorphine implants and with the extended-release injection formulation. If buprenorphine is used during pregnancy, it should generally be transmucosal monoproduct.[307] Refer pregnant patients to prenatal care.
  - **Assess liver function.** If possible, obtain liver function tests, but do not wait for results before starting transmucosal buprenorphine treatment. A patient with chronic hepatitis can receive OUD treatment with buprenorphine. Discuss risks and benefits if the patient's liver enzymes are at or above five times the normal level and monitor liver function during treatment. Patients with transaminase levels less than five times normal levels, including patients with hepatitis C virus, appear to tolerate buprenorphine well.[308,309] Exhibit 3D.2 gives more information about hepatic impairment and buprenorphine. **Liver function tests should be obtained and reviewed before initiating buprenorphine implants or extended-release buprenorphine because these formulations are long acting.**

RESOURCE ALERT

Opioid Withdrawal Scales

The COWS and other opioid withdrawal scales can be downloaded from Annex 10 of WHO's *Guidelines for the Psychosocially Assisted Pharmacological Treatment of Opioid Dependence* from the National Center for Biotechnology Information website (www.ncbi.nlm.nih.gov/books/NBK143183).

The CINA Scale for Withdrawal Symptoms is also available online (www.ncpoep.org/wp-content/uploads/2015/02/Appendix_7_Clinical_Institute_Narcotic_Assessment_CINA_Scale_for_Withdrawal_Symptoms.pdf).

- **Conduct hepatitis and HIV tests.** Hepatitis B and C are common among patients entering buprenorphine treatment. HIV infection is also prevalent. If possible, test the patient for these infections and refer to treatment as appropriate. The Centers for Disease Control and Prevention recommends hepatitis B vaccination for individuals seeking treatment for SUDs.[310]

Patient Selection

No evidence clearly predicts which patients are best treated with buprenorphine versus other OUD medications. Inform all patients with OUD about treatment with transmucosal buprenorphine and where it's available. (See "Treatment Planning or Referral" in Part 2 of this TIP for more on shared decision making.)

Patients who responded well to buprenorphine in the past should be considered for this treatment.

Prior use of diverted buprenorphine doesn't rule out OUD treatment with buprenorphine. Diverted buprenorphine is often associated with an inability to access treatment,[311] and it's often used to self-treat opioid withdrawal rather than to "get high."[312,313]

Unsuccessful treatment experiences with buprenorphine in the past do not necessarily indicate that buprenorphine will be ineffective again. Motivation and circumstances change over time. Also, treatment varies by provider, clinic, and setting, as it does for other medical illnesses. Records from previous providers can contextualize the extent of past treatment.

Pregnant women should be considered for transmucosal buprenorphine treatment.

Stable patients are the best candidates for buprenorphine implants. Implants are indicated for patients who have already achieved illicit opioid abstinence and clinical stability while

> Do not taper patients to 8 mg daily solely to switch them to implants.

taking transmucosal buprenorphine for at least 90 days. Their current dose should be 8 mg/day or less.[314] There is no absolute definition of clinical stability, but per the implant package insert, patients may be stable if they are:[315]

- Abstaining currently from illicit opioids.
- Having little or no craving for illicit opioids.
- Living in a stable environment.
- Participating in a structured job or activity.
- Engaging in a positive social support system.
- Lacking recent hospitalizations, emergency department visits, or crisis interventions for substance use or mental illness.
- Adhering to clinic appointments and other aspects of treatment and recovery plans.

Informed Consent

Inform all patients of:

- Their OUD diagnosis and the nature of the disorder.
- Risks and benefits of all available medications for OUD.
- Risks and benefits of nonmedication treatments.

Educate patients about basic buprenorphine pharmacology and induction expectations (Exhibit 3D.5). They should understand the need to be in opioid withdrawal that's visible to the prescriber (or, for home induction, that meets predefined self-assessment criteria) to avoid precipitated withdrawal.

> Use language and written materials appropriate to each patient's comprehension level to ensure that he or she understands the options and can make informed decisions.

EXHIBIT 3D.5. Key Points of Patient Education for Buprenorphine

Before starting OUD treatment with buprenorphine, patients should:

- Tell providers the prescribed and over-the-counter medications they take to allow drug interaction assessment.
- Understand the goal of the first week of treatment: To improve withdrawal symptoms without oversedation.
- Tell providers if they feel sedated or euphoric within 1 to 4 hours after their dose.
- Be given the appropriate buprenorphine medication guide.
- Know possible side effects, including:
  - Headache.
  - Dizziness.
  - Nausea.
  - Vomiting.
  - Sweating.
  - Constipation.
  - Sexual dysfunction.
- Agree to store medication securely and out of the reach of others.
- Alert providers if they discontinue medications, start new ones, or change their medication dose.
- Understand that discontinuing buprenorphine increases risk of overdose death upon return to illicit opioid use.
- Know that use of alcohol or benzodiazepines with buprenorphine increases the risk of overdose and death.
- Understand the importance of informing providers if they become pregnant.
- Tell providers if they are having a procedure that may require pain medication.
- Be aware of resources through which to obtain further education for:
  - Themselves: *Decisions in Recovery: Treatment for Opioid Use Disorder* (https://store.samhsa.gov/product/SMA16-4993)
  - Their families and friends: *Medication-Assisted Treatment for Opioid Addiction: Facts for Families and Friends* (http://www.ct.gov/dmhas/lib/dmhas/publications/MAT-InfoFamilyFriends.pdf)

Initiating Buprenorphine Treatment

It can be helpful to use a buprenorphine treatment agreement for patients treated in office-based settings (see Chapter 3D Appendix for a sample treatment agreement).

Induction can occur in the office or at home. Most clinical trials were conducted with office-based induction, and extant guidance recommends this approach.[316] However, office-based induction can be a barrier to treatment initiation. Home induction is increasingly common.[317]

Office-Based Induction

Providers can perform office-based induction by ordering and storing induction doses in the office or by prescribing medication and instructing patients to bring it to the office on the day of induction. **Office-based induction allows providers to:**

- **Ensure that patients know how to take medication** without swallowing or spitting it out if they have too much saliva or experience unpleasant tastes. Tell them to wait to eat or drink until the medication is totally dissolved.
- **Enhance the therapeutic relationship.**
- **Verify the presence of opioid withdrawal and absence of precipitated opioid withdrawal.**
- **Ensure the lack of sedation 1 to 2 hours after the first dose in patients taking sedatives.**
- **Use time between doses for patient self-assessment.** See the Chapter 3D Appendix for sample goal-setting forms that help patients identify treatment goals and triggers for use.

Home Induction

Home induction can be safe and effective.[318] Retention rates are similar to office inductions,[319] but no comparison data from large randomized controlled studies exist. The American Society of Addiction Medicine National Practice Guideline recommends home induction only if the patient or prescriber has experience with using buprenorphine.[320,321] Clinical experience indicates that patients suitable for home induction:

- Can describe, understand, and rate withdrawal.
- Can understand induction dosing instructions.
- Can and will contact their provider about problems.

Educate patients about how to assess their withdrawal, when to start the first dose, how to take the medication properly, and how to manage withdrawal on induction day. Instruct patients to take their first dose when they experience opioid withdrawal at least 12 hours after last use of heroin or a short-acting prescription opioid. Effectively switching from methadone to buprenorphine can be challenging. This should generally be started with office-based induction. Consult with a medical expert knowledgeable about methadone in these situations until experience is gained. Withdrawal can include:

- Goose bumps.
- Nausea.
- Abdominal cramps.
- Running nose.
- Tearing.
- Yawning.

Be available for phone consultation during the induction period and for an in-office evaluation should the need arise. See patients in the office within approximately 7 days of the start of home induction. (See the Chapter 3D Appendix for a sample buprenorphine/naloxone home dosage schedule.)

> **Advise patients to abstain from tobacco before dosing.** Many patients with OUD use tobacco products. Nicotine causes vasoconstriction, decreasing the surface area of blood vessels that absorb buprenorphine.

Induction

Patients who are currently physically dependent on opioids

Patients should begin buprenorphine when they are exhibiting clear signs of opioid withdrawal. Induction typically starts with a 2 mg to 4 mg dose of buprenorphine or a 2 mg/0.5 mg to 4 mg/1 mg dose of buprenorphine/naloxone.[322] Depending on the formulation used and whether a given patient has a dry mouth, the dose can take between 3 and 10 minutes to dissolve fully. After approximately 2 hours, an additional 2 mg to 4 mg dose of buprenorphine/naloxone can be given if there is continued withdrawal and lack of sedation.

Always individualize dosing. The FDA label recommends a maximum buprenorphine/naloxone dose of 8 mg on Day 1 and 16 mg on Day 2.[323] When dosing outside of FDA recommendations, document the clinical rationale, including risks and benefits. Remember that some patients stabilize on lower doses.

If patients experience sedation upon first dose, stop and reevaluate the following:

- Did they recently take other sedating medications (e.g., benzodiazepines)?
- Have they recently been in a controlled environment, such as a hospital, jail, or residential drug treatment facility?
- Was the history of recency and amount of opioid use inaccurate?
- Was the heroin used of poor quality?
- Was their use mostly of low-potency opioids (e.g., codeine)?

Consider whether a dose decrease, change in treatment plan, or both are necessary. If induction is still indicated, adjust the dose more slowly as needed to minimize sedation. The dose can be adjusted on subsequent days to address continued withdrawal or uncontrollable craving if the patient is not sedated.

Patients with a history of OUD who are not currently physically dependent on opioids

Buprenorphine induction can be appropriate for certain patients with a history of opioid addiction at high risk for return to use of opioids but not currently dependent on them. This includes patients who've been incarcerated or in other controlled environments.[324] Before starting treatment, discuss risks and benefits of buprenorphine and other medications (including extended-release naltrexone [XR-NXT]). Buprenorphine doses should begin at lower-than-usual levels (e.g., 1 mg). They should be increased more slowly than in tolerant patients to avoid oversedation and possible overdose. Take particular care with patients who are being treated with other central nervous system depressant medications.[325] At the beginning of treatment, directly administer doses in an OTP or in the office. This will allow patients to be observed for sedation after dosing and will reduce the risk that patients take more medication than prescribed.

In one study, research participants not currently physically dependent on opioids but with a history of OUD were started on 1 mg buprenorphine with weekly 1 mg dose increases to 4 mg, followed by 2 mg weekly increases to 8 mg. Most patients tolerated this dose induction, and the mean daily dose exceeded 8 mg per day by the fifth week, when the planned dose was 6 mg.[326] As with all opioid agonist treatment, dosing should be individualized and based on careful patient assessment during treatment.

Patients who are currently taking methadone

Some patients who take methadone may wish to switch to buprenorphine treatment for a variety of reasons. This often requires methadone dose reduction before switching medications, which may increase the risk of return to opioid use. Exercise caution with this approach and thoroughly discuss the risks and benefits with the patients before embarking on the change in medication. Experienced prescribers should conduct this procedure in the office, not via home induction. The lower the methadone dose and the longer it's been since the last dose, the easier the transition.

Before initiating buprenorphine, carefully taper methadone to lower the risk of return to illicit opioid use during transition. Patients who take methadone for OUD should taper to 30 mg to 40 mg methadone per day and remain on that dose for at least 1 week before starting buprenorphine.[327] With patients' permission, OTPs can confirm the time and amount of patients' last methadone dose.

Do not start buprenorphine until the patient manifests signs of opioid withdrawal. At least 24 hours should pass between the last dose of methadone and the first dose of buprenorphine. Waiting 36 hours or more reduces risk of precipitated withdrawal. Lower doses of buprenorphine/naloxone are less likely to precipitate methadone withdrawal.[328] For example, once opioid withdrawal is verified, an initial dose of 2 mg/0.5 mg can be given. If patients continue to have unrelieved opioid withdrawal after the first 2 mg dose, administer another 2 mg/0.5 mg dose approximately every 2 hours as needed (holding for sedation). Induction should be conducted slowly; consider palliating unrelieved withdrawal with nonopioid therapies for the first few days of transition to buprenorphine. Be alert to any increase in withdrawal symptoms, as this may suggest precipitated withdrawal.

Dose Stabilization

Stabilization occurs when there is evidence of:

- Markedly reduced or eliminated illicit opioid use.
- Reduced craving.
- Suppression of opioid withdrawal.
- Minimal side effects.
- Patient-reported blunted or blocked euphoria during illicit opioid use.

Remind patients to take their dose once daily rather than splitting it. Document reduced illicit drug use via patient self-report and urine drug testing. Consecutive negative urine test results suggest a positive prognosis.

Continue monitoring dose effectiveness during early stabilization. Dose adjustments may still be necessary (Exhibit 3D.6). Buprenorphine treatment should substantially reduce opioid cravings. See Chapter 3E: Medical Management Strategies for detailed information on the management of patients taking buprenorphine in office-based treatment settings.

Once patients have stabilized, continue to screen and evaluate for mental disorders and psychosocial problems that may need to be addressed (e.g., having a spouse or cohabitant who is using illicit opioids). Support patients' engagement in prosocial activities and progress toward treatment goals and recovery as they decrease use of illicit substances.

Offer referrals for adjunctive counseling and recovery support services as needed. It may not be possible to eliminate opioid craving completely, regardless of the dose. Counseling can help patients reduce and manage craving.

EXHIBIT 3D.6. Adjusting the Buprenorphine Dose

When to increase the dose:

- Are patients taking medication correctly and as scheduled?
  - If they take at least 16 mg per day, mu-opioid receptors are approximately 80 to 95 percent occupied.[329]
  - If there are adherence problems, assess causes and intervene to promote adherence and proper administration (e.g., offer supervised dosing at the clinic, by a network support, at a pharmacy).
  - **If patients are taking doses correctly, a dose increase may be indicated, if certain conditions exist.**
- Are patients taking other medications that may interfere with buprenorphine metabolism?
- If patients are taking doses properly, **increase the dose if they still have opioid withdrawal** (document with a clinical tool like COWS), **opioid craving, or "good" effects (e.g., feeling "high") from using illicit opioids.**
  - **Craving can be a conditioned response.** It may not decrease with dose increases if patients spend time with people who use opioids in their presence.
  - Dose increases typically occur in 2 mg to 4 mg increments.
  - It will take about 5 to 7 days to reach steady-state plasma concentrations after a dose increase.
  - Offer psychosocial referrals to help decrease and manage cravings.
- **Determine whether nonpharmacological problems are contributing to the need for increase.**
  - For example, do patients show signs and symptoms of untreated major depressive or generalized anxiety disorders? Are they living in a chaotic household? Do they have childcare problems or financial difficulties? Are they experiencing trauma or trauma-related mental disorders?
  - **Address or refer to counseling to address these problems.**

When to decrease the dose:

- Decrease the dose **when there is evidence of dose toxicity** (i.e., sedation or, rarely, clearly linked clinically relevant increases in liver function tests).
- Hold the dose **when there is acute alcohol or benzodiazepine intoxication.**

A more important measure of dose adequacy than craving is whether patients report that the feeling of euphoria associated with self-administered illicit opioids is blunted or blocked. **Patients who were not interested in adjunctive addiction or mental health counseling during induction may become receptive to it when they are feeling more stable.**

Be cautious when increasing doses above 24 mg/6 mg per day. Nearly all patients stabilize on daily doses of 4 mg/1 mg to 24 mg/6 mg. Very limited data show additional benefits of doses higher than the FDA label's recommended maximum of 24 mg/6 mg.[330] Carefully document clinical justification for higher doses and always have a diversion control plan in place. Doses above 24 mg/6 mg a day may unintentionally heighten diversion risk. Patients not responding to high doses of buprenorphine at the upper limit approved by FDA should be considered for methadone treatment.

Risk Evaluation and Mitigation Strategy

Practitioners should **become familiar with the FDA-approved REMS for buprenorphine.** It provides useful information and checklists for providers. REMS can be found online for:

- Buprenorphine monoproduct and buprenorphine/naloxone (www.accessdata.fda.gov/scripts/cder/rems/index.cfm?event=IndvRemsDetails.page&REMS=352)
- Transmucosal buprenorphine (www.accessdata.fda.gov/scripts/cder/rems/index.cfm?event=RemsDetails.page&REMS=9)
- Buprenorphine implants (www.accessdata.fda.gov/scripts/cder/rems/index.cfm?event=IndvRemsDetails.page&REMS=356)
- Buprenorphine extended-release injection (www.accessdata.fda.gov/scripts/cder/rems/index.cfm?event=indvremsdetails.page&rems=376)

See also "Buprenorphine Induction and Maintenance Appropriate Use Checklists" in Chapter 3D Appendix.

Transmucosal Buprenorphine Dosing Summary

Induction and stabilization

The goal is to reduce or eliminate opioid withdrawal and craving without causing sedation:

- Induction and stabilization strategies can vary based on patient variables and use of short- versus long-acting opioids. For more discussion on induction models, see the Providers' Clinical Support System's Models of Buprenorphine Induction (http://pcssmat.org/wp-content/uploads/2015/01/Models-of-Buprenorphine-Induction.pdf).
- The combination buprenorphine/naloxone product is safe to use for induction for most patients.
- The buprenorphine monoproduct (without naloxone) has been recommended for the treatment of pregnant women[331] because of the danger to the fetus of precipitated opioid withdrawal if the combination product were to be injected. Although there are some publications with small sample sizes that indicate that the combination product appears to be safe in pregnancy,[332,333] the safety data are insufficient at this time to recommend its use.[334] This is an area of some uncertainty. An expert panel on the treatment of OUD in pregnancy was unable to agree whether pregnant women should be treated with the monoproduct or combination product.[335]
- Prescribers should observe the patient taking the medication to ensure proper use, especially if the patient is new to buprenorphine treatment. It can be helpful to do this periodically after induction, especially when the prescribed dose is not providing the expected benefit.
- Before the first dose, the patient should be in opioid withdrawal (to avoid precipitated withdrawal).

- The first dose is typically 4 mg/1 mg (2 mg if withdrawal is from methadone).
- Repeat dose as needed for continuing withdrawal every 2 hours up to typically 8 mg on the first day.

At the start of the next day, patients typically take the first day's total dose all at once:

- If necessary, an additional 2 mg to 4 mg can be given every 2 hours up to approximately a 16 mg total daily dose to treat continuing opioid withdrawal and craving on Day 2 or 3, barring sedation.
- The initial stabilization dose can often be achieved within the first several days of treatment.

Maintenance

Typical maintenance doses range from 4 mg/1 mg to 24 mg/6 mg per day. An effective maintenance dose is the lowest dose that can:

- Eliminate withdrawal.
- Reduce or eliminate opioid craving.
- Reduce or stop illicit opioid use's desirable effects.
- Be well tolerated (e.g., not produce sedation).

Duration of treatment

- Treatment should last for as long as patients benefit from treatment.
- Longer treatment length is associated with positive treatment outcomes.

Initiation of Buprenorphine Implants

Prescribers and implanters of buprenorphine implants require special certification to make this formulation available to their patients. In addition, implanters must get special training in the Probuphine REMS program to obtain certification to implant and remove this formulation. After completing training, providers can order implants through a central pharmacy for delivery, along with an implant insertion kit that contains all necessary implant procedure materials except a local anesthetic. If the prescriber is not performing the procedure, the prescriber should ensure that the implanter has completed the required training. For more information, see the Probuphine REMS program webpage (http://probuphinerems.com/probuphine-locator).

The prescriber and implanter/remover must record the number of implanted/removed rods and their serial numbers and location, the date of the implant, and who performed the procedure. The implanter should document implant and inspection procedures, as with any other standard procedure.

Instruct patients to take the last transmucosal dose of buprenorphine 12 to 24 hours before insertion. Remind them to shower and thoroughly wash the nondominant arm, which is preferred for insertion.

Implant procedure

Subdermal insertion of the four rods takes less than 30 minutes. Local anesthetic (lidocaine) is typically used. The implant procedure includes the following steps:

- Provide education about what to expect during the procedure.
- Obtain appropriate consent form(s).
- Provide a local anesthetic (e.g., lidocaine).
- Using sterile procedures, make a single incision in the inner upper arm between the biceps and triceps muscles, about 8 cm to 10 cm from the medial epicondyle.
- Using a cannula and an obturator, insert rods serially, pivoting the cannula slightly after each rod insertion in the subdermal space so that the rods lie next to one another, nearly parallel in a fanlike pattern.
- After implantation, apply butterfly strips and a pressure bandage.
- **Review wound care with the patient,** and provide a copy of the instructions.
- **Advise the patient not to drive or engage in heavy physical activity** for approximately 24 hours.
- **Do not give the patient a prescription for transmucosal buprenorphine** at this time.

Wound care

The patient should return within 1 week of the implant procedure for a wound care check. Check for signs of infection, trouble healing, or implant extrusion. The rods are subdermal, so they should remain palpable. Document that all four rods were palpated.

Stabilization

Maintain contact with patients after implant placement. Even among highly stable patients, return to illicit opioid use can occur. Explain the risk of unintentional overdose if patients return to illicit opioid or alcohol or benzodiazepine use while implants are in place. It is important to monitor the patient between implant placements.

Schedule office visits no less than once a month for continued assessment of maintenance of stability, manual palpation of the four implanted rods, and ongoing psychosocial support and counseling per the FDA label (www.accessdata.fda.gov/drugsatfda_docs/label/2016/204442Orig1s000lbl.pdf). If the patient returns to illicit opioid use, consider whether adequate psychosocial treatment has been given.

Consider transmucosal medication supplementation if a patient with implants destabilizes and reports inadequate opioid blockade. In one study,[336] 17.9 percent of participants with buprenorphine implants needed supplemental sublingual buprenorphine/naloxone. Most required small doses, such as 2 mg/0.5 mg per day. Consider more frequent assessment and higher intensity of treatment for patients who continue using illicit opioids or other substances.

Removal

After 6 months, have a certified implanter remove them. Implantation of a second set of rods in the opposite arm can then occur. There is no experience with inserting additional implants into other sites or second insertion into a previously used arm. After one insertion in each arm, most patients should transition to a transmucosal buprenorphine-containing product for continued treatment. Patients should follow the same directions to prepare for implant removal as they did for insertion. The removal procedure may require stitches. Patients should visit the clinic for removal of stitches and wound assessment within 1 week of removal. Store and dispose of rods safely in accordance with local and federal regulations.

Initiation of Buprenorphine Extended-Release Injection

Healthcare settings and pharmacies need special certification to order and dispense extended-release injectable buprenorphine to ensure long-acting preparations are dispensed directly to healthcare providers for administration and by healthcare providers to patients (see www.accessdata.fda.gov/scripts/cder/rems/index.cfm?event=indvremsdetails.page&rems=376 for more details).

Before initiating extended-release buprenorphine treatment, patients with moderate-to-severe OUD should be stabilized on transmucosal buprenorphine (8 mg to 24 mg daily) for at least 7 days. Do not use in opioid-naïve patients. Obtain liver function and pregnancy tests. Extended-release buprenorphine is not recommended for patients with severe hepatic impairment and may not be appropriate for patients with moderate hepatic impairment because of the long-acting nature of this formulation. There are insufficient data on its use in pregnancy to recommend initiating this formulation during pregnancy.

Inform patients that:

- The medication is only available in a restricted program (the Sublocade REMS Program) via specific pharmacies and healthcare providers, as intravenous self-injection by patients can cause death.
- After abdominal injection, a lump may be present at the injection site for a few weeks. It will get gradually smaller. Patients should not rub or massage it or let belts or waistbands rub against it.

- Patients should tell their healthcare providers that they are being treated with this medication.
- Using alcohol, benzodiazepines, sleeping pills, antidepressants, or some other medications with extended-release buprenorphine can lead to drowsiness or overdose.
- The most common side effects are constipation, headache, nausea, vomiting, increased liver enzymes, tiredness, and injection site itching or pain.
- Patients should inform their provider if they become pregnant during treatment with this formulation. They should have a risk/benefit discussion about continuing with this formulation given the limited safety data on its impact on the developing fetus. They should be informed that their newborn can have symptoms of opioid withdrawal at birth.

Storage
Follow package insert directions for medication storage under refrigeration. Keep at room temperature for at least 15 minutes before injection (discard if left at room temperature for more than 7 days).

Administration
Rotate the abdominal subcutaneous injection site with each injection, following the instructions in the package insert. Record the location of each injection in the medical record. Each of the first two monthly doses (with at least 26 days between doses) should be 300 mg. Subsequent monthly doses should be 100 mg. Some patients may benefit from increasing the maintenance dose to 300 mg monthly if they have tolerated the 100 mg dose but continue to use illicit opioids.

Medical management
Monitor patient progress and response to treatment during regular office visits and with periodic urine drug testing. Examine the injection site for reactions, infections, or evidence of attempts to remove the depot medication. If the medication is discontinued, the patient should continue to be seen and evaluated for several months for sustained progress in treatment and for signs and symptoms of opioid withdrawal, which should be treated as clinically appropriate.

Duration of Buprenorphine Treatment

There is no known duration of therapy with buprenorphine (or methadone or XR-NTX) after which patients can stop medication and be certain not to return to illicit opioid use. Those who stay in treatment often abstain longer from illicit opioid use and show increasing clinical stability. Long-term treatment outcomes up to 8 years after buprenorphine treatment entry show lower illicit opioid use among those with more time on medication.[337]

Patients should take buprenorphine as long as they benefit from it and wish to continue.

Successful Buprenorphine Treatment

The goal of buprenorphine treatment is full remission from OUD. Maintaining illicit opioid abstinence is ideal, but imperfect abstinence does not preclude treatment benefits. Patients should do better in treatment than before treatment. If not, seek alternatives.

Do not judge treatment progress and success on the amount of medication a patient needs or how long treatment is required. Rather, gauge treatment progress and success based on patients' achievement of specific goals that were agreed on in a shared decision-making and treatment planning process.

> Given the often-chronic nature of OUD and the potentially fatal consequences of unintended opioid overdose, it is critical that you **base patients' length of time in treatment on their individual needs.**

Consider this analogy: A patient with poorly controlled diabetes was previously unable to work and was admitted to the hospital several times for diabetic ketoacidosis. When taking insulin regularly, the patient worked part time, had fewer hospitalizations for diabetic ketoacidosis despite a nondiabetic diet, and had lower (but still high) hemoglobin A1C. This patient's treatment with insulin is not a "failure" because perfect control and function were not restored, and the patient would not be discharged from care against his or her will.

Dose Tapering and Buprenorphine Discontinuation

Following short-term medically supervised withdrawal, patients frequently restart illicit opioid use.[338] In contrast to short-term medically supervised withdrawal, dose tapering refers to gradually reducing the buprenorphine dose in patients who have been stabilized on the medication for some time.

Base decisions to decrease dose or stop buprenorphine on patients' circumstances and preferences. Successful dose reductions may be more likely when patients have sustained abstinence from opioids and other drugs, psychosocial support, housing, effective coping strategies, stable mental health, employment, and involvement in mutual-help programs or other meaningful activities.[339] However, there is no guarantee that even patients with years of abstinence, full-time employment, stable housing, and psychosocial supports can remain abstinent after discontinuing buprenorphine.

It is up to patients to decide whether to taper or eventually discontinue medication. Help them make informed choices by educating them about the process and fully including them in decision making. Invite them to reenter treatment if they believe they may return or have already returned to opioid use.

Before beginning to taper the dose of medication, explore these considerations with patients:

- **How have they responded to treatment so far?** Are they in full remission from OUD? Do they have adequate mental and social supports to remain in remission and maintain recovery?
- **Why do they want to taper?** They may be motivated by inconvenience, expense, loss of insurance coverage, side effects, feelings of shame, pressure from family, and lack of recovery supports. Many of these reasons are not predictive of a successful outcome.
- **What do they expect to be different** after tapering or discontinuing buprenorphine?
- **Do they understand the risks and benefits** of dose decrease and discontinuation of buprenorphine?
- **What strategies do they have for engaging family members and recovery supports to reduce the risk of return to illicit substance use?**
- **Do they grasp the risk of overdose associated with a return to illicit opioid use?**
- **Do they have a safety plan?** To reduce overdose risk after a return to use, plans should include:
  - A prescription for naloxone or a naloxone kit.
  - Instructions on recognizing and responding to an overdose.
  - Information on naloxone use for family members and others in the patient's recovery support network.
  - See the *SAMHSA Opioid Overdose Prevention Toolkit* (https://store.samhsa.gov/shin/content/SMA16-4742/SMA16-4742.pdf) for more guidance.
  - If patients return to opioid use, it may be appropriate for them to restart buprenorphine or switch to methadone or XR-NTX treatment. These options should be discussed with them.

- **Have they thought about how they will feel if they attempt to taper off of medication but cannot do so?** Convey to patients that the inability to taper is not a failure and that they should not be afraid or embarrassed to discuss stopping the taper.

Document the discussion, patient education, and decision in the medical record.

There is no ideal tapering protocol. Providers and patients should understand this before beginning a taper. Whether buprenorphine is ultimately discontinued, patients need additional psychosocial and recovery support during this time. Generally, taper occurs over several months to permit patients to acclimate to the lower dose and to reduce potential discomfort from opioid withdrawal and craving.

For patients who wish to discontinue buprenorphine, national and international guidelines recommend gradual dose reductions and advice to patients that they can stop the taper at any time.[340,341,342]

Consider increased monitoring and proactive discussions about how to address and manage cravings and withdrawal symptoms. Taper protocols vary in duration and may include use of ancillary medication, such as clonidine, if needed (Exhibit 3A.2).[343]

Continue to monitor patients who successfully taper off buprenorphine completely. Establish a post-taper monitoring and support plan (see Chapter 3E for more information on medical management strategies). Continue to assess and monitor patients' progress and how they cope with stress and triggers to use. Discuss the role of XR-NTX in preventing return to opioid use after completing treatment with an opioid agonist (see Chapter 3C for more information on naltrexone).

Chapter 3D Appendix

Buprenorphine Induction and Maintenance Appropriate Use Checklists

Patient Name: _____

BTOD|REMS

APPROPRIATE USE CHECKLIST:
BUPRENORPHINE-CONTAINING TRANSMUCOSAL PRODUCTS FOR OPIOID DEPENDENCE

This checklist is a useful reminder of the safe use conditions and monitoring requirements for prescribing buprenorphine-containing transmucosal products for opioid dependence.

Requirements to address during each patient's appointment include:
- understanding and reinforcement of safe use conditions
- the importance of psychosocial counseling
- screening and monitoring patients to determine progress towards treatment goals

If a patient continues to abuse various drugs or is unresponsive to treatment, including psychosocial intervention, it is important that you assess the need to refer the patient to a specialist and/or a more intensive behavioral treatment environment.

Additional resource: Physician Clinical Support System: http://pcssb.org/

This checklist may be used during the induction period and filed in patient's medical record to document safe use conditions. Once a maintenance dose has been established, use the maintenance checklist.

MEASUREMENT TO ENSURE APPROPRIATE USE	NOTES
Date:	
INDUCTION	
☐ Verified patient meets appropriate diagnostic criteria for opioid dependence	
☐ Discussed risks described in professional labeling and Medication Guide with patient	
☐ Explained or reviewed conditions of safe storage of medication, including keeping it out of the sight and reach of children	
☐ Provided induction doses under appropriate supervision	
☐ Prescribed limited amount of medication at first visit	
☐ Scheduled next visit at interval commensurate with patient stability • Weekly, or more frequent visits recommended for the first month	

Continued on next page

Part 3 of 5—Pharmacotherapy for Opioid Use Disorder

TIP 63

Patient Name: _____

BTOD|REMS

APPROPRIATE USE CHECKLIST:
BUPRENORPHINE-CONTAINING TRANSMUCOSAL PRODUCTS FOR OPIOID DEPENDENCE

This checklist may be used for visits following the induction period and filed in patient's medical record to document safe use conditions.

MEASUREMENT TO ENSURE APPROPRIATE USE	NOTES
Date: Visit #	
MAINTENANCE	
☐ Assessed and encouraged patient to take medication as prescribed • Consider pill/film count/dose reconciliation	

☐ Assessed appropriateness of dosage
• Buprenorphine combined with naloxone is recommended for maintenance:
  • Buprenorphine/Naloxone SL tablet and film (Suboxone®): doses ranging from 12 mg to 16 mg of buprenorphine are recommended for maintenance
  • Buprenorphine/Naloxone SL tablet (Zubsolv®): a target dose of 11.4 mg buprenorphine is recommended for maintenance
  • Buprenorphine/Naloxone Buccal Film (Bunavail®): a target dose of 8.4 mg of buprenorphine is recommended for maintenance
• Doses higher than this should be an exception
• The need for higher dose should be carefully evaluated	

☐ Conduct urine drug screens as appropriate to assess use of illicit substances	
☐ Assessed participation in professional counseling and support services	
☐ Assessed whether benefits of treatment with buprenorphine-containing products outweigh risks associated with buprenorphine-containing products	
☐ Assessed whether patient is making adequate progress toward treatment goals • Considered results of urine drug screens as part of the evidence of the patient complying with the treatment program • Consider referral to more intensive forms of treatment for patients not making progress	
☐ Scheduled next visit at interval commensurate with patient stability • Weekly, or more frequent visits are recommended for the first month	

2

Available online (www.accessdata.fda.gov/drugsatfda_docs/rems/BTOD_2017-01-23_Appropriate_Use_Checklist.pdf).
Reprinted from material in the public domain.[344]

Sample Goal Sheet and Coping Strategies Form

Patient's Name: _____ **Date:** _____

3-MONTH GOALS

1 _____
_____

2 _____
_____

3 _____
_____

6-MONTH GOALS

1 _____
_____

2 _____
_____

3 _____
_____

1-YEAR GOALS

1 _____
_____

2 _____
_____

3 _____
_____

List of Triggers to Using Drugs
_____

People To Stay Away From
_____

Places To Stay Away From
_____

Ways To Cope or Manage Stress Without Using Drugs
_____

M. Lofwall, February 27, 2017 (personal communication). Adapted with permission.

Sample Goal-Setting Form

Patient's Name: _____ Date: _____

GOAL CATEGORY	CURRENT SITUATION SCORE 10 = major problems and 0 = no problems	What would need to change to decrease this score?	PRIORITY SCORE 10 = highest priority ("I really want to work on this") and 1 = lowest priority ("I really do not want to work on this")
Opioid use			
Other illicit drug use: _____			
Alcohol use			
Tobacco use			
Physical health			
Mental health			
Legal/court issues			
Finances			
Job/employment			
Hobbies			
Family relations			
Partner relations			
Supportive drug-free network			
Education			
Keeping medication safe (e.g., not giving it away, selling it, having it stolen)			
Other			
Other			

M. Lofwall, February 27, 2017 (personal communication). Adapted with permission.

Buprenorphine/Naloxone Home Dosage Schedule: Films or Tablets

Name: _____ **Date:** _____

Procedure for taking buprenorphine:
- Let the medication dissolve under your tongue for at least 10 minutes. Do not suck on it.*
- Do not eat, drink, or smoke cigarettes for 30 minutes after you take your medication.
- Wait 2 hours between each dose.

The maximum dose is 16 mg/4 mg. If you reach this dose, you cannot increase further without calling the office first.

The office phone number is _____ [insert phone number].

Day 1 Induction Day (In Office): You have taken a total dose of _____ mg.

Day 2 in the Morning: Take the total dose you took on **Day 1** = _____ mg.
- If you experience withdrawal 2 hours later, you may take one 2 mg/0.5 mg film or tablet.
- Record your withdrawal symptoms: _____.
- If you continue to experience withdrawal 2 hours later, you may take one more 2 mg/0.5 mg film or tablet.
- Record your withdrawal symptoms: _____.

Your total dose on **Day 2 cannot exceed** _____ mg. Record your total dose on **Day 2:** _____ mg.

Day 3 in the Morning: Take the total dose you took on **Day 2** = _____ mg.
- If you experience withdrawal 2 hours later, you may take one more 2 mg/0.5 mg film or tablet.
- Record your withdrawal symptoms: _____.
- If you continue to experience withdrawal 2 hours later, you may take one more 2 mg/0.5 mg film or tablet.
- Record your withdrawal symptoms: _____.

Your total dose on **Day 3 cannot exceed** _____ mg. Record your total dose on **Day 3:** _____ mg.

Day 4 in the Morning: Take the total dose you took on **Day 3** = _____ mg.
- If you experience withdrawal 2 hours later, you may take one more 2 mg/0.5 mg film or tablet.
- Record your withdrawal symptoms: _____.
- If you continue to experience withdrawal 2 hours later, you may take one more 2 mg/0.5 mg film or tablet.
- Record your withdrawal symptoms: _____.

Your total dose on **Day 4 cannot exceed** _____ mg. Record your total dose on **Day 4:** _____ mg.

Day 5 to next visit: In the morning, take the total dose you took on **Day 4** = _____ mg.

General Rules
- The maximum dose is 16 mg/4 mg. If you reach this dose, you cannot increase further without calling the office first. The office phone number is _____ [insert phone number].
- Please call if you have any questions. There are no "stupid" questions.
- Call us if you feel sleepy after your dose.
- Please bring this record to your next visit.
- It's okay to take Tylenol (acetaminophen) or Motrin (ibuprofen) for aches/pains.

BRING THIS WITH YOU TO YOUR NEXT APPOINTMENT, scheduled for _____ [insert date and time].

Notes:

---

*If prescribing the buccal film, ensure the patient understands that the buccal film is placed on the inner cheek (buccal mucosa) rather than sublingually (under the tongue).

M. Lofwall, February 27, 2017 (personal communication). Adapted with permission.

Part 3 of 5—Pharmacotherapy for Opioid Use Disorder TIP 63

Buprenorphine Treatment Agreement

This form is for educational/informational purposes only. It doesn't establish a legal or medical standard of care. Healthcare professionals should use their judgment in interpreting this form and applying it in the circumstances of their individual patients and practice arrangements. The information provided in this form is provided "as is" with no guarantee as to its accuracy or completeness.

TREATMENT AGREEMENT

I agree to accept the following treatment contract for buprenorphine office-based opioid addiction treatment:

1. The risks and benefits of buprenorphine treatment have been explained to me.
2. The risks and benefits of other treatment for opioid use disorder (including methadone, naltrexone, and nonmedication treatments) have been explained to me.
3. I will keep my medication in a safe, secure place away from children (for example, in a lockbox). My plan is to store it [describe where and how _____].
4. I will take the medication exactly as my healthcare provider prescribes. If I want to change my medication dose, I will speak with my healthcare provider first. Taking more medication than my healthcare provider prescribes or taking it more than once daily as my healthcare provider prescribes is medication misuse and may result in supervised dosing at the clinic. Taking the medication by snorting or by injection is also medication misuse and may result in supervised dosing at the clinic, referral to a higher level of care, or change in medication based on my healthcare provider's evaluation.
5. I will be on time to my appointments and respectful to the office staff and other patients.
6. I will keep my healthcare provider informed of all my medications (including herbs and vitamins) and medical problems.
7. I agree not to obtain or take prescription opioid medications prescribed by any other healthcare provider without consulting my buprenorphine prescriber.
8. If I am going to have a medical procedure that will cause pain, I will let my healthcare provider know in advance so that my pain will be adequately treated.
9. If I miss an appointment or lose my medication, I understand that I will not get more medication until my next office visit. I may also have to start having supervised buprenorphine dosing.
10. If I come to the office intoxicated, I understand that my healthcare provider will not see me, and I will not receive more medication until the next office visit. I may also have to start having supervised buprenorphine dosing.
11. I understand that it's illegal to give away or sell my medication; this is diversion. If I do this, my treatment will no longer include unsupervised buprenorphine dosing and may require referral to a higher level of care, supervised dosing at the clinic, and/or a change in medication based on my healthcare provider's evaluation.
12. Violence, threatening language or behavior, or participation in any illegal activity at the office will result in treatment termination from the clinic.
13. I understand that random urine drug testing is a treatment requirement. If I do not provide a urine sample, it will count as a positive drug test.
14. I understand that I will be called at random times to bring my medication container into the office for a pill or film count. Missing medication doses could result in supervised dosing or referral to a higher level of care at this clinic or potentially at another treatment provider based on my individual needs.
15. I understand that initially I will have weekly office visits until I am stable. I will get a prescription for 7 days of medication at each visit.
16. I can be seen every 2 weeks in the office starting the second month of treatment if I have two negative urine drug tests in a row. I will then get a prescription for 14 days of medication at each visit.
17. I will go back to weekly visits if I have a positive drug test. I can go back to visits every 2 weeks when I have two negative drug tests in a row again.
18. I may be seen less than every 2 weeks based on goals made by my healthcare provider and me.
19. I understand that people have died by mixing buprenorphine with alcohol and other drugs like benzodiazepines (drugs like Valium, Klonopin, and Xanax).

Continued on next page

20. I understand that treatment of opioid use disorder involves more than just taking medication. I agree to comply with my healthcare provider's recommendations for additional counseling and/or for help with other problems.
21. I understand that there is no fixed time for being on buprenorphine and that the goal of treatment is for me to stop using all illicit drugs and become successful in all aspects of my life.
22. I understand that I may experience opioid withdrawal symptoms when I stop taking buprenorphine.
23. I have been educated about the other two FDA-approved medications used for opioid dependence treatment, methadone and naltrexone.
24. I have been educated about the increased chance of pregnancy when stopping illicit opioid use and starting buprenorphine treatment and been informed about methods for preventing pregnancy.

Other specific items unique to my treatment include:

Patient's Name (print): _____

Patient's Signature: _____ Date: _____

This form is adapted from the American Society of Addiction Medicine's Sample Treatment Agreement, which is updated periodically; the most current version of the agreement is available online (https://www.asam.org/docs/default-source/advocacy/sample-treatment-agreement30fa159472bc604ca5b7ff000030b21a.pdf?sfvrsn=bd4675c2_0).

Adapted with permission.[345]

Part 3 of 5—Pharmacotherapy for Opioid Use Disorder   TIP 63

Patient Urine Drug Screen and Medication Count Monitoring Form

Patient's Name: _____   **Date To Be Called:** _____

Called for:
☐ Urine Drug Screen
☐ Medication Count at ☐ Office or ☐ Pharmacy FOR: _____
☐ Buprenorphine/Naloxone
☐ Other (list drug: _____, _____, _____)

Documentation of Phone Call to Patient

Patient was called at _____ (insert phone #) on _____ (date) at ____:____ (time) and informed of monitoring required (described above) within the next _____ hours.

Check One:
☐ I spoke with patient
☐ Message left on answering machine/voicemail
☐ Message left with _____
☐ Other _____

Signature of Staff Member Making Phone Call: _____

M. Lofwall, February 27, 2017 (personal communication). Adapted with permission.

Pharmacy Tablet/Film Count Form

(Note: Before sending this form, discuss with the pharmacist first to explain goals and procedures and to ensure agreement and understanding.)

Date: _____

To: Pharmacists @ _____ Pharmacy

From: Healthcare Provider: _____

Clinic Address: _____

Phone Number: _____

My patient, _____, is starting office-based buprenorphine treatment for opioid dependence.

As part of monitoring this treatment, we ask the patient to do buprenorphine tablet/film counts at random times (we call the patient when it's time for a pill/film count).

The above-named patient lives much closer to your pharmacy than to our treatment clinic. It would be a big help to me and this patient if you would be able to perform periodic tablet/film counts on his/her buprenorphine and then fax this form to us.

On the days we call the patient for a random tablet/film count, the patient would come to your pharmacy with his or her pill bottle. When we call the patient to go for a random tablet/film count, we will fax this form to you. We would appreciate if you could record the tablet/film count results on this form and fax it back to us the same day. This would be a real help to me in monitoring my patient's treatment and also a great service to the patient.

Thank you very much for your help with this! Sincerely,

_____
Signature

Buprenorphine/Naloxone formulation: _____

Dose per tablet/film: _____

Total # of tablets/films remaining in bottle: _____ Fill date on bottle: _____

Total # of tablets/films dispensed on fill date: _____ Tablet/film count correct? ☐ Yes ☐ No

Please fax this back to: _____
Thank You!

M. Lofwall, February 27, 2017 (personal communication). Adapted with permission.

Chapter 3E: Medical Management Strategies for Patients Taking OUD Medications in Office-Based Settings

Chapter 3E examines key issues in medical management of patients who are prescribed buprenorphine or naltrexone in office-based opioid treatment (OBOT) settings. It covers regulatory and administrative concerns specific to buprenorphine and naltrexone that affect medical management of patients in office settings.

Management of patients taking medications for opioid use disorder (OUD) varies by setting. OBOT stabilize on buprenorphine or naltrexone, providers focus on medication management and treatment of other substance use, medical co-morbidities, and psychosocial needs. Treatment of comorbid conditions should be offered onsite or via referral and should be verified as having been received.

Exhibit 3E.1 addresses use of terminology in this chapter.

EXHIBIT 3E.1. Key Terms

In addition to the key terms defined in Exhibit 3.1 of this Treatment Improvement Protocol (TIP), these terms appear in Chapter 3E:

Psychosocial support: Ancillary services to enhance a patient's overall functioning and well-being, including recovery support services, case management, housing, employment, and educational services.

Psychosocial treatment: Interventions that seek to enhance patient's social and mental functioning, including addiction counseling, contingency management, and mental health services.

Patient Selection

To assess patients' chances of success with standard office-based treatment, consider:

- **Concurrent substance use disorder (SUD) involving alcohol or benzodiazepines.** Benzodiazepine (illicit and prescription) and alcohol use are common in patients with OUD. This use presents clinical challenges, including increased risk of respiratory depression and unintentional overdose or death. Some patients may have taken appropriately prescribed benzodiazepines for years with limited or no evidence of misuse. For such patients, tapering benzodiazepines may be contraindicated and unrealistic. Others may require treatment for a benzodiazepine use disorder. (See Exhibit 3B.1 for strategies for assessing and managing patients in OUD treatment who have concurrent benzodiazepine use disorder.)
- Although concomitant use of buprenorphine with benzodiazepines increases the risk of an adverse reaction, including overdose death, opioid agonist treatment should not be denied to patients solely because they take benzodiazepines,[346] because untreated OUD can pose a greater risk of morbidity and mortality. The Food and Drug Administration (FDA) advises that careful medication management by healthcare professionals can reduce risk (see www.fda.gov/Drugs/DrugSafety/ucm575307.htm for more information).

Approaches to addressing concurrent benzodiazepine use include:

- Get patients' permission to contact their benzodiazepine prescribers to confirm their histories. Speaking with close family members or friends (with patients' permission) can also help in evaluating evidence of alcohol or benzodiazepine misuse (e.g., intoxication, accidents, withdrawal seizures).
- Make sure patients understand that combining buprenorphine with alcohol, benzodiazepines, or other central nervous system depressants risks potential respiratory depression and unintentional overdose death.[347] Overdose death with buprenorphine is most often associated with intravenous benzodiazepine and heavy alcohol use.
- For patients misusing benzodiazepines (e.g., taking in high doses, bingeing, using intravenously), the TIP expert panel recommends referral to higher intensity addiction treatment with medically supervised benzodiazepine withdrawal if available (e.g., intensive outpatient programs, residential treatment). Do not rule out concurrent use of buprenorphine or extended-release injectable naltrexone (XR-NTX) for treatment of OUD in more structured settings for these patients.
- For patients who are physically dependent on illicit benzodiazepines but do not inject or binge, a gradual outpatient medically supervised withdrawal can be attempted using long-acting benzodiazepines, under certain conditions that promote safety and reduce risk. These conditions may include:
  - Requiring frequent office visits with observation of patients taking medication.
  - Having significant others monitor patients and report back to the office.
  - Offering a short-duration prescription supply.
  - Monitoring prescription drug monitoring program (PDMP) reports more frequently.
  - Conducting frequent urine tests.
  - Using written treatment agreements outlining conditions for dual buprenorphine and benzodiazepine prescriptions.
- Review patient progress regularly; adjust treatment plans as needed. Document treatment decisions, as research showing the effectiveness and safety of these approaches is lacking.[348]

- **Significant comorbid mental illness or suicidal or homicidal ideation.** Patients who are actively suicidal, homicidal, severely depressed, or psychotic or who are having other significant psychiatric problems may need assessment and treatment by a mental health professional who can treat both the psychiatric comorbidity and the OUD. Depending on the severity, they may need higher levels of mental health services in a crisis center, emergency department, or inpatient setting. An addiction psychiatrist can treat such patients upon discharge.
- **Significant medical comorbidity, including infections.** Severe abscesses, endocarditis, or osteomyelitis from injecting drugs may require hospitalization. If hospitalization is necessary, buprenorphine can be initiated.[349] Initiation of HIV and hepatitis C virus treatments do not contraindicate buprenorphine treatment.[350]

Patient Management and Treatment Monitoring

Base management of OUD on a comprehensive assessment that is updated throughout treatment (see Part 2 of this TIP for more information on conducting assessments). Tailor the management approach to patients' needs and goals. Components of the management approach include:

- The length and frequency of office visits.
- The length of time between prescriptions or XR-NTX injections.
- The frequency of drug testing.
- Ancillary psychosocial and medical treatments and referrals.

Course of Treatment

The typical course of OUD treatment is varied. There is often not a direct pathway from heavy illicit opioid use to no illicit opioid use.[351] Some patients have only occasional returns to use and do not require reinduction on buprenorphine or naltrexone. Other patients may return to use in the context of medication nonadherence, requiring reinduction and restabilization on buprenorphine or medically supervised withdrawal from opioids and an appropriate period of abstinence before restarting naltrexone. Some patients may have sustained abstinence and choose to remain on their maintenance buprenorphine or naltrexone dose. However, others may try to taper their buprenorphine dose, discontinue naltrexone, consider a change in pharmacotherapy (e.g., from buprenorphine to naltrexone or naltrexone to buprenorphine), or attempt maintenance of remission of OUD without any medication.

Because OUD is often a chronic and relapsing illness, patients may have different types and durations of treatment over their lifetimes. Some may have periods of successful outpatient treatment at different times with all three available FDA-approved medications for OUD. Others may experience forced medication discontinuation (e.g., insurance lapse, time in controlled environments that disallow or discriminate against OUD medication, cases in family and drug courts, parole and probation). A relative few may remain in remission after successfully discontinuing medication voluntarily. Different treatment journeys occur in different treatment settings (e.g., intensive outpatient, residential programs) and with different pharmacotherapies and ancillary psychosocial and recovery support services.

To the extent possible, coordinate primary care, behavioral health, and wraparound services needed and desired by the patients to address their medical, social, and recovery needs. Individuals with co-occurring physical, mental, and substance use disorders may benefit from collaborative care.[352]

RESOURCE ALERT

Substance Abuse and Mental Health Services Administration (SAMHSA) Treatment Guidance for Individuals With Co-Occurring Disorders

TIP 42, *Substance Abuse Treatment for Persons With Co-Occurring Disorders,* provides treatment strategies for SUD treatment for individuals with mental disorders (https://store.samhsa.gov/shin/content//SMA13-3992/SMA13-3992.pdf).

General Principles for the Use of Pharmacological Agents To Treat Individuals With Co-Occurring Mental and Substance Use Disorders offers assistance for the planning, delivery, and evaluation of pharmacotherapy for individuals with co-occurring mental and substance use disorders (https://store.samhsa.gov/shin/content//SMA12-4689/SMA12-4689.pdf).

Pharmacologic Guidelines for Treating Individuals With Post-Traumatic Stress Disorder and Co-Occurring Opioid Use Disorders is tailored to the provision of medication for OUD to individuals also diagnosed with posttraumatic stress disorder (https://store.samhsa.gov/shin/content//SMA12-4688/SMA12-4688.pdf).

Role of the Treatment Plan and Treatment Agreement in Medical Management

The initial treatment plan should include:

- **Treatment goals.**
- **Conditions for changing or stopping treatment** (the Chapter 3E Appendix has a sample goal-setting form).
- **Therapeutic contingencies for nonadherence and failure to meet initial goals,** such as:
  - Increase in the intensity or scope of services at the office or through referral.
  - More intensive psychosocial treatment, including inpatient treatment or transfer to an opioid treatment program (OTP) for observed buprenorphine dosing if the office-based practice is unable to provide such services.
  - Reassessment to ensure psychiatric and other comorbid addictions are adequately addressed via consultation with mental health, addiction treatment, or pain management providers as available and indicated.

Some patients may need a more structured environment when there is continued opioid use or comorbid use of substances other than opioids or when mental disorders are impeding their progress toward remission and recovery. In these cases, medication for OUD should not be interrupted.

Treatment agreements can help clarify expectations for patients and healthcare professionals (see the Chapter 3C Appendix and Chapter 3D Appendix for sample treatment agreement forms for naltrexone and buprenorphine, respectively). Review and amend treatment plans and treatment agreements periodically as patients progress (or destabilize) and new goals emerge. This will help healthcare professionals across settings deliver coordinated, effective care. Updating treatment plans and agreements helps patients recognize their progress and supports their motivation to remain engaged. Involving patients' support networks makes patients accountable to a group of caring people rather than to a single healthcare professional.

If a patient does not discontinue all illicit drugs for extended periods, it doesn't mean treatment has failed and should not result in automatic discharge. It means the treatment plan may require modification to meet the patient's needs.

Engage patients' family members and other recovery supports (with patients' written consent) by sharing their treatment goals and agreements. Identify specific ways they can support patients' goals.[353]

Medical Management Strategies

Medical management includes:

- Providing brief supportive counseling.
- Referring to ancillary psychosocial services.
- Referring to psychiatric and medical care if not directly provided by the healthcare professional prescribing or administering OUD medication.
- Adjusting the frequency of office visits.
- Conducting drug tests.
- Monitoring patient adherence to medication with occasional observed dosing, random medication inventorying, or both.
- Addressing patient concerns about side effects.

The TIP expert panel recommends medication management and brief supportive counseling at each visit. Refer for adjunctive addiction counseling and other psychosocial supports as clinically indicated.

- Discussing any concerns with the patient or their support network.
- Prescribing medication for co-occurring alcohol use disorder (e.g., disulfiram, acamprosate).

Strategies for optimizing medical management and brief supportive counseling involve:

- **Helping the patient manage stressors and identify triggers** for a return to illicit opioid use.
- **Providing empathic listening and nonjudgmental discussion** of triggers that precede use or increased craving and how to manage them.
- **Providing ongoing assessment to mark progress.** Revise treatment goals via shared decision making to incorporate new insights. (See "Treatment Planning or Referral" in Part 2 of this TIP for more on shared decision making.)
- **Providing medical care for comorbid health conditions.**
- **Referring patients as needed** to:
  - Adjunctive psychiatric treatment.
  - Addiction counseling.
  - Case management.
  - Community-based recovery support groups.
- **Inviting supportive family members and friends to medical visits** to discuss strategies to support patients.
- **Engaging and educating family members and friends** who are reluctant to accept medication's role in treatment.
- **Advocating for patients as needed** if their treatment becomes threatened by their employer, housing provider, insurance company, the courts, or criminal justice agencies. These threats, refusal of service, or frank coercion may constitute potential violations of the Americans with Disabilities Act or other discrimination or parity violations.

Referral to counseling and other psychosocial supports

Prescribers of buprenorphine must be able to refer patients for appropriate adjunctive counseling and ancillary services as needed according to federal law.[354] (However, patients can still receive buprenorphine treatment even if they do not use such services.) There's no such referral requirement for naltrexone treatment, but patients should receive medical management and be referred as needed for adjunctive addiction, mental health, or recovery services.

To achieve clinical stability and abstinence from illicit drug use, many patients need psychosocial counseling and support services beyond what their buprenorphine prescriber's practice offers. For example, patients with mental disorders (e.g., depression, posttraumatic stress disorder)[355] should be assessed and treated with appropriate medications (as indicated) and adjunctive mental health services.

Some patients are reluctant to engage in addiction counseling or recovery support groups until they stabilize on medication. Once stabilized, they may see benefits to participating in these supports. Recommend additional addiction, mental health, and social services as appropriate if patients:

- Do not achieve full remission.
- Continue to misuse nonopioid substances.
- Do not reach their treatment goals with medication management alone.

Behavioral treatment with contingency management (e.g., rewards for illicit drug abstinence) is highly effective and is offered in some specialty treatment programs. It can motivate the patient to reduce illicit drug use, including opioids and stimulants, and increase medication adherence.[356]

Alcoholics Anonymous, Narcotics Anonymous, Self-Management and Recovery Training, and other **peer recovery support groups can be** helpful to patients, especially if they find groups with accepting attitudes toward OUD medication and people who take it. (See Part 5 of this TIP for resources on recovery support groups.) Some peer recovery support groups consider patients taking methadone and buprenorphine for OUD treatment as not being abstinent from opioids. Check with local groups before referring a patient. Groups not accepting of OUD medications are not appropriate for patients taking them. Patients are most likely to benefit from peer support programs if they actively participate in offered recovery activities.[357] Monitor recovery activities to ensure that patients are accessing appropriate supports and are benefiting from them (Exhibit 3E.2)

Patients may need many other psychosocial services. Case managers can help patients obtain:

- Housing support.
- Medicaid or other health insurance.
- Income support.
- Food assistance services.
- Vocational and educational services.
- Mental health and family therapy.

Refer to psychosocial services as appropriate. Get patient consent to share information and make provider introductions, just as referrals to other medical specialists would occur. Strategies include:

- Referring per program availability, affordability, and patients' needs, preferences, and treatment responses. Ensure referrals to programs that accept and support patients receiving OUD medication.
- If possible, personally introducing patients to the new behavioral health service providers or peer recovery support specialists if changing settings, to encourage a successful transition.
- Developing and maintaining a list of referral resources, including:
  - Drug and alcohol counselors.
  - Inpatient, residential, and outpatient addiction counseling programs.
  - OTPs.
  - Inpatient/outpatient behavioral health programs.
  - Primary care and mental health providers.
  - Community-based services.
  - Recovery support groups.

EXHIBIT 3E.2. Monitoring Recovery Activities

At medical management visits, do not simply ask about attendance at recovery support meetings—explore the level of participation and engagement in those activities. Some activities include:

- Finding and working closely with a sponsor.
- "Working" the 12 Steps at 12-Step meetings and with a sponsor.
- Doing service at meetings (e.g., setting up chairs, making coffee, going on a "commitment" to speak at a meeting in a jail or an inpatient drug and alcohol program).
- Having and frequently attending a regular "home" group.[358]

Remember this statement from recovery experts A. Thomas McLellan and William White:

Recovery status is best defined by factors other than medication status. Neither medication-assisted treatment of opioid addiction nor the cessation of such treatment by itself constitutes recovery. Recovery status instead hinges on broader achievements in health and social functioning—with or without medication support."[359]

- Using active referral procedures (e.g., linking patients directly via phone to a specific program staff member) instead of passive ones (e.g., giving a patient a name and a phone number to call).
- Avoiding leaving patients to find their own referrals.
- Monitoring patients' follow-through via phone contact or at the next office visit.

Frequency of medical management visits

The TIP expert panel and the American Society of Addiction Medicine (ASAM) recommend that patients be seen approximately once a week until they demonstrate significant reductions in or abstinence from illicit substance use.[360] This is also a time to ensure adherence to pharmacotherapy. Nonadherence to naltrexone or buprenorphine prevents optimal treatment outcomes. In scheduling patient visits, be sensitive to treatment barriers such as:

- Work and childcare obligations.
- Cost of care and lack of insurance coverage.
- Driving time.
- Lack of public transportation to visits, which may be particularly challenging for patients in rural areas.

Goals of weekly visits include:

- Assessing patients' clinical needs and challenges.
- Assessing medication effectiveness and side effects.
- Assessing functional status (e.g., home, work, school).
- Assessing and monitoring stress coping strategies and potential triggers for return to substance use.
- Assessing adherence to the recommended frequency of attendance for XR-NTX injections or the prescribed buprenorphine dosing regimen and responsible handling of the medication (e.g., safely storing out of reach of children, taking as prescribed, not sharing or losing it).
- Monitoring use of alcohol and illicit drugs and ensuring adequate therapeutic dosing (e.g., opioid blockade if there is ongoing illicit opioid use and adherence to medication).
- Following up on any referrals made, such as adjunctive counseling, recovery support groups, or other psychosocial services (the Chapter 3E Appendix has a sample medical management visit form).

Once patients adhere to therapeutic doses of OUD medication, decrease illicit drug and alcohol use, and increase negative opioid toxicological samples, consider less frequent visits. Monthly visits (or less for carefully selected patients who have been stable on buprenorphine for extended periods with adequate support) are reasonable for patients taking naltrexone or buprenorphine who show progress toward treatment objectives. Indications that a patient is ready to come less than weekly include:

- Several weeks of illicit opioid abstinence based on self-report and negative drug tests.
- Adherence to appointments and treatment plan.
- No ongoing drug use that may risk patient safety (e.g., alcohol or benzodiazepine misuse).
- Absence of significant medication side effects.
- Stable mental health and medical conditions.
- Responsible handling of medication (e.g., safe storage, no requests for early refills).
- Absence of unexpected controlled medication prescriptions from other providers in the PDMP.

As visits become less frequent, consider random urine drug testing, medication counts (buprenorphine tablets or films), and involvement of network supports if available.

Buprenorphine implants are indicated only for stable patients already taking transmucosal buprenorphine with positive treatment response. Extended-release buprenorphine is indicated for patients treated with transmucosal buprenorphine for at least 1 week. It's expected that patients with the implants or those

Visit frequency should not depend only on dosing schedule for long-acting OUD medications. Also consider patients' treatment needs, preferences, and responses. To ensure continued engagement, consider adding to the treatment agreement the expected visit frequency and frequency of other ancillary treatments tailored to patients' needs, goals, and preferences.

treated with extended-release buprenorphine will receive medication management services with visits approximately weekly at the start and then less frequently as clinically indicated based on patient treatment response. Likewise, patients treated with XR-NTX should be seen more than once per month when initiating the medication to monitor progress and assess and address any side effects.

Drug testing in ongoing medical management

Ongoing clinical monitoring that includes drug testing of urine or oral fluid specimens is part of good practice. Objective evidence of any ongoing illicit substance use is important to consider along with patient reports. Patients may not wish to disclose recent drug use because of shame, fear of punishment, or even fear of discharge from treatment.

Explain to patients that testing will help them meet treatment goals and is not performed to render punishments. Results help:

- Detect medication nonadherence that could cause harm (e.g., unintentional overdose).
- Monitor abstinence and response to medication treatment.
- Counsel and improve treatment plans.
- Detect a return to illicit opioid use or other substance use.

The TIP expert panel recommends periodic random testing. Drug testing frequency should be clinically determined. It should occur at least at the time of the initial evaluation and initiation of medication (naltrexone, buprenorphine) and at a frequency consistent with office visits (e.g., weekly initially).

Point-of-service tests give immediate results, allowing findings and implications to be discussed with patients during visits. However, some circumstances require confirmatory laboratory testing, such as when the patient contests the results and when testing for employment or legal monitoring. In these cases, samples may need to be collected and sent to a Department of Health and Human Services-certified laboratory under strict chain-of-custody procedure. In addition, norbuprenorphine may not be available in point-of-service tests and therefore, periodically, a specimen should be sent to a laboratory for testing. Important aspects of testing include:

- Testing technology.
- The cutoffs for positive tests.
- Any administrative requirements.
- Time windows to detect a positive result.
- Cross-reactivity, sensitivity, and specificity.
- Test interpretation. (See Part 2 for more information about how to interpret drug testing results.)
- Consideration of panels based on drugs most commonly used in the region.

Conduct point-of-service drug tests following the manufacturer's instructions. Use Clinical Laboratory Improvement Amendments-waived testing kits. A provider's office must enroll and pay a modest fee for certification. The application is available online (www.cms.gov/Medicare/CMS-Forms/CMS-Forms/downloads/cms116.pdf).

Sample collection via oral swab is straightforward; follow the manufacturer's directions. **If collecting urine samples, take steps to reduce the likelihood of tampering.** In settings that treat many patients or treat patients potentially facing criminal justice sanctions, consider taking these measures:

- Have patients visit the bathroom alone, without bags or jackets, to deter use of another person's urine specimen.
- Set the sink to run only cold water and use a colored toilet bowl cleaner to prevent dilution of urine specimens.
- Use specimen cups with specific gravity testing, if possible, to identify diluted samples.
- Use temperature-sensitive strips in collection cups to identify tampered specimens.

Ongoing positive opioid tests during treatment indicate the need to reassess the patient and revise the treatment plan. Repeated positives may indicate that patients:

- Are not taking some or all of their medication or may be taking the medication incorrectly.
- Need a different medication.
- Need directly observed medication administration in the office or at an OTP.
- Need a buprenorphine dose increase.
- Need more counseling or a higher level of a specialty addiction treatment program.
- Need to participate in recovery support services.

For more information on drug testing in the primary care setting, see Technical Assistance Publication 32, *Clinical Drug Testing in Primary Care*[361] (https://store.samhsa.gov/shin/content//SMA12-4668/SMA12-4668.pdf) and ASAM's Consensus Statement on Appropriate Use of Drug Testing in Clinical Addiction Medicine.[362]

Opioids and opiates in point-of-service tests

Point-of-service and laboratory screening tests for opiates only test for opioids metabolized to morphine (e.g., codeine, heroin). Semisynthetic and synthetic opioids, such as methadone, buprenorphine, and others (e.g., fentanyl, oxycodone), are not metabolized to morphine and do not test positive on most opiate tests. Specific point-of-service tests exist for these opioids.

Some point-of-service and laboratory tests can detect methadone, buprenorphine, and other opioids. Patients taking buprenorphine should have buprenorphine specifically included in their urine test panel to assure the prescriber that the patient is indeed taking the medication. Some patients may put some of their buprenorphine in the urine to mask nonadherence. Periodically testing for a buprenorphine metabolite (e.g., norbuprenorphine, buprenorphine glucuronide) is advised.

Assessing buprenorphine adherence

Medication nonadherence and diversion can signal inadequately treated OUD (e.g., return to use with positive urine drug tests). Assess such behaviors clinically and develop therapeutic responses to them.

Remember that nonadherence, misuse, and diversion occur with other medications as well—those with and without abuse potential. For instance, it's clear that opioid analgesics have been overprescribed for pain, misused, and diverted; they have contributed to deaths among individuals prescribed as well as those not prescribed these medications. Antibiotics for bacterial infections are also overprescribed, and patient nonadherence (e.g., not completing the full course), misuse (e.g., saving leftover medication for a later self-diagnosed and self-treated infection), and diversion (e.g., giving leftover medication to ill family members or friends) can cause significant public health harm, given the spread of drug-resistant bacteria. **Medication nonadherence has largely fueled development of longer acting medications** (e.g., depot antipsychotics, long-acting contraceptives, XR-NTX, buprenorphine implants).

Strategies for addressing medication non-adherence and diversion include carefully assessing the patient to understand underlying causes of the behavior. Address these causes and monitor adherence. For instance, if a patient gives his or her medication to a relative on a waiting list for treatment, getting the relative into treatment can help that patient become adherent. Monitor adherence by:

- Asking patients to bring their unused medication into the office for counting.
- Increasing the frequency of office visits.
- Increasing urine drug testing.
- Talking with family members or significant others.
- Writing prescriptions for shorter duration.
- Observing medication administration at the office, pharmacy, or OTP.
- Checking urine for buprenorphine and its metabolites.
- Checking the PDMP.
- Avoiding doses over 24 mg (save in rare cases).

Chapter 3D Appendix includes a sample patient urine drug screen and medication count form, as well as a pharmacy tablet/film count form.

If these steps have no positive effect, patients may need referral to higher levels of care at OTPs or residential addiction treatment programs. Different formulations or pharmacotherapy may need to be considered.[363] If a change in setting is required, consider patients for return to OBOT once they stabilize.

Discontinuing medication for OUD

Patients should decide whether to taper off or discontinue pharmacotherapy with the support of their healthcare professional and, if applicable, their addiction or mental health counselor, family, and peer recovery supports (e.g., peer support specialist, recovery coach). If patients' goals include stopping medication, discuss the risks and benefits of discontinuing. Work closely with patients to develop a buprenorphine dose taper plan, if needed, and a robust plan to sustain recovery and reengage in treatment before any return to substance use. Before patients begin a buprenorphine dose taper or discontinue XR-NTX, they should demonstrate:

- Medication adherence.
- Abstinence from illicit opioid use.
- A stable living environment.
- Social support.
- Sustained improvements in functioning at home and at school or work.

Consider treatment with XR-NTX following successful taper from an opioid agonist or partial agonist (after an appropriate period of abstinence). Data are limited on the effectiveness of this approach.

The TIP expert panel recommends that providers not discharge patients from treatment solely because of continued illicit opioid use if the benefits of treatment continue to outweigh the risks. If risks outweigh benefits or alternative treatments may offer more benefit, refer patients to alternative treatment (e.g., OTP). Discharging patients without attempting meaningful referral when illicit opioid use is ongoing can worsen the patient's condition and may be considered patient abandonment.

Forced tapers or abrupt discontinuation

Forcing a patient to taper off of medication for nonmedical reasons or because of ongoing substance misuse is generally inappropriate. Many patients are abruptly discontinued or tapered from OUD medication against their will

> Do not require discontinuation of pharmacotherapy because of incomplete treatment response. Doing so is not a rational therapeutic response to the predicted course of a chronic condition.

while detained or awaiting trial. A randomized trial of continuing versus tapering off methadone for detainees found that those who kept taking medication in detention were significantly more likely to return to treatment on release.[364] It's likely that the same holds true for forced discontinuation from buprenorphine during detention.

As is sometimes the case in general medical practice, **patients who are unable to pay their bills should not be discontinued from treatment without attempting meaningful referral.** Attempt referrals to publicly funded addiction treatment services (e.g., specialty treatment programs, federally qualified health centers). If patients cannot continue treatment because of inability to pay, providers can contact the pharmaceutical company about patient assistance programs to help defer the cost of medications.

Forced dose tapers against the patient's desire may be clinically indicated when risks of treatment outweigh benefits or, in unusual cases, where the patient has been violent toward staff or other patients. In these cases, attempt to place the patient in a higher level of care and document the attempt. In some circumstances, forced tapering or abrupt discontinuation may violate the Americans with Disabilities Act. The Legal Action Center (www.lac.org) and the National Alliance for Medication Assisted Recovery (www.methadone.org) offer information on how to legally manage forced tapers.

Patient follow-up

Medical management should not end when patients taper off of medication. The TIP expert panel recommends regular follow-up visits (or phone checkups by clinical staff or recovery support specialists) to help patients manage their condition, address potential concerns about returning to illicit opioid use, and discuss reinitiating OUD maintenance medication if warranted. Attendance at drug counseling or mutual-help groups can be helpful, as can periodic drug testing.

Administrative Considerations

Patient Limits

Physicians

After taking the necessary training, qualified physicians can obtain waivers to prescribe buprenorphine to up to 30 active patients at any one time. Such providers may apply to SAMHSA to increase their patient limit to up to 100 patients if they've had a waiver for at least 1 year. Physicians with a waiver to prescribe to up to 100 patients for at least 1 year may apply to SAMHSA to prescribe to up to 275 patients under more restrictive conditions. More information on patient limits and applying for limit increases is available from SAMHSA (www.samhsa.gov/sites/default/files/programs_campaigns/medication_assisted/understanding-patient-limit275.pdf).

Nurse practitioners and physician assistants

Qualified nurse practitioners and physician assistants can obtain waivers to prescribe buprenorphine to up to 30 patients the first year and 100 patients thereafter. These practitioners must complete 24 hours of additional training to qualify. More information is available from SAMHSA (www.samhsa.gov/medication-assisted-treatment/qualify-nps-pas-waivers).

Diversion Control Policies for OBOT With Buprenorphine

Controlled substance diversion refers to unauthorized provision of medication to someone for whom it was not prescribed.[365] **Patients may divert buprenorphine for various reasons, such as:**

- To "help" someone who needs medically supervised withdrawal or awaits treatment.[366,367]
- To provide income for the seller.
- To enable someone else to experience the euphoric effect of the medication.[368]

Address diversion of controlled substances with patients using the following strategies:

- Clarify that continuing in office-based treatment depends largely on taking medication as prescribed; nonadherence and diversion are thus problematic.
- In a nonjudgmental way, discuss to whom within their network of family, friends, and acquaintances they might be tempted to divert their medication and why they might be tempted to do so.
- **Instruct patients to store medication securely** (children may inadvertently ingest it and overdose, or other people may take the medication for their own use or to sell).[369]
    - Discuss patients' plans to safely store buprenorphine. Advise patients to keep the medication in the original packaging and out of the reach of children.[370]
    - Tell patients not to store their medication in common areas (e.g., kitchen, bathroom) where others may access it.
    - Educate patients that any portion of a dose taken by a child or pet can be deadly and that they should call 9-1-1 immediately if this occurs.
- Explain how diversion causes negative views of treatment, leading to discrimination against people with OUD. Therefore, healthcare professionals must proactively address diversion to help prevent it.

Possible signs that a patient is diverting buprenorphine[371] include:

- Frequently missed appointments.
- Requests for early refills because medication was reportedly lost or stolen.
- Negative buprenorphine urine screens.
- Positive buprenorphine urine screens that are negative for buprenorphine metabolites.
- Specific requests for the buprenorphine monoproduct owing to naloxone allergy.
- Specific requests for doses of buprenorphine greater than 24 mg/6 mg.
- PDMP shows prescription fills for opioids or other medications that are not positive on his or her drug tests.
- Failed film/pill callback counts.

Establish a diversion control plan to minimize OUD medication diversion. The plan provides measures to reduce diversion and assigns specific responsibility to medical and administrative staff members for carrying out these measures.[372] It should address medication storage, dispensing and administration (if applicable), and prescribing[373] (see the Chapter 3E Appendix for a sample diversion control policy). For providers who store buprenorphine for administration and dispensing, plans should indicate how they will control diversion and which approaches they will use to ensure that patients take their medication. Exhibit 3E.3 summarizes key elements of a diversion control plan.

Physicians who prescribe buprenorphine to more than 100 patients need a diversion control plan. Document diversion incidents and responses to incidents in the patient record. More information about Drug Enforcement Administration (DEA) requirements for Drug Addiction Treatment Act of 2000 (DATA 2000)-waivered healthcare professionals is available online (www.deadiversion.usdoj.gov/pubs/docs/dwp_buprenorphine.htm).

Storage of Buprenorphine

Practices that store buprenorphine onsite must have appropriate security, which includes storing the medication in a securely locked, substantially constructed cabinet.[374] If a significant amount of stored buprenorphine is lost or stolen, providers must notify the local DEA office in writing within 1 business day and complete a Form DEA-106 (https://apps.deadiversion.usdoj.gov/webforms/dtlLogin.jsp).

Employees convicted of a felony related to a controlled substance or who had a DEA registration denied, revoked, or surrendered "for cause" are not permitted to have access to buprenorphine.

EXHIBIT 3E.3. Key Elements of an OBOT Clinic Diversion Control Plan[375]

New Patients

Check the state's PDMP before admission to determine whether patients are receiving opioids or benzodiazepine prescriptions from other providers.

Ask patients to sign a release of information to speak with the other prescribers. Patients who are unwilling to sign a release of information are poor candidates for outpatient treatment.

Review the clinic diversion control policy with new patients. This should include counseling patients to:

- Keep buprenorphine locked up and out of children's reach.
- Never share medication with anyone.
- Never sell medication to anyone.
- Acknowledge giving or selling medication to others as illegal.
- Take medication only as prescribed.
- Review, understand, and agree to the practice's buprenorphine treatment agreement before they start.

Prescribe buprenorphine/naloxone when possible rather than monoproduct. Exceptions include prescribing the monoproduct for pregnant women with OUD.

Prescribe an adequate but not excessive dose. Most patients respond to doses at or below 24 mg per day. Carefully evaluate requests for higher doses and confirm, document, and assess medication adherence continuously.

Ongoing Patients

Periodically check the state's PDMP.

Conduct random urine tests that include a wide spectrum of opioids—including morphine, oxycodone, and buprenorphine—and periodically include buprenorphine metabolites. This will help monitor response to treatment and determine whether patients are taking at least some of their prescribed buprenorphine.

Use **unobserved** specimen collection to preserve patient privacy and dignity:

- Do not let patients bring backpacks, jackets, or other items into the bathroom.
- Do not let others enter bathrooms with patients.
- Temperature test the urine sample.

Use **observed** specimen collection (obtained by a staff member of the same gender) or oral fluid testing if there is reason to suspect tampering or falsification.

Contact patients at random; ask them to bring in their medication within a reasonable period (24 to 48 hours) to count the tablets/films to ensure that all medication is accounted for.

Provide a limited number of days of medication per prescription without refills (e.g., several days or 1 week per prescription) until the patient has demonstrated stability and lowered diversion risk.

Records for Dispensers

Office-based practices that dispense buprenorphine must keep records of:[376]

- The number of units and doses dispensed with the names and addresses of the patients.
- The dates the medication was dispensed.
- The names (or initials) of the staff members who dispensed or administered the medication.

The diversion control plan should include approaches to ensuring that patients take the medication and do not divert it to others.

Recordkeeping for ordering, storing, and dispensing buprenorphine in the office

All prescribers and staff members must follow federal and state laws for ordering, storing, administering, and dispensing buprenorphine in outpatient settings. Records of inventories of medication received, dispensed, destroyed, and lost or stolen must be maintained. For guidance on how to comply with federal requirements, see:

- Diversion Control Division's *Practitioner's Manual* (www.deadiversion.usdoj.gov/pubs/manuals/pract).
- FDA Recordkeeping Requirements for Buprenorphine Treatment (www.buppractice.com/node/12246).

Recordkeeping for prescribing buprenorphine

Consider writing an initial prescription for only a few days. An example of a 1-day in-office induction prescription is:

> *Buprenorphine/naloxone 2mg /0.5 mg: Dispense #4 for in-office induction, no refills, fill on _____ [insert date that is 1 day before the scheduled induction to make it less tempting for patients to use on their own before induction]*

Keep a log for possible DEA inspection that includes:

- Patients' names (or ID numbers).
- Dates of prescriptions.
- The names, strengths, and quantities of the medications.

Although not required, such a log facilitates inspection and indicates that the provider is within the approved patient limits. Alternatively, electronic health records can be used for this purpose.

DEA Inspections

Under DATA 2000, DEA must ensure that providers administering, dispensing, or prescribing buprenorphine are following recordkeeping, security, and other requirements. To fulfill this requirement, **DEA conducts routine, unannounced onsite inspections.** A description of the inspection process and how to comply with its requirements is available online (https://pcssmat.org/wp-content/uploads/2014/02/FINAL-How-to-Prepare-for-a-DEA-Inspection.pdf).

Emergency Protocols and Patient Safety Measures

Clinics that provide buprenorphine or naltrexone do not need special emergency protocols, crash carts, or other special equipment. However, for patient safety, **the TIP expert panel recommends having injectable or intranasal naloxone onsite.** Clinics that administer XR-NTX or buprenorphine should have a written policy and procedure for responding to precipitated withdrawal and medication allergies.

On-call services and backup during absences should be available either directly or through contracts or cooperative agreements with other local providers with waivers. Qualified medical staff can offer routine medical and psychiatric coverage even without a buprenorphine waiver.

Recommendations for Staff Member Training

All staff members who interact with patients are part of the treatment environment. They can affect patients' treatment experiences and, ultimately, their outcomes. Staff members who interact with patients can include receptionists, billing clerks, urine specimen collection clerks, and all clinical staff members. Therefore, it is useful to **educate and train all staff members in key areas,** including:

- Organizational mission.
- The scientific and empirical underpinnings for the use of FDA-approved medications for OUD, how these medications work, and the evidence for their effectiveness.
- The similarity of medical management and support of patients with OUD to that of patients with other chronic illnesses.

> **Providers who give more than 100 patients buprenorphine must have on-call services.** Such services are valuable regardless of the number of patients in treatment.

- The importance of maintaining a nonjudgmental and welcoming attitude toward patients.
- How to hold discussions about negative perceptions and prejudices associated with OUD.
- Side effects of OUD medications and procedures to alert staff members when patients exhibit them.
- The effect of OUD and other substance use and mental disorders (including posttraumatic stress disorder) on patients' behavior and how staff members can respond appropriately.
- Procedures for seeking help from other staff members to deescalate disagreements or solve problems.
- Procedures for protecting patients' confidentiality and safety.

Treating OUD can be a challenging yet rewarding part of a clinical practice.
Addressing key administrative issues keeps the focus on the rewarding aspects of developing long-term relationships with patients as they work to overcome negative effects of OUD on their lives and improve their health.

RESOURCE ALERT

Training and Mentorship for Prescribers

The Providers' Clinical Support System, with the American Academy of Addiction Psychiatry as the lead organization along with partners from ASAM and other professional organizations, delivers education, training, and mentorship to providers who wish to treat OUD with medications. More information about training and professional mentorship is available online (http://pcssmat.org).

TIP 63 — Medications for Opioid Use Disorder

Chapter 3E Appendix

Sample Goal-Setting Form

Patient's Name: _____ Date: _____

GOAL CATEGORY	CURRENT SITUATION SCORE 10 = major problems and 0 = no problems	What would need to change to decrease this score?	PRIORITY SCORE 10 = highest priority ("I really want to work on this") and 1 = lowest priority ("I really do not want to work on this")
Opioid use			
Other illicit drug use: _____			
Alcohol use			
Tobacco use			
Physical health			
Mental health			
Legal/court issues			
Finances			
Job/employment			
Hobbies			
Family relations			
Partner relations			
Supportive drug-free network			
Education			
Keeping medication safe (e.g., not giving it away, selling it, having it stolen)			
Other			
Other			

M. Lofwall, February 27, 2017 (personal communication). Adapted with permission.

Part 3 of 5—Pharmacotherapy for Opioid Use Disorder   TIP 63

Sample Medical Management Visit Form

Patient's Name: _____ **ID#** _____

Date: _____ **Week#:** _____ **Dose:** _____ mg ☐ No Show

Heroin/cocaine or other illicit drug use since last visit?
_____

Symptoms or signs that might indicate return to use (e.g., changes in mood, physical appearance)?
_____

Since the last visit, are there any problems with the following:

If yes, explain

Drug Use	☐ Yes	☐ No	_____
Alcohol Use	☐ Yes	☐ No	_____
Psychiatric	☐ Yes	☐ No	_____
Medical	☐ Yes	☐ No	_____
Employment	☐ Yes	☐ No	_____
Social/Family	☐ Yes	☐ No	_____
Legal	☐ Yes	☐ No	_____

Any new problem to add to Treatment Plan Review?   ☐ Yes   ☐ No
_____

Plan to address any new problem _____
_____

Participation in Narcotics Anonymous or Alcoholics Anonymous since last visit?   ☐ Yes   ☐ No

Length of Session: _____ Healthcare Professional Signature: _____

D. Fiellin, December 3, 2016 (personal communication). Adapted with permission.

Sample Buprenorphine Diversion Control Policy

XYZ Medical Practice
Office-Based Opioid Use Disorder Policy and Procedure Manual

Policy Title: Diversion Control for Patients Prescribed Transmucosal (Sublingual) Buprenorphine
Effective Date: _____ (Month, Day, Year)

This Diversion Control Policy is provided for educational and informational purposes only. It is intended to offer healthcare professionals guiding principles and policies regarding best practices in diversion control for patients who are prescribed buprenorphine. This policy is not intended to establish a legal or medical standard of care. Healthcare professionals should use their personal and professional judgment in interpreting these guidelines and applying them to the particular circumstances of their individual patients and practice arrangements. The information provided in this Policy is provided "as is" with no guarantee as to its accuracy or completeness.

Preamble: Healthcare professionals can now treat up to 275 patients with buprenorphine. This increased access may contribute to increased diversion, misuse, and related harms. Signs that a patient is misusing or diverting buprenorphine include (1) missed appointments; (2) requests for early refills because pills were lost, stolen, or other reasons; (3) urine screens negative for buprenorphine, positive for opioids; (4) claims of being allergic or intolerant to naloxone and requesting monotherapy; (5) nonhealing or fresh track marks; or (5) police reports of selling on the streets. Likewise, there are a range of reasons for diversion and misuse (e.g., diverting to family/friends with untreated opioid addiction with the intent of trying to "help" convince them to also get treatment; diverting to family/friends on a treatment waiting list; selling some or all of the medication to pay off old drug debts/purchase preferred opioid of misuse/pay for treatment in places where there are inadequate addiction treatment professionals taking private insurance or Medicaid for such reasons as inadequate reimbursement/no reimbursement/burdensome prior authorization process).

The safety and health of patients and others in the community could be at risk if misuse and diversion are not addressed proactively throughout treatment. The reputation of XYZ Medical Practice may also be put at risk.

Definitions: *Diversion* is defined as the unauthorized rerouting or misappropriation of prescription medication to someone other than for whom it was intended (including sharing or selling a prescribed medication); *misuse* includes taking medication in a manner, by route or by dose, other than prescribed.[377]

Purpose: Misuse and diversion should be defined and discussed with patients at the time of treatment entry; periodically throughout treatment, particularly when there have been returns to illicit drug use; and when suspected (e.g., incorrect buprenorphine pill/film count) or confirmed. These procedures will establish the steps to be taken to prevent, monitor, and respond to misuse and diversion of buprenorphine. The response should be therapeutic and matched to the patients' needs, as untreated opioid use disorder and treatment dropout/administrative discharges may lead to increased patient morbidity and mortality and further use of diverted medications or illicit opioids associated with overdose death.

Procedures for Prevention:

- Use buprenorphine/naloxone combination products when medically indicated and cost is not an issue. Reserve the daily buprenorphine monoproducts for pregnant patients and patients who could not afford treatment if the combination product were required, who have a history of stability in treatment and low diversion risk, or who have arrangements for observed dosing. Buprenorphine monoproducts are recommended for pregnant women.
- Counsel patients on safe storage of, and nonsharing of, medications. Patients must agree to safe storage of their medication. This is even more critical if there are children in the home where the patient lives. Counsel patients about acquiring locked devices and avoiding storage in parts of the home frequented by visitors (e.g., do not recommend storage in the kitchen or common bathrooms). Proactively discuss how medication should be stored and transported when traveling to minimize risk of unintended loss.
- Counsel patients on taking medication as instructed and not sharing medication. Explicitly explain to patients the definitions of diversion and misuse, with examples. Patients are required to take medication as instructed by the healthcare professional; for example, they may not crush or inject the medication.
- Check the prescription drug monitoring program for new patients and check regularly thereafter. Prescription drug monitoring program reports can be a useful resource when there is little history available or when there is a concern based on observation. Check for prescriptions that interact with buprenorphine and for other buprenorphine prescribers.

- Prescribe a therapeutic dose that is tailored to the patient's needs. Do not routinely provide an additional supply "just in case." Question patients who say they need a significantly higher dose, particularly when they are already at 24 mg per day of buprenorphine equivalents.
- Make sure the patient understands the practice's treatment agreement and prescription policies. The XYZ Medical Practice's treatment agreement and other documentation are clear about policies regarding number of doses in each prescription, refills, and rules on "lost" prescriptions. Review the policies in person with the patient. Offer an opportunity for questions. Patient and provider must sign the agreement. Review the policies again with the patient at subsequent appointments. See Sample Buprenorphine Treatment Agreement or Sample XR-NTX Treatment Agreement as needed.

Procedures for Monitoring:

- Request random urine tests. The presence of buprenorphine in the urine indicates that the patient has taken some portion of the prescribed dose. Absence of buprenorphine in the urine supports nonadherence. Testing for buprenorphine metabolites (which are present only if buprenorphine is metabolized) should periodically be included to minimize the possibility that buprenorphine is added directly to the urine sample. Dipstick tests can be subverted or replaced. A range of strategies can be used to minimize falsified urine collections, including (1) observed collection; (2) disallowing carry-in items (e.g., purses, backpacks) in the bathroom; (3) turning off running water and coloring toilet water to eliminate the possibility of dilution; (4) monitoring the bathroom door so that only one person can go in; and (5) testing the temperature of the urine immediately after voiding.
- Schedule unannounced pill/film counts. Periodically ask patients who are at high risk at initial or subsequent appointments to bring in their medication containers for a pill/film count.
- With unannounced monitoring (both pill/film counts and urine tests), the patient is contacted and must appear within a specified time period (e.g., 24 hours) after the phone call. If the patient doesn't show, then the provider should consider this as a positive indicator of misuse or diversion.
- Directly observe ingestion. Patients take medication in front of the healthcare professional or another qualified clinician and are observed until the medication dissolves in the mouth (transmucosal [sublingual or buccal] absorption). Patients who are having difficulty adhering to their buprenorphine can have their medication provided under direct observation in the office for a designated frequency (e.g., three times/week).
- Limit medication supply. When directly observed doses in the office are not practical, short prescription time spans can be used (e.g., weekly, 3 days at a time).

Procedures To Respond to Misuse or Diversion:

Misuse or diversion doesn't mean automatic discharge from the practice. However, it will require consideration of one or more of the following procedures:

- Evaluate the misuse and diversion. For instance, describe the incident of misuse (e.g., "the patient took the prescribed dose on three or more occasions by intravenous route immediately after starting treatment, stating that she believed the dose would not be adequate by sublingual route; she has just initiated treatment") or diversion ("the patient gave half of dose to his wife, who is still using heroin and was withdrawing, because he did not want her to have to buy heroin off the street; she is on a waiting list for treatment") and tailor the response to the behavior (e.g., reeducation of the patient on buprenorphine pharmacology in the first example above; assistance with treatment entry for the spouse in the second example). Reassess the treatment plan and patient progress. Strongly consider smaller supplies of medication and supervised dosing for any patient who is taking medication intravenously or intranasally or diverting, regardless of reason. Treatment structure may need to be increased, including more frequent appointments, supervised administration, and increased psychosocial support.
- Intensify treatment or level of care, if needed. Some patients may require an alternative treatment setting or pharmacotherapy such as methadone. The clinician will discuss these alternatives with the patient to ensure optimal patient outcome. This should be discussed at treatment onset so the patient is aware of the consequences of misuse and diversion.
- Document and describe the misuse and diversion incident. Also document the clinical thinking that supports the clinical response, which should be aimed at minimizing risk of diversion and misuse and treating the patient's opioid use disorder at the level of care needed.

Policy adapted from ASAM's *Office-Based Opioid Use Disorder Policy and Procedure Manual*, which is updated periodically; the most current version is available online (https://www.asam.org/docs/default-source/advocacy/sample-diversion-policy.pdf?sfvrsn=6).

Adapted with permission.[378]

This page intentionally left blank.

Chapter 3F: Medical Management of Patients Taking OUD Medications in Hospital Settings

Chapter 3F guides the management of patients taking OUD medications in hospital settings. The audience is healthcare professionals in emergency, general medical, surgical, psychiatric, and obstetric units.

Patients with opioid use disorder (OUD) who present to emergency departments (EDs) or are admitted to hospitals for acute medical or psychiatric care can benefit from medication to treat OUD in the hospital setting. During acute medical illness, patients experiencing consequences of opioid use may be motivated to change.[379] Hospital-based providers can take this opportunity to initiate long-term medication maintenance.[380,381]

Unfortunately, less than one-quarter of patients with an opioid-related hospitalization are offered Food and Drug Administration-approved medication for OUD within 30 days of discharge.[382] Patients who already take OUD medication may also present to the hospital. Thus, a broad understanding of how to manage their OUD medication during hospitalization is necessary.

The keys to effective patient management in general hospital settings are:

- **Balancing pharmacotherapy for OUD with other medical concerns** (e.g., surgery, pain management) during hospitalization.
- **Careful management after discharge.**
- **Seamless transfer to opioid treatment** via an opioid treatment program (OTP) or office-based opioid treatment (OBOT) provider after discharge.

OPIOID-RELATED inpatient hospital stays **INCREASED 64%** nationally from 2005–2014.[383]

Hospitalized or ED Patients Taking Medication for OUD

Buprenorphine, methadone, and naltrexone may be ordered in EDs or inpatient hospital units. It's essential for the patient to continue receiving OUD medication while hospitalized.

Pain Management

Pain management for hospitalized patients who take OUD medication is a key element of medical management. Discuss pain management and engage in a shared decision-making process with patients being treated for OUD with buprenorphine, methadone, or naltrexone. Patients may have strong preferences and opinions about pain and use of opioid analgesics for pain treatment. Some patients may want to avoid opioid analgesics. For others, inadequately treated pain may be a trigger for illicit drug use. Involve primary care pain specialists and addiction treatment providers in discussing options for managing OUD medication and pain during patient hospitalization.

Buprenorphine

The hospital team will need to manage buprenorphine for patients who present to the ED or are hospitalized on buprenorphine maintenance. **Physicians in inpatient settings can legally order buprenorphine without a waiver if a patient is admitted primarily for other medical reasons.**[384] Key medication management strategies include:

- **Obtaining written consent to contact the patient's providers,** including:
    - Primary care provider.
    - Buprenorphine prescriber.
    - Pharmacy.
- **Confirming the patient's outpatient buprenorphine dose** by:
    - Checking prescribing records.
    - Contacting the prescriber or pharmacy.
    - Examining recent prescription bottles.
    - Checking the prescription drug monitoring program database before administering buprenorphine.
- Providing the usual daily dose to the patient, once that dose is confirmed.
- Ensuring the patient's outpatient prescriber understands the reason for any missed visits.
- Informing the patient's outpatient prescriber that the patient may test positive for opioids if treated with opioid analgesics while in the hospital.
- Maintaining contact with the patient's prescriber, especially when a buprenorphine dose change is considered and in discharge planning.

Patients with pain may continue their buprenorphine while in the hospital. For mild-to-moderate pain, dividing the patient's usual buprenorphine dose three times per day (TID) may provide sufficient pain relief.[385] In some cases, increased buprenorphine dose may be appropriate. For moderate-to-severe pain, additional analgesia will be necessary. Two approaches to consider:

1. **Continue buprenorphine treatment and use full agonist opioids for added pain relief.** Because of the partial blockade caused by buprenorphine, higher-than-usual doses of opioids will probably be required for pain relief. Fentanyl, hydromorphone, and morphine have relatively high binding affinities for the mu-opioid receptor and are most likely to displace buprenorphine from receptors and provide improved analgesia. Once the painful condition has improved, if mild-to-moderate pain persists, buprenorphine can be divided TID to manage residual pain. This approach is usually successful and allows the patient to remain stable on buprenorphine.

2. **Discontinue buprenorphine upon hospitalization and use full agonist opioids to treat pain and prevent withdrawal.** This approach avoids the blockade effect of buprenorphine on the mu-opioid receptors but leaves the patient vulnerable to a return to illicit opioid use. It may be useful if the first approach does not achieve adequate pain control.[386] Consider a consult by an addiction medicine, psychiatric, or pain management provider if appropriate and available.

Pregnant women on buprenorphine can continue buprenorphine through their labor. Labor pain for pregnant patients on buprenorphine can be managed effectively with epidural analgesia or intravenous opioids. Spinal anesthesia is effective in patients on buprenorphine; patients can receive general anesthesia if needed.[387]

Perioperative pain management of patients on buprenorphine requires further study, but multiple approaches have been found effective. **Most patients can continue buprenorphine through the operative period.** Treat postoperative pain with regional anesthesia, nonopioid pain management, or full agonist opioids. Remember that higher doses are likely to be necessary. Some data suggest that buprenorphine divided TID may even be as effective as morphine for postoperative pain control.[388] Alternatively, buprenorphine can be discontinued 72 hours before a planned surgery and restarted after resolution of acute postoperative pain. The risk of this approach is that it leaves the patient vulnerable to a return to use of illicit opioids.[389]

Methadone

The hospital team will need to manage methadone for patients who present to the ED or are hospitalized on methadone maintenance treatment. This includes pregnant women. Generally, only physicians in OTPs can order methadone to treat OUD. However, **physicians in an inpatient setting can legally order methadone administration to patients admitted primarily for other reasons.**[390]

Contact the patient's OTP directly to confirm the outpatient methadone dose, the last day of dose administration, and whether the patient was dispensed take-home doses (and how many doses) after the last dose administration at the OTP. This is to avoid double dosing and to avoid providing a full dose to a patient who hasn't been to the OTP for several days. Notify the OTP of the patient's admission and discharge so that OTP staff is aware of:

- The patient's upcoming missed visits.
- Medications received during hospitalization.
- Medications prescribed at discharge.

Patients in pain should receive their full usual daily dose of methadone, barring contraindications. This is their baseline dose and should not be considered a dose for pain management.

The expert panel for this Treatment Improvement Protocol (TIP) recommends restarting buprenorphine before discharge when possible, with a proper handoff between inpatient and outpatient providers.

They'll need pain medication in addition to their usual methadone dose. If their condition is painful enough to require opioids, prescribe short-acting opioids as scheduled, not as-needed, treatment. Because these patients are already opioid tolerant, they'll likely require higher doses of opioids than patients without tolerance.[391] However, as with any patient, use nonopioid multimodal pain management when possible to minimize reliance on opioids and maximize pain control.[392]

CLINICAL CAUTION

Do Not Rely Solely on Patient Self-Report of Methadone Dosage

Do not administer the methadone dose based on patient self-report of OTP enrollment and methadone dose; get OTP confirmation. This is important because doses above 30 mg can be lethal if the patient is not currently receiving methadone treatment and has relatively low tolerance to opioids. If it's not possible to confirm the patient's methadone dose because the OTP is closed on nights or weekends and has no emergency contact, up to 20 mg per day can be administered to treat opioid withdrawal symptoms, but monitor for signs of opioid intoxication. If the patient shows no signs of sedation or opioid intoxication 3 to 4 hours after the initial dose and continues to display symptoms of withdrawal, an additional 5 mg to 10 mg may be safe to administer.

It is important to tell patients who receive take-home doses that they should not take their own medication while in the hospital. They will receive methadone from the treatment team. Patients can be asked to lock their take-home medications with their other valuables. It is also important to monitor these patients closely after the initial and subsequent methadone administration in the hospital. Some patients who receive take-home doses do not take their entire dose every day, so they may display signs of intoxication or frank overdose if the hospital staff gives them the full dose.

Naltrexone

Patients taking oral naltrexone for OUD treatment may continue naltrexone when admitted to the hospital if they do not have and are not at risk for developing a painful condition requiring opioid analgesia. Oral naltrexone provides full blockade of opioid receptors for up to 72 hours. Extended-release injectable naltrexone (XR-NTX) provides measurable naltrexone levels for 1 month or longer. Thus, managing acute pain in patients taking XR-NTX is complicated.

In patients who have taken naltrexone, manage severe pain intensively via nonopioid approaches, such as regional anesthesia or injected nonsteroidal anti-inflammatory drugs.

Naltrexone blockade can be overcome with very high doses of opioids, but patients must be closely monitored for respiratory depression in a setting with anesthesia services. This is especially true upon discontinuation of oral naltrexone, which dissociates from opioid receptors.

Hospitalized or ED Patients Not Taking Medication for OUD

Patients with OUD who present to the ED or are admitted to the hospital for an acute medical problem may benefit from initiating medications for OUD during their hospitalization. A thoughtful and respectful discussion of treatment options and patient-centered provision of medication can be a critical entry point into care. Research supports the efficacy of initiating either buprenorphine or methadone during acute hospital stays[393,394] and starting patients on buprenorphine in the ED.[395]

Buprenorphine Induction in the Hospital Setting

Patients admitted to the hospital for medical conditions incident to OUD can undergo medically supervised withdrawal or receive buprenorphine maintenance treatment during their inpatient stay.[396] It is important to adequately address opioid withdrawal because hospital patients may otherwise sign out against medical advice or use illicit opioids in the hospital. **Buprenorphine can also be initiated for maintenance treatment** if there is a system in place that allows smooth and reliable discharge to an outpatient buprenorphine prescriber. Unlike methadone, a several-day delay between discharge and the first visit to the outpatient provider is acceptable for stable patients, as long as sufficient medication is provided until the patient begins outpatient treatment. The prescription for medication to be taken outside the hospital must be written by a prescriber with a buprenorphine waiver. If there is no prescriber with a waiver, it is possible to have a patient return to the hospital ED or a clinic within the hospital to have the buprenorphine dose administered by a physician (who does not need to be waivered) for up to 3 days.

To provide continuity of care at discharge, use these strategies:

- **Develop and maintain a network of local buprenorphine prescribers and other drug treatment providers.**
- **Discharge patients directly to a specific outpatient prescriber** for stabilization and maintenance after inpatient buprenorphine induction.
- **Send discharge information directly to the outpatient prescriber,** including treatment course, medications administered, and medications prescribed.

To initiate buprenorphine during hospitalization:

- Confirm that there are no contraindications to buprenorphine before initiation.
- Discontinue opioids for pain management only when no longer needed and the patient is stable enough to tolerate withdrawal.
- Wait for patients to develop opioid withdrawal symptoms.
- Initiate buprenorphine treatment.
- Individualize buprenorphine dosing.
- Follow the dosing guidance found in Chapter 3D of this TIP.

A clinical trial found that starting buprenorphine in the ED to treat OUD was more effective in linking patients to buprenorphine treatment in the community than were two other approaches without medication.[397] When patients presented in opioid withdrawal, they received 8 mg of buprenorphine in the ED. Patients who were not in withdrawal received a detailed self-medication guide and were provided buprenorphine for an unobserved home induction. In both cases, patients were given sufficient buprenorphine to take 16 mg per day at home until they could see an outpatient prescriber within 72 hours. Close follow-up with an outpatient buprenorphine prescriber was critical for dose stabilization and ongoing medication management.

Methadone Induction in the Hospital Setting

Offer to treat hospitalized patients in opioid withdrawal with methadone (or buprenorphine) maintenance if they can continue the medication in an OTP seamlessly after discharge. Do not start patients on methadone maintenance in the hospital without a clear follow-up plan. Form relationships with local OTPs that allow discharging of patients directly into methadone maintenance treatment.

RESOURCE ALERT

Telehealth Tools for the Treatment of OUD

The Substance Abuse and Mental Health Services Administration and other federal agencies have developed numerous resources to guide healthcare professionals in their use of telehealth and telemedicine approaches for OUD. These resources include information on:

- Guidance on the use of telemedicine in OTPs (https://store.samhsa.gov/shin/content/PEP15-FEDGUIDEOTP/PEP15-FEDGUIDEOTP.pdf).
- The policies that must be put in place (to comply with the Controlled Substances Act) by physicians who wish to use telehealth in treating patients with buprenorphine for OUD under the Drug Addiction Treatment Act of 2000. Federal (and sometimes state) restrictions apply, which can be reviewed by accessing 21 USC § 802 (www.gpo.gov/fdsys/pkg/USCODE-2011-title21/pdf/USCODE-2011-title21-chap13-subchapI-partA-sec802.pdf).
- Centers for Medicare and Medicaid guidance on telehealth (www.cms.gov/Medicare/Medicare-General-Information/Telehealth/index.html).
- Challenges and opportunities in using telehealth for rural populations (https://store.samhsa.gov/shin/content/SMA16-4989/SMA16-4989.pdf).
- How certified community behavioral health clinics can use telehealth approaches to expand their services (www.samhsa.gov/section-223/care-coordination/telehealth-telemedicine).

> **The TIP expert panel urges providers not to force patients to withdraw from opioid agonist treatment in the hospital, especially if they have acute illness, pain, or a mental illness.**

Inpatient methadone inductions should follow the same "start low, go slow" principles that outpatient inductions do (see Chapter 3B of this TIP). The initial dose should be from 10 mg to 20 mg per day. Increase slowly by 5 mg every few days in response to symptoms of opioid withdrawal and level of sedation at the peak plasma level 2 to 4 hours after dosing.

Naltrexone Induction in the Hospital Setting

Consider XR-NTX initiation for patients who complete withdrawal in the hospital and are opioid free for 7 days (short acting) and up to 14 days (long acting). Only do so if:

- There are no contraindications (such as the need for opioid analgesia).
- The patient prefers it after a risk/benefit discussion that covers alternative treatments.
- There are available follow-up opportunities for ongoing medication maintenance upon discharge.

No published data indicate this approach's effectiveness.

If a patient desires and gives informed consent for medically supervised withdrawal and naltrexone initiation while in the hospital, a first dose of naltrexone can be given before discharge. As with other medications for OUD, discharge coordination is critical. Hospitals that develop naltrexone induction protocols need to have a clear discharge plan in place for patients who will then need to continue naltrexone in the outpatient setting. Patients should be advised about the risk of overdose if return to opioid use occurs after discontinuing naltrexone.

Medical Management Plan

The key to effective treatment is to **involve patients and all treating healthcare professionals in developing a comprehensive plan for managing treatment with OUD medication during and after hospitalization.** This plan should include:

- Strategies for pain management (if required).
- In-hospital dosing procedures.
- Postdischarge coordination of care with outpatient programs and outpatient providers.

This plan ensures effective pain relief as well as continuity of ongoing care for patients taking medication for OUD.[398]

Notes

1. Department of Health and Human Services. (2016). *The opioid epidemic: By the numbers.* Washington, DC: Author.

2. Center for Behavioral Health Statistics and Quality. (2017). *Key substance use and mental health indicators in the United States: Results from the 2016 National Survey on Drug Use and Health.* Rockville, MD: Substance Abuse and Mental Health Services Administration.

3. American Psychiatric Association. (2013). *Diagnostic and statistical manual of mental disorders* (5th ed.). Arlington, VA: American Psychiatric Publishing.

4. Weiss, A. J., Elixhauser, A., Barrett, M. L., Steiner, C. A., Bailey, M. K., & O'Malley, L. (2017, January). *Opioid-related inpatient stays and emergency department visits by state, 2009–2014.* HCUP Statistical Brief No. 219. Rockville, MD: Agency for Healthcare Research and Quality.

5. American Society of Addiction Medicine. (2011). Definition of addiction. Chevy Chase, MD: American Society of Addiction Medicine. Retrieved January 5, 2018, from www.asam.org/resources/definition-of-addiction

6. American Psychiatric Association. (2013). *Diagnostic and statistical manual of mental disorders* (5th ed.). Arlington, VA: American Psychiatric Publishing.

7. Substance Abuse and Mental Health Services Administration. (2015). *Federal guidelines for opioid treatment programs.* HHS Publication No. (SMA) PEP15-FEDGUIDEOTP. Rockville, MD: Substance Abuse and Mental Health Services Administration.

8. Substance Abuse and Mental Health Services Administration. (2016). *Pocket guide: Medication-assisted treatment of opioid use disorder.* HHS Publication No. (SMA) 16-4892PG. Rockville, MD: Substance Abuse and Mental Health Services Administration.

9. Substance Abuse and Mental Health Services Administration. (2015). *Clinical use of extended-release injectable naltrexone in the treatment of opioid use disorder: A brief guide.* HHS Publication No. (SMA) 14-4892R. Rockville, MD: Substance Abuse and Mental Health Services Administration.

10. Kreek, M. J., Borg, L., Ducat, E., & Ray, B. (2010). Pharmacotherapy in the treatment of addiction: Methadone. *Journal of Addictive Diseases, 29*(2), 200–216.

11. Mattick, R. P., Breen, C., Kimber, J., & Davoli, M. (2009). Methadone maintenance therapy versus no opioid replacement therapy for opioid dependence. *Cochrane Database of Systematic Reviews, 2009*(3), 1–19.

12. World Health Organization. (2015). *19th WHO model list of essential medicines.* Geneva, Switzerland: Author.

13. Mattick, R. P., Breen, C., Kimber, J., & Davoli, M. (2014). Buprenorphine maintenance versus placebo or methadone maintenance for opioid dependence. *Cochrane Database of Systematic Reviews, 2014*(2), 1–84.

14. Sees, K. L., Delucchi, K. L., Masson, C., Rosen, A., Clark, H. W., Robillard, H., ... Hall, S. M. (2000). Methadone maintenance vs 180-day psychosocially enriched detoxification for treatment of opioid dependence: A randomized controlled trial. *JAMA, 283*(10), 1303–1310.

15. Nielsen, S., Larance, B., Degenhardt, L., Gowing, L., Kehler, C., & Lintzeris, N. (2016). Opioid agonist treatment for pharmaceutical opioid dependent people. *Cochrane Database of Systematic Reviews, 2016*(5), 1–61.

16. Stoller, K. B., Stephens, M. A. C., & Schorr, A. (2016). Integrated service delivery models for opioid treatment programs in an era of increasing opioid addiction, health reform, and parity. Retrieved October 16, 2017, from www.aatod.org/wp-content/uploads/2016/07/2nd-Whitepaper-.pdf

17. Comer, S. D., Sullivan, M. A., Yu, E., Rothenberg, J. L., Kleber, H. D., Kampman, K., ... O'Brien, C. P. (2006). Injectable, sustained-release naltrexone for the treatment of opioid dependence: A randomized, placebo-controlled trial. *Archives of General Psychiatry, 63*(2), 210–218.

18. Krupitsky, E., Nunes, E. V., Ling, W., Illeperuma, A., Gastfriend, D. R., & Silverman, B. L. (2011). Injectable extended-release naltrexone for opioid dependence: A double-blind, placebo-controlled, multicentre randomised trial. *Lancet, 377*(9776), 1506–1513.

19. Lee, J. D., Friedmann, P. D., Kinlock, T. W., Nunes, E. V., Boney, T. Y., Hoskinson, R. A., Jr., ... O'Brien, C. P. (2016). Extended-release naltrexone to prevent opioid relapse in criminal justice offenders. *New England Journal of Medicine, 374*(13), 1232–1242.

20. American Society of Addiction Medicine. (2015). *The ASAM national practice guideline for the use of medications in the treatment of addiction involving opioid use.* Chevy Chase, MD: Author.

21. Lee, J. D., McDonald, R., Grossman, E., McNeely, J., Laska, E., Rotrosen, J., & Gourevitch, M. N. (2015). Opioid treatment at release from jail using extended-release naltrexone: A pilot proof-of-concept randomized effectiveness trial. *Addiction, 110*(6), 1008–1014.

22. Leslie, D. L., Milchak, W., Gastfriend, D. R., Herschman, P. L., Bixler, E. O., Velott, D. L., & Meyer, R. E. (2015). Effects of injectable extended-release naltrexone (XR-NTX) for opioid dependence on residential rehabilitation outcomes and early follow-up. *American Journal on Addictions, 24*(3), 265–270.

23. Sullivan, M. A., Garawi, F., Bisaga, A., Comer, S. D., Carpenter, K., Raby, W. N., ... Nunes, E. V. (2007). Management of relapse in naltrexone maintenance for heroin dependence. *Drug and Alcohol Dependence, 91*(2–3), 289–292.

24. Mattick, R. P., Breen, C., Kimber, J., & Davoli, M. (2014). Buprenorphine maintenance versus placebo or methadone maintenance for opioid dependence. *Cochrane Database of Systematic Reviews, 2014*(2), 1–84.

25. World Health Organization. (2015). *19th WHO model list of essential medicines.* Geneva, Switzerland: Author.

26. Jaffe, J. H., & O'Keeffe, C. (2003). From morphine clinics to buprenorphine: Regulating opioid agonist treatment of addiction in the United States. *Drug and Alcohol Dependence, 70*(2 Suppl.), S3–S11.

27. Ling, W., Casadonte, P., Bigelow, G., Kampman, K. M., Patkar, A., Bailey, G. L., ... Beebe, K. L. (2010). Buprenorphine implants for treatment of opioid dependence: A randomized controlled trial. *JAMA, 304*(14), 1576–1583.

28. Substance Abuse and Mental Health Services Administration. (2015). *Clinical use of extended-release injectable naltrexone in the treatment of opioid use disorder: A brief guide.* HHS Publication No. (SMA) 14-4892R. Rockville, MD: Substance Abuse and Mental Health Services Administration.

29. Kinlock, T. W., Gordon, M. S., Schwartz, R. P., Fitzgerald, T. T., & O'Grady, K. E. (2009). A randomized clinical trial of methadone maintenance for prisoners: Results at twelve-months post-release. *Journal of Substance Abuse Treatment, 37*(3), 277–285.

30. McKenzie, M., Zaller, N., Dickman, S. L., Green, T. C., Parihk, A., Friedmann, P. D., & Rich, J. D. (2012). A randomized trial of methadone initiation prior to release from incarceration. *Substance Abuse, 33*(1), 19–29.

31. Gordon, M. S., Kinlock, T. W., Schwartz, R. P., O'Grady, K. E., Fitzgerald, T. T., & Vocci, F. J. (2017). A randomized trial of buprenorphine for prisoners: Findings at 12-months post-release. *Drug and Alcohol Dependence, 172,* 34–42.

32. Vocci, F. J., Schwartz, R. P., Wilson, M. E., Gordon, M. S., Kinlock, T. W., Fitzgerald, T. T., O'Grady, K. E., & Jaffe, J. H. (2015). Buprenorphine dose induction in non-opioid-tolerant pre-release prisoners. *Drug and Alcohol Dependence, 156,* 133–138.

33. Substance Abuse and Mental Health Services Administration. (2018). *Clinical guidance for treating pregnant and parenting women with opioid use disorder and their infants.* HHS Publication No. (SMA) 18-5054. Rockville, MD: Substance Abuse and Mental Health Services Administration.

34. Binder, T., & Vavrinková, B. (2008). Prospective randomised comparative study of the effect of buprenorphine, methadone and heroin on the course of pregnancy, birthweight of newborns, early postpartum adaptation and course of the neonatal abstinence syndrome (NAS) in women followed up in the outpatient department. *Neuro Endocrinology Letters, 29*(1), 80–86.

35. Fajemirokun-Odudeyi, O., Sinha, C., Tutty, S., Pairaudeau, P., Armstrong, D., Phillips, T., & Lindow, S. W. (2006). Pregnancy outcome in women who use opiates. *European Journal of Obstetrics & Gynecology and Reproductive Biology, 126*(2), 170–175.

36. Stimmel, B., & Adamsons, K. (1976). Narcotic dependency in pregnancy. Methadone maintenance compared to use of street drugs. *JAMA, 235,* 1121–1124.

37. Substance Abuse and Mental Health Services Administration. (2018). *Clinical guidance for treating pregnant and parenting women with opioid use disorder and their infants.* HHS Publication No. (SMA) 18-5054. Rockville, MD: Substance Abuse and Mental Health Services Administration.

38. Substance Abuse and Mental Health Services Administration. (2015). *Clinical use of extended-release injectable naltrexone in the treatment of opioid use disorder: A brief guide.* HHS Publication No. (SMA) 14-4892R. Rockville, MD: Substance Abuse and Mental Health Services Administration.

39. American College of Obstetricians and Gynecologists Committee Opinion. (2017, August). Opioid use and opioid use disorder in pregnancy. Number 711. Retrieved October 30, 2017, from www.acog.org/Resources-And-Publications/Committee-Opinions/Committee-on-Obstetric-Practice/Opioid-Use-and-Opioid-Use-Disorder-in-Pregnancy

40. Substance Abuse and Mental Health Services Administration. (2018). *Clinical guidance for treating pregnant and parenting women with opioid use disorder and their infants.* HHS Publication No. (SMA) 18-5054. Rockville, MD: Substance Abuse and Mental Health Services Administration.

41. American College of Obstetricians and Gynecologists Committee Opinion. (2017, August). Opioid use and opioid use disorder in pregnancy. Number 711. Retrieved October 30, 2017, from www.acog.org/Resources-And-Publications/Committee-Opinions/Committee-on-Obstetric-Practice/Opioid-Use-and-Opioid-Use-Disorder-in-Pregnancy

42. American Society of Addiction Medicine. (2015). *The ASAM national practice guideline for the use of medications in the treatment of addiction involving opioid use.* Chevy Chase, MD: Author.

43. Mattick, R. P., Breen, C., Kimber, J., & Davoli, M. (2014). Buprenorphine maintenance versus placebo or methadone maintenance for opioid dependence. *Cochrane Database of Systematic Reviews, 2014*(2). CD002207.

44. Lee, J. D., Nunes, E. V., Jr., Novo, P., Bachrach, K., Bailey, G. L., Bhatt, S., ... Rotrosen, J. (2018). Comparative effectiveness of extended-release naltrexone versus buprenorphine-naloxone for opioid relapse prevention (X:BOT): A multicentre, open-label, randomised controlled trial. *Lancet, 391*(10118), 309–318.

45. Tanum, L., Solli, K. K., Latif, Z. E., Benth, J. Š., Opheim, A., Sharma-Haase, K., ... Kunøe, N. (2017). The effectiveness of injectable extended-release naltrexone vs daily buprenorphine-naloxone for opioid dependence: A randomized clinical noninferiority trial. *JAMA Psychiatry, 74*(12), 1197–1205.

46. Department of Veterans Affairs & Department of Defense. (2015). *VA/DoD clinical practice guideline for the management of substance use disorders*. Retrieved October 16, 2017, from www.healthquality.va.gov/guidelines/MH/sud/VADoDSUDCPGRevised22216.pdf

47. Sees, K. L., Delucchi, K. L., Masson, C., Rosen, A., Clark, H. W., Robillard, H., ... Hall, S. M. (2000). Methadone maintenance vs 180-day psychosocially enriched detoxification for treatment of opioid dependence: A randomized controlled trial. *JAMA, 283*(10), 1303–1310.

48. Weiss, R. D., Potter, J. S., Fiellin, D. A., Byrne, M., Connery, H. S., Dickinson, W., ... Ling, W. (2011). Adjunctive counseling during brief and extended buprenorphine-naloxone treatment for prescription opioid dependence: A 2-phase randomized controlled trial. *Archives of General Psychiatry, 68*(12), 1238–1246.

49. Lee, J. D., Friedmann, P. D., Kinlock, T. W., Nunes, E. V., Boney, T. Y., Hoskinson, R. A., Jr., ... O'Brien, C. P. (2016). Extended-release naltrexone to prevent opioid relapse in criminal justice offenders. *New England Journal of Medicine, 374*(13), 1232–1242.

50. Gowing, L., Ali, R., White, J. M., & Mbewe, D. (2017). Buprenorphine for managing opioid withdrawal. *Cochrane Database of Systematic Reviews, 2017*(2). CD002025.

51. Degenhardt, L., Randall, D., Hall, W., Law, M., Butler, T., & Burns, L. (2009). Mortality among clients of a state-wide opioid pharmacotherapy program over 20 years: Risk factors and lives saved. *Drug and Alcohol Dependence, 105*(1–2), 9–15.

52. Hser, Y. I., Huang, D., Saxon, A. J., Woody, G., Moskowitz, A. L., Matthews, A. G., & Ling, W. (2017). Distinctive trajectories of opioid use over an extended follow-up of patients in a multisite trial on buprenorphine + naloxone and methadone. *Journal of Addiction Medicine, 11*(1), 63–69.

53. Novick, D. M., Salsitz, E. A., Joseph, H., & Kreek, M. J. (2015). Methadone medical maintenance: An early 21st-century perspective. *Journal of Addictive Diseases, 34*(2–3), 226–237.

54. Fiellin, D. A., Moore, B. A., Sullivan, L. E., Becker, W. C., Pantalon, M. V., Chawarski, M. C., ... Schottenfeld, R. S. (2008). Long-term treatment with buprenorphine/naloxone in primary care: Results at 2-5 years. *American Journal on Addictions, 17*(2), 116–120.

55. Krupitsky, E., Nunes, E. V., Ling, W., Gastfriend, D. R., Memisoglu, A., & Silverman, B. L. (2013). Injectable extended-release naltrexone (XR-NTX) for opioid dependence: long-term safety and effectiveness. *Addiction, 108*(9), 162–1637.

56. Kreek, M. J., Levran, O., Reed, B., Schlussman, S. D., Zhou, Y., & Butelman, E. R. (2012). Opiate addiction and cocaine addiction: Underlying molecular neurobiology and genetics. *Journal of Clinical Investigation, 122*(10), 3387–3393.

57. Volkow, N. D., Koob, G. F., & McLellan, A. T. (2016). Neurobiologic advances from the brain disease model of addiction. *New England Journal of Medicine, 374*(4), 363–371.

58. Ling, W., Hillhouse, M., Domier, C., Doraimani, G., Hunter, J., Thomas, C., ... Bilangi, R. (2009). Buprenorphine tapering schedule and illicit opioid use. *Addiction, 104*(2), 256–265.

59. Senay, E. C., Dorus, W., & Thornton, W. (1977). Withdrawal from methadone maintenance: Rate of withdrawal and expectation. *Archives of General Psychiatry, 34*(3), 361–367.

60. Sigmon, S. C., Dunn, K. E., Saulsgiver, K., Patrick, M. E., Badger, G. J., Heil, S. H., ... Higgins, S. T. (2013). A randomized, double-blind evaluation of buprenorphine taper duration in primary prescription opioid abusers. *JAMA Psychiatry, 70*(12), 1347–1354.

61. Department of Veterans Affairs & Department of Defense. (2015). *VA/DoD clinical practice guideline for the management of substance use disorders*. Retrieved October 16, 2017, from www.healthquality.va.gov/guidelines/MH/sud/VADoDSUDCPGRevised22216.pdf

62. Fullerton, C. A., Kim, M., Thomas, C. P., Lyman, D. R., Montejano, L. B., Dougherty, R. H., ... Delphin-Rittmon, M. E. (2014). Medication-assisted treatment with methadone: Assessing the evidence. *Psychiatric Services, 65*(2), 146–157.

63. Weiss, R. D., Potter, J. S., Fiellin, D. A., Byrne, M., Connery, H. S., Dickinson, W., ... Ling, W. (2011). Adjunctive counseling during brief and extended buprenorphine-naloxone treatment for prescription opioid dependence: A 2-phase randomized controlled trial. *Archives of General Psychiatry, 68*(12), 1238–1246.

64. Amato, L., Davoli, M., Minozzi, S., Ferroni, E., Ali, R., & Ferri M. (2013). Methadone at tapered doses for the management of opioid withdrawal. *Cochrane Database of Systematic Reviews, 2013*(2). CD003409.

65. Weiss, R. D., Potter, J. S., Fiellin, D. A., Byrne, M., Connery, H. S., Dickinson, W., ... Ling, W. (2011). Adjunctive counseling during brief and extended buprenorphine-naloxone treatment for prescription opioid dependence: A 2-phase randomized controlled trial. *Archives of General Psychiatry, 68*(12), 1238–1246.

66. Ling, W., Hillhouse, M., Domier, C., Doraimani, G., Hunter, J., Thomas, C., & Bilangi, R. (2009) Buprenorphine tapering schedule and illicit opioid use. *Addiction, 104*(2), 256–265.

67. Amato, L., Minozzi, S., Davoli, M., & Vecchi, S. (2011). Psychosocial and pharmacological treatments versus pharmacological treatments for opioid detoxification. *Cochrane Database of Systematic Reviews, 2011*(9). CD005031.

68. Nunes, E. V., Gordon, M., Friedmann, P. D., Fishman, M. J., Lee, J. D., Chen, D. T., ... O'Brien, C. P. (2018). Relapse to opioid use disorder after inpatient treatment: Protective effect of injection naltrexone. *Journal of Substance Abuse Treatment, 85*, 49–55.

69. Satoh, M., & Minami, M. (1995). Molecular pharmacology of the opioid receptors. *Pharmacology & Therapeutics, 68*(3), 343–364.

70. Akbarali, H. I., Inkisar, A., & Dewey, W. L. (2014). Site and mechanism of morphine tolerance in the gastrointestinal tract. *Neurogastroenterology and Motility, 26*(10), 1361–1367.

71. Bodnar, R. J. (2017). Endogenous opiates and behavior, 2015. *Peptides, 88*, 126–188.

72. Johnson, R. E., Strain, E. C., & Amass, L. (2003). Buprenorphine: How to use it right. *Drug and Alcohol Dependence, 70*(Suppl.), S59–S77.

73. Minozzi, S., Amato, L., Vecchi, S., Davoli, M., Kirchmayer, U., & Verster, A. (2011). Oral naltrexone maintenance treatment for opioid dependence. *Cochrane Database of Systematic Reviews, 2011*(2). CD001333.

74. Substance Abuse and Mental Health Services Administration. (2016). Sublingual and transmucosal buprenorphine for opioid use disorder: Review and update. *Advisory*, Vol. 15, Issue 1. Rockville, MD: Substance Abuse and Mental Health Services Administration.

75. Kreek, M. J., Borg, L., Ducat, E., & Ray, B. (2010). Pharmacotherapy in the treatment of addiction: Methadone. *Journal of Addictive Diseases, 29*(2), 200–216.

76. Mattick, R. P., Breen, C., Kimber, J., & Davoli, M. (2009). Methadone maintenance therapy versus no opioid replacement therapy for opioid dependence. *Cochrane Database of Systematic Reviews, 2009*(3), 1–19.

77. Mattick, R. P., Breen, C., Kimber, J., & Davoli, M. (2009). Methadone maintenance therapy versus no opioid replacement therapy for opioid dependence. *Cochrane Database of Systematic Reviews, 2009*(3), 1–19.

78. Degenhardt, L., Randall, D., Hall, W., Law, M., Butler, T., & Burns, L. (2009). Mortality among clients of a state-wide opioid pharmacotherapy program over 20 years: Risk factors and lives saved. *Drug and Alcohol Dependence, 105*(1–2), 9–15.

79. Metzger, D. S., Woody, G. E., McLellan, A. T., O'Brien, C. P., Druley, P., Navaline, H., ... Abrutyn, E. J. (1993). Human immunodeficiency virus seroconversion among intravenous drug users in- and out-of-treatment: An 18-month prospective follow-up. *Journal of Acquired Immune Deficiency Syndromes, 6*(9), 1049–1056.

80. Ball, J. C., & Ross, A. (1991). *The effectiveness of methadone maintenance treatment*. New York, NY: Springer Verlag.

81. Mattick, R. P., Breen, C., Kimber, J., & Davoli, M. (2014). Buprenorphine maintenance versus placebo or methadone maintenance for opioid dependence. *Cochrane Database of Systematic Reviews, 2014*(2). CD002207.

82. Walsh, S. L., & Strain, E. C. (2006). Pharmacology of methadone. In E. C. Strain & M. L. Stitzer (Eds.), *The treatment of opioid dependence* (pp. 59–76). Baltimore, MD: John Hopkins University Press.

83. Mallinckrodt Pharmaceuticals. (2017). Label: Methadose - methadone hydrochloride concentrate; Methadose sugar-free- methadone hydrochloride concentrate. Retrieved on January 9, 2018, from https://dailymed.nlm.nih.gov/dailymed/drugInfo.cfm?setid=808a9d0b-720b-4034-a862-5122ff514608

84. Walsh, S. L., & Strain, E. C. (2006). Pharmacology of methadone. In E. C. Strain & M. L. Stitzer (Eds.), *The treatment of opioid dependence* (pp. 59–76). Baltimore, MD: John Hopkins University Press.

85. Payte, J. T., & Zweben, J. E. (1998). Opioid maintenance therapies. In A. W. Graham, T. K. Schultz, & B. B. Wilford (Eds.), *Principles of addiction medicine* (pp. 557–570). Chevy Chase, MD: American Society of Addiction Medicine.

86. Eap, C. B., Buclin, T., & Baumann, P. (2002). Interindividual variability of the clinical pharmacokinetics of methadone: Implications for the treatment of opioid dependence. *Clinical Pharmacokinetics, 41*(14), 1153–1193.

87. Mallinckrodt Pharmaceuticals. (2017). Label: Methadose - methadone hydrochloride concentrate; Methadose sugar-free- methadone hydrochloride concentrate. Retrieved on January 9, 2018, from https://dailymed.nlm.nih.gov/dailymed/drugInfo.cfm?setid=808a9d0b-720b-4034-a862-5122ff514608

88 Oda, Y., & Kharasch, E. D. (2001). Metabolism of methadone and levo-alpha-acetylmethadol (LAAM) by human intestinal cytochrome P450 3A4 (CYP3A4): Potential contribution of intestinal metabolism to presystemic clearance and bioactivation. *Journal of Pharmacology and Experimental Therapeutics, 298*(3), 1021–1032.

89 Eap, C. B., Buclin, T., & Baumann, P. (2002). Interindividual variability of the clinical pharmacokinetics of methadone: Implications for the treatment of opioid dependence. *Clinical Pharmacokinetics, 41*(14), 1153–1193.

90 Eap, C. B., Buclin, T., & Baumann, P. (2002). Interindividual variability of the clinical pharmacokinetics of methadone: Implications for the treatment of opioid dependence. *Clinical Pharmacokinetics, 41*(14), 1153–1193.

91 American Psychiatric Association. (2013). *Diagnostic and statistical manual of mental disorders* (5th ed.). Arlington, VA: American Psychiatric Publishing.

92 Federal opioid treatment standards, 42 CFR § 8.12 (2015).

93 Chou, R., Cruciani, R. A., Fiellin, D. A., Compton, P., Farrar, J. T., Haigney, M. C., … Zeltzer, L. (2014). Methadone safety: A clinical practice guideline from the American Pain Society and College on Problems of Drug Dependence, in collaboration with the Heart Rhythm Society. *Journal of Pain, 15*(4), 321–337.

94 Baxter, L. E., Sr., Campbell, A., Deshields, M., Levounis, P., Martin, J. A., McNicholas, L., … Wilford, B. B. (2013). Safe methadone induction and stabilization: Report of an expert panel. *Journal of Addiction Medicine, 7*(6), 377–386.

95 Food and Drug Administration. (2016, March). FDA Drug Safety Communications, FDA urges caution about withholding opioid addiction medications from patients taking benzodiazepines or CNS depressant: Careful medication management can reduce risks. Retrieved January 3, 2018, from www.fda.gov/downloads/Drugs/DrugSafety/UCM576377.pdf

96 Lintzeris, N., & Nielsen, S. (2010). Benzodiazepines, methadone and buprenorphine: Interactions and clinical management. *American Journal on Addictions, 19*(1), 59–72.

97 Bart, G., Wyman, Z., Wang, Q., Hodges, J. S., Karim, R., & Bart, B. A. (2017). Methadone and the QTc interval: Paucity of clinically significant factors in a retrospective cohort. *Journal of Addiction Medicine, 11*(6), 489–493.

98 Chou, R., Cruciani, R. A., Fiellin, D. A., Compton, P., Farrar, J. T., Haigney, M. C., … Zeltzer, L. (2014). Methadone safety: A clinical practice guideline from the American Pain Society and College on Problems of Drug Dependence, in collaboration with the Heart Rhythm Society. *Journal of Pain, 15*(4), 321–337.

99 Bednar, M. M., Harrigan, E. P., & Ruskin, J. N. (2002). Torsades de pointes associated with nonantiarrhythmic drugs and observations on gender and QTc. *American Journal of Cardiology, 89*(11), 1316–1319.

100 Al-Khatib, S. M., LaPointe, N. M. A., Kramer, J. M., & Califf, R. M. (2003). What clinicians should know about the QT interval. *JAMA, 289*(16), 2120–2127.

101 Martin, J. A., Campbell, A., Killip, T., Kotz, M., Krantz, M. J., Kreek, M. J., … Wilford, B. B. (2011). QT interval screening in methadone maintenance treatment: Report of a SAMHSA expert panel. *Journal of Addictive Diseases, 30*(4), 283–306.

102 Bazett, H. C. (1997). An analysis of the time-relations of electrocardiograms. *Annals of Noninvasive Electrocardiology, 2*(2), 177–194.

103 Martin, J. A., Campbell, A., Killip, T., Kotz, M., Krantz, M. J., Kreek, M. J., … Wilford, B. B. (2011). QT interval screening in methadone maintenance treatment: Report of a SAMHSA expert panel. *Journal of Addictive Diseases, 30*(4), 283–306.

104 Mallinckrodt Pharmaceuticals. (2015). Methadose™ dispersible tablets, 40 mg (Methadone hydrochloride tablets for oral suspension USP), CII - Generic products. Retrieved October 16, 2017, from https://dailymed.nlm.nih.gov/dailymed/archives/fdaDrugInfo.cfm?archiveid=8731

105 Chou, R., Cruciani, R. A., Fiellin, D. A., Compton, P., Farrar, J. T., Haigney, M. C., … Zeltzer, L. (2014). Methadone safety: A clinical practice guideline from the American Pain Society and College on Problems of Drug Dependence, in collaboration with the Heart Rhythm Society. *Journal of Pain, 15*(4), 321–337.

106 Krantz, M. J., Martin, J., Stimmel, B., Mehta, D., & Haigney, M. C. (2009). QTc interval screening in methadone treatment. *Annals of Internal Medicine, 150*(6), 387–395.

107 Bart, G., Wyman, Z., Wang, Q., Hodges, J. S., Karim, R., & Bart, B. A. (2017). Methadone and the QTc interval: Paucity of clinically significant factors in a retrospective cohort. *Journal of Addiction Medicine, 11*(6), 489–493.

108 Pani, P. P., Trogu, E., Maremmani, I., & Pacini, M. (2013). QTc interval screening for cardiac risk in methadone treatment of opioid dependence. *Cochrane Database of Systematic Reviews, 2013*(6). CD008939.

109 Martin, J. A., Campbell, A., Killip, T., Kotz, M., Krantz, M. J., Kreek, M. J., … Wilford, B. B. (2011). QT interval screening in methadone maintenance treatment: Report of a SAMHSA expert panel. *Journal of Addictive Diseases, 30*(4), 283–306.

110 Chou, R., Cruciani, R. A., Fiellin, D. A., Compton, P., Farrar, J. T., Haigney, M. C., … Zeltzer, L. (2014). Methadone safety: A clinical practice guideline from the American Pain Society and College on Problems of Drug Dependence, in collaboration with the Heart Rhythm Society. *Journal of Pain, 15*(4), 321–337.

111 Chou, R., Cruciani, R. A., Fiellin, D. A., Compton, P., Farrar, J. T., Haigney, M. C., ... Zeltzer, L. (2014). Methadone safety: A clinical practice guideline from the American Pain Society and College on Problems of Drug Dependence, in collaboration with the Heart Rhythm Society. *Journal of Pain, 15*(4), 321–337.

112 Jones, H. E., Dengler, E., Garrison, A., O'Grady, K. E., Seashore, C., Horton, E., ... Thorp, J. (2014). Neonatal outcomes and their relationship to maternal buprenorphine dose during pregnancy. *Drug and Alcohol Dependence, 134*, 414–417.

113 Cleary, B. J., Reynolds, K., Eogan, M., O'Connell, M. P., Fahey, T., Gallagher, P. J., ... Murphy, D. J. (2014). Methadone dosing and prescribed medication use in a prospective cohort of opioid-dependent pregnant women. *Addiction, 108*(4), 762–770.

114 Kaltenbach, K., Holbrook, A. M., Coyle, M. G., Heil, S. H., Salisbury, A. L., Stine, S. M., ... Jones, H. E. (2012). Predicting treatment for neonatal abstinence syndrome in infants born to women maintained on opioid agonist medication. *Addiction, 107*(Suppl. 1), 45–52.

115 Food and Drug Administration. (2016, March). FDA Drug Safety Communication: FDA warns about several safety issues with opioid pain medicines; requires label changes. Retrieved December 18, 2017, from www.fda.gov/downloads/Drugs/DrugSafety/UCM491302.pdf

116 McCance-Katz, E. F., Sullivan, L. E., & Nallani, S. (2010). Drug interactions of clinical importance among the opioids, methadone and buprenorphine, and other frequently prescribed medications: A review. *American Journal on Addictions, 19*(1), 4–16.

117 Martin, J., Zweben, J. E., & Payte, J. T. (2014). Opioid maintenance treatment. In R. K. Ries, D. A. Fiellin, S. C. Miller, & R. Saitz (Eds.), *The ASAM principles of addiction medicine* (5th ed., pp. 759–777). Philadelphia, PA: Wolters Kluwer Health.

118 Saxon, A. J., & Miotto, K. (2011). Methadone maintenance. In P. Ruiz & E. Strain (Eds.), *Lowinson and Ruiz's substance abuse: A comprehensive textbook* (5th ed., pp. 419–436). Philadelphia, PA: Wolters Kluwer Health.

119 McCance-Katz, E. F., Rainey, P. M., Jatlow, P., & Friedland, G. (1998). Methadone effects on zidovudine disposition (AIDS Clinical Trials Group 262). *Journal of Acquired Immune Deficiency Syndromes and Human Retrovirology, 18*(5), 435–443.

120 World Health Organization. (2009). *Guidelines for the psychosocially assisted pharmacological treatment of opioid dependence*. Geneva, Switzerland: WHO Press.

121 American College of Obstetricians and Gynecologists Committee Opinion. (2017, August). Opioid use and opioid use disorder in pregnancy. Number 711. Retrieved October 30, 2017, from www.acog.org/Resources-And-Publications/Committee-Opinions/Committee-on-Obstetric-Practice/Opioid-Use-and-Opioid-Use-Disorder-in-Pregnancy

122 Substance Abuse and Mental Health Services Administration. (2018). *Clinical guidance for treating pregnant and parenting women with opioid use disorder and their infants*. HHS Publication No. (SMA) 18-5054. Rockville, MD: Substance Abuse and Mental Health Services Administration.

123 Centers for Disease Control and Prevention. (2016). Viral hepatitis. Retrieved December 1, 2017, from www.cdc.gov/hepatitis/hbv/bfaq.htm

124 Baxter, L. E., Sr., Campbell, A., Deshields, M., Levounis, P., Martin, J. A., McNicholas, L., ... Wilford, B. B. (2013). Safe methadone induction and stabilization: Report of an expert panel. *Journal of Addiction Medicine, 7*(6), 377–386.

125 McCance-Katz, E. F., Sullivan, L. E., & Nallani, S. (2010). Drug interactions of clinical importance among the opioids, methadone and buprenorphine, and other frequently prescribed medications: A review. *American Journal on Addictions, 19*(1), 4–16.

126 Baxter, L. E., Sr., Campbell, A., Deshields, M., Levounis, P., Martin, J. A., McNicholas, L., ... Wilford, B. B. (2013). Safe methadone induction and stabilization: Report of an expert panel. *Journal of Addiction Medicine, 7*(6), 377–386.

127 Jones, H. E. (2004). Practical considerations for the clinical use of buprenorphine. *Science and Practice Perspectives, 2*(2), 4–20.

128 Vocci, F. J., Schwartz, R. P., Wilson, M. E., Gordon, M. S., Kinlock, T. W., Fitzgerald, T. T., ... Jaffe, J. H. (2015). Buprenorphine dose induction in non-opioid-tolerant pre-release prisoners. *Drug and Alcohol Dependence, 156*, 133–138.

129 Kinlock, T. W., Gordon, M. S., Schwartz, R. P., & O'Grady, K. E. (2008). A study of methadone maintenance for male prisoners: 3-month postrelease outcomes. *Criminal Justice and Behavior, 35*(1), 34–47.

130 Martin, J., Zweben, J. E., & Payte, J. T. (2014). Opioid maintenance treatment. In R. K. Ries, D. A. Fiellin, S. C. Miller, & R. Saitz (Eds.), *The ASAM principles of addiction medicine* (5th ed., pp. 759–777). Philadelphia, PA: Wolters Kluwer.

131 Baxter, L. E., Sr., Campbell, A., Deshields, M., Levounis, P., Martin, J. A., McNicholas, L., ... Wilford, B. B. (2013). Safe methadone induction and stabilization: Report of an expert panel. *Journal of Addiction Medicine, 7*(6), 377–386.

132 Center for Substance Abuse Treatment. (1993). *State methadone treatment guidelines*. HHS Publication No. (SMA) 93-1991. Rockville, MD: Substance Abuse and Mental Health Services Administration.

133 Chou, R., Cruciani, R. A., Fiellin, D. A., Compton, P., Farrar, J. T., Haigney, M. C., … Zeltzer, L. (2014). Methadone safety: A clinical practice guideline from the American Pain Society and College on Problems of Drug Dependence, in collaboration with the Heart Rhythm Society. *Journal of Pain, 15*(4), 321–337.

134 Gowing, L., Ali, R., Dunlop, A., Farrell, M., & Lintzeris, N. (2014). *National guidelines for medication-assisted treatment of opioid dependence*. Retrieved January 4, 2018, from www.nationaldrugstrategy.gov.au/internet/drugstrategy/Publishing.nsf/content/AD14DA97D8EE00E8CA257CD1001E0E5D/$File/National_Guidelines_2014.pdf

135 Leavitt, S. B., Shinderman, M., Maxwell, S., Eap, C. B., & Paris, P. (2000). When "enough" is not enough: New perspectives on optimal methadone maintenance dose. *Mount Sinai Journal of Medicine, 67*(5–6), 404–411.

136 Payte, J. T. (2002). Opioid agonist treatment of addiction. Slide presentation at ASAM Review Course in Addiction Medicine.

137 Leavitt, S. B. (2003). The methadone dose debate continues. *Addiction Treatment Forum, 12*(1), 1,3.

138 Substance Abuse and Mental Health Services Administration. (2018). *Clinical guidance for treating pregnant and parenting women with opioid use disorder and their infants*. HHS Publication No. (SMA) 18-5054. Rockville, MD: Substance Abuse and Mental Health Services Administration.

139 Benmebarek, M., Devaud, C., Gex-Fabry, M., Powell Golay, K., Brogli, C., Baumann, P., … Eap, C. B. (2004). Effects of grapefruit juice on the pharmacokinetics of the enantiomers of methadone. *Clinical Pharmacology and Therapeutics, 76*(1), 55–63.

140 Drozdick, J., III, Berghella, V., Hill, M., & Kaltenbach, K. (2002). Methadone trough levels in pregnancy. *American Journal of Obstetrics and Gynecology, 187*(5), 1184–1188.

141 Leavitt, S. B., Shinderman, M., Maxwell, S., Eap, C. B., & Paris, P. (2000). When "enough" is not enough: New perspectives on optimal methadone maintenance dose. *Mount Sinai Journal of Medicine, 67*(5–6), 404–411.

142 Hallinan, R., Ray, J., Byrne, A., Agho, K., & Attia, J. (2006). Therapeutic thresholds in methadone maintenance treatment: A receiver operating characteristic analysis. *Drug and Alcohol Dependence, 81*, 129–136.

143 Stine, S. M., & Kosten, T. R. (2014). Pharmacologic interventions for opioid dependence. In R. K. Ries, D. A. Fiellin, S. C. Miller, & R. Saitz (Eds.), *The ASAM principles of addiction medicine* (5th ed., pp. 745–758). Philadelphia, PA: Wolters Kluwer.

144 Drozdick, J., III, Berghella, V., Hill, M., & Kaltenbach, K. (2002). Methadone trough levels in pregnancy. *American Journal of Obstetrics and Gynecology, 187*(5), 1184–1188.

145 Substance Abuse and Mental Health Services Administration. (2018). *Clinical guidance for treating pregnant and parenting women with opioid use disorder and their infants*. HHS Publication No. (SMA) 18-5054. Rockville, MD: Substance Abuse and Mental Health Services Administration.

146 Food and Drug Administration. (2008). Methadose™ oral concentrate. Retrieved October 16, 2017, from www.accessdata.fda.gov/drugsatfda_docs/label/2008/017116s021lbl.pdf

147 Department of Veterans Affairs & Department of Defense. (2015). *VA/DoD clinical practice guideline for the management of substance use disorders*. Retrieved October 16, 2017, from www.healthquality.va.gov/guidelines/MH/sud/VADoDSUDCPGRevised22216.pdf

148 Stitzer, M. L., Iguchi, M. Y., & Felch, L. J. (1992). Contingent take-home incentive: Effects on drug use of methadone maintenance patients. *Journal of Consulting and Clinical Psychology, 60*(6), 927–934.

149 Gwin Mitchell, S., Kelly, S. M., Brown, B. S., Schacht Reisinger, H., Peterson, J. A., Ruhf, A., … Schwartz, R. P. (2009). Uses of diverted methadone and buprenorphine by opioid-addicted individuals in Baltimore, Maryland. *American Journal on Addictions, 18*(5), 346–355.

150 Vlahov, D., O'Driscoll, P., Mehta, S. H., Ompad, D. C., Gern, R., Galai, N., & Kirk, G. D. (2007). Risk factors for methadone outside treatment programs: Implications for HIV treatment among injection drug users. *Addiction, 102*(5), 771–777.

151 Timko, C., Schultz, N. R., Cucciare, M. A., Vittorio, L., & Garrison-Diehn, C. (2016). Retention in medication-assisted treatment for opiate dependence: A systematic review. *Journal of Addictive Diseases, 35*(1), 22–35.

152 Woody, G. E., Kane, V., Lewis, K., & Thompson, R. (2007). Premature deaths after discharge from methadone maintenance: A replication. *Journal of Addiction Medicine, 1*(4), 180–185.

153 Sordo, L., Barrio, G., Bravo, M. J., Indave, I., Degenhardt, L., Wiessing, L., Ferri, M., & Pastor-Barriuso, R. (2017). Mortality risk during and after opioid substitution treatment: Systematic review and meta-analysis of cohort studies. *BMJ, 357*, j1550.

154 Gibson, A., Degenhardt, L., Mattick, R. P., Ali, R., White, J., & O'Brien, S. (2008). Exposure to opioid maintenance treatment reduces long-term mortality. *Addiction, 103*(3), 462–468.

155 Schwartz, R. P., Highfield, D. A., Jaffe, J. H., Brady, J. V., Butler, C. B., Rouse, C. O., ... Battjes, R. J. (2006). A randomized controlled trial of interim methadone maintenance. *Archives of General Psychiatry, 63*(1), 102–109.

156 Yancovitz, S. R., Des Jarlais, D. C., Peyser, N. P., Drew, E., Friedmann, P., Trigg, H. L., & Robinson, J. W. (1991). A randomized trial of an interim methadone maintenance clinic. *American Journal of Public Health, 81*(9), 1185–1191.

157 Substance Abuse and Mental Health Services Administration. (2015). *Federal guidelines for opioid treatment programs.* HHS Publication No. (SMA) PEP15-FEDGUIDEOTP. Rockville, MD: Substance Abuse and Mental Health Services Administration.

158 Martin, W. R., Jasinski, D. R., & Mansky, P. A. (1973). Naltrexone, an antagonist for the treatment of heroin dependence: Effects in man. *Archives of General Psychiatry, 28*(6), 784–791.

159 Sullivan, M. A., Garawi, F., Bisaga, A., Comer, S. D., Carpenter, K., Raby, W. N., ... Nunes, E. V. (2007). Management of relapse in naltrexone maintenance for heroin dependence. *Drug and Alcohol Dependence, 91*(2–3), 289–292.

160 American Society of Addiction Medicine. (2015). *National practice guideline for the use of medications in the treatment of addiction involving opioid use.* Retrieved December 1, 2017, from www.asam.org/docs/default-source/practice-support/guidelines-and-consensus-docs/asam-national-practice-guideline-supplement.pdf?sfvrsn=24

161 Minozzi, S., Amato, L., Vecchi, S., Davoli, M., Kirchmayer, U., & Verster, A. (2011). Oral naltrexone maintenance treatment for opioid dependence. *Cochrane Database of Systematic Reviews, 2011*(2), 1–45. doi:10.1002/14651858.CD001333.pub3

162 Alkermes. (2015). Vivitrol. Retrieved May 21, 2017, from http://medlibrary.org/lib/rx/meds/vivitrol/page/6

163 Krupitsky, E., Nunes, E. V., Ling, W., Illeperuma, A., Gastfriend, D. R., & Silverman, B. L. (2011). Injectable extended-release naltrexone for opioid dependence: A double-blind, placebo-controlled, multicentre randomised trial. *Lancet, 377*(9776), 1506–1513.

164 Lee, J. D., Friedmann, P. D., Kinlock, T. W., Nunes, E. V., Boney, T. Y., Hoskinson, R. A., Jr., ... O'Brien, C. P. (2016). Extended-release naltrexone to prevent opioid relapse in criminal justice offenders. *New England Journal of Medicine, 374*(13), 1232–1242.

165 Krupitsky, E., Nunes, E. V., Ling, W., Illeperuma, A., Gastfriend, D. R., & Silverman, B. L. (2011, April 30). Injectable extended-release naltrexone for opioid dependence: A double-blind, placebo-controlled, multicentre randomised trial. *Lancet, 377*(9776), 1506–1513.

166 Lee, J. D., Nunes, E. V., Jr., Novo, P., Bachrach, K., Bailey, G. L., Bhatt, S., ... Rotrosen J. (2018). Comparative effectiveness of extended-release naltrexone versus buprenorphine-naloxone for opioid relapse prevention (X:BOT): A multicentre, open-label, randomised controlled trial. *Lancet, 391*(10118), 309–318.

167 Tanum, L., Solli, K. K., Latif, Z. E., Benth, J. Š., Opheim, A., Sharma-Haase, K., ... Kunøe, N. (2017). The effectiveness of injectable extended-release naltrexone vs daily buprenorphine-naloxone for opioid dependence: A randomized clinical noninferiority trial. *JAMA Psychiatry, 74*(12), 1197–1205.

168 Meyer, M. C., Straughn, A. B., Lo, M. W., Schary, W. L., & Whitney, C. C. (1984). Bioequivalence, dose-proportionality, and pharmacokinetics of naltrexone after oral administration. *Journal of Clinical Psychiatry, 45*(9 Pt 2), 15–19.

169 Alkermes. (2015). Vivitrol (naltrexone for extended release injectable suspension) 380 mg/vial. Retrieved on January 9, 2018, from www.vivitrol.com/content/pdfs/prescribing-information.pdf

170 Alkermes. (2015). Vivitrol (naltrexone for extended release injectable suspension) 380 mg/vial. Retrieved on January 9, 2018, from www.vivitrol.com/content/pdfs/prescribing-information.pdf

171 Meyer, M. C., Straughn, A. B., Lo, M. W., Schary, W. L., & Whitney, C. C. (1984). Bioequivalence, dose-proportionality, and pharmacokinetics of naltrexone after oral administration. *Journal of Clinical Psychiatry, 45*(9, Pt. 2), 15–19.

172 Bigelow, G. E., Preston, K. L., Schmittner, J., Dong, Q., & Gastfriend, D. R. (2012). Opioid challenge evaluation of blockade by extended-release naltrexone in opioid-abusing adults: Dose-effects and time-course. *Drug and Alcohol Dependence, 123*(1–3), 57–65.

173 Tetrault, J. M., Tate, J. P., McGinnis, K. A., Goulet, J. L., Sullivan, L. E., Bryant, K., ... Fiellin, D. A. (2012). Hepatic safety and antiretroviral effectiveness in HIV-infected patients receiving naltrexone. *Alcoholism: Clinical and Experimental Research, 36*(2), 318–324.

174 Jones, H. E., Kaltenbach, K., Heil, S. H., Stine, S. M., Coyle, M. G., Arria, A. M., ... Fischer, G. (2010). Neonatal abstinence syndrome after methadone or buprenorphine exposure. *New England Journal of Medicine, 363*(24), 2320–2331.

175 Mozurkewich, E. L., & Rayburn, W. F. (2014). Buprenorphine and methadone for opioid addiction during pregnancy. *Obstetrics and Gynecology Clinics of North America, 41*(2), 241–253.

176 Alkermes. (2015). Vivitrol. Retrieved October 16, 2017, from http://medlibrary.org/lib/rx/meds/vivitrol/page/6

177 Sullivan, M., Bisaga, A., Pavlicova, M., Choi, C. J., Mishlen, K., Carpenter, K. M., ... Nunes, E. V. (2017). Long-acting injectable naltrexone induction: A randomized trial of outpatient opioid detoxification with naltrexone versus buprenorphine. *American Journal of Psychiatry, 174*(5), 459–467.

178 Tetrault, J. M., Tate, J. P., McGinnis, K. A., Goulet, J. L., Sullivan, L. E., Bryant, K., ... Fiellin, D. A. (2012). Hepatic safety and antiretroviral effectiveness in HIV-infected patients receiving naltrexone. *Alcoholism: Clinical and Experimental Research, 36*(2), 318–324.

179 Crowley, T. J., Wagner, J. E., Zerbe, G., & Macdonald, M. (1985). Naltrexone-induced dysphoria in former opioid addicts. *American Journal of Psychiatry, 142*(9), 1081–1084.

180 Miotto, K., McCann, M., Basch, J., Rawson, R., & Ling, W. (2002). Naltrexone and dysphoria: Fact or myth? *American Journal on Addictions, 11*(2), 151–160.

181 Substance Abuse and Mental Health Services Administration. (2015). *Clinical use of extended-release injectable naltrexone in the treatment of opioid use disorder: A brief guide.* HHS Publication No. (SMA) 14-4892R. Rockville, MD: Substance Abuse and Mental Health Services Administration.

182 National Library of Medicine. (2014). NALTREXONE HYDROCHLORIDE - naltrexone hydrochloride tablet, film coated DAILY MED. Retrieved October 16, 2017, from https://dailymed.nlm.nih.gov/dailymed/drugInfo.cfm?setid=06ff2d5a-e62b-4fa4-bbdb-01938535bc65

183 Substance Abuse and Mental Health Services Administration. (2015). *Clinical use of extended-release injectable naltrexone in the treatment of opioid use disorder: A brief guide.* HHS Publication No. (SMA) 14-4892R. Rockville, MD: Substance Abuse and Mental Health Services Administration.

184 Substance Abuse and Mental Health Services Administration. (2018). *Clinical guidance for treating pregnant and parenting women with opioid use disorder and their infants.* HHS Publication No. (SMA) 18-5054. Rockville, MD: Substance Abuse and Mental Health Services Administration.

185 Substance Abuse and Mental Health Services Administration. (2015). *Clinical use of extended-release injectable naltrexone in the treatment of opioid use disorder: A brief guide.* HHS Publication No. (SMA) 14-4892R. Rockville, MD: Substance Abuse and Mental Health Services Administration.

186 Centers for Disease Control and Prevention. (2016). Viral hepatitis. Retrieved October 16, 2017, from www.cdc.gov/hepatitis/hbv/bfaq.htm

187 Nunes, E. V., Krupitsky, E., Ling, W., Zummo, J., Memisoglu, A., Silverman, B. L., & Gastfriend, D. R. (2015). Treating opioid dependence with injectable extended-release naltrexone (XR-NTX): Who will respond? *Journal of Addiction Medicine, 9*(3), 238–243.

188 Substance Abuse and Mental Health Services Administration. (2015). *Clinical use of extended-release injectable naltrexone in the treatment of opioid use disorder: A brief guide.* HHS Publication No. (SMA) 14-4892R. Rockville, MD: Substance Abuse and Mental Health Services Administration.

189 Sigmon, S. C., Bisaga, A., Nunes, E. V., O'Connor, P. G., Kosten, T., & Woody, G. (2012). Opioid detoxification and naltrexone induction strategies: Recommendations for clinical practice. *American Journal of Drug and Alcohol Abuse, 38*(3), 187–199.

190 Substance Abuse and Mental Health Services Administration. (2015). *Clinical use of extended-release injectable naltrexone in the treatment of opioid use disorder: A brief guide.* HHS Publication No. (SMA) 14-4892R. Rockville, MD: Substance Abuse and Mental Health Services Administration.

191 Sullivan, M. A., Bisaga, A., Mariani, J. J., Glass, A., Levin, F. R., Comer, S. D., & Nunes, E. V. (2013). Naltrexone treatment for opioid dependence: Does its effectiveness depend on testing the blockade? *Drug and Alcohol Dependence, 133*(1), 80–85.

192 Substance Abuse and Mental Health Services Administration. (2015). *Clinical use of extended-release injectable naltrexone in the treatment of opioid use disorder: A brief guide.* HHS Publication No. (SMA) 14-4892R. Rockville, MD: Substance Abuse and Mental Health Services Administration.

193 Kosten, T. R., Morgan, C., & Kleber, H. D. (1992). Phase II clinical trials of buprenorphine: Detoxification and induction onto naltrexone. *NIDA Research Monograph, 121,* 101–119.

194 Bisaga, A., Sullivan, M. A., Glass, A., Mishlen, K., Pavlicova, M., Haney, M., ... Nunes, E. V. (2015). The effects of dronabinol during detoxification and the initiation of treatment with extended release naltrexone. *Drug and Alcohol Dependence, 154,* 38–45.

195 Sigmon, S. C., Bisaga, A., Nunes, E. V., O'Connor, P. G., Kosten, T., & Woody, G. (2012). Opioid detoxification and naltrexone induction strategies: Recommendations for clinical practice. *American Journal of Drug and Alcohol Abuse, 38*(3), 187–199.

196 Sullivan, M., Bisaga, A., Pavlicova, M., Choi, C. J., Mishlen, K., Carpenter, K. M., ... Nunes, E. V. (2017). Long-acting injectable naltrexone induction: A randomized trial of outpatient opioid detoxification with naltrexone versus buprenorphine. *American Journal of Psychiatry, 174*(5), 459–467.

197 Sullivan, M., Bisaga, A., Pavlicova, M., Choi, C. J., Mishlen, K., Carpenter, K. M., ... Nunes, E. V. (2017). Long-acting injectable naltrexone induction: A randomized trial of outpatient opioid detoxification with naltrexone versus buprenorphine. *American Journal of Psychiatry, 174*(5), 459–467.

198 Bisaga, A. (2015). *Implementing antagonist-based relapse prevention treatment for buprenorphine-treated individuals.* Providence, RI: Providers' Clinical Support System for Medication-Assisted Treatment.

199 Shearer, J., Wodak, A. D., & Dolan, K. A. (2007). Evaluation of a prison-based naltrexone program. *International Journal of Prisoner Health, 3*(3), 214–224.

200 Adi, Y., Juarez-Garcia, A., Wang, D., Jowett, S., Frew, E., Day, E., … Burls, A. (2007). Oral naltrexone as a treatment for relapse prevention in formerly opioid-dependent drug users: A systematic review and economic evaluation. *Health Technology Assessment, 11*(6), iii–iv, 1–85.

201 Department of Veterans Affairs & Department of Defense. (2015). *VA/DoD clinical practice guideline for the management of substance use disorders.* Retrieved October 16, 2017, from www.healthquality.va.gov/guidelines/MH/sud/VADoDSUDCPGRevised22216.pdf

202 Minozzi, S., Amato, L., Vecchi, S., Davoli, M., Kirchmayer, U., & Verster, A. (2011). Oral naltrexone maintenance treatment for opioid dependence. *Cochrane Database of Systematic Reviews, 2011*(2), 1–45.

203 Ling, W., & Wesson, D. R. (1984). Naltrexone treatment for addicted health-care professionals: A collaborative private practice experience. *Journal of Clinical Psychiatry, 45*(9 Pt. 2), 46–48.

204 Washton, A. M., Gold, M. S., & Pottash, A. C. (1984). Successful use of naltrexone in addicted physicians and business executives. *Advances in Alcohol and Substance Abuse, 4*(2), 89–96.

205 Sullivan, M. A., Rothenberg, J. L., Vosburg, S. K., Church, S. H., Feldman, S. J., Epstein, E. M., … Nunes, E. V. (2006). Predictors of retention in naltrexone maintenance for opioid dependence: Analysis of a Stage I trial. *American Journal on Addictions, 15*(2), 150–159.

206 Sullivan, M. A., Garawi, F., Bisaga, A., Comer, S. D., Carpenter, K., Raby, W. N., … Nunes, E. V. (2007). Management of relapse in naltrexone maintenance for heroin dependence. *Drug and Alcohol Dependence, 91*(2–3), 289–292.

207 Sullivan, M. A., Garawi, F., Bisaga, A., Comer, S. D., Carpenter, K., Raby, W. N., … Nunes, E. V. (2007). Management of relapse in naltrexone maintenance for heroin dependence. *Drug and Alcohol Dependence, 91*(2–3), 289–292.

208 American Society of Addiction Medicine. (2017). Sample treatment agreement. Retrieved October 19, 2017, from www.asam.org/docs/default-source/advocacy/sample-treatment-agreement30fa159472bc604ca5b7ff000030b21a.pdf?sfvrsn=0

209 Alkermes. (2013). Patient counseling tool: VIVITROL (naltrexone for extended-release injectable suspension. Retrieved January 9, 2018, from www.vivitrolrems.com/content/pdf/patinfo-counseling-tool.pdf

210 Alkermes. (2015). Key techniques to reduce severe injection site reactions: VIVITROL (naltrexone for extended release injectable suspension) intramuscular injection. Retrieved January 9, 2018, from www.vivitrolrems.com/content/pdf/patinfo-injection-poster.pdf

211 Mattick, R. P., Breen, C., Kimber, J., & Davoli, M. (2014). Buprenorphine maintenance versus placebo or methadone maintenance for opioid dependence. *Cochrane Database of Systematic Reviews, 2014*(2), 1–84.

212 Caldiero, R. M., Parran, T. J., Adelman, C. L., & Piche, B. (2006). Inpatient initiation of buprenorphine maintenance vs. detoxification: Can retention of opioid-dependent patients in outpatient counseling be improved? *American Journal on Addictions, 15*(1), 1–7.

213 Weiss, R. D., Potter, J. S., Fiellin, D. A., Byrne, M., Connery, H. S., Dickinson, W., … Ling, W. (2011). Adjunctive counseling during brief and extended buprenorphine-naloxone treatment for prescription opioid dependence: A 2-phase randomized controlled trial. *Archives of General Psychiatry, 68*(12), 1238–1246.

214 Fiellin, D. A., Moore, B. A., Sullivan, L. E., Becker, W. C., Pantalon, M. V., Chawarski, M. C., … Schottenfeld, R. S. (2008). Long-term treatment with buprenorphine/naloxone in primary care: Results at 2–5 years. *American Journal on Addictions, 17*(2), 116–120.

215 Edelman, E. J., Chantarat, T., Caffrey, S., Chaudhry, A., O'Connor, P. G., Weiss, L., … Fiellin, L. E. (2014). The impact of buprenorphine/naloxone treatment on HIV risk behaviors among HIV-infected, opioid-dependent patients. *Drug and Alcohol Dependence, 139*, 79–85.

216 Sullivan, L. E., Moore, B. A., Chawarski, M. C., Pantalon, M. V., Barry, D., O'Connor, P. G., … Fiellin, D. A. (2008). Buprenorphine/naloxone treatment in primary care is associated with decreased human immunodeficiency virus risk behaviors. *Journal of Substance Abuse Treatment, 35*(1), 87–92.

217 Auriacombe, M., Fatséas, M., Dubernet, J., Daulouède, J. P., & Tignol, J. (2004). French field experience with buprenorphine. *American Journal on Addictions, 13*(Suppl. 1), S17–S28.

218 Degenhardt, L., Randall, D., Hall, W., Law, M., Butler, T., & Burns, L. (2009). Mortality among clients of a state-wide opioid pharmacotherapy program over 20 years: Risk factors and lives saved. *Drug and Alcohol Dependence, 105*(1–2), 9–15.

219 Herget, G. (2005). Methadone and buprenorphine added to the WHO list of essential medicines. *HIV/AIDS Policy and Law Review, 10*(3), 23–24.

220 Department of Veterans Affairs & Department of Defense. (2015). *VA/DoD clinical practice guideline for the management of substance use disorders.* Retrieved October 16, 2017, from substance use disorders. Retrieved October 16, 2017, from www.healthquality.va.gov/guidelines/MH/sud/VADoDSUDCPG Revised22216.pdf

221 Orexo US. (2016). Zubsolv (buprenorphine and naloxone) sublingual tablets: Full prescribing information. Retrieved October 16, 2017, from www.zubsolv.com/wp-content/uploads/2015/01/ZubsolvFullPrescribingInformation.pdf

222 BioDelivery Sciences International. (2015). Bunavail (buprenorphine and naloxone) buccal film: Full prescribing information. Retrieved from https://bunavail.com/hcp/assets/pdfs/BUNAVAIL_Full_Prescribing_Information.pdf

223 BioDelivery Sciences International. (2015). Bunavail (buprenorphine and naloxone) buccal film: Full prescribing information. Retrieved October 16, 2017, from https://bunavail.com/hcp/assets/pdfs/BUNAVAIL_Full_Prescribing_Information.pdf

224 Food and Drug Administration. (n.d.). Drugs@FDA: FDA approved drug products. Retrieved October 16, 2017, through www.accessdata.fda.gov/scripts/cder/drugsatfda/index.cfm

225 Roxane Laboratories. (2015). Buprenorphine and naloxone sublingual tablets: Full prescribing information. Retrieved October 16, 2017, from http://dailymed.nlm.nih.gov/dailymed/drugInfo.cfm?setid=713db2c6-0544-4633-b874-cfbeaf93db89

226 Food and Drug Administration. (n.d.). Drugs@FDA: FDA approved drug products. Retrieved October 16, 2017, through www.accessdata.fda.gov/scripts/cder/drugsatfda/index.cfm

227 Roxane Laboratories. (2015). Buprenorphine HCl sublingual tablets: Full prescribing information. Retrieved October 16, 2017, from http://dailymed.nlm.nih.gov/dailymed/drugInfo.cfm?setid=1bf8b35a-b769-465c-a2f8-099868dfcd2f

228 Food and Drug Administration. (n.d.). Drugs@FDA: FDA approved drug products. Retrieved October 16, 2017, from www.accessdata.fda.gov/scripts/cder/drugsatfda/index.cfm

229 Indivior. (2015). Suboxone (buprenorphine and naloxone) sublingual film: Full prescribing information. Retrieved October 16, 2017, from www.suboxone.com/content/pdfs/prescribing-information.pdf

230 Orexo US. (2015). Zubsolv (buprenorphine and naloxone) sublingual tablets: Full prescribing information. Retrieved October 16, 2017, from www.zubsolv.com/wp-content/uploads/2015/01/ZubsolvFullPrescribingInformation.pdf

231 Food and Drug Administration. (n.d.). Drugs@FDA: FDA approved drug products. Retrieved October 16, 2017, from www.accessdata.fda.gov/scripts/cder/drugsatfda/index.cfm

232 Roxane Laboratories. (2015). Buprenorphine HCl sublingual tablets: Full prescribing information. Retrieved October 16, 2017, from http://dailymed.nlm.nih.gov/dailymed/drugInfo.cfm?setid=1bf8b35a-b769-465c-a2f8-099868dfcd2f

233 Indivior. (2015). Suboxone (buprenorphine and naloxone) sublingual film: Full prescribing information. Retrieved October 16, 2017, from www.suboxone.com/content/pdfs/prescribing-information.pdf

234 Substance Abuse and Mental Health Services Administration. (2016). Sublingual and transmucosal buprenorphine for opioid use disorder: Review and update. *Advisory,* Vol. 15, Issue 1. Rockville, MD: Substance Abuse and Mental Health Services Administration.

235 Indivor. (2017). Label: Sublocade (buprenorphine extended-release injection, for subcutaneous use. Retrieved January 9, 2018, from www.accessdata.fda.gov/drugsatfda_docs/label/2017/209819s000lbl.pdf

236 Amass, L., Kamien, J. B., & Mikulich, S. K. (2001). Thrice-weekly supervised dosing with the combination buprenorphine-naloxone tablet is preferred to daily supervised dosing by opioid-dependent humans. *Drug and Alcohol Dependence, 61*(2), 173–181.

237 Schottenfeld, R. S., Pakes, J., O'Connor, P., Chawarski, M., Oliveto, A., & Kosten, T. R. (2000). Thrice-weekly versus daily buprenorphine maintenance. *Biological Psychiatry, 47*(12), 1072–1079.

238 Walsh, S. L., Preston, K. L., Stitzer, M. L., Cone, E. J., & Bigelow, G. E. (1994). Clinical pharmacology of buprenorphine: Ceiling effects at high doses. *Clinical Pharmacology and Therapeutics, 55*(5), 569–580.

239 Elkader, A., & Sproule, B. (2005). Buprenorphine: Clinical pharmacokinetics in the treatment of opioid dependence. *Clinical Pharmacokinetics, 44*(7), 661–680.

240 Kuhlman, J. J., Jr., Levine, B., Johnson, R. E., Fudala, P. J., & Cone, E. J. (1998). Relationship of plasma buprenorphine and norbuprenorphine to withdrawal symptoms during dose induction, maintenance and withdrawal from sublingual buprenorphine. *Addiction, 93*(4), 549–559.

241 Indivor. (2016). Label: Suboxone – buprenorphine hydrochloride, naloxone hydrochloride film, soluble. Retrieved January 9, 2018, from https://dailymed.nlm.nih.gov/dailymed/drugInfo.cfm?setid=8a5edcf9-828c-4f97-b671-268ab13a8ecd

242 Marsch, L. A., Bickel, W. K., Badger, G. J., & Jacobs, E. A. (2005). Buprenorphine treatment for opioid dependence: The relative efficacy of daily, twice and thrice weekly dosing. *Drug & Alcohol Dependence, 77*(2), 195–204.

243 Jones, J. D., Sullivan, M. A., Vosburg, S. K., Manubay, J. M., Mogali, S., Metz, V., & Comer, S. D. (2015). Abuse potential of intranasal buprenorphine versus buprenorphine/naloxone in buprenorphine-maintained heroin users. *Addiction Biology, 20*(4), 784–798.

244 Walsh, S. L., Nuzzo, P. A., Babalonis, S., Casselton, V., & Lofwall, M. R. (2016). Intranasal buprenorphine alone and in combination with naloxone: Abuse liability and reinforcing efficacy in physically dependent opioid abusers. *Drug and Alcohol Dependence, 162*, 190–198.

245 Indivior. (2017). Sublocade (buprenorphine extended-release) injection: Full prescribing information. Retrieved December 18, 2017, from www.accessdata.fda.gov/drugsatfda_docs/label/2017/209819s000lbl.pdf

246 Elkader, A., & Sproule, B. (2005). Buprenorphine: Clinical pharmacokinetics in the treatment of opioid dependence. *Clinical Pharmacokinetics, 44*(7), 661–680.

247 Zhang, W., Ramamoorthy, Y., Tyndale, R. F., & Sellers, E. M. (2003). Interaction of buprenorphine and its metabolite norbuprenorphine with cytochromes p450 in vitro. *Drug Metabolism and Disposition: The Biological Fate of Chemicals, 31*(6), 768–772.

248 McCance-Katz, E. F., Sullivan, L. E., & Nallani, S. (2010). Drug interactions of clinical importance among the opioids, methadone and buprenorphine, and other frequently prescribed medications: A review. *American Journal on Addictions, 19*(1), 4–16.

249 Lofwall, M. R., & Walsh, S. L. (2014). A review of buprenorphine diversion and misuse: The current evidence base and experiences from around the world. *Journal of Addiction Medicine, 8*(5), 315–326.

250 Lofwall, M. R., & Walsh, S. L. (2014). A review of buprenorphine diversion and misuse: The current evidence base and experiences from around the world. *Journal of Addiction Medicine, 8*(5), 315–326.

251 Selden, T., Ahlner, J., Druid, H., & Kronstrand, R. (2012). Toxicological and pathological findings in a series of buprenorphine related deaths. Possible risk factors for fatal outcome. *Forensic Science International, 220*(1–3), 284–290.

252 Hakkinen, M., Launiainen, T., Vuori, E., & Ojanpera, I. (2012). Benzodiazepines and alcohol are associated with cases of fatal buprenorphine poisoning. *European Journal of Clinical Pharmacology, 68*(3), 301–309.

253 Indivior. (2015). Suboxone (buprenorphine and naloxone) sublingual film: Full prescribing information. Retrieved October 16, 2017, from www.suboxone.com/content/pdfs/prescribing-information.pdf

254 Toce, M. S., Burns, M. M., & O'Donnell, K. A. (2017). Clinical effects of unintentional pediatric buprenorphine exposures: Experience at a single tertiary care center. *Clinical Toxicology (Philadelphia, Pa.), 55*(1), 12–17.

255 Saxon, A. J., Ling, W., Hillhouse, M., Thomas, C., Hasson, A., Ang, A., … Jacobs, P. (2013). Buprenorphine/naloxone and methadone effects on laboratory indices of liver health: A randomized trial. *Drug and Alcohol Dependence, 128*(1–2), 71–76.

256 Roxane Laboratories. (2015). Buprenorphine HCl sublingual tablets: Full prescribing information. Retrieved October 16, 2017, from http://dailymed.nlm.nih.gov/dailymed/drugInfo.cfm?setid=1bf8b35a-b769-465c-a2f8-099868dfcd2f

257 Roxane Laboratories. (2015). Buprenorphine HCl sublingual tablets: Full prescribing information. Retrieved October 16, 2017, from http://dailymed.nlm.nih.gov/dailymed/drugInfo.cfm?setid=1bf8b35a-b769-465c-a2f8-099868dfcd2f

258 Nasser, A. F., Heidbreder, C., Liu, Y., & Fudala, P. J. (2015). Pharmacokinetics of sublingual buprenorphine and naloxone in subjects with mild to severe hepatic impairment (Child-Pugh classes A, B, and C), in hepatitis C virus-seropositive subjects, and in healthy volunteers. *Clinical Pharmacokinetics, 54*(8), 837–849.

259 Durand, F., & Valla, D. (2008). Assessment of prognosis of cirrhosis. *Seminars in Liver Disease, 28*(1), 110–122.

260 Durand, F., & Valla, D. (2008). Assessment of prognosis of cirrhosis. *Seminars in Liver Disease, 28*(1), 110–122.

261 Indivior. (2015). Suboxone (buprenorphine and naloxone) sublingual film: Full prescribing information. Retrieved October 16, 2017, from www.suboxone.com/content/pdfs/prescribing-information.pdf

262 Nasser, A. F., Heidbreder, C., Liu, Y., & Fudala, P. J. (2015). Pharmacokinetics of sublingual buprenorphine and naloxone in subjects with mild to severe hepatic impairment (Child-Pugh classes A, B, and C), in hepatitis C virus-seropositive subjects, and in healthy volunteers. *Clinical Pharmacokinetics, 54*(8), 837–849.

263 Roxane Laboratories. (2015). Buprenorphine HCl sublingual tablets: Full prescribing information. Retrieved October 16, 2017, from http://dailymed.nlm.nih.gov/dailymed/drugInfo.cfm?setid=1bf8b35a-b769-465c-a2f8-099868dfcd2f

264 Indivior. (2015). Suboxone (buprenorphine and naloxone) sublingual film: Full prescribing information. Retrieved October 16, 2017, from www.suboxone.com/content/pdfs/prescribing-information.pdf

265 Nasser, A. F., Heidbreder, C., Liu, Y., & Fudala, P. J. (2015). Pharmacokinetics of sublingual buprenorphine and naloxone in subjects with mild to severe hepatic impairment (Child-Pugh classes A, B, and C), in hepatitis C virus-seropositive subjects, and in healthy volunteers. *Clinical Pharmacokinetics, 54*(8), 837–849.

266 Durand, F., & Valla, D. (2008). Assessment of prognosis of cirrhosis. *Seminars in Liver Disease, 28*(1), 110–122.

267 Nasser, A. F., Heidbreder, C., Liu, Y., & Fudala, P. J. (2015). Pharmacokinetics of sublingual buprenorphine and naloxone in subjects with mild to severe hepatic impairment (Child-Pugh classes A, B, and C), in hepatitis C virus-seropositive subjects, and in healthy volunteers. *Clinical Pharmacokinetics, 54*(8), 837–849.

268 Roxane Laboratories. (2015). Buprenorphine HCl sublingual tablets: Full prescribing information. Retrieved October 16, 2017, from http://dailymed.nlm.nih.gov/dailymed/drugInfo.cfm?setid=1bf8b35a-b769-465c-a2f8-099868dfcd2f

269 Nasser, A. F., Heidbreder, C., Liu, Y., & Fudala, P. J. (2015). Pharmacokinetics of sublingual buprenorphine and naloxone in subjects with mild to severe hepatic impairment (Child-Pugh classes A, B, and C), in hepatitis C virus-seropositive subjects, and in healthy volunteers. *Clinical Pharmacokinetic, 54*(8), 837–849.

270 Substance Abuse and Mental Health Services Administration. (2016). Sublingual and transmucosal buprenorphine for opioid use disorder: Review and update. *Advisory*, Vol. 15, Issue 1. Rockville, MD: Substance Abuse and Mental Health Services Administration.

271 Lofwall, M. R., & Walsh, S. L. (2014). A review of buprenorphine diversion and misuse: The current evidence base and experiences from around the world. *Journal of Addiction Medicine, 8*(5), 315–326.

272 Lofwall, M. R., Martin, J., Tierney, M., Fatseas, M., Auriacombe, M., & Lintzeris, N. (2014). Buprenorphine diversion and misuse in outpatient practice. *Journal of Addiction Medicine, 8*(5), 327–332.

273 Indivior. (2016). Suboxone (buprenorphine and naloxone) sublingual film: Full prescribing information. Retrieved October 16, 2017, from www.suboxone.com/content/pdfs/prescribing-information.pdf

274 Indivior. (2016). Suboxone (buprenorphine and naloxone) sublingual film: Full prescribing information. Retrieved October 16, 2017, from www.suboxone.com/content/pdfs/prescribing-information.pdf

275 Strain, E. C., & Lofwall, M. R. (Eds.). (2008). Buprenorphine. *The American Psychiatric Publishing textbook of substance abuse treatment* (4th ed.). Arlington, VA: American Psychiatric Publishing.

276 Walsh, S. L., June, H. L., Schuh, K. J., Preston, K. L., Bigelow, G. E., & Stitzer, M. L. (1995). Effects of buprenorphine and methadone in methadone-maintained subjects. *Psychopharmacology, 119*(3), 268–276.

277 Strain, E. C., Preston, K. L., Liebson, I. A., & Bigelow, G. E. (1995). Buprenorphine effects in methadone-maintained volunteers: Effects at two hours after methadone. *Journal of Pharmacology and Experimental Therapeutics, 272*(2), 628–638.

278 Rosado, J., Walsh, S. L., Bigelow, G. E., & Strain, E. C. (2007). Sublingual buprenorphine/naloxone precipitated withdrawal in subjects maintained on 100mg of daily methadone. *Drug and Alcohol Dependence, 90*(2–3), 261–269.

279 Walsh, S. L., June, H. L., Schuh, K. J., Preston, K. L., Bigelow, G. E., & Stitzer, M. L. (1995). Effects of buprenorphine and methadone in methadone-maintained subjects. *Psychopharmacology, 119*(3), 268–276.

280 Jones, H. E., Dengler, E., Garrison, A., O'Grady, K. E., Seashore, C., Horton, E., ... Thorp, J. (2014). Neonatal outcomes and their relationship to maternal buprenorphine dose during pregnancy. *Drug and Alcohol Dependence, 134*, 414–417.

281 Cleary, B. J., Reynolds, K., Eogan, M., O'Connell, M. P., Fahey, T., Gallagher, P. J., ... Murphy, D. J. (2014). Methadone dosing and prescribed medication use in a prospective cohort of opioid-dependent pregnant women. *Addiction, 108*(4), 762–770.

282 Kaltenbach, K., Holbrook, A. M., Coyle, M. G., Heil, S. H., Salisbury, A. L. Stine, S. M., ... Jones, H. E. (2012). Predicting treatment for neonatal abstinence syndrome in infants born to women maintained on opioid agonist medication. *Addiction, 107*(Suppl. 1), 45–52.

283 McCance-Katz, E. F., Sullivan, L. E., & Nallani, S. (2010). Drug interactions of clinical importance among the opioids, methadone and buprenorphine, and other frequently prescribed medications: A review. *American Journal on Addictions, 19*(1), 4–16.

284 Center for Substance Abuse Treatment. (2004). *Clinical guidelines for the use of buprenorphine in the treatment of opioid addiction.* Treatment Improvement Protocol (TIP) Series 40. HHS Publication No. (SMA) 04-3939. Rockville, MD: Substance Abuse and Mental Health Services Administration.

285 Indivior. (2016). Suboxone (buprenorphine and naloxone) sublingual film: Full prescribing information. Retrieved October 16, 2017, from www.suboxone.com/content/pdfs/prescribing-information.pdf

286 McCance-Katz, E. F., Moody, D. E., Morse, G. D., Ma, Q., DiFrancesco, R., Friedland, G., ... Rainey, P. M. (2007). Interaction between buprenorphine and atazanavir or atazanavir/ritonavir. *Drug and Alcohol Dependence, 91*(2–3), 269–278.

287 Bruce, R. D., & Altice, F. L. (2006). Three case reports of a clinical pharmacokinetic interaction with buprenorphine and atazanavir plus ritonavir. *AIDS, 20*(5), 783–784.

288 Vergara-Rodriguez, P., Tozzi, M. J., Botsko, M., Nandi, V., Altice, F., Egan, J. E., ... Fiellin, D. A. (2011). Hepatic safety and lack of antiretroviral interactions with buprenorphine/naloxone in HIV-infected opioid-dependent patients. *Journal of Acquired Immune Deficiency Syndromes, 56*(Suppl. 1), S62–S67.

289 McCance-Katz, E. F., Moody, D. E., Prathikanti, S., Friedland, G., & Rainey, P. M. (2011). Rifampin, but not rifabutin, may produce opiate withdrawal in buprenorphine-maintained patients. *Drug and Alcohol Dependence, 118*(2–3), 326–334.

290 Roxane Laboratories. (2015). Buprenorphine HCl sublingual tablets: Full prescribing information. Retrieved October 16, 2017, from http://dailymed.nlm.nih.gov/dailymed/drugInfo.cfm?setid=1bf8b35a-b769-465c-a2f8-099868dfcd2f

291 McCance-Katz, E. F., Moody, D. E., Morse, G. D., Ma, Q., DiFrancesco, R., Friedland, G., ... Rainey, P. M. (2007). Interaction between buprenorphine and atazanavir or atazanavir/ritonavir. *Drug and Alcohol Dependence, 91*(2–3), 269–278.

292 McCance-Katz, E. F., Moody, D. E., Morse, G. D., Ma, Q., DiFrancesco, R., Friedland, G., ... Rainey, P. M. (2007). Interaction between buprenorphine and atazanavir or atazanavir/ritonavir. *Drug and Alcohol Dependence, 91*(2–3), 269–278.

293 Bruce, R. D., Moody, D. E., Altice, F. L., Gourevitch, M. N., & Friedland, G. H. (2013). A review of pharmacological interactions between HIV or hepatitis C virus medications and opioid agonist therapy: Implications and management for clinical practice. *Expert Review of Clinical Pharmacology, 6*(3), 249–269.

294 Roxane Laboratories. (2015). Buprenorphine HCl sublingual tablets: Full prescribing information. Retrieved October 16, 2017, from http://dailymed.nlm.nih.gov/dailymed/drugInfo.cfm?setid=1bf8b35a-b769-465c-a2f8-099868dfcd2f

295 Bruce, R. D., Moody, D. E., Altice, F. L., Gourevitch, M. N., & Friedland, G. H. (2013). A review of pharmacological interactions between HIV or hepatitis C virus medications and opioid agonist therapy: Implications and management for clinical practice. *Expert Review of Clinical Pharmacology, 6*(3), 249–269.

296 Gruber, V. A., Rainey, P. M., Moody, D. E., Morse, G. D., Ma, Q., Prathikanti, S., ... McCance-Katz, E. F. (2012). Interactions between buprenorphine and the protease inhibitors darunavir-ritonavir and fosamprenavir-ritonavir. *Clinical Infectious Diseases, 54*(3), 414–423.

297 Bruce, R. D., Moody, D. E., Altice, F. L., Gourevitch, M. N., & Friedland, G. H. (2013). A review of pharmacological interactions between HIV or hepatitis C virus medications and opioid agonist therapy: Implications and management for clinical practice. *Expert Review of Clinical Pharmacology, 6*(3), 249–269.

298 McCance-Katz, E. F., Moody, D. E., Morse, G. D., Friedland, G., Pade, P., Baker, J., ... Rainey, P. M. (2006). Interactions between buprenorphine and antiretrovirals. I. The nonnucleoside reverse-transcriptase inhibitors efavirenz and delavirdine. *Clinical Infectious Diseases, 43*(Suppl. 4), S224–S234.

299 McCance-Katz, E. F., Moody, D. E., Morse, G. D., Friedland, G., Pade, P., Baker, J., ... Rainey, P. M. (2006). Interactions between buprenorphine and antiretrovirals. I. The nonnucleoside reverse-transcriptase inhibitors efavirenz and delavirdine. *Clinical Infectious Diseases, 43*(Suppl. 4), S224–S234.

300 Bruce, R. D., Winkle, P., Custodio, J., Yin, X., Rhee, M., Andrews, J., ... Ramanathan, S. (2012, September). Pharmacokinetics of cobicistat-boosted elvitegravir administered in combination with methadone or buprenorphine/naloxone. Paper presented at the 52nd Interscience Conference on Antimicrobial Agents and Chemotherapy, San Francisco, CA.

301 McCance-Katz, E. F., Moody, D. E., Morse, G. D., Ma, Q., & Rainey, P. M. (2010). Lack of clinically significant drug interactions between nevirapine and buprenorphine. *American Journal on Addictions, 19*(1), 30–37.

302 McCance-Katz, E. F., Moody, D. E., Smith, P. F., Morse, G. D., Friedland, G., Pade, P., ... Rainey, P. (2006). Interactions between buprenorphine and antiretrovirals. II. The protease inhibitors nelfinavir, lopinavir/ritonavir, and ritonavir. *Clinical Infectious Diseases, 43*(Suppl. 4), S235–S246.

303 Bruce, R. D., Altice, F. L., Moody, D. E., Lin, S. N., Fang, W. B., Sabo, J. P., ... Friedland, G. H. (2009). Pharmacokinetic interactions between buprenorphine/naloxone and tipranavir/ritonavir in HIV-negative subjects chronically receiving buprenorphine/naloxone. *Drug and Alcohol Dependence, 105*(3), 234–239.

304 Substance Abuse and Mental Health Services Administration. (2016). Sublingual and transmucosal buprenorphine for opioid use disorder: Review and update. *Advisory*, Vol. 15, Issue 1. Rockville, MD: Substance Abuse and Mental Health Services Administration.

305 Isenberg, D., Wong, S. C., & Curtis, J. A. (2008). Serotonin syndrome triggered by a single dose of Suboxone. *American Journal of Emergency Medicine, 26*(7), 840.e3–840.e5.

306 Substance Abuse and Mental Health Services Administration. (2018). *Clinical guidance for treating pregnant and parenting women with opioid use disorder and their infants.* HHS Publication No. (SMA) 18-5054. Rockville, MD: Substance Abuse and Mental Health Services Administration.

307 Soyka, M. (2013). Buprenorphine use in pregnant opioid users: A critical review. *CNS Drugs, 27*(8), 653–662.

308 Saxon, A. J., Ling, W., Hillhouse, M., Thomas, C., Hasson, A., Ang, A., ... Jacobs, P. (2013). Buprenorphine/naloxone and methadone effects on laboratory indices of liver health: A randomized trial. *Drug and Alcohol Dependence, 128*(1–2), 71–76.

309 Vergara-Rodriguez, P., Tozzi, M. J., Botsko, M., Nandi, V., Altice, F., Egan, J. E., ... Fiellin, D. A. (2011). Hepatic safety and lack of antiretroviral interactions with buprenorphine/naloxone in HIV-infected opioid-dependent patients. *Journal of Acquired Immune Deficiency Syndromes, 56*(Suppl. 1), S62–S67.

310 Centers for Disease Control and Prevention. (2016). Viral hepatitis. Retrieved October 16, 2017, from www.cdc.gov/hepatitis/hbv/bfaq.htm

311 Lofwall, M. R., & Havens, J. R. (2012). Inability to access buprenorphine treatment as a risk factor for using diverted buprenorphine. *Drug and Alcohol Dependence, 126*(3), 379–383.

312 Bazazi, A. R., Yokell, M., Fu, J. J., Rich, J. D., & Zaller, N. D. (2011). Illicit use of buprenorphine/naloxone among injecting and noninjecting opioid users. *Journal of Addiction Medicine, 5*(3), 175–180.

313 Moratti, E., Kashanpour, H., Lombardelli, T., & Maisto, M. (2010). Intravenous misuse of buprenorphine: Characteristics and extent among patients undergoing drug maintenance therapy. *Clinical Drug Investigation, 30*(Suppl. 1), 3–11.

314 Braeburn Pharmaceuticals. (2016). Probuphine (buprenorphine) implant: Full prescribing information. Retrieved October 16, 2017, from www.accessdata.fda.gov/drugsatfda_docs/label/2016/204442Orig1s000lbl.pdf

315 Braeburn Pharmaceuticals. (2016). Probuphine (buprenorphine) implant: Full prescribing information. Retrieved October 16, 2017, from www.accessdata.fda.gov/drugsatfda_docs/label/2016/204442Orig1s000lbl.pdf

316 Center for Substance Abuse Treatment. (2004). *Clinical guidelines for the use of buprenorphine in the treatment of opioid addiction.* Treatment Improvement Protocol (TIP) Series 40. HHS Publication No. (SMA) 04-3939. Rockville, MD: Substance Abuse and Mental Health Services Administration.

317 Walley, A. Y., Alperen, J. K., Cheng, D. M., Botticelli, M., Castro-Donlan, C., Samet, J. H., & Alford, D. P. (2008). Office-based management of opioid dependence with buprenorphine: Clinical practices and barriers. *Journal of General Internal Medicine, 23*(9), 1393–1398.

318 Gunderson, E. W., Wang, X. Q., Fiellin, D. A., Bryan, B., & Levin, F. R. (2010). Unobserved versus observed office buprenorphine/naloxone induction: A pilot randomized clinical trial. *Addictive Behaviors, 35*(5), 537–540.

319 Lee, J. D., Vocci, F., & Fiellin, D. A. (2014). Unobserved "home" induction onto buprenorphine. *Journal of Addiction Medicine, 8*(5), 299–308.

320 American Society of Addiction Medicine. (2015). *The ASAM national practice guideline for the use of medications in the treatment of addiction involving opioid use.* Chevy Chase, MD: Author.

321 Providers Clinical Support System for Medication Assisted Treatment. (2013, November). PCSS Guidance. Retrieved December 18, 2017, from http://pcssmat.org/wp-content/uploads/2014/02/PCSS-MAT GuidanceBuprenorphineInduction.Casadonte.pdf

322 Tompkins, D. A., & Strain, E. C. (2011). Buprenorphine in the treatment of opioid dependence. In P. Ruiz & E. C. Strain (Eds.), *Substance abuse. A comprehensive textbook* (5th ed., pp. 437–446). Philadelphia, PA: Wolters Kluwer.

323 Indivior. (2016). Suboxone (buprenorphine and naloxone) sublingual film: Full prescribing information. Retrieved October 16, 2017, from www.suboxone.com/content/pdfs/prescribing-information.pdf

324 Strain, E. C. (2006). Clinical use of buprenorphine. In E. C. Strain & M. L. Stitzer (Eds.) *The treatment of opioid dependence* (pp. 230–252). Baltimore, MD: Johns Hopkins University Press.

325 Rich, J. D., McKenzie, M., Dickman, S., Bratberg, J., Lee, J. D., & Schwartz, R. P. (2011). An adverse reaction to buprenorphine/naloxone induction in prison: A case report. *Addictive Disorders and Their Treatment, 10*(4), 199–200.

326 Vocci, F. J., Schwartz, R. P., Wilson, M. E., Gordon, M. S., Kinlock, T. W., Fitzgerald, T. T., ... Jaffe, J. H. (2015). Buprenorphine dose induction in non-opioid-tolerant pre-release prisoners. *Drug and Alcohol Dependence, 156*, 133–138.

327 Tompkins, D. A., & Strain, E. C. (2011). Buprenorphine in the treatment of opioid dependence. In P. Ruiz & E. C. Strain (Eds.), *Substance abuse: A comprehensive textbook* (5th ed., pp. 437–446). Philadelphia, PA: Wolters Kluwer.

328 Rosado, J., Walsh, S. L., Bigelow, G. E., & Strain, E. C. (2007). Sublingual buprenorphine/naloxone precipitated withdrawal in subjects maintained on 100mg of daily methadone. *Drug and Alcohol Dependence, 90*(2–3), 261–269.

329 Zubieta, J., Greenwald, M. K., Lombardi, U., Woods, J. H., Kilbourn, M. R., Jewett, D. M., ... Johanson, C. E. (2000). Buprenorphine-induced changes in mu-opioid receptor availability in male heroin-dependent volunteers: A preliminary study. *Neuropsychopharmacology, 23*(3), 326–334.

330 Hser, Y., Saxon, A. J., Huang, D., Hasson, A., Thomas, C., Hillhouse, M. ... Ling, W. (2014). Treatment retention among patients randomized to buprenorphine/naloxone compared to methadone in a multi-site trial. *Addiction, 109*(1), 79–87.

331 American College of Obstetricians and Gynecologists Committee Opinion. (2017, August). Opioid use and opioid use disorder in pregnancy. Number 711. Retrieved October 30, 2017, from www.acog.org/Resources-And-Publications/Committee-Opinions/Committee-on-Obstetric-Practice/Opioid-Use-and-Opioid-Use-Disorder-in-Pregnancy

332 Debelak, K., Morrone, W. R., O'Grady, K. E., & Jones, H. E. (2013). Buprenorphine + naloxone in the treatment of opioid dependence during pregnancy-initial patient care and outcome data. *American Journal on Addictions, 22*, 252–254.

333 Wiegand, S. L., Stringer, E. M., Stuebe, A. M., Jones, H., Seashore, C., & Thorp, J. (2015). Buprenorphine and naloxone compared with methadone treatment in pregnancy. *Obstetrics & Gynecology, 125*, 363–368.

334 American Society of Addiction Medicine. (2015). *The ASAM national practice guideline for the use of medications in the treatment of addiction involving opioid use.* Chevy Chase, MD: Author.

335 Substance Abuse and Mental Health Services Administration. (2018). *Clinical guidance for treating pregnant and parenting women with opioid use disorder and their infants.* HHS Publication No. (SMA) 18-5054. Rockville, MD: Substance Abuse and Mental Health Services Administration.

336 Chavoustie, S., Frost, M., Snyder, O., Owen, J., Darwish, M., Dammerman, R., & Sanjurjo, V. (2017). Buprenorphine implants in medical treatment of opioid addiction. *Expert Review of Clinical Pharmacology, 10*(8), 799–807.

337 Hser, Y. I., Huang, D., Saxon, A. J., Woody, G., Moskowitz, A. L., Matthews, A. G., & Ling, W. (2017). Distinctive trajectories of opioid use over an extended follow-up of patients in a multisite trial on buprenorphine + naloxone and methadone. *Journal of Addiction Medicine, 11*(1), 63–69.

338 Ling, W., Hillhouse, M., Domier, C., Doraimani, G., Hunter, J., Thomas, C., ... Bilangi, R. (2009). Buprenorphine tapering schedule and illicit opioid use. *Addiction, 104*(2), 256–265.

339 Substance Abuse and Mental Health Services Administration. (2016). Sublingual and transmucosal buprenorphine for opioid use disorder: Review and update. *Advisory*, Vol. 15, Issue 1. Rockville, MD: Substance Abuse and Mental Health Services Administration.

340 American Society of Addiction Medicine. (2015). *The ASAM national practice guideline for the use of medications in the treatment of addiction involving opioid use.* Chevy Chase, MD: Author.

341 Henry-Edwards, S., Gowing, L., White, J., Ali, R., Bell, J., Brough, R., ... Quigley, A. (2003). *Clinical guidelines and procedures for the use of methadone in the maintenance treatment of opioid dependence.* Publication approval number: 3263 (JN 7616).

342 World Health Organization. (2009). *Guidelines for the psychosocially assisted pharmacological treatment of opioid dependence.* Geneva, Switzerland: WHO Press.

343 Ling, W., Hillhouse, M., Domier, C., Doraimani, G., Hunter, J., Thomas, C., ... Bilangi, R. (2009). Buprenorphine tapering schedule and illicit opioid use. *Addiction, 104*(2), 256–265.

344 Food and Drug Administration. (2017, May). *Appropriate use checklist: Buprenorphine-containing transmucosal products for opioid dependence.* Silver Spring, MD: Author.

345 American Society of Addiction Medicine. (2017). Sample treatment agreement. Retrieved October 19, 2017, from www.asam.org/docs/default-source/advocacy/sample-treatment-agreement30fa159472bc604ca5b7ff000030b21a.pdf?sfvrsn=0

346 Food and Drug Administration. (2017). FDA Drug Safety Communication: FDA urges caution about withholding opioid addiction medications from patients taking benzodiazepines or CNS depressants: Careful medication management can reduce risks. Retrieved December 18, 2017, from www.fda.gov/Drugs/DrugSafety/ucm575307.htm

347 Lintzeris, N., & Nielsen, S. (2010). Benzodiazepines, methadone and buprenorphine: Interactions and clinical management. *American Journal on Addictions, 19*(1), 59–72.

348 Lofwall, M. R., & Walsh, S. L. (2014). A review of buprenorphine diversion and misuse: The current evidence base and experiences from around the world. *Journal of Addiction Medicine, 8*(5), 315–326.

349 Liebschutz, J. M., Crooks, D., Herman, D., Anderson, B., Tsui, J., Meshesha, L. Z., ... Stein, M. (2014). Buprenorphine treatment for hospitalized, opioid-dependent patients: A randomized clinical trial. *JAMA Internal Medicine, 174*(8), 1369–1376.

350 Weiss, L., Netherland, J., Egan, J. E., Flanigan, T. P., Fiellin, D. A., Finkelstein, R., & Altice, F. L. (2011). Integration of buprenorphine/naloxone treatment into HIV clinical care: Lessons from the BHIVES collaborative. *Journal of Acquired Immune Deficiency Syndromes, 56*(Suppl. 1), S68–S75.

351 Weiss, R. D., Potter, J. S., Griffin, M. L., Provost, S. E., Fitzmaurice, G. M., McDermott, K. A., ... Carroll, K. M. (2015). Long-term outcomes from the National Drug Abuse Treatment Clinical Trials Network Prescription Opioid Addiction Treatment Study. *Drug and Alcohol Dependence, 150*, 112–119.

352 Substance Abuse and Mental Health Services Administration. (2005). *Substance abuse treatment for persons with cooccurring disorders.* Treatment Improvement Protocol (TIP) Series 42. HHS Publication No. (SMA) 133992. Rockville, MD: Substance Abuse and Mental Health Services Administration.

353 Center for Substance Abuse Treatment. (2004). *Clinical guidelines for the use of buprenorphine in the treatment of opioid addiction.* Treatment Improvement Protocol (TIP) Series 40. HHS Publication No. (SMA) 04-3939. Rockville, MD: Substance Abuse and Mental Health Services Administration.

354 Drug Addiction Treatment Act of 2000, H. R. 2634 (1999–2000).

355 Vujanovic, A. A., Bonn-Miller, M. O., & Petry, N. M. (2016). Co-occurring posttraumatic stress and substance use: Emerging research on correlates, mechanisms, and treatments—Introduction to the special issue. *Psychology of Addictive Behaviors, 30*(7), 713–719.

356 Stitzer, M. L., & Vandrey, R. (2008). Contingency management: Utility in the treatment of drug abuse disorders. *Clinical Pharmacology and Therapeutics, 83*(4), 644–647.

357 Donovan, D. M., Ingalsbe, M. H., Benbow, J., & Daley, D. C. (2013). 12-step interventions and mutual support programs for substance use disorders: An overview. *Social Work in Public Health, 28*(3–4), 313–332.

358 Donovan, D. M., Ingalsbe, M. H., Benbow, J., & Daley, D. C. (2013). 12-step interventions and mutual support programs for substance use disorders: An overview. *Social Work in Public Health, 28*(3–4), 313–332.

359 McLellan, A. T., & White, W. (2012). *Opioid maintenance and recovery-oriented systems of care: It is time to integrate* (p. 2). London, England: National Treatment Agency for Substance Misuse.

360 American Society of Addiction Medicine. (2015). *The ASAM national practice guideline for the use of medications in the treatment of addiction involving opioid use.* Chevy Chase, MD: Author.

361 Substance Abuse and Mental Health Services Administration. (2012). *Clinical drug testing in primary care.* Technical Assistance Publication (TAP) Series 32. HHS Publication No. (SMA) 12-4668. Rockville, MD: Substance Abuse and Mental Health Services Administration.

362 Jarvis, M., Williams, J., Hurford, M., Lindsay, D., Lincoln, P., Giles, L., ... Safarian, T. (2017.) Appropriate use of drug testing in clinical addiction medicine. *Journal of Addiction Medicine, 11*(3), 163–173.

363 Stoller, K. B., Stephens, M. A. C., & Schorr, A. (2016). Integrated service delivery models for opioid treatment programs in an era of increasing opioid addiction, health reform, and parity. Retrieved May 21, 2017, from www.aatod.org/wp-content/uploads/2016/07/2nd-Whitepaper-.pdf

364 Rich, J. D., McKenzie, M., Larney, S., Wong, J. B., Tran, L., Clarke, J., ... Zaller, N. (2015, July 25). Methadone continuation versus forced withdrawal on incarceration in a combined US prison and jail: A randomised, open-label trial. *Lancet, 386*(9991), 350–359.

365 Lofwall, M. R., & Walsh, S. L. (2014). A review of buprenorphine diversion and misuse: The current evidence base and experiences from around the world. *Journal of Addiction Medicine, 8*(5), 315–326.

366 Genberg, B. L., Gillespie, M., Schuster, C. R., Johanson, C.-E., Astemborski, J., Kirk, G. D., ... Mehta, S. H. (2013). Prevalence and correlates of street-obtained buprenorphine use among current and former injectors in Baltimore, Maryland. *Addictive Behaviors, 38*(12), 2868–2873.

367 Schuman-Olivier, Z., Albanese, M., Nelson, S. E., Roland, L., Puopolo, F., Klinker, L., & Shaffer, H. J. (2010). Self-treatment: Illicit buprenorphine use by opioid-dependent treatment seekers. *Journal of Substance Abuse Treatment, 39*(1), 41–50.

368 Cicero, T. J., Ellis, M. S., Surratt, H. L., & Kurtz, S. P. (2014). Factors contributing to the rise of buprenorphine misuse: 2008-2013. *Drug and Alcohol Dependence, 142,* 98–104.

369 Lofwall, M. R., & Walsh, S. L. (2014). A review of buprenorphine diversion and misuse: The current evidence base and experiences from around the world. *Journal of Addiction Medicine, 8*(5), 315–326.

370 United States National Library of Medicine. (2017, October). Buprenorphine sublingual and buccal (opioid dependence). Retrieved December 18, 2017, from https://medlineplus.gov/druginfo/meds/a605002.html

371 American Society of Addiction Medicine. (2016). Sample office-based opioid use disorder policy and procedure manual. Retrieved October 19, 2017, from www.asam.org/docs/default-source/advocacy/sample-diversion-policy.pdf?sfvrsn=0

372 Substance Abuse and Mental Health Services Administration. (2015). *Federal guidelines for opioid treatment programs.* HHS Publication No. (SMA) PEP15-FEDGUIDEOTP. Rockville, MD: Substance Abuse and Mental Health Services Administration.

373 Medication Assisted Treatment for Opioid Use Disorders. HHS Final Rule, Fed. Reg. 81 44711 (July 8, 2016) (to be codified at 42 CFR pt. 8).

374 Physical security controls for practitioners, 21 CFR § 1301.75 (2016).

375 American Society of Addiction Medicine. (2016). Sample office-based opioid use disorder policy and procedure manual. Retrieved October 19, 2017, from www.asam.org/docs/default-source/advocacy/sample-diversion-policy.pdf?sfvrsn=0

376 Records for manufacturers, distributors, dispensers, researchers, importers, exporters, registrants that reverse distribute, and collectors, 21 CFR § 1304.22 (2014).

377 Lofwall, M., & Walsh, S. (2014). A review of buprenorphine diversion and misuse: The current evidence base and experiences from around the world (p. 316). *Journal of Addiction Medicine, 8*(5), 315–326.

378 American Society of Addiction Medicine. (2016). Sample office-based opioid use disorder policy and procedure manual. Retrieved October 19, 2017, from www.asam.org/docs/default-source/advocacy/sample-diversion-policy.pdf?sfvrsn=0

379 Velez, C. M., Nicolaidis, C., Korthuis, P. T., & Englander, H. (2016). "It's been an experience, a life learning experience": A qualitative study of hospitalized patients with substance use disorders. *Journal of General Internal Medicine, 32*(3), 296–303.

380 Liebschutz, J. M., Crooks, D., Herman, D., Anderson, B., Tsui, J., Meshesha, L. Z., … Stein, M. (2014). Buprenorphine treatment for hospitalized, opioid-dependent patients: A randomized clinical trial. *JAMA Internal Medicine, 174*(8), 1369–1376.

381 D'Onofrio, G., O'Connor, P. G., Pantalon, M. V., Chawarski, M. C., Busch, S. H., Owens, P. H., … Fiellin, D. A. (2015). Emergency department-initiated buprenorphine/naloxone treatment for opioid dependence: A randomized clinical trial. *JAMA, 313*(16), 1636–1644.

382 Naeger, S., Ali, M. M., Mutter, R., Mark, T., & Hughey, L. (2016). Post-discharge prescription fills following an opioid hospitalization. *Psychiatric Services, 67*(11), 1264–1267.

383 Weiss, A. J., Elixhauser, A., Barrett, M. L., Steiner, C. A., Bailey, M. K., & O'Malley, L. (2017, January). *Opioid-related inpatient stays and emergency department visits by state, 2009–2014*. HCUP Statistical Brief No. 219. Rockville, MD: Agency for Healthcare Research and Quality.

384 Administering or dispensing of narcotic drugs, 21 CFR § 1306.07 (2005).

385 Alford, D., Compton, P., & Samet, H. (2006). Acute pain management for patients receiving maintenance methadone or buprenorphine therapy. *Annals of Internal Medicine, 144*(2), 127–134.

386 Sen, S., Arulkumar, S., Cornett, E. M., Gayle, J. A., Flower, R. R., Fox, C. J., & Kaye, A. D. (2016). New pain management options for the surgical patient on methadone and buprenorphine. *Current Pain and Headache Reports, 20*(3), 16.

387 Jones, H. E., Deppen, K., Hudak, M. L., Leffert, L., McClelland, C., Sahin, L., … Creanga, A. A. (2014). Clinical care for opioid-using pregnant and postpartum women: The role of obstetric providers. *American Journal of Obstetrics and Gynecology, 210*(4), 302–310.

388 Alizadeh, S., Mahmoudi, G. A., Solhi, H., Sadeghi-Sedeh, B., Behzadi, R., & Kazemifar, A. M. (2015). Post-operative analgesia in opioid dependent patients: Comparison of intravenous morphine and sublingual buprenorphine. *Addiction and Health, 7*(1–2), 60–65.

389 Sen, S., Arulkumar, S., Cornett, E. M., Gayle, J. A., Flower, R. R., Fox, C. J., & Kaye, A. D. (2016). New pain management options for the surgical patient on methadone and buprenorphine. *Current Pain and Headache Reports, 20*(3),16.

390 Administering or dispensing of narcotic drugs, 21 CFR § 1306.07 (2005).

391 Alford, D. P., Compton, P., & Samet, J. H. (2006). Acute pain management for patients receiving maintenance methadone or buprenorphine therapy. *Annals of Internal Medicine, 144*(2), 127–134.

392 Devin, C. J., & McGirt, M. J. (2015). Best evidence in multimodal pain management in spine surgery and means of assessing postoperative pain and functional outcomes. *Journal of Clinical Neuroscience, 22*(6), 930–938.

393 Noska, A., Mohan, A., Wakeman, S., Rich, J., & Boutwell, A. (2015). Managing opioid use disorder during and after acute hospitalization: A case-based review clarifying methadone regulation for acute care settings. *Journal of Addictive Behaviors, Therapy and Rehabilitation, 4*(2), 1000138.

394 Liebschutz, J. M., Crooks, D., Herman, D., Anderson, B., Tsui, J., Meshesha, L. Z., … Stein, M. (2014). Buprenorphine treatment for hospitalized, opioid-dependent patients: A randomized clinical trial. *JAMA Internal Medicine, 174*(8), 1369–1376.

395 D'Onofrio, G., O'Connor, P. G., Pantalon, M. V., Chawarski, M. C., Busch, S. H., Owens, P. H., … Fiellin, D. A. (2015). Emergency department-initiated buprenorphine/naloxone treatment for opioid dependence: A randomized clinical trial. *JAMA, 313*(16), 1636–1644.

396 Substance Abuse and Mental Health Services Administration. (2016, March). Special circumstances for providing buprenorphine. Retrieved December 18, 2017, from www.samhsa.gov/medication-assisted-treatment/legislation-regulations-guidelines/special-circumstances-providing-buprenorphine

397 D'Onofrio, G., O'Connor, P. G., Pantalon, M. V., Chawarski, M. C., Busch, S. H., Owens, P. H., … Fiellin, D. A. (2015). Emergency department-initiated buprenorphine/naloxone treatment for opioid dependence: A randomized clinical trial. *JAMA, 313*(16), 1636–1644.

398 Huxtable, C. A., Roberts, L. J., Somogyi, A. A., & Macintyre, P. E. (2011). Acute pain management in opioid-tolerant patients: A growing challenge. *Anaesthesia and Intensive Care, 39*(5), 804–823.

This page intentionally left blank.

TIP 63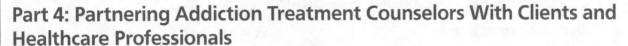

MEDICATIONS FOR OPIOID USE DISORDER

Part 4: Partnering Addiction Treatment Counselors With Clients and Healthcare Professionals

For Healthcare and Addiction Professionals

Part 4 of this **Treatment Improvement Protocol (TIP)** is for addiction treatment professionals and peer recovery support specialists who work with individuals who take a Food and Drug Administration (FDA)-approved medication to treat opioid use disorder (OUD).

TIP Navigation

Executive Summary
For healthcare and addiction professionals, policymakers, patients, and families

Part 1: Introduction to Medications for Opioid Use Disorder Treatment
For healthcare and addiction professionals, policymakers, patients, and families

Part 2: Addressing Opioid Use Disorder in General Medical Settings
For healthcare professionals

Part 3: Pharmacotherapy for Opioid Use Disorder
For healthcare professionals

Part 4: Partnering Addiction Treatment Counselors With Clients and Healthcare Professionals
For healthcare and addiction professionals

Part 5: Resources Related to Medications for Opioid Use Disorder
For healthcare and addiction professionals, policymakers, patients, and families

KEY MESSAGES

- Many patients taking OUD medication benefit from counseling as part of their treatment.
- Counselors play the same role for clients with OUD who take medication as for clients with any other SUD.
- Counselors help clients recover by addressing the challenges and consequences of addiction.
- OUD is often a chronic illness requiring ongoing communication among patients and providers to ensure that patients fully benefit from both pharmacotherapy and psychosocial treatment and support.
- OUD medications are safe and effective when prescribed and taken appropriately.
- Medication is integral to recovery for many people with OUD. Medication usually produces better treatment outcomes than outpatient treatment without medication.
- Supportive counseling environments for clients who take OUD medication can promote treatment and help build recovery capital.

PART 4: PARTNERING ADDICTION TREATMENT COUNSELORS WITH CLIENTS AND HEALTHCARE PROFESSIONALS

Overview and Context 4-1

Quick Guide to Medications 4-12

Counselor–Prescriber Communications 4-18

Creation of a Supportive Counseling Experience 4-20

Other Common Counseling Concerns 4-34

Notes 4-37

PART 4 of 5
Partnering Addiction Treatment Counselors With Clients and Healthcare Professionals

Part 4 of this TIP is for addiction treatment professionals and peer recovery support specialists who work with individuals who take an FDA-approved medication for OUD—methadone, naltrexone, or buprenorphine. These providers have direct helping relationships with clients. They don't prescribe or administer OUD medications, but they interact with healthcare professionals who do. They also help people who take OUD medication access supportive services (e.g., transportation, child care, housing).

Overview and Context

Scope of the Problem

Opioid misuse has caused a growing nationwide epidemic of OUD and unintentional overdose deaths.[1] This epidemic affects people in all regions, of all ages, and from all walks of life. Opioid misuse devastates families, burdens emergency departments and first responders, fuels increases in hospital admissions, and strains criminal justice and child welfare systems.

Counselors can play an integral role in addressing this crisis. Counseling helps people with OUD and other substance use disorders (SUDs) change how they think, cope, react, and acquire the skills and confidence necessary for recovery. Counseling can provide support for people who take medication to treat their OUD. Patients may get counseling from prescribers or other staff members in the prescribers' practices or by referral to counselors at specialty addiction treatment programs or in private practice.

Counselors and peer recovery support specialists can work with patients who take OUD medication and refer patients with active OUD to healthcare professionals for an assessment for treatment with medication.

2.1 MILLION people in the U.S., ages 12 and older, had OUD involving **PRESCRIPTION OPIOIDS, HEROIN,** or both in 2016.[2]

Part 4 uses "counselor" to refer to the range of professionals—including recovery coaches and other peer recovery support services specialists—who may counsel, coach, or mentor people who take OUD medication, although their titles, credentials, and range of responsibilities vary. At times, Part 4 refers to individuals as "clients." For other key terms, see Exhibit 4.1. Part 5 of this TIP provides a full glossary and other resources related to the treatment of OUD.

Counseling clients who take OUD medication requires understanding:

- Basic information about OUD.
- The role and function of OUD medications.
- Ways to create a supportive environment that helps clients work toward recovery.
- Counseling's role within a system of whole-person, recovery-oriented OUD care.

EXHIBIT 4.1. Key Terms

Addiction: As defined by the American Society of Addiction Medicine,[3] "a primary, chronic disease of brain reward, motivation, memory, and related circuitry" (p. 1). It is characterized by inability to consistently abstain, impairment in behavioral control, craving, diminished recognition of significant problems with one's behaviors and interpersonal relationships, and a dysfunctional emotional response. Like other chronic diseases, addiction often involves cycles of **relapse** and **remission.** The *Diagnostic and Statistical Manual of Mental Disorders,* Fifth Edition[4] (DSM-5), does not use the term for diagnostic purposes, but it commonly describes the more severe forms of OUD.

Care provider: Encompasses both **healthcare professionals** and other professionals who do not provide medical services, such as counselors or providers of supportive services. Often shortened to "provider."

Healthcare professionals: Physicians, nurse practitioners, physician assistants, and other medical service professionals who are eligible to prescribe medications for and treat patients with OUD. The term **"prescribers"** also refers to these healthcare professionals.

Maintenance treatment: Providing medications to achieve and sustain clinical remission of signs and symptoms of OUD and support the individual process of recovery without a specific endpoint (as is the typical standard of care in medical and psychiatric treatment of other chronic illnesses).

Mutual-help groups: Groups of people who work together on obtaining and maintaining recovery. Unlike peer support (e.g., the use of recovery coaches), mutual-help groups consist entirely of people who volunteer their time and typically have no official connection to treatment programs. Most are self-supporting. Although 12-Step groups such as Alcoholics Anonymous (AA) and Narcotics Anonymous (NA) are the most widespread and well-researched type of mutual-help groups, other groups may be available in some areas. They range from groups affiliated with a religion (e.g., Celebrate Recovery, Millati Islami) to purely secular groups (e.g., SMART Recovery, Women for Sobriety).

Opioid misuse: The use of prescription opioids in any way other than as directed by a doctor; the use of any opioid in a manner, situation, amount, or frequency that can cause harm to self or others.[5]

Opioid receptor agonist: A substance that has an affinity for and stimulates physiological activity at cell receptors in the central nervous system (CNS) that are normally stimulated by opioids. **Mu-opioid receptor full agonists** (e.g., methadone) bind to the mu-opioid receptor and produce actions similar to those produced by the endogenous opioid beta-endorphin. Increasing the dose increases the effect. **Mu-opioid receptor partial agonists** (e.g., buprenorphine) bind to the mu-opioid receptor. Unlike with full agonists, increasing their dose may not produce additional effects once they have reached their maximal effect. At low doses, partial agonists may produce effects similar to those of full agonists.

Opioid receptor antagonist: A substance that has an affinity for opioid receptors in the CNS without producing the physiological effects of opioid agonists. Mu-opioid receptor antagonists (e.g., naltrexone) can block the effects of exogenously administered opioids.

Opioids: All natural, synthetic, and semisynthetic substances that have effects similar to morphine. They can be used as medications having such effects (e.g., methadone, buprenorphine, oxycodone).

Opioid treatment program (OTP): An accredited treatment program with Substance Abuse and Mental Health Services Administration (SAMHSA) certification and Drug Enforcement Administration registration to administer and dispense opioid agonist medications that are approved by FDA to treat opioid addiction. Currently, these include methadone and buprenorphine. Other pharmacotherapies, such as naltrexone, may be provided but are not subject to these regulations. OTPs must provide adequate medical, counseling, vocational, educational, and other assessment and treatment services either onsite or by referral to an outside agency or practitioner through a formal agreement.[6]

EXHIBIT 4.1. Key Terms (continued)

Opioid use disorder (OUD): Per DSM-5,[7] a disorder characterized by loss of control of opioid use, risky opioid use, impaired social functioning, tolerance, and withdrawal. Tolerance and withdrawal do not count toward the diagnosis in people experiencing these symptoms when using opioids under appropriate medical supervision. OUD covers a range of severity and replaces what the *Diagnostic and Statistical Manual of Mental Disorders,* Fourth Edition, termed "opioid abuse" and "opioid dependence." An OUD diagnosis is applicable to a person who uses opioids and experiences at least 2 of the 11 symptoms in a 12-month period. (See Exhibit 2.13 and the Appendix in Part 2 for full DSM-5 diagnostic criteria for OUD.)

Peer support: The use of peer support specialists in recovery to provide nonclinical (i.e., not requiring training in diagnosis or treatment) recovery support services to individuals in recovery from addiction and to their families.

Peer support specialist: Someone in recovery who has lived experience in addiction plus skills learned in formal training. Peer support specialists may be paid professionals or volunteers. They are distinguished from members of mutual-help groups because they maintain contact with treatment staff. They offer experiential knowledge that treatment staff often lack.

Prescribers: Healthcare professionals who are eligible to prescribe medications for OUD.

Psychosocial support: Ancillary services to enhance a patient's overall functioning and well-being, including recovery support services, case management, housing, employment, and educational services.

Psychosocial treatment: Interventions that seek to enhance a patient's social and mental functioning, including addiction counseling, contingency management, and mental health services.

Recovery: A process of change through which individuals improve their health and wellness, live a self-directed life, and strive to reach their full potential. Even individuals with severe and chronic SUDs can, with help, overcome their SUDs and regain health and social function. Although abstinence from all substance misuse is a cardinal feature of a recovery lifestyle, it is not the only healthy, prosocial feature. Patients taking FDA-approved medication to treat OUD can be considered in recovery.

Recovery capital: The sum of the internal (e.g., motivation, self-efficacy, spirituality) and external (e.g., access to health care, employment, family support) resources that an individual can draw upon to begin and sustain recovery from SUDs.

Recovery-oriented care: A service orientation that supports individuals with behavioral health conditions in a process of change through which they can improve their health and wellness, live self-directed lives, and strive to reach their full potential.

Relapse: A process in which a person with OUD who has been in **remission** experiences a return of symptoms or loss of remission. A relapse is different from a **return to opioid use** in that it involves more than a single incident of use. Relapses occur over a period of time and can be interrupted. Relapse need not be long lasting. The TIP uses relapse to describe relapse prevention, a common treatment modality.

Remission: A medical term meaning a disappearance of signs and symptoms of the disease.[8] DSM-5 defines remission as present in people who previously met OUD criteria but no longer meet any OUD criteria (with the possible exception of craving).[9] Remission is an essential element of **recovery.**

Return to opioid use: One or more instances of **opioid misuse** without a return of symptoms of OUD. A return to opioid use may lead to **relapse.**

Setting the Stage

Since the 1990s, dramatic increases in controlled medication prescriptions—particularly opioid pain relievers—have coincided with increases in their misuse.[10] Since the mid-2000s, heroin[11,12] and fentanyl (mainly illicit formulations)[13] consumption has also sharply increased. People who turn to illicit drugs after misusing opioid medications have driven greater use of heroin and fentanyl, which are cheaper and easier to obtain.

Approximately 1,500 OTPs currently dispense methadone, buprenorphine, or both.[14] They may also offer naltrexone. Historically, OTPs were the only source of OUD medication and offered only methadone.

Buprenorphine is increasingly available in general medical settings. Physicians, nurse practitioners, and physician assistants (whether or not they're addiction specialists) can get a federal waiver to prescribe buprenorphine. These healthcare professionals can also prescribe and administer naltrexone, which does not require a waiver or OTP program certification.

People with OUD should have access to the medication most appropriate for them. Medication helps establish and maintain OUD remission. By controlling withdrawal and cravings and blocking the euphoric effects of illicit opioids, OUD medication helps patients stop illicit opioid use and resolve OUD's psychosocial problems. For some people, OUD medication may be lifesaving. Ideally, patients with OUD should have access to all three FDA-approved pharmacotherapies. (See the "Quick Guide to Medications" section for an overview of each medication.)

Many patients taking OUD medication benefit from counseling as part of their treatment. Counseling helps people with OUD change how they think, cope, react, and acquire the skills and confidence needed for recovery. Patients may get counseling from medication prescribers or staff members in prescribers' practices or by referral to counselors at specialty addiction treatment programs or in private practice. Exhibit 4.2

> The counselor's role with clients who take OUD medication is the same as it is with all clients who have SUDs: Help them achieve recovery by addressing addiction's challenges and consequences.

discusses recommending versus requiring counseling as part of medication treatment for OUD.

Distinguishing OUD From Physical Dependence on Opioid Medications

According to DSM-5,[15] OUD falls under the general category of SUDs and is marked by:

- Compulsion and craving.
- Tolerance.
- Loss of control.
- Withdrawal when use stops.
- Continued opioid use despite adverse consequences.

Properly taken, some medications cause tolerance and physical dependence. Medications for some chronic illnesses (e.g., steroids for systemic lupus erythematosus) can make the body build tolerance to the medications over time. If people abruptly stop taking medications on which they've become physically dependent, they can experience withdrawal symptoms. This can be serious, even fatal.

Physical dependence on a prescribed, properly taken opioid medication is distinct from OUD and opioid addiction. OUD is a behavioral disorder associated with loss of control of opioid use, use despite adverse consequences, reduction in functioning, and compulsion to use. The professionals who revised DSM-5 diagnostic criteria for OUD made several significant changes. Among the most notable was differentiating physical dependence from OUD:

- Tolerance or withdrawal symptoms related to FDA-approved medications appropriately prescribed and taken to treat OUD (buprenorphine, methadone) don't count toward diagnostic criteria for OUD.

> **EXHIBIT 4.2. Recommending Versus Requiring Counseling**
>
> The TIP expert panel affirms that counseling and ancillary services greatly benefit many patients. However, such **counseling and ancillary services should target patients' needs and shouldn't be arbitrarily required as a condition for receiving OUD medication (although they are required by regulations in OTPs),** especially when the benefits of medication outweigh the risks of not receiving counseling.
>
> **The TIP expert panel recommends individualized treatment.** Patients who choose to start medication and medication management with their prescriber without adjunctive counseling and don't adequately respond to such treatment should be referred to adjunctive counseling and more intensive services as needed.[16]
>
> **The law requires buprenorphine prescribers to be able to refer patients taking OUD medication to counseling and ancillary services.** Buprenorphine prescribers may meet this requirement by keeping a list of referrals or by providing counseling themselves. **The law doesn't require naltrexone prescribers to refer patients to additional services.** However, FDA labels for both medications recommend counseling as part of treatment.
>
> **Some treatment environments require counseling by regulation or contractual obligation.** In other cases, a healthcare professional may believe that a patient taking OUD medication would benefit from counseling. Some healthcare professionals may require counseling, particularly if patients aren't responding well to medication.

OUD is often a chronic medical illness.[17] Treatment isn't a cure.

- If the individual is being treated with an OUD medication and meets no OUD criteria other than tolerance, withdrawal, or craving (but did meet OUD criteria in the past), he or she is considered in remission on pharmacotherapy.

Accepting this distinction is essential to working with clients taking OUD medication. One common question about patients taking medication for OUD is "Aren't they still addicted?" The new DSM-5 distinction makes the answer to this question "No, they're not still addicted." A person can require OUD medication and be physically dependent on it but still be in remission and recovery from OUD.

Understanding the Benefits of Medication for OUD

Medication is an effective treatment for OUD.[18,19,20] People with OUD should be referred for an assessment for pharmacotherapy unless they decline.[21] To be supportive and effective when counseling clients who could benefit from or who take medication for OUD, know that:

- **Treatment with methadone and buprenorphine is associated with lower likelihood of overdose death compared with not taking these medications.**[22,23,24,25,26]
- **Medication helps people reduce or stop opioid misuse.**[27,28,29,30] As Jessica's story in Exhibit 4.3 shows, even if people return to opioid use during treatment or don't achieve abstinence in the short term, medication lessens misuse and its health risks (e.g., overdose, injection-related infections).[31]
- **Patients taking FDA-approved medication used to treat OUD can join residential or outpatient treatment.** Decades of clinical experience in OTPs, which must provide counseling, suggest that patients taking OUD medication can fully participate in group and individual counseling, both cognitively and emotionally. Patients with concurrent SUDs (involving stimulants or alcohol) can benefit from residential treatment while continuing to take their OUD medication.

EXHIBIT 4.3. Jessica's Story About Medication

Jessica is a 32-year-old who unsuccessfully quit heroin dozens of times. She had been in and out of treatment but says, "It just never stuck. I'd always start using again when I left the program." Three years ago, her primary care doctor started prescribing her buprenorphine. Now Jessica says:

Some days I pinch myself. I can't believe I got my life back. I tried quitting so many times but always got pulled back into the scene. Ever since I've been on buprenorphine, I haven't had any cravings. Even when I'm around triggers, they just don't set me off the same way. I've been able to get a job and I'm starting to build a community of friends who don't use. The hardest part about being on buprenorphine is that my emotions aren't masked anymore. I have to feel all of the sadness and fear that I was avoiding all these years. But it's good. I'm getting a chance to work through it.

- **Randomized clinical trials indicate that OUD medication improves treatment retention and reduces illicit opioid use.**[32,33,34] Retention in treatment increases the opportunity to provide counseling and supportive services that can help patients stabilize their lives and maintain recovery.
- **The longer patients take medication, the less likely they are to return to opioid use,** whereas short-term medically supervised withdrawal rarely prevents return to use:[35,36,37,38,39]
  - Conducting short-term medically supervised withdrawal may increase the risk of unintentional fatal overdose because of decreased tolerance after withdrawal completion.[40,41]
  - Providing short-term medical treatment for OUD is the same as treating a heart attack without managing the underlying coronary disease.
  - Providing longer courses of medication that extend beyond withdrawal can allow patients to stabilize.
  - Getting stabilized, which may take months or even years, allows patients to focus on building and maintaining a healthy lifestyle.
- **Patients taking OUD medication can achieve long-term recovery.** People who continue to take medication can be in remission from OUD and live healthy, productive lives.[42]

Reviewing the Evidence on Counseling in Support of Medication To Treat OUD

Dedicated counseling can help clients address the challenges of extended recovery. For clients who seek a self-directed, purposeful life, counseling can help them:

- Improve problem-solving and interpersonal skills.
- Find incentives for reduced use and abstinence.
- Build a set of techniques to resist drug use.
- Replace drug use with constructive, rewarding activities.

Moreover, evidence shows that counseling can be a useful part of OUD treatment for people who take OUD medication. Impact studies of counseling for people with SUDs show that:

- **Motivational enhancement/interviewing is generally beneficial.**[43] This approach helps get people into treatment. It also supports behavior change and, thus, recovery.

- **Cognitive–behavioral therapy (CBT) has demonstrated efficacy in the treatment of SUDs,** whether used alone or in combination with other strategies.[44] Clinical trials have not shown that CBT added to buprenorphine treatment with medical management is associated with significantly lower rates of illicit opioid use.[45,46] However, a secondary analysis of one of those trials found that CBT added to buprenorphine and medical management was associated with significantly greater reduction in any drug use among participants whose OUD was primarily linked to misuse of prescription opioids than among those whose OUD involved only heroin.[47] Thus, CBT may be helpful to those patients receiving buprenorphine treatment who have nonopioid drug use problems.
- **Case management helps establish the stability necessary for SUD remission.**[48,49,50] Case management helps some people in SUD treatment get or sustain access to services and necessities, such as:
  - Food.
  - Shelter.
  - Income support.
  - Legal aid.
  - Dental services.
  - Transportation.
  - Vocational services.
- **Family therapy can address SUDs and various other family problems** (e.g., family conflict, unemployment, conduct disorders). Several forms of family therapy are effective with adolescents[51] and can potentially address family members' biases about use of medication for OUD.[52]
- **There is more research on combined methadone treatment and various psychosocial treatments (e.g., different levels of counseling, contingency management) than on buprenorphine or naltrexone treatment in office-based settings.** More research is needed to identify the best interventions to use with specific medications, populations, and treatment phases in outpatient settings.[53]
- **Motivational intervention, case management, or both can improve likelihood of entry into medication treatment for OUD** among people who inject opioids, according to a systematic review of 13 studies plus data from a prior systematic review.[54]
- **Clinical trials have shown no differences in outcomes for buprenorphine with medical management between participants who get adjunctive counseling and those who don't** (i.e., prescriber-provided guidance focused specifically on use of the medication).[55,56,57,58]

RESOURCE ALERT

Principles of Effective Treatment

In its *Principles of Drug Addiction Treatment*, the National Institute on Drug Abuse lists 13 principles of effective treatment (p. 2).[59] Two principles that pertain to counseling are:

- "**No single treatment is effective for everyone.** Treatment varies depending on the type of drug and the characteristics of the patients. Matching treatment settings, interventions, and services to an individual's particular problems and needs is critical to his or her ultimate success in returning to productive functioning in the family, workplace, and society."
- "**Effective treatment attends to multiple needs of the individual, not just his or her drug abuse.** To be effective, treatment must address the individual's drug abuse and any associated medical, psychological, social, vocational, and legal problems. It is also important that treatment be appropriate to the individual's age, gender, ethnicity, and culture."

Yet those trials:
- Relied on well-structured medical management sessions that may not be typical in practice.
- Excluded patients with certain co-occurring disorders or factors that complicated treatment.

- **Benefits from counseling may depend on factors such as the number of sessions and adherence.**[60]

Using a Recovery-Oriented Approach to Treating Patients With OUD

Counseling for OUD gives patients tools to manage their illness, achieve and sustain better health, and improve their quality of life. There are limits to how much medication alone can accomplish. OUD medication will improve quality of life,[61] but many clients in addiction treatment have complex issues that may decrease quality of life, such as:

- Other SUDs (e.g., alcohol use disorder, cannabis use disorder).[62,63,64]
- Mental distress[65] (i.e., high levels of symptoms) and disorders[66,67,68] (e.g., major depressive disorder, posttraumatic stress disorder).
- Medical problems (e.g., hepatitis, diabetes).[69]
- History of trauma.[70,71]
- Poor diet, lack of physical activity, or both.[72]
- Lack of social support.[73]
- Unemployment.[74]

Acknowledge many pathways to recovery

Recovery occurs via many pathways.[75] OUD medication may play a role in the beginning, middle, or entire continuum of care.

Support clients in making their own informed decisions about treatment. Counselors don't need to agree with clients' decisions but must respect them. Educate new clients about:

- Addiction as a chronic disease influenced by genetics and environment.
- How medications for OUD work.

RESOURCE ALERT

Recovery-Oriented Treatment

Recovery-Oriented Methadone Maintenance: This guide by White and Mojer-Torres is the most thorough document on this topic currently available and is applicable to clients receiving other medications for OUD (www.attcnetwork.org/userfiles/file/GreatLakes/5th%20Monograph_RM_Methadone.pdf).

Supporting Recovery From Opioid Addiction: Community Care Best Practice Guidelines for Recovery-Oriented Methadone Maintenance (www.ccbh.com/pdfs/providers/healthchoices/bestpractice/MethadoneBestPracticeGuideline.pdf) and ***Supporting Recovery From Opioid Addiction: Community Care Best Practice Guidelines for Buprenorphine and Suboxone*** (www.ccbh.com/pdfs/providers/healthchoices/bestpractice/Community_Care_BP_Guidelines_for_Buprenorphine_and_Suboxone.pdf) outline phase-specific tasks and accompanying strategies for programs that provide services to clients who take these medications.

SAMHSA'S GUIDING PRINCIPLES OF RECOVERY[76]

- Recovery emerges from hope.
- Recovery is person driven.
- Recovery occurs via many pathways.
- Recovery is holistic.
- Recovery is supported by peers and allies.
- Recovery is supported through relationships and social networks.
- Recovery is culturally based and influenced.
- Recovery is supported by addressing trauma.
- Recovery involves individual, family, and community strengths and responsibilities.
- Recovery is based on respect.

- What occurs during dose stabilization.
- The benefits of longer term medication use and the risks of abruptly ending treatment.

Promote recovery for clients with OUD

Focus on addressing personal and practical problems of greatest concern to clients, which can improve their engagement in treatment.[77] Recovery supports can sustain the progress clients made in treatment and further improve their quality of life. Addressing the full range of client needs can improve clients' quality of life and lead to better long-term recovery outcomes. A recovery-oriented approach to traditional SUD counseling may help address client needs.[78,79]

Increasing recovery capital supports long-term abstinence and improved quality of life, especially for clients who decide to stop medication. Clients with substantial periods of abstinence from illicit drugs identify these strategies for increasing recovery capital as helpful:[80,81,82]

- Forging new relationships with friends/family
- Obtaining support from friends, family, partners, and communities
- Using positive coping strategies
- Finding meaning or a sense of purpose in life
- Engaging in a church or in spiritual practices
- Pursuing education, employment, or both
- Engaging in new interests or activities (e.g., joining a community group, exercising)
- Building confidence in ability to maintain abstinence (i.e., increasing abstinence-related self-efficacy)
- Finding ways to help other individuals who are new to recovery

Help clients further grow recovery capital by offering or connecting them to a range of services, such as:

- Ancillary services (e.g., vocational rehabilitation, supported housing).
- Additional counseling.
- Medical services.
- Mental health services.

Provide person-centered care

Clients' confidence in their ability to stay away from illicit substances, or self-efficacy, is an important factor in successful change. In person-centered care, also known as patient-centered care:

- Clients control the amount, duration, and scope of services they receive.
- They select the professionals they work with.
- Care is holistic; it respects and responds to clients' cultural, linguistic, and socioenvironmental needs.[83]
- Providers implement services that recognize patients as equal partners in planning, developing, and monitoring care to ensure that it meets each patient's unique needs.[84]

RESOURCE ALERT

Decision-Making Tool

Decisions in Recovery: Treatment for Opioid Use Disorders is a SAMHSA web-based tool (http://brsstacs.com/Default.aspx) and handbook (https://store.samhsa.gov/product/SMA16-4993) to help people with OUD make decisions about treatment and recovery.

RESOURCE ALERT

Relapse Prevention and Recovery Promotion TIP

Relapse Prevention and Recovery Promotion in Behavioral Health Services is a planned TIP, which will be available on the SAMHSA Publications Ordering webpage (https://store.samhsa.gov), that will cover the closely related topics of relapse prevention and recovery promotion for SUDs and many mental disorders.[85]

> The confrontational/expert model that characterized much of SUD treatment in the past may harm some patients and inhibit or prevent recovery.[86]

A person-centered approach to OUD treatment empowers clients in making decisions, such as:[87]

- Whether to take OUD medication.
- Which medication to take.
- Which counseling and ancillary services to receive.

Fragmented healthcare services are less likely to meet the full range of patients' needs. Integrated medical and behavioral healthcare delivery provides patient-focused, comprehensive treatment that meets the wide range of symptoms and service needs that patients with OUD may have. Significant demand remains for better integrated and coordinated SUD treatment (including OTP), medical, and mental health services.[88] Such improvements are particularly important for the many individuals with co-occurring substance use and mental disorders who receive OUD medication.[89,90] In a randomized trial of methadone patients with co-occurring mental disorders receiving onsite versus offsite mental health services, those receiving services onsite had less psychiatric distress at follow-up.[91]

Promote family and social support

Support from family and friends can be the most important factor in long-term recovery, according to many people who have achieved long-term recovery from OUD.[92,93] Support from intimate partners helps all clients, especially women, avoid return to opioid use.[94,95] But the more people in clients' social networks who use drugs, the more likely clients are to return to use.[96,97]

Most clients are willing to invite a substance-free family member or friend to support their recovery.[98] Most have at least one nearby family member who does not use illicit drugs.[99] A client's community may provide a cultural context for their recovery and culturally specific supports that may not otherwise be available in treatment.[100]

Help clients develop and support positive relations with their families by:

- Suggesting that clients invite family and friends to aid in the recovery planning process (Exhibit 4.4).
- Emphasizing the importance of relationships with family and friends who actively support recovery.
- Supporting clients in mending broken relationships with loved ones.
- Helping clients cut ties with individuals who still use drugs or enable clients' drug use.
- Encouraging clients to build new relationships that support recovery.

RESOURCE ALERT

Treatment Guidance for Co-Occurring Substance Use and Mental Disorders

TIP 42, *Substance Abuse Treatment for Persons With Co-Occurring Disorders*, provides SUD treatment strategies for people with mental disorders (https://store.samhsa.gov/shin/content//SMA13-3992/SMA13-3992.pdf).

Integrated Treatment for Co-Occurring Disorders Evidence-Based Practices KIT provides practical guidance for integrating mental health services and SUD treatment (https://store.samhsa.gov/product/Integrated-Treatment-for-Co-Occurring-Disorders-Evidence-Based-Practices-EBP-KIT/SMA08-4367).

EXHIBIT 4.4. Engaging Reluctant Family Members in a Client's Treatment

If the client agrees and has signed the appropriate releases, help even reluctant family members engage in the client's treatment to offer support. To reach out to family members who hesitate to engage, try to:

- **Recognize that they have been harmed** by their family member's substance use and that their participation in his or her recovery can help them heal too.
- **Ask them to recall some positive experiences** they have had with the client.
- **Introduce them to mutual-help groups and other supports** for families (e.g., Nar-Anon, Learn to Cope, Parents of Addicted Loved Ones Group). Ensure that suggested groups don't have an antimedication bias.
- **Help them understand OUD, the treatment process, and medication's role in recovery.** This knowledge can keep family members from pressuring the client to taper medication prematurely.
- **Hold multifamily therapy groups or informal discussion sessions for families** (with or without clients present) so that family members can learn from one another and share their experiences.
- **Offer family or couples therapy** as an option for additional support.

Provide trauma-informed care

Trauma-informed service requires providers to realize the significance of trauma. According to SAMHSA,[101] trauma-informed counselors know what trauma is and also:

- Understand how trauma can affect clients, families, and communities.
- Apply knowledge of trauma extensively and consistently in both practice and policy.
- Know ways to promote recovery from trauma.
- Recognize the signs and symptoms of trauma in clients, families, staff members, and others.
- Resist things that may retraumatize or harm clients or staff.

Incorporate trauma-informed principles of care into recovery promotion efforts, because:

- Trauma histories and trauma-related disorders may increase clients' risk for various problems, including early drop-out from treatment[102] and greater problems with pain.[103]
- Childhood trauma is highly prevalent among people with OUD.[104,105]
- People often suffer multiple traumas during opioid misuse.[106]
- An intervention that integrated trauma treatment and standard care (which goes further than the trauma-informed care detailed here) had better outcomes than standard care alone in a diverse group of women treated in various settings, including an OTP.[107]

RESOURCE ALERT

Trauma-Informed Care TIP

TIP 57, *Trauma-Informed Care in Behavioral Health Services*, has more information on providing trauma-informed care in SUD treatment programs (https://store.samhsa.gov/product/TIP-57-Trauma-Informed-Care-in-Behavioral-Health-Services/SMA14-4816).

Quick Guide to Medications

This section introduces the neurochemistry and biology of OUD and the medications that treat it. Reading this section will familiarize counselors with terminology healthcare professionals may use in discussing patients who take OUD medication (see also Exhibit 4.1 and the comprehensive glossary in Part 5).

Understanding the Neurobiology of OUD

Opioid receptors are a part of the body's natural endorphin system. Endorphins are chemicals our bodies release to help reduce our experience of pain. They can also contribute to euphoric feelings like the "runner's high" that some people experience. When endorphins or opioids bind to opioid receptors, the receptors activate, causing a variety of effects.

After taking opioids, molecules bind to and activate the brain's opioid receptors and release dopamine in a brain area called the nucleus accumbens (NAc), causing euphoria. Like opioid receptors, the NAc has a natural, healthy function. For example, when a person eats, the NAc releases dopamine to reinforce this essential behavior. The NAc is a key part of the brain's reward system.

Opioid use leads to an above-normal release of dopamine, essentially swamping the natural reward pathway and turning the brain strongly toward continued use. The brain also learns environmental cues associated with this dopamine release. It associates specific people, places, and things (e.g., music, drug paraphernalia) with the euphoria; these environmental cues then become triggers for drug use.

Intermittent opioid use causes periods of euphoria followed by periods of withdrawal. The brain's strong draw toward euphoria drives repeated and continued use. Few people with OUD reexperience the euphoria they obtained early in their opioid use, yet they continue to seek it.

Changes in brain function that result from repeated drug use cause a person who once took the drug for euphoria to seek it out of habit, then compulsion. People with OUD use opioids to stave off withdrawal. Without opioids, the person feels dysphoric and physically ill, only feeling normal by taking opioids again. At the same time, other areas of the brain begin to change:[108]

- The amygdala, which is associated with feelings of danger, fear, and anger, becomes overactive.
- The frontal cortex, which is associated with planning and self-control, becomes underactive.
- The ability to control impulses diminishes, and drug use becomes compulsive.
- The need to escape the discomfort and intensely negative emotional states of withdrawal becomes the driving force of continued use.

Even after opioid use stops, brain changes linger. A person's ability to make plans and manage impulses stays underactive. That's why return to substance use is very common even after a period of abstinence.

Medications for OUD promote emotional, psychological, and behavioral stabilization. By acting directly on the same opioid receptors as misused opioids (**but in different ways**), medications can **stabilize** abnormal brain activity.

Learning How OUD Medications Work

The following sections describe how each of the OUD medications functions (Exhibit 4.5; see also Part 3 of this TIP for greater detail). Discuss questions or concerns about a patient's medication, side effects, or dosage with the patient's prescriber after getting the patient's consent.

EXHIBIT 4.5. FDA-Approved Medications Used To Treat OUD: Key Points

MEDICATION	HOW IT'S TAKEN	WHY IT WORKS	SIDE EFFECTS	NOTES
Buprenorphine	Tablet dissolved under the tongue or film dissolved under the tongue or against the inside of the cheek. Taken once daily, every other day, or 3 times a week. It also comes as an implant that lasts 6 months or as an injection that lasts 1 month.	Partially activates the opioid receptor. Reduces craving and blocks the euphoric effect of opioids.	Can cause constipation, headache, nausea, insomnia, excessive sweating, or opioid withdrawal. Overdose is possible but less likely than with methadone. Overdose death risk is increased if buprenorphine is taken with alcohol or intravenously in combination with benzodiazepines or other CNS depressants. Neonatal abstinence syndrome (NAS)	Less sedating than methadone. Prescribers must have a special SAMHSA waiver but don't need to be part of a federally certified OTP. Can be prescribed through pharmacies or provided via OTPs.
Methadone	Liquid or tablet once daily. Dose may be divided for twice-daily dosing if medically necessary.	Fully activates the opioid receptor. Reduces craving and blocks the euphoric effect of opioids.	Can cause constipation, sleepiness, sweating, swelling of hands and feet, sexual dysfunction, heart arrhythmias, low blood pressure, fainting, and substance misuse. Can cause overdose death if increased too rapidly, taken in a much higher than usual dose, or taken concurrently with some substances and medications, particularly CNS depressants such as alcohol or benzodiazepines. NAS	Initially requires visits 6 to 7 times per week to an OTP. Patients can decrease attendance gradually based on time in treatment and clinical stability.
Naltrexone	Daily tablet (can also be taken 3 times a week) or monthly injection in buttock.	Occupies the opioid receptors. Reduces craving and blocks the euphoric effect of opioids.	Can cause nausea, headache, dizziness, fatigue, liver toxicity, depression and suicidality, muscle cramps, fainting, and loss of or decreased appetite or other appetite disorders; in the extended-release injectable formulation, can cause pain, swelling, and other complications at the injection site. Patient must complete withdrawal and stay opioid abstinent for at least 7 days before starting naltrexone and longer (e.g., 10 or more days) for long-acting opioids, such as methadone.	Tablets are rarely effective. Monthly injections are more effective than tablets.

Buprenorphine

Buprenorphine reduces opioid misuse, HIV risk behaviors, and risk of overdose death.[109,110,111,112] Buprenorphine only partially activates opioid receptors; it is a partial agonist. It binds to and activates receptors sufficiently to prevent craving and withdrawal and to block the effects of illicit opioids. Appropriate doses of buprenorphine shouldn't make patients feel euphoric, sleepy, or foggy headed.

Buprenorphine has the benefit of a ceiling effect. Its effectiveness and sedation or respiratory effects don't increase after a certain dosing level, even if more is taken. This lowers risk of overdose and misuse.[113] Groups at particular risk for buprenorphine overdose include children who accidentally ingest the medication[114] and patients who also use CNS depressants like benzodiazepines or alcohol.[115,116] (See Part 3 of this TIP for more information on concurrent use of CNS depressants and buprenorphine.)

Buprenorphine is available outside of OTPs, through non-OTP healthcare settings (e.g., physicians' offices, outpatient drug treatment programs). Healthcare professionals (including nurse practitioners and physician assistants, per the Comprehensive Addiction and Recovery Act of 2016) can prescribe it outside of an OTP provided they have a specific federal waiver. This is often referred to as "being waivered" to prescribe buprenorphine.

Buprenorphine can cause opioid withdrawal in patients who have recently taken a full opioid agonist (e.g., heroin, oxycodone). This occurs because buprenorphine pushes the full opioid activator molecules off the receptors and replaces them with its weaker, partially activating effect. For this reason, patients must be in opioid withdrawal when they take their first dose of buprenorphine.

The most common buprenorphine formulation contains naloxone to reduce misuse. Naloxone is an opioid antagonist. It blocks rather than activates receptors and lets no opioids sit on receptors to activate them. Naloxone is poorly absorbed under the tongue/against the cheek, so when taking the combined medication as directed, it has no effect. If injected, naloxone causes sudden opioid withdrawal.

Buprenorphine comes in two forms that melt on the inside of the cheek or under the tongue: films (combined with naloxone) or tablets (buprenorphine/naloxone or buprenorphine alone). For treatment of OUD, patients take the films or tablets once daily, every other day, or three times a week. Various companies manufacture these forms of the medication. Some are brand name, and some are generic. The different kinds vary in strength or number of milligrams, but they have been designed and tested to provide roughly the same amount of medication as the first approved product (Exhibit 3A.5 in Part 3).

Buprenorphine is also available in a long-acting implant that specially trained healthcare professionals place under the skin (subdermal implant) and an extended-release formulation that is administered under the skin (subcutaneous injection). The implant is appropriate for patients who have been stable on low doses of the films or tablets. It lasts for 6 months and can be replaced once after 6 months. The extended-release formulation lasts for 1 month and can be repeated monthly. It is appropriate for patients who have been stabilized on the films or tablets for at least 7 days.

Healthcare professionals with waivers can prescribe buprenorphine. Physicians who take an 8-hour training and get a waiver can prescribe buprenorphine. Nurse practitioners and physician assistants are eligible to apply for waivers after 24 hours of training. Providers who wish to deliver buprenorphine implants must receive special training on how to insert and remove them.

Buprenorphine can cause side effects including constipation, headache, nausea, and insomnia. These often improve over time and can be managed with dosage adjustments or other approaches.

Methadone

Methadone is highly effective. Many studies over decades of research show that it:[117,118,119]

- Increases treatment retention.
- Reduces opioid misuse.
- Reduces drug-related HIV risk behavior.
- Lowers risk of overdose death.

Methadone is slow in onset and long acting, avoiding the highs and lows of short-acting opioids. It is a full agonist. Patients who take the same appropriate dose of methadone daily as prescribed will neither feel euphoric from the medication nor experience opioid withdrawal.

Methadone is an oral medication that is taken daily under observation by a nurse or pharmacist and under the supervision of an OTP physician. Methadone is available as a liquid concentrate, a tablet, or an oral solution made from a dispersible tablet or powder.

Methadone blunts or blocks the euphoric effects of illicit opioids because it occupies the opioid receptors. This "opioid blockade" helps patients stop taking illicit opioids because they no longer feel euphoric if they use illicit opioids. When on a proper dose of methadone, patients can:

- Keep regular schedules.
- Lead productive, healthy lives.
- Meet obligations (family, social, work).

Methadone can lead to overdose death in people who use a dose that's considerably higher than usual, as methadone is a full agonist. People who don't usually take opioids or have abstained from them for a while could overdose on a fairly small amount of methadone. Thus, patients start on low doses of methadone and gradually adjust upward to identify the optimal maintenance dose level.

Patients must attend a clinic for dose administration 6 to 7 days per week during the start of treatment. Healthcare professionals can thus observe patients' response to medication and discourage diversion to others. Visit frequency can lessen after patients spend time in treatment and show evidence of progress.

Methadone can cause certain side effects. Common potential side effects of methadone include:

- Constipation.
- Sleepiness.
- Sweating.
- Sexual dysfunction.
- Swelling of the hands and feet.

Sleepiness can be a warning sign of potential overdose. Patients who are drowsy should receive prompt medical assessment to determine the cause and appropriate steps to take—which may require a reduction in methadone dose. Some patients may appear sleepy or have trouble staying awake when idle, even if there is no immediate danger of evolving overdose. These patients may need a lower dose or may be taking other prescribed or nonprescribed medications (e.g., benzodiazepines, clonidine) that are interacting with the methadone.

Naltrexone

Naltrexone stops opioids from reaching and activating receptors, preventing any reward from use. Naltrexone is an antagonist of the opioid receptors—it does not activate them at all. Instead, it sits on the receptors and blocks other opioids from activating them.

Naltrexone appears to reduce opioid craving[120] but not opioid withdrawal (unlike buprenorphine and methadone, which reduce both craving and withdrawal). Someone starting naltrexone must be abstinent from short-acting opioids for at least 7 days and from long-acting opioids for 10 to 14 days before taking the first dose. Otherwise, it will cause opioid withdrawal, which can be more severe than that caused by reducing or stopping opioid use.

Naltrexone comes in two forms: tablet and injection.

- Patients take naltrexone tablets daily or three times per week. Tablets are rarely effective, as patients typically stop taking them after a short time.[121,122,123]
- **Highly externally monitored populations in remission may do well with the tablet,**[124,125,126] such as physicians who have mandatory frequent urine drug testing and are at risk of losing their licenses.
- **The injected form is more effective than the tablet because it lasts for 1 month.** Patients can come to a clinic to receive an intramuscular injection in their buttock.

Naltrexone can produce certain side effects, which may include:

- Nausea.
- Headache.
- Dizziness.
- Fatigue.

For the extended-release injectable formulation, potential reactions at the injection site include:

- Pain.
- Bumps.
- Blistering.
- Skin lesions (may require surgery).

Knowing What Prescribers Do

The following sections will help explain the role healthcare professionals play in providing each OUD medication as part of collaborative care. Part 3 of this TIP offers more detailed clinical information.

Administer buprenorphine

Patients typically begin buprenorphine in opioid withdrawal. Patients may take their first dose in the prescriber's office so the prescriber can observe its initial effects. Increasingly often, patients take their first dose at home and follow up with prescribers by phone. Most people are stable on buprenorphine dosages between 8 mg and 24 mg each day.

Patients who take buprenorphine visit their prescriber regularly to allow monitoring of their response to treatment and side effects and to receive supportive counseling. The visits may result in specific actions, such as adjusting the dosage or making a referral for psychosocial services. Stable patients may obtain up to a 30-day prescription of this medication through community pharmacies. Visits may include urine drug testing. Early in treatment, patients typically see their prescribers at least weekly. Further along, they may visit prescribers every 1 to 2 weeks and then as infrequently as once a month or less.

The prescriber will make dosage adjustments as needed, reducing for side effects or increasing for unrelieved withdrawal or ongoing opioid misuse. OTPs that provide buprenorphine will typically follow a similar process, with the principal difference being that the program will administer or dispense the medication rather than the patient filling a prescription at a pharmacy.

Administer methadone

Only SAMHSA-certified OTPs may provide methadone by physician order for daily observed administration onsite or for self-administration at home by stable patients.[127] The physician will start patients on a low dose of methadone. People in early methadone treatment are required by federal regulation to visit the OTP six to seven times per week to take their medication under observation. The physician will monitor patients' initial response to the methadone and slowly increase the dose until withdrawal is completely relieved for 24 hours.

A prescriber can't predict at the start of treatment what daily methadone dose will work for a patient. An effective dose is one that eliminates withdrawal symptoms and most craving and blunts euphoria from self-administered illicit opioids without producing sedation. On average, higher dosages of methadone (60 mg to 100 mg daily) are associated with better outcomes than lower dosages.[128,129] That said, an effective dose of methadone for a particular patient can be above or below that range.

The prescriber will continue to monitor the patient and adjust dosage slowly up or down to find the optimum dose level. The dose may need further adjustment if the patient returns to opioid use, experiences side effects such as sedation, starts new medications that may interact with methadone, or has a change in health that causes the previously effective dose to become inadequate or too strong.

If patients taking methadone drink heavily or take sedatives (e.g., benzodiazepines), physicians may:

- Treat the alcohol misuse.
- Refer to a higher level of care.
- Address comorbid anxiety or depression.
- Decrease dosage to prevent overdose.

Administer naltrexone

To avoid severe withdrawal, prescribers will ensure that patients are abstinent from opioids at least 7 to 10 days before initiating or resuming naltrexone. Prescribers may require longer periods of abstinence for patients transitioning from buprenorphine or methadone to naltrexone.

Prescribers typically take urine drug screens to confirm abstinence before giving naltrexone. Healthcare professionals can confirm abstinence through a "challenge test" with naloxone, a short-acting opioid antagonist.

Healthcare professionals manage withdrawal symptoms with nonopioid medication. Prescribers are prepared to handle withdrawal caused by naltrexone despite a period of abstinence.[130] Ideally, they administer the first injection before patients' release from residential treatment or other controlled settings (e.g., prison) so qualified individuals can monitor them for symptoms of withdrawal.

Healthcare professionals typically see patients at least monthly to give naltrexone injections. For those taking oral naltrexone, prescribers schedule visits at their discretion. Thus, urine drug testing may be less frequent for these patients than for patients taking buprenorphine. But periodic drug testing should occur.

There is only one dose level for injected naltrexone,[131] so prescribers cannot adjust the dose. However, they can slightly shorten the dosing interval if the medication's effectiveness decreases toward the end of the monthly dosing interval. If the patient is having side effects or intense cravings, the prescriber may recommend switching to a different medication.

Set expectations

Ideally, prescribers will collaborate with counselors and other care providers involved in patients' care to set reasonable patient expectations. Medications can effectively treat OUD, but they don't treat other SUDs (save naltrexone, also FDA-approved to treat alcohol use disorder). Patients may still need:

- Counseling for psychosocial issues.
- Social supports/treatment to get back on track.
- Medications, therapy, or both for co-occurring conditions.

Collaboration between all involved healthcare providers helps patients understand the OUD treatment timeline, which generally lasts months or years. Courses of medically supervised withdrawal or tapering are considerably less effective than longer term maintenance treatment with buprenorphine or methadone and are often associated with return to substance use and a heightened risk of overdose.[132,133,134,135]

> Patients may still benefit from the counseling you can offer in addition to care from other providers, even if you can't communicate with those providers directly.

Counselor–Prescriber Communications

OUD medication can support counselors' work with clients who have OUD, and counseling supports the work prescribers do with them. **Good communication facilitates mutually supportive work** (Exhibit 4.6). A counselor will probably:

- See patients more frequently than prescribers.
- Have a more complete sense of patients' issues.
- Offer providers valuable context and perspective.
- Help patients take medications appropriately.
- Ensure that patients receive high-quality care from their other providers.

Obtaining Consent

Get written consent from patients allowing communication directly with their providers (unless the counselor and the providers work in the same treatment program). The consent must explicitly state that the patient allows

Good communication with prescribers and other treatment team members allows everyone to work together to:

- Assess patient progress.
- Change treatment plans if needed.
- Make informed decisions about OUD medication.

the counselor to discuss substance-use-related issues. It should also specify which kinds of information the counselor can share (e.g., medical records, diagnoses). Consent forms must comply with federal and state confidentiality laws that govern the sharing of information about patients with SUDs.[136,137]

Carefully protect any identifying information about patients and their medical and treatment information. Don't send such information through unsecured channels, such as:

- Text messaging.
- Unsecure, unencrypted emails.
- Faxes to unsecured machines.

EXHIBIT 4.6. Example of Counselor–Prescriber Communication

Counselor:	Dr. Smith, thank you for referring Jeff to my counseling practice. I'd like to review with you the elements of the treatment plan we've developed.
Prescriber:	That would be really helpful.
Counselor:	We agreed to meet weekly while he's getting stabilized on the buprenorphine. The initial focus of our sessions will be helping Jeff expand his recovery support network.
Prescriber:	I'm glad to hear that you're following up on that. My nurse reported that he's alone in the waiting room before his appointments, and he also mentioned to me that he doesn't have anybody to talk with.
Counselor:	I suggested a support group for people taking buprenorphine that's in his neighborhood. We've also begun talking about recreational activities that can help him fill the time he used to spend with drug-using friends.
Prescriber:	I'll reinforce your suggestions when he comes in this Friday.
Counselor:	Also, he seems confused about where the film goes in his mouth. I urged him to discuss that with you.
Prescriber:	I'll make a note to go over that with him again on Friday.

Phone calls are the most secure way to discuss patient cases, although it may be more convenient to reach out to healthcare professionals first through email.

Structuring Communications With Prescribers

Regular, structured communication can improve the flow of information between treatment teams. Some multidisciplinary programs produce regular reports for prescribers about patient progress. Exhibit 4.7 provides some strategies for discussing patient care with healthcare professionals.

Helping Clients Overcome Challenges in Accessing Resources

By collaborating with healthcare professionals in OUD care, counselors can help clients overcome challenges they face in obtaining treatment, such as:

- **Ability to pay for OUD medication.** Counselors are often already skilled in helping clients address treatment costs (e.g., facilitating Medicaid applications, linking them to insurance navigators). Try to refer clients who face difficulty meeting prescription costs or copays back to the agency's financial department for sliding scale adjustments and ability-to-pay assessments. Also try to help patients find and apply for relevant pharmaceutical company medication prescription plans.
- **Transportation.** Options to offer clients may include:
  - Providing vouchers for public transportation.
  - Providing information on other subsidized transportation options.
  - Linking clients to peer support specialists and case managers who can arrange transportation.
  - Assisting eligible clients in navigating Medicaid to obtain transportation services.
  - If available, arranging for telehealth services to overcome clients' transportation barriers.
- **Access to medication in disaster situations.** Counselors can review options with patients for obtaining prescription replacements and refills or daily medicine dosing under various scenarios. This could include if their usual clinic or primary pharmacy is closed or if they're relocated without notice because of an unforeseen emergency. Also advise patients on the items to take with them in such scenarios to facilitate refills from a new

EXHIBIT 4.7. Tips for Discussing Patient Care With Prescribers

- Identify the patient. Once the counselor has established secure communication through encrypted email or by phone, he or she should state the patient's name, date of birth, and medical record number (if obtained).
- Let prescribers know up front the purpose of the call. Begin by clearly describing the question or concern leading to the call. If it is simply to establish contact because of a shared patient, that's fine.
- Share any relevant information about the patient (if the patient has consented). If there is a concern about a side effect, for example, describe observed changes to the healthcare professional. If there is a concern about return to opioid use, describe which elements of the patient's behavior are worrisome.
- Work together to build a shared understanding of the patient's situation. The counselor likely has key information about the patient that the prescriber does not have, and vice versa.
- Discuss next steps with the healthcare provider before ending any communication to help coordinate patient care. Consider scheduling a check-in with each other to assess patient progress.

medication-dispensing facility. Key materials include:
- Photo identification.
- Medication containers of currently prescribed medications (even if empty).
- Written prescriptions.
- Packaging labels that contain dosage, prescriber, and refill information.
- Any payment receipts that contain medication information.

To overcome systemic barriers, help enact collaborative policies and procedures. Work with program management and the community at large to address the following issues:

- **Connection to treatment:** Counselors may be able to participate in community efforts to ensure that information on how to obtain treatment for OUD is available wherever people with OUD:
  - Gather (e.g., all-night diners, bars, free health clinics, injection equipment exchanges).
  - Seek help (e.g., emergency departments, houses of worship, social service agencies).
  - Reveal a need for help (e.g., encounters with law enforcement and child welfare agencies).

  Encourage buprenorphine prescribers to make known their availability if they are prepared to accept new patients. Help disseminate lists of addiction treatment providers and share their information via peer recovery specialists (see Part 5).

- **Rapid assessment and treatment initiation:** Try to help OUD pharmacotherapy providers, particularly in OTPs, streamline counseling intake processes to help patients receive medication efficiently. The expert panel of this TIP recognizes that same-day admission of patients with OUD may not be possible in all settings, but it's a worthwhile goal. Every program should streamline its intake processes and expedite admissions.

- **Return to treatment:** When patients discontinue treatment prematurely and return to use of opioids, it can be hard for them to reengage in treatment because of the shame they feel or because there is a waiting list for admission. The waitlist problem may not be solvable because of capacity limitations, but all collaborative care team members—including counselors and prescribers—should:
  - Inform patients from intake onward that the program will readmit them even if they drop out.
  - Encourage patients to seek readmission if they return to opioid use or feel that they are at risk for returning to opioid use.
  - **Inform patients of the importance of overdose prevention** (see the "Counseling Patients on Overdose Prevention and Treatment" section).
  - Provide continued monitoring if possible; it can range from informal quarterly check-ins to regularly scheduled remote counseling or peer support (e.g., from a recovery coach).
  - Offer an expedited reentry process to encourage patients to return if they need to.
  - Engage in active outreach and reengagement with OTP patients, which can be effective.[138,139] Try to contact patients who have dropped out to encourage them to return.

Creation of a Supportive Counseling Experience

Maintaining the Therapeutic Alliance

The therapeutic alliance is a counselor's most powerful tool for influencing outcomes.[140] It underlies all types and modalities of therapy and helping services. A strong alliance welcomes patients into treatment and creates a sense of safety.

COUNSELING PATIENTS WITH OUD WHO DON'T TAKE MEDICATION

Patients who don't take an OUD medication after withdrawal are at high risk of return to opioid use, which can be fatal given the loss of opioid tolerance. Provide these patients with overdose prevention education and the overdose-reversal medication naloxone, or educate them about naloxone and how they can obtain it in their community. Advise them to report a return to opioid use or a feeling that they are at risk of relapsing. Work with them and their care team to either resume medication for OUD or enter a more intensive level of behavioral care.

Certain counselor skills help build and maintain a therapeutic alliance, including:

- Projecting empathy and warmth.
- Making patients feel respected and understood.
- Not allowing personal opinions, anecdotes, or feelings to influence the counseling process (unless done deliberately and with therapeutic intention).[141]

These skills are relevant for working with all patients, including those taking medication for OUD. Apply them consistently from the very first interaction with a patient through the conclusion of services. For example, recognize and reconcile personal views about medication for OUD so that they don't influence counseling sessions.

Educating Patients About OUD and a Chronic Care Approach to Its Treatment

Help ensure that patients understand the chronic care approach to OUD and their:

- Diagnosis.
- Prognosis.
- Treatment options.
- Available recovery supports.
- Prescribed medications.
- Risk of overdose (and strategies to reduce it).

Seek to understand patients' preferences and goals. Doing so can help convey information meaningfully so patients understand the choices available to them. Also, help communicate patients' preferences and goals to healthcare professionals and family members.

Educate colleagues and other staff members so they can help create a supportive experience for patients with OUD:

- Provide basic education to colleagues about medications for OUD and how they work.
- Share evidence on how these medications reduce risky behavior, improve outcomes, and save lives.
- Note that major U.S. and international guidelines affirm use of medication to treat OUD.
- Ask about and address specific fears and concerns.
- Provide resources for additional information.

Counseling Patients on Overdose Prevention and Treatment

Know how to use naloxone to treat opioid overdose; share this information with patients and their family members and friends. Available by prescription (or without a prescription in some states), naloxone is an opioid antagonist that has successfully reversed many thousands of opioid overdoses. It comes in auto-injector and nasal spray formulations easy for laypeople to administer immediately on the scene of an overdose, before emergency responders arrive.

Ask patients if they have a naloxone prescription or help them get it without one if possible. Providers may prescribe naloxone in addition to OUD medication. Counselors should check state laws to learn their jurisdiction's naloxone prescription and dispensation policies (see "Resource Alert: Overdose Prevention/Treatment").

Inform clients and their friends and families of any Good Samaritan laws in the jurisdiction, which protect against drug offenses for people who call for medical help while experiencing or observing overdose.

Emphasize that a person given naloxone to reverse overdose must go to the emergency department, because overdose can start again when naloxone wears off.

Consider working with the program administrator to place a naloxone rescue kit in the office, if one is not already available. To be ready for an emergency, learn:

- The signs of overmedication (which may progress to overdose) and overdose itself.
- What to do if an overdose is suspected.
- How to administer naloxone.

Consider working with the program administrators to set up a program to distribute naloxone directly to patients. Many states allow organizations to do this under a standing order from a physician. Clients are more likely to access naloxone if their program provides it directly to them rather than sending them to another organization to get it. Learn more at Prescribe to Prevent (http://prescribetoprevent.org).

Helping Patients Cope With Bias and Discrimination

Patients taking medication for OUD must deal with people—including family members, friends, colleagues, employers, and community members—who are misinformed or biased about the nature of OUD and effective treatments for it (Exhibit 4.8).

Wherever possible, such as in a counseling session or a community education forum, counter misunderstandings with accurate information. Emphasize the message that addiction is governed by more powerful brain forces than those that determine habits. As a result, having a lot of positive intent, wanting to quit, and working hard at it sometimes won't be enough.

Remind patients about building recovery capital and sticking with their treatment plan and goals. A particularly good opportunity to do so arises when patients ask how to "get off medication." Statements such as "The longer you take medication, the more of your life you can get back and the less likely you are to return to opioid use" and "We usually recommend continuing medication long term because it helps people maintain recovery" can help clients understand that they are following medical recommendations and doing a good job of caring for themselves (Exhibit 4.9).

> People may think that addiction is just a bad habit or willful self-destruction and that someone who has difficulty stopping opioid misuse is lazy. They may view OUD medication as "just another drug" and urge patients to stop taking it.

RESOURCE ALERT

Overdose Prevention/Treatment

SAMHSA Opioid Overdose Prevention Toolkit (https://store.samhsa.gov/product/SAMHSA-Opioid-Overdose-Prevention-Toolkit/SMA16-4742)

National Conference of State Legislatures' *Drug Overdose Immunity and Good Samaritan Laws* (www.ncsl.org/research/civil-and-criminal-justice/drug-overdose-immunity-good-samaritan-laws.aspx)

Project Lazarus' *Naloxone: The Overdose Antidote* (www.projectlazarus.org/naloxone)

Prescription Drug Abuse Policy System's *Interactive Map of Naloxone Overdose Prevention Laws* (http://pdaps.org/datasets/laws-regulating-administration-of-naloxone-1501695139)

EXHIBIT 4.8. Conversation: Addressing Misinformation

Mother of Patient: They want to put my son on methadone, but it's going to rot his teeth.

Father of Patient: Yeah. I don't want him to look like he's on drugs when he's finally off them.

Counselor: You have the impression that people who use drugs have bad teeth. And in many cases, that's true. But there are a lot of reasons why people with a substance use disorder develop teeth and gum problems—such as a high-sugar diet, co-occurring depression that prevents them from taking good care of themselves, poor health that allows oral disease to develop, and lack of access to preventive dental care or treatment. But if your son practices good oral hygiene, his mouth will stay healthy while he takes methadone.

Mother of Patient: What do you mean by "oral hygiene"?

Counselor: Like all of us, he'll have to limit his sweets and brush and floss regularly. Methadone can reduce the flow of saliva, which means that not as much of the bacteria on his teeth will get washed away. So, he'll want to get good dental advice on how to address dry mouth if that's a problem for him. Regular dental checkups will be really important, too.

Father of Patient: So, he won't trade his teeth for his recovery. Thanks—that's one less thing to worry about!

Review a client's motivation for tapering or quitting medication (Exhibit 4.10) and have a conversation about the best timing for such a change (Exhibit 4.11). If the client has consented to communication with other providers, inform the client's prescriber about the client's desires or intent so that shared decision making can take place.

Be proactive in dispelling myths and providing facts about medications for OUD when countering misconceptions and judgmental attitudes. Point out that multiple organizations consider individuals to be in recovery if they take OUD medication as prescribed, including:

- The American Medical Association.[142]
- The American Society of Addiction Medicine.[143]
- The National Institute on Drug Abuse.[144]
- The Office of the Surgeon General.[145]
- SAMHSA.[146]
- The World Health Organization.[147]

Explain that alcohol and opioids are different substances with different effects on the body and brain. This counters the mistaken belief that people receiving buprenorphine or methadone are always "high" and as impaired as if they drank alcohol all day. People acquire tolerance to impairments that drinking causes in motor control and cognition. But this tolerance is partial; alcohol consumption always results in some deficits. Opioids don't have the same motor or cognitive effects. Complete tolerance develops to the psychoactive effects and related motor impairments opioids cause.

If a person takes a therapeutic dose of opioid agonist medication as prescribed, he or she may be as capable as anyone else of driving, being emotionally open, and working productively. Some people worry that OUD medication causes a "high" because they've seen patients taking OUD medication whose behavior was affected by other substances (e.g., benzodiazepines). Others may assume that someone is high

EXHIBIT 4.9. Addressing the Misconception That an Opioid Medication Is "Just Another Drug"

Concerned Colleague:	These patients are just replacing one drug with another. Instead of heroin, they're using buprenorphine or methadone.
Counselor:	Actually, there's substantial research that medication for opioid use disorder helps patients stop feeling withdrawal and craving and allows them to get their life back on track. These medications keep patients in treatment and reduce crime and HIV risk behavior.
Concerned Colleague:	Yeah, but aren't they still addicted?
Counselor:	Physically dependent, yes; but addicted, no. There's an important difference. Someone addicted to heroin has to take the drug several times a day to avoid withdrawal. This usually leads to craving, loss of control, and taking more than intended. Drug-seeking behavior causes loss of family and friends. It makes the person unable to perform daily roles and meet obligations.
Concerned Colleague:	Yes, I know how addiction works. But isn't taking methadone an addiction, too?
Counselor:	Patients only take methadone once a day, and its makeup is different from heroin. Daily methadone lets the body stabilize so patients don't have the highs and lows that come from heroin use. If patients use heroin, the methadone blocks its effects; they don't get high. Methadone is taken orally, so there isn't the same danger of infection that comes with injection drug use. Taking methadone as part of a treatment program lets patients feel normal and focus on changing the other aspects of their lives that led to drug use.
Concerned Colleague:	But you just said they take methadone every day.
Counselor:	Yes. That is true of most medications for any disease, if you think about it. Patients have a physical dependence on the medication but are in remission from addiction.

on a medication for OUD who isn't taking any such medication at all.

Point out that many thousands of people are prescribed medication for OUD every year, are receiving appropriate treatment, and are indistinguishable from other people. People taking OUD medication rely on it to maintain daily function, like people with diabetes rely on insulin. Nevertheless, some people think that individuals taking buprenorphine or methadone are still addicted to opioids (Exhibit 4.9), even if they don't use illicit drugs. For people with OUD, the medication addresses the compulsion and craving to use. It also blocks the euphoric effects of illicit opioids, which over time helps people stop attempting to use. For people with

EXHIBIT 4.10. When a Patient Wants To Taper Medication or Stop Altogether

- Review the decision with the patient to determine the motivation for tapering or quitting medication and the best timing for such a change.
- Tell the prescriber that the patient wants to taper; shared decision making should guide the patient's decision.
- Avoid encouraging tapering, which can imply that recovery can only truly occur off of the medication.

EXHIBIT 4.11. Responding to a Patient's Desire To Taper Medication for OUD

Patient: I want to taper off the buprenorphine.

Counselor: You'd like to taper—can you tell me why?

Patient: I'm getting married. I want a fresh start.

Counselor: You're saying you'd like to have this all behind you for the new phase in your life.

Patient: Yeah, that's it.

Counselor: Would it be alright if I share my concerns about that?

Patient: Okay.

Counselor: A big change—whether it's having a baby, getting a new job, or getting married like you're about to do—can be very exciting. But it can also be surprisingly stressful. You may want to consider staying on the medication during this transition to make sure you maintain your recovery. I'm just suggesting postponing a taper decision until you start getting settled into married life.

Patient: I hear you. The last thing I want to do is mess up my marriage right away by using again.

It would be inappropriate for a medical team to refuse radiation for cancer patients because the team believes chemotherapy is always needed, or to refuse chemotherapy because they believe that radiation is always needed, regardless of each patient's diagnosis and condition. It would be just as **inappropriate to refuse evidence-based treatment with medication for a patient with OUD, when that may be the most clinically appropriate course of treatment.**

diabetes, medication addresses the problems caused by inadequate production of insulin by the pancreas. Medication allows both populations to live life more fully.

Focus on common ground—all patients want a healthy recovery, and judging or isolating someone for return to use doesn't aid anyone's recovery. A divide may occur between patients in a group setting over return to opioid use. People in the OUD community typically are forgiving of return to opioid use and recognize that it can occur on the path to long-term recovery. However, some people in mutual-help communities judge those who return to use (see the "Helping Clients Find Accepting Mutual-Help Groups" section). Address judgmental attitudes through this analogy: People with diabetes whose blood sugar spikes aren't condemned and ejected from treatment.

Dispel the myth that OUD medications make people sick. In fact, methadone and buprenorphine relieve opioid withdrawal, even if patients don't feel complete relief in the first few days. Taking naltrexone too soon after opioid use can cause opioid withdrawal, but withdrawal symptoms can generally be managed successfully. Point out that people taking medication for OUD sometimes get colds, the flu, or other illnesses, like everyone else. A similar misconception is that OUD medications make all patients sleepy. Exhibit 4.12 offers a sample dialog for responding to this misconception.

EXHIBIT 4.12. Conversation: Redirecting a Concern to the Prescriber

Concerned Colleague: A patient in my group was falling asleep. I think his methadone dose is too high.

Counselor: That's an important observation. That certainly is possible, although there are many other possible explanations. What makes you think it's the medication and not lack of sleep or some other reason?

Concerned Colleague: Because everyone taking methadone falls asleep in group.

Counselor: Our medical staff members work hard to make sure that each patient is on the right dose. If a patient is falling asleep in group, you should alert the patient's physician right away, regardless of what medication they're taking. But I'm wondering if anything besides medication could be causing this issue.

Concerned Colleague: Well, this patient is struggling with having an all-night job.

Counselor: It may be helpful to talk to the patient about moving to a group that meets at a time when he can be more rested. In any case, to be safe, you should call the patient's prescriber about reassessing him.

When return to opioid use comes up in a group counseling setting, messages about getting back on track and avoiding shaming and blaming apply just as much to the patients taking OUD medication as to other participants. This topic is an opportunity to **address the dangers of overdose, especially the dangers of using an opioid after a period of abstinence or together with other CNS depressants.**

Helping Patients Advocate for Themselves

Educate clients so they can advocate for their treatment and personal needs. Key topics include:

- Addiction as a chronic disease influenced by genetics and environment.
- The ways that medications for OUD work.
- The process of dose stabilization.
- The benefits of longer term medication use and risks of abrupt treatment termination.
- The role of recovery supports (e.g., mutual-help groups) in helping achieve goals.

Offer clients' family and friends education on these topics as well so that they can advocate for their loved ones. Encourage patients to let family and friends know how important they are and how valuable their support is. Also urge patients to ask loved ones to help them express concerns or fears.

Role-playing can help patients self-advocate. It allows them to practice what to say, what reactions to expect, and ways to respond. Coach patients in active listening and in focusing on solutions rather than problems. Exhibit 4.13 gives an example of a counselor helping a client self-advocate.

Urge patients to advocate for themselves beyond one-on-one conversations. Options include sharing educational pamphlets, inviting loved ones to a counseling session, or referring them to websites.

Addressing Discrimination Against Clients Who Take OUD Medication

Patients can face discriminatory actions when dealing with individuals, organizations, or systems that make decisions based on misinformation about, or biases against, the use of medication for OUD. The following sections highlight issues patients taking OUD medication may face and how counselors can help.

EXHIBIT 4.13. Conversation: Helping a Client Self-Advocate

Patient:	My mom is driving me to my back surgery. I'm worried that she'll find out I'm taking buprenorphine.
Counselor:	It sounds like you're worried she'll reject you and be upset if she knows you're taking medication.
Patient:	I think she'll be disappointed in me. She thinks people who take addiction medication are still on drugs.
Counselor:	What would you think about finding a time before your surgery to tell your mother that you're taking buprenorphine? You can explain how it works and remind her how well you've been doing maintaining your job, regaining custody of your children, and living a balanced and healthy life. That may help ease her fears.
Patient:	Thanks. I'll give that a try.
Counselor:	If you want, you could invite her to one of our sessions so that I can answer any questions she has.
Patient:	Yeah, she may hear it better from you. I like the idea of having her come in after I've told her.
Counselor:	When would be a good time to bring up this topic?
Patient:	She's driving me to my pre-op appointment on Friday. Maybe I'll suggest we go for coffee after.
Counselor:	That's a good idea. How about we practice that conversation? I'll play the role of your mom.

Help clients address employment-related issues

Under the Americans With Disabilities Act, employers cannot discriminate against patients taking medication for OUD.[148] However, the law doesn't always stop employers from taking such action. For example, some employers conduct workplace urine drug testing, either before offering employment or randomly during employment. The OUD medication they test for most frequently is methadone, but it's possible to test for buprenorphine. Naltrexone is generally not tested for. The TIP expert panel concludes, based on multiple patient experiences, that patients who take OUD medication find it intimidating to explain to their employers why their urine test results are positive for opioids. Yet if they offer no explanation, they don't get the callback for the job or are let go from the job they have.

Direct patients to legal resources and help them consider how to respond to discrimination at work based on misinterpreted drug tests. Offer to speak with their prospective/current employers to address concerns and misperceptions about OUD medication and its effect on their ability to do work tasks.

RESOURCE ALERT

Becoming a Certified Medication-Assisted Treatment Advocate

The National Alliance for Medication Assisted Recovery has a training and credentialing program for interested people—not just those who receive medication for OUD—to become Certified Medication-Assisted Treatment Advocates (www.methadone.org/certification/faq.html).

Understand potential legal issues

This section describes issues that can affect access to care for patients involved in the justice system who take buprenorphine or methadone for OUD. These issues usually don't apply for naltrexone.

Many jails (short term) and prisons (long term) restrict or disallow access to OUD medication despite the federal mandate that people who are incarcerated have access to medical care.[149,150] For example:

- A jail may not continue methadone treatment or allow methadone delivery by patients' OTPs.
- Patients' medication may be seized upon arrest.
- Jail health officials may deny patients' buprenorphine prescriptions.

Help negotiate patient access to OUD medication during incarceration. Negotiating access to OUD medication can be problematic and often requires multiple meetings between care providers and jail staff members to resolve successfully. Patients taking OUD medication may be forced to go without medication during incarceration. This increases their risk for opioid overdose if they return to use after reentering the community, given the decreased tolerance that results from interrupted treatment.

Encourage patients to reengage in treatment as soon as they're released. People with OUD released from prison or jail who don't take OUD medication have higher risk of overdose death during their first few weeks in the community. Early after release, they are at very high risk of overdose, given possible:

- Decrease in opioid tolerance while incarcerated.
- Lack of appropriate OUD therapy while incarcerated.
- OUD medication initiation right before release.
- Release without coordination or a slot for community-based treatment.

Patients who aren't opioid tolerant need a lower starting dose that prescribers will increase more slowly than usual. Extended-release injectable naltrexone can be an effective alternative for these patients.

OPIOID ADDICTION is linked with high rates of ILLEGAL ACTIVITY and INCARCERATION.[151,152]

Support patients in getting legal advice or counsel via their OUD medication prescribers' healthcare organization. Members of the TIP expert panel have observed situations in which law enforcement personnel arrested patients leaving methadone clinics and charged them with driving under the influence or arrested them after finding buprenorphine prescription bottles in their cars. Discussions among treatment organizations and local law enforcement leadership can help address such situations.

Address concerns and advocate for addiction specialists to select treatments best suited for each patient. Sometimes, authorities insist that patients enter a particular kind of treatment or follow particular rules related to their OUD. To ensure a patient-centered focus, help involve addiction specialists in determining what kind of treatment best meets patients' needs. This kind of advocacy works best when counselors and the programs for which they work have preexisting relationships with personnel in local employment, law enforcement, drug court, and child welfare facilities.

Address issues in dealing with healthcare providers

Misunderstandings about OUD and its treatment aren't rare among healthcare providers:

- Patients admitted to the hospital for medical issues may face prejudice from hospital staff members.
- Providers may not know how to manage patients' OUD medication during their hospital stay.
- Some providers don't know how to manage pain in someone taking medication for OUD.

Help communicate issues to patients' prescribers, who can advocate for proper handling of OUD medication. It is also possible to help hospital staff members see the patient as a whole person who deserves respect and to provide them with essential information about treatment for OUD.

Inpatient SUD treatment facilities may refuse admission until patients are off buprenorphine or methadone. Sometimes, patients taking OUD medication seek admission to inpatient facilities for treatment of an additional SUD, a mental disorder, or both. If a facility won't accept someone on OUD medication, call on local or state regulatory authorities (e.g., the State Opioid Treatment Authority) and patients' healthcare professionals to intervene with the facility's professional staff and management.

Demonstrate awareness of pregnancy and parenting issues

Healthcare professionals may be unaware of current guidelines for treating pregnant women with OUD (Exhibit 4.14). As a result, they may inappropriately:

- Deny OUD medication to pregnant women.
- Discourage breastfeeding by mothers taking OUD medication.
- Direct women who become pregnant while taking OUD medication to undergo withdrawal from their medication and attempt abstinence.

Hospital policies on screening infants for prenatal substance exposure vary considerably. A positive screen may trigger involvement of Child Protective Services. This may occur even when the positive screen results from treatment with OUD medication under a physician's care rather than opioid misuse.

Help pregnant and postnatal clients in these situations by:

- **Educating them** and encouraging them to share pertinent information and resources with healthcare professionals involved in their care.
- **Coordinating with their prescribers** to help them get prenatal and postnatal care from well-informed healthcare professionals.
- **Getting involved in efforts to educate the local healthcare community** about best practices for the care of pregnant and postnatal women with OUD.

Legal problems can arise if Child Protective Services or legal personnel don't understand that parents receiving OUD medication are fully capable of caring for children and contributing to their families. Judges, probation or parole officers, or Child Protective Services workers may inappropriately request that patients discontinue medication as a condition of family reunification. Such orders are medically inappropriate and should be challenged. Possible ways to help:

RESOURCE ALERT

Treatment of Pain in Patients With OUD

SAMHSA's TIP 54, *Managing Chronic Pain in Adults With or in Recovery From Substance Use Disorders* (https://store.samhsa.gov/product/TIP-54-Managing-Chronic-Pain-in-Adults-With-or-in-Recovery-From-Substance-Use-Disorders/SMA13-4671)

RESOURCE ALERT

Pregnancy- and Parenting-Related Issues

SAMHSA's *Clinical Guidance for Treating Pregnant and Parenting Women With Opioid Use Disorder and Their Infants* (https://store.samhsa.gov/product/SMA18-5054)

> **EXHIBIT 4.14. Summary of Current Guidance for the Treatment of Pregnant Women With OUD**
>
> - An obstetrician and an addiction treatment provider should comanage care, and the woman should receive counseling and supportive services as needed to assist her in achieving a stable life.
> - Treatment with methadone or buprenorphine without naloxone during pregnancy is recommended. Treatment with naltrexone is not recommended during pregnancy.
> - Medically supervised withdrawal during pregnancy is typically not advisable. If not done with great care in a controlled setting, it can cause premature labor, fetal distress, and miscarriage. Attempts at abstinence from opioids without the support of medication are generally not advised because of the risk of return to opioid use, which can adversely affect both mother and fetus.
> - Newborns of women who take OUD medication often show symptoms of NAS, which is treatable. NAS from opioid agonist treatment is not as harmful to the fetus as continued use of illicit opioids during pregnancy.
> - Mothers stabilized on medication for OUD are encouraged to breastfeed.
>
> Summarized from SAMHSA's publication *A Collaborative Approach to the Treatment of Pregnant Women With Opioid Use Disorders* (https://store.samhsa.gov/product/A-Collaborative-Approach-to-the-Treatment-of-Pregnant-Women-with-Opioid-Use-Disorders/SMA16-4978).[153]

- **Write letters to judges and lawyers** explaining how effective OUD medication can be.
- **Send judges and lawyers literature** about current medical recommendations (including this TIP).
- **Testify in court,** if necessary.

Helping Clients Find Accepting Mutual-Help Groups

Voluntary participation in 12-Step groups can improve abstinence and recovery-related skills and behaviors for some people with SUDs. Greater involvement (e.g., being a 12-Step sponsor) can increase these benefits.[154,155,156,157] However, not much research has explored less widespread types of groups (e.g., groups that follow a given religion's principles, secular groups that downplay the spiritual aspects of 12-Step groups). Research exploring longitudinal outcomes for people with OUD who attend NA is limited, but findings link more frequent attendance with abstinence.[158,159,160]

Clients taking medication for OUD may face challenges in attending mutual-help groups. For example:

- NA, the most widely available program, treats illicit opioids and OUD medications equally in gauging abstinence and recovery. NA doesn't consider people taking OUD medication "clean and sober."[161]
- Local chapters of NA may decide not to allow people taking OUD medication to participate at meetings or may limit their participation (e.g., not allowing service work).
- Clients attending some NA meetings may encounter hostile attitudes toward the use of medication.
- AA's official policy is more accepting of the use of prescribed medication, but clients may still encounter negative attitudes toward their use of medications for OUD.
- Other groups, such as some religious mutual-help programs, SMART Recovery, and LifeRing Secular Recovery, also have policies that could challenge clients for taking medication for OUD.

RESOURCE ALERT

Addressing Bias and Discrimination

Are You in Recovery From Alcohol or Drug Problems? Know Your Rights: Rights for Individuals on Medication-Assisted Treatment: SAMHSA publication explaining patient rights and federal laws that protect people receiving OUD medication. Describes whom these laws protect and what they cover, including employment, housing, services, and public accommodations (http://store.samhsa.gov /product/Rights-for-Individuals-on-Medication -Assisted-Treatment/SMA09-4449)

Know Your Rights: Employment Discrimination Against People With Alcohol/Drug Histories: Legal Action Center webinar (http://lac.org /resources/substance-use-resources /employment-education-housing-resources /webinar-know-rights-employment -discrimination-people-alcoholdrug-histories)

Medication-Assisted Treatment for Opioid Addiction: Myths and Facts: Legal Action Center publication that dispels myths and provides facts about OUD medication (http://lac.org/wp-content/uploads/2016/02 /Myth-Fact-for-MAT.pdf)

Methadone Maintenance Myths and Resources: Missouri Department of Mental Health factsheet (http://dmh.mo.gov/docs/ada /methadonemyths.pdf)

Prepare clients who take medication for OUD to attend mutual-help meetings

Clients will be better able to find supportive mutual-help groups if their counselor and program:

- **Evaluate attitudes** toward medication for OUD among local mutual-help groups.
- **Keep on hand information** about all mutual-help options available in the clients' area.
- **Recruit volunteers from mutual-help groups** to help clients find and attend meetings (e.g., by providing transportation, serving as "sponsors," introducing clients).
- **Do not mandate meeting attendance.** Recommending participation is just as effective.[162]
- **Keep track of clients' experiences at different groups** to ensure that meetings remain welcoming.
- **Help clients start onsite mutual-help groups.**
- **Ask staff members to evaluate their own feelings and beliefs** about mutual-help groups.[163]

Facilitate positive mutual-help group experiences

- **Educate clients about mutual-help groups.** Explore group types, risks and benefits of participation, and limitations of research in support of those risks and benefits.
- **Suggest buddying up.** Clients can attend meetings with other people who take medication for OUD.
- **Review with clients their understanding of and prior experience with mutual help.**
- **Explore clients' understanding of the benefits and risks of disclosure** about taking OUD medication.
- **Develop a risk-reduction plan** for disclosure if clients want to share their use of OUD medication (e.g., talking with an individual group member instead of disclosing to the entire group).

- **Help clients anticipate and learn to handle negative responses:**
  - Develop sample scripts clients can use when questioned about their medication.
  - Role-play scenarios in which clients respond to questions about their use of medication.
- **Respect the privacy of clients' participation** in mutual-help groups and recognize that some groups ask that participants not discuss what occurs in meetings.
- **Make sure clients know they can talk about their experiences** in mutual-help groups but don't pressure them to disclose in these groups that they take OUD medication.
- **Consider mutual-help participation using groups more open to OUD medication** (e.g., attending AA even if the client has no alcohol use disorder; attending groups for co-occurring substance use and mental disorders, such as Dual Recovery Anonymous or Double Trouble in Recovery). Clients with OUD who attend AA and not NA have similar recovery-related outcomes and retention rates.[164]

RESOURCE ALERT

How To Use Technology-Based Tools in Behavioral Health Services

SAMHSA's TIP 60, *Using Technology-Based Therapeutic Tools in Behavioral Health Services*, is available from the SAMHSA Store (https://store.samhsa.gov/product/TIP-60-Using-Technology-Based-Therapeutic-Tools-in-Behavioral-Health-Services/SMA15-4924). In addition to discussing online mutual-help groups, this TIP can help counselors implement technology-assisted care for patients with OUD. It highlights the importance of using technology-based assessments and interventions and discusses how technology reduces barriers to treatment.

Online mutual-help groups

Before recommending an online group, check its content and tone on the use of medication. Mutual help using the Internet (either through real-time chat rooms or discussion boards where one posts and waits for responses) has been growing in popularity. This is an especially valuable resource for clients living in rural and remote areas. Groups range from general meetings for people with a particular SUD (e.g., online AA meetings) to those that are very specific (e.g., Moms on Methadone). Moderated groups are preferable to unmoderated groups. TIP 60, *Using Technology-Based Therapeutic Tools in Behavioral Health Services*, addresses many of the pros and cons of online support groups.[165] Part 5 of this TIP gives links for several groups that the TIP expert panel has identified as helpful.

RESOURCE ALERT

Mutual Help for Clients With OUD

William White's *Narcotics Anonymous and the Pharmacotherapeutic Treatment of Opioid Addiction in the United States:* Publication that gives more information on the pros and cons of 12-Step groups for people receiving medication for OUD and how to prepare them for meetings[166] (http://atforum.com/documents/2011NAandMedication-assistedTreatment.pdf)

White, Galanter, Humphreys, and Kelly's "The Paucity of Attention to Narcotics Anonymous in Current Public, Professional, and Policy Responses to Rising Opioid Addiction": Peer-reviewed journal article on the benefits of NA and the need to include it among the options offered to people receiving medication for OUD[167] (www.tandfonline.com/doi/abs/10.1080/07347324.2016.1217712)

Mutual-help groups specific to OTPs

Although these meetings occur mostly on the premises of OTPs, it may be possible to use the models developed by OTPs in more general SUD treatment settings. Because they serve only patients receiving medication to treat OUD, OTPs can create and sustain onsite mutual-help groups specific to this population. Such groups include Methadone Anonymous (MA),[168] other variations on a 12-Step model,[169,170] and the mutual-help component of Medication-Assisted Recovery Services (MARS). MARS is a recovery community organization, not just a mutual-help program. MARS members design, implement, and evaluate a variety of peer-delivered recovery support services in addition to providing meetings. More information on these programs is in the articles cited and online resources presented in Part 5.

Facilitating Groups That Include Patients Taking OUD Medication

Foster acceptance via attitude and behavior when facilitating groups that include patients taking OUD medication:

- **Establish ground rules** about being respectful, avoiding negative comments about group members, and keeping statements made in the group confidential—as with any group.
- **Be proactive.** State up front that ground rules apply to everyone, regardless of a given person's decisions about whether to include OUD medication in his or her path to recovery.
- **Ask members to discuss how to address any negative comments,** should they occur. This is especially important for mixed groups.
- **Ask group members to affirm that they will abide by the rules.**
- **Provide consistent reminders** throughout each session about the ground rules.

Group members may still make negative comments about medication for OUD. Avoid feeding the negativity with attention, which can worsen the situation. **Reframe negative comments to express underlying motivations, often based on fear or misunderstanding.** Remain positive; model expected behavior, which can benefit the person who made the negative remark (Exhibit 4.15).

Additional tips for leading mixed groups include the following:

- **Treat patients taking OUD medication the same as other patients in the group.** Patients taking medication can participate in and benefit from individual and group counseling just like other patients. There is no need to have separate counseling tracks

EXHIBIT 4.15. Redirecting Negative Comments

Petra:	How can you say Joni is in recovery when she's still taking a drug every day? I struggled every day and never took anything for 10 years.
Counselor:	I hear your concern for Joni. You want her recovery to follow the same path you took in yours.
Petra:	Right! And she's taking methadone, which is an opioid. People use opioids to get high.
Counselor:	In this treatment program, we see addiction as a brain disease. Methadone treats the brain disease part of addiction. It stabilizes the brain and allows the person to focus on learning new ways of thinking and reacting. It works by blocking the effects of other opioids. Patients on a proper dose can't get high even if they try to use. This helps discourage future drug use. Joni, would you like to add anything?
Joni:	Petra, it's great that you stopped using opioids and stayed in recovery without medication—but everyone has a different path to recovery. For me, medication helps me hold a job, take care of my kids, stay focused in my counseling sessions, and feel normal.

based on OUD medication status, nor should that status limit a participant's responsibilities, leadership role, or level of participation.

- **Meet with patients taking OUD medication in advance to prepare them for mixed-group settings.** Advise them that they don't have to disclose their medication status to the group, just as they don't have to disclose any other health issues. Counsel them that if they choose to talk about their medication status, it helps to talk about how medication has helped shape their personal recovery.
- **Don't single out patients taking OUD medication.** Let participants decide whether to tell the group about any issue they want to share, including medication status. If a patient chooses to disclose that status, follow up after the session to ensure that he or she is in a positive space and feels supported.
- **Keep the session's focus on the topic and not on the pros and cons of medication for OUD.** If the person receiving medication for OUD or other group members have specific questions about such medications, have them ask their healthcare professionals.
- **Reinforce messages of acceptance.** During the wrap-up discussion at the end of a session, members may comment on points that stood out for them. This is a chance to restate information accurately and model respect for each patient's road to recovery, whether it includes OUD medication or not.
- **Review confidentiality rules.** Affirm that patients' OUD medication status will not be shared with other group members. Remind participants to think carefully before sharing personal details such as their medication status with the group, because other participants may not respect confidentiality even if they have agreed to do so as part of the group guidelines.

Other Common Counseling Concerns

Patients must sign releases to permit ongoing conversations between care providers in accordance with federal regulations on confidentiality of medical records for patients in treatment for an SUD (42 CFR Part 2). When patients' primary care providers, prescribers of medication for OUD, and addiction-specific counselors don't work for the same entity, patients must consent for them to share information.

It can be challenging when a patient refuses to consent to collaborative communication among his or her healthcare team members. In these cases, the professionals involved must decide whether they will continue to provide either medication or counseling services without permission to collaborate. In other words, is cross-communication among all providers required for collaborative care? The answer to this complicated question depends on each patient's circumstances.

> **The TIP expert panel recommends communication among providers as the standard of care for OUD treatment and recovery support.** Carefully consider deviations from this standard, which should occur only rarely. That said, individualize decisions about collaborative communication among providers to each patient's unique preferences, needs, and circumstances.

Patients may not consent to communication among providers if they:

- **Have experienced discrimination in healthcare systems.**
- **Have developed OUD after taking opioid pain medication.**
- **Have legitimate cause not to trust providers** (e.g., perceiving themselves as having been abused by a healthcare professional).[171]
- **Are not ready to make primary care providers aware of their disorder,** even (or especially) if those providers have been prescribing opioid pain medication.
- **Encounter problems in making progress toward recovery.** After typically consenting to communication among providers, a patient's sudden revocation may signal trouble in recovery.

Exhibit 4.16 lists common collaborative care issues and responses counselors can consider. Suggested responses assume that patients have consented to open exchange of information among all providers.

EXHIBIT 4.16. Common Collaborative Care Issues and Possible Counselor Responses

POTENTIAL MEDICATION-RELATED ISSUE	COUNSELOR RESPONSE
The patient complains of continued cravings.	Talk with the patient about his or her medication adherence. Review with the patient strategies for overcoming cravings using a CBT model.
	Communicate with the prescriber to see whether dosage can be adjusted to subdue the cravings.
A patient taking methadone does not appear engaged in counseling sessions and seems drowsy during conversations.	Ask the patient whether drowsiness is caused by lack of sleep, disturbed sleep, substance use, or overmedication. Consider obtaining a spot urine test (if available).
	In all cases of drowsiness, alert the prescriber immediately so that the cause can be determined. This is particularly important during the first few weeks of treatment.
The patient is at risk for return to opioid use.	Inform the prescriber if the patient appears at risk for return to use given cravings, life stressors, changes in social circumstances, new triggers, or the like. This alerts the prescriber to monitor the patient more closely and consider medication changes to reduce likelihood of return to use.
The patient has recently returned to opioid misuse after a period of abstinence.	Gather details about circumstances surrounding the incident of use and, in collaboration with the prescriber and the patient, adjust the treatment plan accordingly. Reinforce the patient's understanding of the increased risk of opioid overdose given altered levels of tolerance.

Continued on next page

EXHIBIT 4.16. Common Collaborative Care Issues and Possible Counselor Responses (continued)

POTENTIAL MEDICATION-RELATED ISSUE	COUNSELOR RESPONSE
The patient is discussing chronic pain with the counselor.	Direct the patient to a healthcare professional for assessment of pain and medical treatment as necessary. If indicated as appropriate by a healthcare professional, provide CBT for dealing with pain or instruct the patient in adjunct methods for pain relief (e.g., meditation, exercise, physical therapy).
The patient is asking the counselor for medical advice on what dose to take, side effects, how long to stay on the medication, and the like.	Answer questions based on your knowledge of medications for treatment of OUD but don't provide medical advice. Refer the patient to the prescriber for that. As appropriate, contact the prescriber with the patient to have a three-way discussion.
The counselor or patient is concerned that the prescriber is not giving quality care.	As appropriate, advocate for the patient with the prescribing medical team.
The patient discloses use of other drugs.	Use motivational interviewing techniques to have a collaborative conversation about the details of this drug use. For example, give a response like "Tell me more about this," followed by questions about the specific drugs used, why they were used, and what the patient's thoughts are about changing that drug use.
The patient discloses that she is pregnant.	Advise the patient to contact her prescriber immediately no matter what medication she is taking. Work with her to help her get access to prenatal care (if she doesn't have it already) and other health services related to pregnancy as needed.
The patient has a positive urine screen.	Using motivational interviewing tools, discuss with the patient the context of the substance use and what implications this use may have for the treatment plan. If the patient denies the substance use, reconsider the patient's readiness to change and how it affects the treatment plan.

Notes

1. Centers for Disease Control and Prevention. (2016). Increases in drug and opioid-involved overdose deaths—United States, 2010–2015. *Morbidity and Mortality Weekly Report, 65*(50–51),1445–1452.

2. Center for Behavioral Health Statistics and Quality. (2017). *Key substance use and mental health indicators in the United States: Results from the 2016 National Survey on Drug Use and Health.* Rockville, MD: Substance Abuse and Mental Health Services Administration.

3. American Society of Addiction Medicine. (2011). Definition of addiction. Retrieved October 30, 2017, from www.asam.org/resources/definition-of-addiction

4. American Psychiatric Association. (2013). *Diagnostic and statistical manual of mental disorders* (5th ed.). Arlington, VA: American Psychiatric Publishing.

5. Department of Health and Human Services, Office of the Surgeon General. (2016). *Facing addiction in America: The Surgeon General's report on alcohol, drugs, and health.* Washington, DC: Department of Health and Human Services.

6. Substance Abuse and Mental Health Services Administration. (2015). *Federal guidelines for opioid treatment programs.* HHS Publication No. (SMA) PEP15-FEDGUIDEOTP. Rockville, MD: Substance Abuse and Mental Health Services Administration.

7. American Psychiatric Association. (2013). *Diagnostic and statistical manual of mental disorders* (5th ed.). Arlington, VA: American Psychiatric Association.

8. National Cancer Institute. (n.d.). Remission. In *NCI dictionary of cancer terms.* Retrieved November, 22, 2017, from www.cancer.gov/publications/dictionaries/cancer-terms?cdrid=45867

9. American Psychiatric Association. (2013). *Diagnostic and statistical manual of mental disorders* (5th ed.). Arlington, VA: American Psychiatric Publishing.

10. Manchikanti, L. (2007). National drug control policy and prescription drug abuse: Facts and fallacies. *Pain Physician, 10,* 399–424.

11. Jones, C. M. (2013). Heroin use and heroin use risk behaviors among nonmedical users of prescription opioid pain relievers—United States, 2002–2004 and 2008–2010. *Drug and Alcohol Dependence, 132*(1–2), 95–100.

12. Hedegaard, H., Chen, L. H, & Warner, M. (2015). *Drug-poisoning deaths involving heroin: United States, 2000–2013.* NCHS Data Brief, No. 190. Hyattsville, MD: National Center for Health Statistics.

13. Centers for Disease Control and Prevention. (2016). Increases in drug and opioid-involved overdose deaths—United States, 2010–2015. *Morbidity and Mortality Weekly Report, 65*(50–51),1445–1452.

14. Substance Abuse and Mental Health Services Administration. (n.d.). Opioid treatment program directory. Retrieved October 19, 2017, from https://dpt2.samhsa.gov/treatment/directory.aspx

15. American Psychiatric Association. (2013). *Diagnostic and statistical manual of mental disorders* (5th ed.). Arlington, VA: American Psychiatric Publishing.

16. Carroll, K. M., & Weiss, R. D. (2016). The role of behavioral interventions in buprenorphine maintenance treatment: A review. *American Journal of Psychiatry, 174*(8), 738–747.

17. McLellan, A. T., Lewis, D. C., O'Brien, C. P., & Kleber, H. D. (2000). Drug dependence, a chronic medical illness: Implications for treatment, insurance, and outcomes evaluation. *JAMA, 284*(13), 1689–1695.

18. Connery, H. S. (2015). Medication-assisted treatment of opioid use disorder: Review of the evidence and future directions. *Harvard Review of Psychiatry, 23*(2), 63–75.

19. Fullerton, C. A., Kim, M., Thomas, C. P., Lyman, D. R., Montejano, L. B., Dougherty, R. H., ... Delphin-Rittmon, M. E. (2014). Medication-assisted treatment with methadone: Assessing the evidence. *Psychiatric Services, 65*(2), 146–157.

20. Thomas, C. P., Fullerton, C. A., Kim, M., Montejano, L., Lyman, D. R., Dougherty, R. H., ... Delphin-Rittman, M. E. (2014). Medication-assisted treatment with buprenorphine: Assessing the evidence. *Psychiatric Services, 65*(2), 158–170.

21. American Society of Addiction Medicine. (2015). *The ASAM national practice guideline for the use of medications in the treatment of addiction involving opioid use.* Chevy Chase, MD: Author.

22. Sordo, L., Barrio, G., Bravo, M. J., Indave, B. I., Degenhardt, L., Wiessing, L., ... Pastor-Barriuso, R. (2017). Mortality risk during and after opioid substitution treatment: Systematic review and meta-analysis of cohort studies. *British Medical Journal (Clinical Research Ed.), 357,* j1550.

23. Mattick, R. P., Breen, C., Kimber, J., & Davoli, M. (2014). Buprenorphine maintenance versus placebo or methadone maintenance for opioid dependence. *Cochrane Database of Systematic Reviews, 2014*(2), 1–84.

24. Auriacombe, M., Fatséas, M., Dubernet, J., Daulouède, J. P., & Tignol, J. (2004). French field experience with buprenorphine. *American Journal on Addictions, 13*(Suppl. 1), S17–S28.

25. Degenhardt, L., Randall, D., Hall, W., Law, M., Butler, T., & Burns, L. (2009). Mortality among clients of a state-wide opioid pharmacotherapy program over 20 years: Risk factors and lives saved. *Drug and Alcohol Dependence, 105*(1–2), 9–15.

26. Gibson, A., Degenhardt, L., Mattick, R. P., Ali, R., White, J., & O'Brien, S. (2008). Exposure to opioid maintenance treatment reduces long-term mortality. *Addiction, 103*(3), 462–468.

27. Merlo, L. J., Greene, W. M., & Pomm, R. (2011). Mandatory naltrexone treatment prevents relapse among opiate-dependent anesthesiologists returning to practice. *Journal of Addiction Medicine, 5*(4), 279–283.

28. Minozzi, S., Amato, L., Vecchi, S., Davoli, M., Kirchmayer, U., & Verster, A. (2011). Oral naltrexone maintenance treatment for opioid dependence. *Cochrane Database of Systematic Reviews, 2011*(4), 1–45.

29. Fullerton, C. A., Kim, M., Thomas, C. P., Lyman, D. R., Montejano, L. B., Dougherty, R. H., ... Delphin-Rittmon, M. E. (2014). Medication-assisted treatment with methadone: Assessing the evidence. *Psychiatric Services, 65*(2), 146–157.

30. Mattick, R. P., Breen, C., Kimber, J., & Davoli, M. (2014). Buprenorphine maintenance versus placebo or methadone maintenance for opioid dependence. *Cochrane Database of Systematic Reviews, 2014*(2), 1–84.

31. Kresina, T. F., & Lubran, R. (2011). Improving public health through access to and utilization of medication assisted treatment. *International Journal of Environmental Research and Public Health, 8*(10), 4102–4117.

32. Krupitsky, E., Nunes, E. V., Ling, W., Illeperuma, A., Gastfiend, D. R., & Silverman, B. L. (2011). Injectable extended-release naltrexone for opioid dependence: A double-blind, placebo-controlled, multicentre randomized trial. *Lancet, 377*(9776), 1506–1533.

33. Mattick, R. P., Breen, C., Kimber, J., & Davoli, M. (2014). Buprenorphine maintenance versus placebo or methadone maintenance for opioid dependence. *Cochrane Database of Systematic Reviews, 2014*(2), 1–84.

34. Timko, C., Schultz, N. R., Cucciare, M. A., Vittorio, L., & Garrison-Diehn, C. (2016). Retention in medication-assisted treatment for opiate dependence: A systematic review. *Journal of Addictive Diseases, 35*(1), 22–35.

35. Fiellin, D. A., Schottenfeld, R. S., Cutter, C. J., Moore, B. A., Barry, D. T., & O'Connor, P. G. (2014). Primary care-based buprenorphine taper vs maintenance therapy for prescription opioid dependence: A randomized clinical trial. *JAMA Internal Medicine, 174*(12), 1947–1954.

36. Kakko, J., Svanborg, K. D., Kreek, M. J., & Heilig, M. (2003). 1-year retention and social function after buprenorphine-assisted relapse prevention treatment for heroin dependence in Sweden: A randomised, placebo-controlled trial. *Lancet, 361*(9358), 662–668.

37. Sees, K. L., Delucchi, K. L., Masson, C., Rosen, A., Clark, H. W., Robillard, H., ... Hall, S. M. (2000). Methadone maintenance vs 180-day psychosocially enriched detoxification for treatment of opioid dependence: A randomized controlled trial. *JAMA, 283*(10), 1303–1310.

38. Weiss, R. D., Potter, J. S., Fiellin, D. A., Byrne, M., Connery, H. S., Dickinson, W., ... Ling, W. (2011). Adjunctive counseling during brief and extended buprenorphine-naloxone treatment for prescription opioid dependence: A 2-phase randomized controlled trial. *Archives of General Psychiatry, 68*(12), 1238–1246.

39. Amato, L., Davoli, M., Minozzi, S., Ferroni, E., Ali, R., & Ferri, M. (2013). Methadone at tapered doses for the management of opioid withdrawal. *Cochrane Database of Systematic Reviews, 2013*(2), 1–68.

40. Bart, G. (2012). Maintenance medication for opiate addiction: The foundation of recovery. *Journal of Addictive Diseases, 31*(3), 207–225.

41. Fiellin, D. A., Schottenfeld, R. S., Cutter, C. J., Moore, B. A., Barry, D. T., & O'Connor, P. G. (2014). Primary care-based buprenorphine taper vs maintenance therapy for prescription opioid dependence: A randomized clinical trial. *JAMA Internal Medicine, 174*(12), 1947–1954.

42. White, W. L. (2012). Medication-assisted recovery from opioid addiction: Historical and contemporary perspectives. *Journal of Addictive Diseases, 31*(3), 199–206.

43. Substance Abuse and Mental Health Services Administration. (1999). *Enhancing motivation for change in substance abuse treatment.* Treatment Improvement Protocol (TIP) Series 35. HHS Publication No. (SMA) 13-4212. Rockville, MD: Substance Abuse and Mental Health Services Administration.

44. McHugh, R. K., Hearon, B. A., & Otto, M. W. (2010). Cognitive behavioral therapy for substance use disorders. *Psychiatric Clinics of North America, 33*(3), 511–525.

45. Ling, W., Hillhouse, M., Ang, A., Jenkins, J., & Fahey, J. (2013). Comparison of behavioral treatment conditions in buprenorphine maintenance. *Addiction, 108*(10), 1788–1798.

46. Fiellin, D. A., Barry, D. T., Sullivan, L. E., Cutter, C. J., Moore, B. A., O'Connor, P. G., & Schottenfeld, R. S. (2013). A randomized trial of cognitive behavioral therapy in primary care-based buprenorphine. *American Journal of Medicine, 126*(1), 74.e11–74.e17.

47. Moore, B. A., Fiellin, D. A., Cutter, C. J., Biondo, F. D., Barry, D. C., Fiellin, L. E., ... Schottenfeld, R. S. (2016). Cognitive behavioral therapy improves treatment outcomes for prescription opioid users in primary care buprenorphine treatment. *Journal of Substance Abuse Treatment, 71*, 54–57.

48. Abbott, P. J. (2010). Case management: Ongoing evaluation of patients' needs in an opioid treatment program. *Professional Case Management, 15*(3), 145–152.

49. Morgenstern, J., Neighbors, C. J., Kermis, A., Riordan, A., Blanchard, K. A., McVeigh, K. H., ... McCredie, B. (2009). Improving 24-month abstinence and employment outcomes for substance-dependent women receiving temporary assistance for needy families with intensive case management. *American Journal of Public Health, 99*(2), 328–333.

50. Substance Abuse and Mental Health Services Administration. (2000). *Comprehensive case management for substance abuse treatment.* Treatment Improvement Protocol (TIP) Series 27. HHS Publication No. (SMA) 15-4215. Rockville, MD: Substance Abuse and Mental Health Services Administration.

51. National Institute on Drug Abuse. (2012). *Principles of drug addiction treatment: A research-based guide* (3rd ed.). NIH Publication No. 12–4180. Bethesda, MD: Author.

52. Woo, J., Bhalerao, A., Bawor, M., Bhatt, M., Dennis, B., Mouravska, N., ... Samaan, Z. (2017). "Don't judge a book by its cover": A qualitative study of methadone patients' experiences of stigma. *Substance Abuse: Research and Treatment, 11,* 1–12.

53. Dugosh, K., Abraham, A., Seymour, B., McLoyd, K., Chalk, M., & Festinger, D. (2016). A systematic review on the use of psychosocial interventions in conjunction with medications for the treatment of opioid addiction. *Journal of Addiction Medicine, 10*(2), 93–103.

54. Roberts, J., Annett, H., & Hickman, M. (2011). A systematic review of interventions to increase the uptake of opiate substitution therapy in injecting drug users. *Journal of Public Health, 33*(3), 378–384.

55. Fiellin, D. A., Barry, D. T., Sullivan, L. E., Cutter, C. J., Moore, B. A., O'Connor, P. G., & Schottenfeld, R. S. (2013). A randomized trial of cognitive behavioral therapy in primary care-based buprenorphine. *American Journal of Medicine, 126*(1), 74.e11–74.e17.

56. Ling, W., Hillhouse, M., Ang, A., Jenkins, J., & Fahey, J. (2013). Comparison of behavioral treatment conditions in buprenorphine maintenance. *Addiction, 108*(10), 1788–1798.

57. Weiss, R. D., Potter, J. S., Fiellin, D. A., Byrne, M., Connery, H. S., Dickinson, W., ... Ling, W. (2011). Adjunctive counseling during brief and extended buprenorphine-naloxone treatment for prescription opioid dependence: A 2-phase randomized controlled trial. *Archives of General Psychiatry, 68*(12), 1238–1246.

58. Ling, W., Hillhouse, M., Ang, A., Jenkins, J., & Fahey, J. (2013). Comparison of behavioral treatment conditions in buprenorphine maintenance. *Addiction, 108*(10), 1788–1798.

59. National Institute on Drug Abuse. (2012). *Principles of drug addiction treatment: A research-based guide* (3rd ed.). NIH Publication No. 12–4180. Bethesda, MD: Author.

60. Weiss, R. D., Griffin, M. L., Potter, J. S., Dodd, D. R., Dreifuss, J. A., Connery, H. S., & Carroll, K. M. (2014). Who benefits from additional drug counseling among prescription opioid-dependent patients receiving buprenorphine-naloxone and standard medical management? *Drug and Alcohol Dependence, 140,* 118–122.

61. Connock, M., Juarez-Garcia, A., Jowett, S., Frew, E., Liu, Z., Taylor, R. J., ... Taylor, R. S. (2007). Methadone and buprenorphine for the management of opioid dependence: A systematic review and economic evaluation. *Health Technology Assessment, 11*(9), 1–171, iii–iv.

62. De Maeyer, J., Vanderplasschen, W., & Broekaert, E. (2010). Quality of life among opiate-dependent individuals: A review of the literature. *International Journal on Drug Policy, 21*(5), 364–380.

63. Carpentier, P. J., Krabbe, P. F., van Gogh, M. T., Knapen, L. J., Buitelaar, J. K., & de Jong, C. A. (2009). Psychiatric comorbidity reduces quality of life in chronic methadone maintained patients. *American Journal on Addictions, 18*(6), 470–480.

64. Muller, A. E., Skurtveit, S., & Clausen, T. (2016). Many correlates of poor quality of life among substance users entering treatment are not addiction-specific. *Health and Quality of Life Outcomes, 14,* 1–10.

65. De Maeyer, J., Vanderplasschen, W., & Broekaert, E. (2010). Quality of life among opiate-dependent individuals: A review of the literature. *International Journal on Drug Policy, 21*(5), 364–380.

66. Carpentier, P. J., Krabbe, P. F., van Gogh, M. T., Knapen, L. J., Buitelaar, J. K., & de Jong, C. A. (2009). Psychiatric comorbidity reduces quality of life in chronic methadone maintained patients. *American Journal on Addictions, 18*(6), 470–480.

67. Fei, J. T. B., Yee, A., Habil, M. H. B., & Danaee, M. (2016). Effectiveness of methadone maintenance therapy and improvement in quality of life following a decade of implementation. *Journal of Substance Abuse Treatment, 69,* 50–56.

68. Millson, P., Challacombe, L., Villeneuve, P. J., Strike, C. J., Fischer, B., Myers, T., ... Hopkins, S. (2006). Determinants of health-related quality of life of opiate users at entry to low-threshold methadone programs. *European Addiction Research, 12*(2), 74–82.

69. Krebs, E., Kerr, T., Wood, E., & Nosyk, B. (2016). Characterizing long-term health related quality of life trajectories of individuals with opioid use disorder. *Journal of Substance Abuse Treatment, 67,* 30–37.

70. Millson, P., Challacombe, L., Villeneuve, P. J., Strike, C. J., Fischer, B., Myers, T., ... Hopkins, S. (2006). Determinants of health-related quality of life of opiate users at entry to low-threshold methadone programs. *European Addiction Research, 12*(2), 74–82.

71. De Maeyer, J., Vanderplasschen, W., & Broekaert, E. (2010). Quality of life among opiate-dependent individuals: A review of the literature. *International Journal on Drug Policy, 21*(5), 364–380.

72. Muller, A. E., Skurtveit, S., & Clausen, T. (2016). Many correlates of poor quality of life among substance users entering treatment are not addiction-specific. *Health and Quality of Life Outcomes, 14*, 1–10.

73. Cavaiola, A. A., Fulmer, B. A., & Stout, D. (2015). The impact of social support and attachment style on quality of life and readiness to change in a sample of individuals receiving medication-assisted treatment for opioid dependence. *Substance Abuse, 36*(2), 183–191.

74. Millson, P., Challacombe, L., Villeneuve, P. J., Strike, C. J., Fischer, B., Myers, T., ... Hopkins, S. (2006). Determinants of health-related quality of life of opiate users at entry to low-threshold methadone programs. *European Addiction Research, 12*(2), 74–82.

75. Center for Substance Abuse Treatment. (2007). *National Summit on Recovery: Conference report.* HHS Publication No. (SMA) 07-4276. Rockville, MD: Substance Abuse and Mental Health Services Administration.

76. Substance Abuse and Mental Health Services Administration. (2012). SAMHSA's working definition of recovery. Retrieved November 24, 2017, from https://store.samhsa.gov/shin/content/PEP12-RECDEF/PEP12-RECDEF.pdf

77. Jackson, L. A., Buxton, J. A., Dingwell, J., Dykeman, M., Gahagan, J., Gallant, K., ... Davison, C. (2014). Improving psychosocial health and employment outcomes for individuals receiving methadone treatment: A realist synthesis of what makes interventions work. *BMC Psychology, 2*, 1–20.

78. Kaplan, L. (2008). *The role of recovery support services in recovery-oriented systems of care.* HHS Publication No. (SMA) 08-4315. Rockville, MD: Substance Abuse and Mental Health Services Administration.

79. White, W. L., & Mojer-Torres, L. (2010). *Recovery-oriented methadone maintenance.* Retrieved October 23, 2017, from www.attcnetwork.org/userfiles/file/GreatLakes/5th%20Monograph_RM_Methadone.pdf

80. Hser, Y. I. (2007). Predicting long-term stable recovery from heroin addiction: Findings from a 33-year follow-up study. *Journal of Addictive Diseases, 26*(1), 51–60.

81. Laudet, A. B., & White, W. L. (2008). Recovery capital as prospective predictor of sustained recovery, life satisfaction, and stress among former poly-substance users. *Substance Use and Misuse, 43*(1), 27–54.

82. Skinner, M. L., Haggerty, K. P., Fleming, C. B., Catalano, R. F., & Gainey, R. R. (2011). Opiate-addicted parents in methadone treatment: Long-term recovery, health, and family relationships. *Journal of Addictive Diseases, 30*(1), 17–26.

83. Substance Abuse and Mental Health Services Administration. (2016). Person- and family-centered care and peer support. Retrieved October 23, 2017, from https://www.samhsa.gov/section-223/care-coordination/person-family-centered

84. Robinson, J. H., Callister, L. C., Berry, J. A., & Dearing, K. A. (2008). Patient-centered care and adherence: Definitions and applications to improve outcomes. *Journal of the American Academy of Nurse Practitioners, 20*(12), 600–607.

85. Substance Abuse and Mental Health Services Administration. (planned). *Relapse prevention and recovery promotion in behavioral health services.* Treatment Improvement Protocol (TIP) Series. Rockville, MD: Substance Abuse and Mental Health Services Administration.

86. White, W., & Miller, W. (2007). The use of confrontation in addiction treatment: History, science and time for change. *Counselor, 8*(4), 12–30.

87. Lindgren, B. M., Eklund, M., Melin, Y., & Graneheim, U. H. (2015). From resistance to existence—Experiences of medication-assisted treatment as disclosed by people with opioid dependence. *Issues in Mental Health Nursing, 36*(12), 963–970.

88. Stoller, K. B., Stephens, M. A. C., & Schorr, A. (2016). Integrated service delivery models for opioid treatment programs in an era of increasing opioid addiction, health reform, and parity. Retrieved October 23, 2017, from www.aatod.org/wp-content/uploads/2016/07/2nd-Whitepaper-.pdf

89. Brooner, R. K., King, V. L., Kidorf, M., Schmidt, C. W., Jr., & Bigelow, G. E. (1997). Psychiatric and substance use comorbidity among treatment-seeking opioid abusers. *Archives of General Psychiatry, 54*(1), 71–80.

90. Savant, J. D., Barry, D. T., Cutter, C. J., Joy, M. T., Dinh, A., Schottenfeld, R. S., & Fiellin, D. A. (2013). Prevalence of mood and substance use disorders among patients seeking primary care office-based buprenorphine/naloxone treatment. *Drug and Alcohol Dependence, 127*(1–3), 243–247.

91. Brooner, R. K., Kidorf, M. S., King, V. L., Peirce, J., Neufeld, K., Stoller, K., & Kolodner, K. (2013). Managing psychiatric comorbidity within versus outside of methadone treatment settings: A randomized and controlled evaluation. *Addiction, 108*(11), 1942–1951.

92. Hser, Y. I., Evans, E., Grella, C., Ling, W., & Anglin, D. (2015). Long-term course of opioid addiction. *Harvard Review of Psychiatry, 23*(2), 76–89.

93 Flynn, P. M., Joe, G. W., Broome, K. M., Simpson, D. D., & Brown, B. S. (2003). Recovery from opioid addiction in DATOS. *Journal of Substance Abuse Treatment, 25*(3), 177–186.

94 Havassy, B. E., Hall, S. M., & Wasserman, D. A. (1991). Social support and relapse: Commonalities among alcoholics, opiate users, and cigarette smokers. *Addictive Behaviors, 16*(5), 235–246.

95 Tuten, M., & Jones, H. E. (2003). A partner's drug-using status impacts women's drug treatment outcome. *Drug and Alcohol Dependence, 70*(3), 327–330.

96 Schroeder, J. R., Latkin, C. A., Hoover, D. R., Curry, A. D., Knowlton, A. R., & Celentano, D. D. (2001). Illicit drug use in one's social network and in one's neighborhood predicts individual heroin and cocaine use. *Annals of Epidemiology, 11*(6), 389–394.

97 Trocchio, S., Chassler, D., Storbjörk, J., Delucchi, K., Witbrodt, J., & Lundgren, L. (2013). The association between self-reported mental health status and alcohol and drug abstinence 5 years post-assessment for an addiction disorder in U.S. and Swedish samples. *Journal of Addictive Diseases, 32*(2), 180–193.

98 Kidorf, M., Latkin, C., & Brooner, R. K. (2016). Presence of drug-free family and friends in the personal social networks of people receiving treatment for opioid use disorder. *Journal of Substance Abuse Treatment, 70*, 87–92.

99 Kidorf, M., Latkin, C., & Brooner, R. K. (2016). Presence of drug-free family and friends in the personal social networks of people receiving treatment for opioid use disorder. *Journal of Substance Abuse Treatment, 70*, 87–92.

100 Substance Abuse and Mental Health Services Administration. (2014). *Improving cultural competence.* Treatment Improvement Protocol (TIP) Series 59. HHS Publication No. (SMA) 14-4849. Rockville, MD: Substance Abuse and Mental Health Services Administration.

101 Substance Abuse and Mental Health Services Administration. (2014). *SAMHSA's concept of trauma and guidance for a trauma-informed approach.* HHS Publication No. (SMA) 14-4884. Rockville, MD: Substance Abuse and Mental Health Services Administration.

102 Kumar, N., Stowe, Z. N., Han, X., & Mancino, M. J. (2016). Impact of early childhood trauma on retention and phase advancement in an outpatient buprenorphine treatment program. *American Journal on Addictions, 25*(7), 542–548.

103 Barry, D. T., Beitel, M., Cutter, C. J., Garnet, B., Joshi, D., Rosenblum, A., & Schottenfeld, R. S. (2011). Exploring relations among traumatic, posttraumatic, and physical pain experiences in methadone-maintained patients. *Journal of Pain, 12*(1), 22–28.

104 Sansone, R. A., Whitecar, P., & Wiederman, M. W. (2009). The prevalence of childhood trauma among those seeking buprenorphine treatment. *Journal of Addictive Disorders, 28*(1), 64–67.

105 Lawson, K. M., Back, S. E., Hartwell, K. J., Moran-Santa, M. M., & Brady, K. T. (2013). A comparison of trauma profiles among individuals with prescription opioid, nicotine, or cocaine dependence. *American Journal of Addiction, 22*(2), 127–131.

106 Jessell, L., Mateu-Gelabert, P., Guarino, H., Vakharia, S. P., Syckes, C., Goodbody, E., … Friedman, S. (2017). Sexual violence in the context of drug use among young adult opioid users in New York City. *Journal of Interpersonal Violence, 32*(19), 2885–2907.

107 Amaro, H., Dai, J., Arévalo, S., Acevedo, A., Matsumoto, A., Nieves, R., & Prado, G. (2007). Effects of integrated trauma treatment on outcomes in a racially/ethnically diverse sample of women in urban community-based substance abuse treatment. *Journal of Urban Health, 84*(4), 508–522.

108 Volkow, N. D., Koob, G. F., & McLellan, A. T. (2016). Neurobiologic advances from the brain disease model of addiction. *New England Journal of Medicine, 374*(4), 363–371.

109 Edelman, E. J., Chantarat, T., Caffrey, S., Chaudhry, A., O'Connor, P. G., Weiss, L., … Fiellin, L. E. (2014). The impact of buprenorphine/naloxone treatment on HIV risk behaviors among HIV-infected, opioid-dependent patients. *Drug and Alcohol Dependence, 139*, 79–85.

110 Gibson, A., Degenhardt, L., Mattick, R. P., Ali, R., White, J., & O'Brien, S. (2008). Exposure to opioid maintenance treatment reduces long-term mortality. *Addiction, 103*(3), 462–468.

111 Rosenthal, R. N., Ling, W., Casadonte, P., Vocci, F., Bailey, G. L., Kampman, K., … Beebe, K. L. (2013). Buprenorphine implants for treatment of opioid dependence: Randomized comparison to placebo and sublingual buprenorphine/naloxone. *Addiction, 108*(12), 2141–2149.

112 Sullivan, L. E., Moore, B. A., Chawarski, M. C., Pantalon, M. V., Barry, D., O'Connor, P. G., … Fiellin, D. A. (2008). Buprenorphine/naloxone treatment in primary care is associated with decreased human immunodeficiency virus risk behaviors. *Journal of Substance Abuse Treatment, 35*(1), 87–92.

113 Substance Abuse and Mental Health Services Administration. (2016). Buprenorphine. Retrieved October 23, 2017, from www.samhsa.gov/medication-assisted-treatment/treatment/buprenorphine

114 Lovegrove, M. C., Mathew, J., Hampp, C., Governale, L., Wysowski, D. K., & Budnitz, D. S. (2014). Emergency hospitalizations for unsupervised prescription medication ingestions by young children. *Pediatrics, 134*(4), e1009–e1016.

115 Hakkinen, M., Launiainen, T., Vuori, E., & Ojanpera, I. (2012). Benzodiazepines and alcohol are associated with cases of fatal buprenorphine poisoning. *European Journal of Clinical Pharmacology, 68*(3), 301–309.

116 Schuman-Olivier, Z., Hoeppner, B. B., Weiss, R. D., Borodovsky, J., Shaffer, H. J., & Albanese, M. J. (2013). Benzodiazepine use during buprenorphine treatment for opioid dependence: Clinical and safety outcomes. *Drug and Alcohol Dependence, 132*(3), 580–586.

117 Fullerton, C. A., Kim, M., Thomas, C. P., Lyman, D. R., Montejano, L. B., Dougherty, R. H., ... Delphin-Rittmon, M. E. (2014). Medication-assisted treatment with methadone: Assessing the evidence. *Psychiatric Services, 65*(2), 146–157.

118 Gibson, A., Degenhardt, L., Mattick, R. P., Ali, R., White, J., & O'Brien, S. (2008). Exposure to opioid maintenance treatment reduces long-term mortality. *Addiction, 103*(3), 462–468.

119 Gowing, L. R., Farrell, M., Bornemann, R., Sullivan, L. E., & Ali, R. L. (2006). Brief report: Methadone treatment of injecting opioid users for prevention of HIV infection. *Journal of General Internal Medicine, 21*(2), 193–195.

120 Lee, J. D., Friedmann, P. D., Kinlock, T. W., Nunes, E. V., Boney, T. Y., Hoskinson, R. A., Jr., ... O'Brien, C. P. (2016). Extended-release naltrexone to prevent opioid relapse in criminal justice offenders. *New England Journal of Medicine, 374*(13), 1232–1242.

121 Merlo, L. J., Greene, W. M., & Pomm, R. (2011). Mandatory naltrexone treatment prevents relapse among opiate-dependent anesthesiologists returning to practice. *Journal of Addiction Medicine, 5*(4), 279–283.

122 Washton, A. M., Gold, M. S., & Pottash, A. C. (1984). Successful use of naltrexone in addicted physicians and business executives. *Advances in Alcohol and Substance Abuse, 4*(2), 89–96.

123 Minozzi, S., Amato, L., Vecchi, S., Davoli, M., Kirchmayer, U., & Verster, A. (2011). Oral naltrexone maintenance treatment for opioid dependence. *Cochrane Database of Systematic Reviews, 2011*(4), 1–45.

124 Cornish, J. W., Metzger, D., Woody, G. E., Wilson, D., McLellan, A. T., Vandergrift, B., & O'Brien, C. (1997). Naltrexone pharmacotherapy for opioid dependent federal probationers. *Journal of Substance Abuse Treatment, 14*(6), 529–534.

125 Minozzi, S., Amato, L., Vecchi, S., Davoli, M., Kirchmayer, U., & Verster, A. (2011). Oral naltrexone maintenance treatment for opioid dependence. *Cochrane Database of Systematic Reviews, 2011*(4), 1–45.

126 Merlo, L. J., Greene, W. M., & Pomm, R. (2011). Mandatory naltrexone treatment prevents relapse among opiate-dependent anesthesiologists returning to practice. *Journal of Addiction Medicine, 5*(4), 279–283.

127 Substance Abuse and Mental Health Services Administration. (2016). *Medication-assisted treatment of opioid use disorder pocket guide.* HHS No. (SMA) 16-4892PG. Rockville, MD: Substance Abuse and Mental Health Services Administration.

128 Faggiano, F., Vigna-Taglianti, F., Versino, E., & Lemma, P. (2003). Methadone maintenance at different dosages for opioid dependence. *Cochrane Database of Systematic Reviews, 2003*(3), 1–45.

129 Fareed, A., Casarella, J., Amar, R., Vayalapalli, S., & Drexler, K. (2010). Methadone maintenance dosing guideline for opioid dependence, a literature review. *Journal of Addictive Diseases, 29*(1), 1–14.

130 Substance Abuse and Mental Health Services Administration. (2015). *Clinical use of extended-release injectable naltrexone in the treatment of opioid use disorder: A brief guide.* HHS Publication No. (SMA) 14-4892R. Rockville, MD: Substance Abuse and Mental Health Services Administration.

131 National Library of Medicine. (2015). VIVITROL – naltrexone. Retrieved October 23, 2017, from https://dailymed.nlm.nih.gov/dailymed/drugInfo.cfm?setid=cd11c435-b0f0-4bb9-ae78-60f101f3703f

132 Fiellin, D. A., Schottenfeld, R. S., Cutter, C. J., Moore, B. A., Barry, D. T., & O'Connor, P. G. (2014). Primary care-based buprenorphine taper vs maintenance therapy for prescription opioid dependence: A randomized clinical trial. *JAMA Internal Medicine, 174*(12), 1947–1954.

133 Kakko, J., Svanborg, K. D., Kreek, M. J., & Heilig, M. (2003, February 22). 1-year retention and social function after buprenorphine-assisted relapse prevention treatment for heroin dependence in Sweden: A randomised, placebo-controlled trial. *Lancet, 361*(9358), 662–668.

134 Sees, K. L., Delucchi, K. L., Masson, C., Rosen, A., Clark, H. W., Robillard, H., ... Hall, S. M. (2000). Methadone maintenance vs 180-day psychosocially enriched detoxification for treatment of opioid dependence: A randomized controlled trial. *JAMA, 283*(10), 1303–1310.

135 Weiss, R. D., Potter, J. S., Fiellin, D. A., Byrne, M., Connery, H. S., Dickinson, W., ... Ling, W. (2011). Adjunctive counseling during brief and extended buprenorphine-naloxone treatment for prescription opioid dependence: A 2-phase randomized controlled trial. *Archives of General Psychiatry, 68*(12), 1238–1246.

136 Confidentiality of Substance Use Disorder Patient Records. ; HHS Final Rule, 82 Fed. Reg. 6052 (January 18, 2017) (to be codified at 42 CFR pt. 2). Retrieved November 13, 2017, from https://www.federalregister.gov/documents/2017/01/18/2017-00719/confidentiality-of-substance-use-disorder-patient-records

137 Jost, T. S. (2006). Appendix B: Constraints on sharing mental health and substance-use treatment information imposed by federal and state medical records privacy laws. In Institute of Medicine (US) Committee on Crossing the Quality Chasm: Adaptation to Mental Health and Addictive Disorders, *Improving the quality of healthcare for mental and substance-use conditions*. Quality Chasm Series. Washington, DC: National Academies Press. Retrieved January 3, 2018, from https://www.ncbi.nlm.nih.gov/books/NBK19829

138 Coviello, D. M., Zanis, D. A., Wesnoski, S. A., & Alterman, A. I. (2006). The effectiveness of outreach case management in re-enrolling discharged methadone patients. *Drug and Alcohol Dependence, 85*(1), 56–65.

139 Goldstein, M. F., Deren, S., Kang, S. Y., Des Jarlais, D. C., & Magura, S. (2002). Evaluation of an alternative program for MMTP drop-outs: Impact on treatment re-entry. *Drug and Alcohol Dependence, 66*(2), 181–187.

140 Duncan, B. (2010). On becoming a better therapist. *Psychotherapy in Australia, 16*(4), 42–51.

141 Wampold, B. E. (2011). Qualities and actions of effective therapists. Retrieved October 23, 2017, from www.apa.org/education/ce/effective-therapists.pdf

142 American Medical Association. (2017). End the epidemic. Retrieved October 23, 2017, from https://www.end-opioid-epidemic.org/types/ama

143 Kampman, K., & Jarvis, M. (2015). American Society of Addiction Medicine (ASAM) national practice guideline for the use of medications in the treatment of addiction involving opioid use. *Journal of Addiction Medicine, 9*(5), 358–367.

144 National Institute on Drug Abuse. (n.d.). Effective treatments for opioid addiction. Retrieved October 23, 2017, from https://www.drugabuse.gov/publications/effective-treatments-opioid-addiction/effective-treatments-opioid-addiction

145 Office of the Surgeon General. (2016). *Facing addiction in America: The Surgeon General's report on alcohol, drugs, and health*. Washington, DC: Department of Health and Human Services.

146 Center for Substance Abuse Treatment. (2005). *Medication-assisted treatment for opioid addiction in opioid treatment programs*. Treatment Improvement Protocol (TIP) Series 43. HHS Publication No. (SMA) 12-4214. Rockville, MD: Substance Abuse and Mental Health Services Administration.

147 Carter, A., & Hall, W. (2007). The ethical use of psychosocially assisted pharmacological treatments for opioid dependence. Retrieved October 23, 2017, from www.who.int/substance_abuse/activities/ethical_use_opioid_treatment.pdf

148 Equal Employment Opportunity Commission. (1992). *A technical assistance manual on the employment provisions (Title I) of the Americans with Disabilities Act*. Washington, DC: Author.

149 Friedmann, P. D., Hoskinson, R., Gordon, M., Schwartz, R., Kinlock, T., Knight, K., ... Frisman, L. K. (2012). Medication-assisted treatment in criminal justice agencies affiliated with the Criminal Justice-Drug Abuse Treatment Studies (CJ-DATS): Availability, barriers & intentions. *Substance Abuse, 33*(1), 9–18.

150 Legal Action Center. (2011). *Legality of denying access to medication assisted treatment in the criminal justice system*. Retrieved October 23, 2017, from www.lac.org/wp-content/uploads/2014/12/MAT_Report_FINAL_12-1-2011.pdf

151 World Health Organization. (2009). *Guidelines for the psychosocially assisted pharmacological treatment of opioid dependence*. Geneva, Switzerland: WHO Press.

152 Soyka, M., Träder, A., Klotsche, J., Haberthür, A., Bühringer, G., Rehm, J., & Wittchen, H. U. (2012). Criminal behavior in opioid-dependent patients before and during maintenance therapy: 6-year follow-up of a nationally representative cohort sample. *Journal of Forensic Sciences, 57*(6), 1524–1530.

153 Substance Abuse and Mental Health Services Administration. (2016). *A collaborative approach to the treatment of pregnant women with opioid use disorders*. HHS Publication No. (SMA) 16-4978. Rockville, MD: Substance Abuse and Mental Health Services Administration.

154 Donovan, D. M., Ingalsbe, M. H., Benbow, J., & Daley, D. C. (2013). 12-step interventions and mutual support programs for substance use disorders: An overview. *Social Work in Public Health, 28*(3–4), 313–332.

155 Humphreys, K., Blodgett, J. C., & Wagner, T. H. (2014). Estimating the efficacy of Alcoholics Anonymous without self-selection bias: An instrumental variables re-analysis of randomized clinical trials. *Alcoholism: Clinical and Experimental Research, 38*(11), 2688–2694.

156 McCrady, B. S., & Tonigan, S. (2014). Recent research into twelve-step programs. In R. K. Ries, D. A. Fiellin, S. C. Miller, & R. Saitz (Eds.), *The ASAM principles of addiction medicine* (pp. 1043–1059). Philadelphia, PA: Wolters Kluwer.

157 Crape, B. L., Latkin, C. A., Laris, A. S., & Knowlton, A. R. (2002). The effects of sponsorship in 12-step treatment of injection drug users. *Drug and Alcohol Dependence, 65*(3), 291–301.

158 Monico, L. B., Gryczynski, J., Mitchell, S. G., Schwartz, R. P., O'Grady, K. E., & Jaffe, J. H. (2015). Buprenorphine treatment and 12-step meeting attendance: Conflicts, compatibilities, and patient outcomes. *Journal of Substance Abuse Treatment, 57*, 89–95.

159 Gossop, M., Stewart, D., & Marsden, J. (2008). Attendance at Narcotics Anonymous and Alcoholics Anonymous meetings, frequency of attendance and substance use outcomes after residential treatment for drug dependence: A 5-year follow-up study. *Addiction, 103*(1), 119–125.

160 Parran, T. V., Adelman, C. A., Merkin, B., Pagano, M. E., Defranco, R., Ionescu, R. A., & Mace, A. G. (2010). Long-term outcomes of office-based buprenorphine/naloxone maintenance therapy. *Drug and Alcohol Dependence, 106*(1), 56–60.

161 Narcotics Anonymous World Services. (2016). *Narcotics Anonymous and persons receiving medication-assisted treatment.* Chatsworth, CA: Author.

162 Monico, L. B., Gryczynski, J., Mitchell, S. G., Schwartz, R. P., O'Grady, K. E., & Jaffe, J. H. (2015). Buprenorphine treatment and 12-step meeting attendance: Conflicts, compatibilities, and patient outcomes. *Journal of Substance Abuse Treatment, 57,* 89–95.

163 White, W., Galanter, M., Humphreys, K., & Kelly, J. (2016). The paucity of attention to Narcotics Anonymous in current public, professional, and policy responses to rising opioid addiction. *Alcoholism Treatment Quarterly, 34*(4), 437–462.

164 Kelly, J. F., Greene, M. C., & Bergman, B. G. (2014). Do drug-dependent patients attending Alcoholics Anonymous rather than Narcotics Anonymous do as well? A prospective, lagged, matching analysis. *Alcohol and Alcoholism, 49*(6), 645–653.

165 Substance Abuse and Mental Health Services Administration. (2015). *Using technology-based therapeutic tools in behavioral health services.* Treatment Improvement Protocol (TIP) Series 60. HHS Publication No. (SMA) 15-4924. Rockville, MD: Substance Abuse and Mental Health Services Administration.

166 White, W. L. (2011). *Narcotics Anonymous and the pharmacotherapeutic treatment of opioid addiction in the United States.* Chicago, IL: Great Lakes Addiction Technology Transfer Center and Philadelphia Department of Behavioral Health and Intellectual Disability Services.

167 White, W., Galanter, M., Humphreys, K., & Kelly, J. (2016). The paucity of attention to Narcotics Anonymous in current public, professional, and policy responses to rising opioid addiction. *Alcoholism Treatment Quarterly, 34*(4), 437–462.

168 Ginter, W. (2012). Methadone Anonymous and mutual support for medication-assisted recovery. *Journal of Groups in Addiction and Recovery, 7*(2–4), 189–201.

169 Ronel, N., Gueta, K., Abramsohn, Y., Caspi, N., & Adelson, M. (2011). Can a 12-step program work in methadone maintenance treatment? *International Journal of Offender Therapy and Comparative Criminology, 55*(7), 1135–1153.

170 Glickman, L., Galanter, M., Dermatis, H., Dingle, S., & Hall, L. (2004). Pathways to recovery: Adapting 12-step recovery to methadone treatment. *Journal of Maintenance in the Addictions, 2*(4), 77–90.

171 Palis, H., Marchand, K., Peng, D., Fikowski, J., Harrison, S., Spittal, P., … Oviedo-Joekes, E. (2016). Factors associated with perceived abuse in the health care system among long-term opioid users: A cross-sectional study. *Substance Use and Misuse, 51*(6), 763–776.

TIP 63

MEDICATIONS FOR OPIOID USE DISORDER

Part 5: Resources Related to Medications for Opioid Use Disorder
For Healthcare and Addiction Professionals, Policymakers, Patients, and Families

Part 5 of this Treatment Improvement Protocol (TIP) provides a collection of resources by audience and a glossary of key terms to help readers better understand how Food and Drug Administration (FDA)-approved medications can be used to treat opioid use disorder (OUD).

TIP Navigation

Executive Summary
For healthcare and addiction professionals, policymakers, patients, and families

Part 1: Introduction to Medications for Opioid Use Disorder Treatment
For healthcare and addiction professionals, policymakers, patients, and families

Part 2: Addressing Opioid Use Disorder in General Medical Settings
For healthcare professionals

Part 3: Pharmacotherapy for Opioid Use Disorder
For healthcare professionals

Part 4: Partnering Addiction Treatment Counselors With Clients and Healthcare Professionals
For healthcare and addiction professionals

Part 5: Resources Related to Medications for Opioid Use Disorder
For healthcare and addiction professionals, policymakers, patients, and families

KEY MESSAGES

- Practice guidelines and decision-making tools can help healthcare professionals with OUD screening, assessment, diagnosis, treatment planning, and referral.
- Patient- and family-oriented resources provide information about opioid addiction in general; the role of medication, behavioral and supportive services, and mutual-help groups in the treatment of OUD; how-tos for identifying recovery support services; and how-tos for locating medical and behavioral health service providers who specialize in treating OUD or other substance use disorders (SUDs).

Substance Abuse and Mental Health Services Administration
www.samhsa.gov • 1-877-SAMHSA-7 (1-877-726-4727)

PART 5: RESOURCES RELATED TO MEDICATIONS FOR OPIOID USE DISORDER

General Resources 5-1

Resources for Counselors and Peer Providers 5-10

Resources for Clients and Families 5-11

Provider Tools and Sample Forms 5-17

Glossary of TIP Terminology 5-57

Notes 5-60

PART 5 of 5
Resources Related to Medications for Opioid Use Disorder

There are numerous resources to help healthcare professionals and behavioral health service providers better understand the use of FDA-approved medications for OUD. Many other resources are available to help patients, their families and friends, and the general public better understand OUD and the medications available to treat it and support recovery from it. Part 5 of this TIP provides an audience-segmented collection of resources and a glossary of key terms related to OUD. It is of use to all interested readers.

General Resources

Facts and Figures

American Association for the Treatment of Opioid Dependence (AATOD), Frequently Asked Questions (www.aatod.org/resources/frequently-asked-questions).

Centers for Disease Control and Prevention (CDC), Smoking & Tobacco Use (www.cdc.gov/tobacco/index.htm).

Legal Action Center (LAC), Medication-Assisted Treatment for Opioid Addiction: Myths and Facts (http://lac.org/wp-content/uploads/2016/02/Myth-Fact-for-MAT.pdf).

Missouri Department of Mental Health, Methadone Maintenance Myths and Resources (https://dmh.mo.gov/docs/ada/methadonemyths.pdf).

National Institute on Drug Abuse (NIDA) (www.drugabuse.gov):

- Addiction Science (www.drugabuse.gov/related-topics/addiction-science). Provides two short videos that explain the nature of addiction. These are useful in educating people in primary care who suffer from addiction. This site has links to publications for professionals that explain the nature of addiction.

- NIDAMED, Medical and Health Professionals (www.drugabuse.gov/nidamed-medical-health-professionals). Disseminates science-based resources to healthcare professionals on the causes and consequences of drug use and addiction and advances in pain management.

> Opioid overdose caused **42,249 DEATHS** nationwide in 2016—this exceeded the # caused by motor vehicle crashes.[1,2]

Office of National Drug Control Policy, Medication-Assisted Treatment for Opioid Addiction (https://online.ndbh.com/docs/providers/SubstanceUseCenter/Medication-Assisted-Treatment-Edited.pdf): Offers a factsheet with a useful summary of pharmacotherapy for OUD and its effectiveness.

Partnership for Drug-Free Kids, Commentary: Countering the Myths About Methadone (www.drugfree.org/news-service/commentary-countering-the-myths-about-methadone).

Substance Abuse and Mental Health Services Administration (SAMHSA):

- Addiction Technology Transfer Center **(ATTC)** (http://attcnetwork.org/home). Network with 10 regional centers across the country that provide training and information on evidence-based practices to practitioners. The ATTC website's section on OUD medication has many resources for clinicians, patients, and family members (www.attcnetwork.org/explore/priorityareas/wfd/mat/mat.pubs.asp).
- State Opioid Treatment Authorities (SOTAs) (https://dpt2.samhsa.gov/regulations/smalist.aspx).

United States Surgeon General's Report, *Facing Addiction in America: The Surgeon General's Report on Alcohol, Drugs, and Health* (https://addiction.surgeongeneral.gov).

Groups and Organizations

AATOD (www.aatod.org): Works with federal and state agencies on opioid treatment policy throughout the United States. Convenes conferences every 18 months on evidence-based clinical practice, current research, and organizational developments related to OUD treatment. AATOD develops publications that serve as resources for addiction counselors and peer support providers.

American Academy of Addiction Psychiatry (AAAP) (www.aaap.org): Offers education and training materials on addiction psychiatry (e.g., webinars, continuing medical education courses).

American Society of Addiction Medicine (ASAM) (www.asam.org): Provides medical education and resources on the treatment of SUDs, including OUD.

LAC (https://lac.org): Offers information about the rights of people with criminal records, HIV/AIDS, and SUDs.

Medical Assisted Treatment of America (www.medicalassistedtreatment.org): Raises awareness and understanding of substance misuse, the problems it creates, and ways to address these problems.

National Alliance for Medication Assisted Recovery (NAMA Recovery) (www.methadone.org): Supports quality opioid agonist treatment through its many U.S. chapters and its international network of affiliate chapters. Thousands of methadone clients and healthcare professionals belong to the organization.

National Alliance of Advocates for Buprenorphine Treatment (www.naabt.org): Aims to educate the public about opioid addiction and buprenorphine as a treatment option, to reduce prejudice and discrimination against clients who have SUDs, and to connect clients in need to qualified treatment providers.

SAMHSA (www.samhsa.gov):

- Buprenorphine Practitioner Verification for Pharmacists (www.samhsa.gov/bupe/lookup-form)
- National Recovery Month (https://recoverymonth.gov)
- Opioid Treatment Program (OTP) Directory (https://dpt2.samhsa.gov/treatment)
- SOTAs (https://dpt2.samhsa.gov/regulations/smalist.aspx)

SAMHSA Publications

All publications listed in this section are available for free from SAMHSA's publications ordering webpage (https://store.samhsa.gov) or by calling 1-877-SAMHSA-7 (1-877-726-4727):

- TIP 42: *Substance Abuse Treatment for Persons With Co-Occurring Disorders* (https://store.samhsa.gov/product/TIP-42-Substance-Abuse-Treatment-for-Persons-With-Co-Occurring-Disorders/SMA13-3992)
- TIP 54: *Managing Chronic Pain in Adults With or in Recovery From Substance Use Disorders* (https://store.samhsa.gov/product/TIP-54-Managing-Chronic-Pain-in-Adults-With-or-in-Recovery-From-Substance-Use-Disorders/SMA13-4671)
- TIP 57: *Trauma-Informed Care in Behavioral Health Services* (https://store.samhsa.gov/product/TIP-57-Trauma-Informed-Care-in-Behavioral-Health-Services/SMA14-4816)
- TIP 62: *Relapse Prevention and Recovery Promotion in Behavioral Health Services* (Once published, this TIP will be available on SAMHSA's publications ordering webpage, https://store.samhsa.gov)
- *Advisory:* An Introduction to Extended-Release Injectable Naltrexone for the Treatment of People With Opioid Dependence (https://store.samhsa.gov/product/An-Introduction-to-Extended-Release-Injectable-Naltrexone-for-the-Treatment-of-People-with-Opioid-Dependence/SMA12-4682)
- *Advisory:* Sublingual and Transmucosal Buprenorphine for Opioid Use Disorder: Review and Update (https://store.samhsa.gov/product/Advisory-Sublingual-and-Transmucosal-Buprenorphine-for-Opioid-Use-Disorder-Review-and-Update/SMA16-4938)
- *Clinical Guidance for Treating Pregnant and Parenting Women With Opioid Use Disorder and Their Infants* (https://store.samhsa.gov/product/Clinical-Guidance-for-Treating-Pregnant-and-Parenting-Women-With-Opioid-Use-Disorder-and-Their-Infants/All-New-Products/SMA18-5054)
- *Clinical Use of Extended-Release Injectable Naltrexone in the Treatment of Opioid Use Disorders: A Brief Guide* (https://store.samhsa.gov/shin/content//SMA14-4892/SMA14-4892.pdf)
- *A Collaborative Approach to the Treatment of Pregnant Women With Opioid Use Disorders* (https://store.samhsa.gov/product/A-Collaborative-Approach-to-the-Treatment-of-Pregnant-Women-with-Opioid-Use-Disorders/SMA16-4978)
- *Decisions in Recovery: Treatment for Opioid Use Disorders, Handbook* (https://store.samhsa.gov/product/SMA16-4993)
- Integrated Treatment for Co-Occurring Disorders Evidence-Based Practices (EBP) Kit (https://store.samhsa.gov/product/Integrated-Treatment-for-Co-Occurring-Disorders-Evidence-Based-Practices-EBP-KIT/SMA08-4367)
- Technical Assistance Publication 32: *Clinical Drug Testing in Primary Care* (https://store.samhsa.gov/shin/content//SMA12-4668/SMA12-4668.pdf)
- *What Are Peer Recovery Support Services?* (https://store.samhsa.gov/shin/content/SMA09-4454/SMA09-4454.pdf)

General Information

Agency for Healthcare Research and Quality:

- *Medication-Assisted Treatment Models of Care for Opioid Use Disorder in Primary Care Settings* (www.ncbi.nlm.nih.gov/books/NBK402352)
- Academy for Integrating Behavioral Health and Primary Care (https://integrationacademy.ahrq.gov)

American Academy of Family Physicians:

- Chronic Pain Management and Opioid Misuse: A Public Health Concern (Position Paper) (www.aafp.org/about/policies/all/pain-management-opioid.html)
- Pain Management and Opioid Use Resources (www.aafp.org/patient-care/public-health/pain-opioids/resources.html)

ATTC Network (http://attcnetwork.org/home): This nationwide network of SAMHSA-sponsored regional centers is a multidisciplinary resource for professionals in the addiction treatment and recovery services fields. The network has many valuable resources and projects of interest to people involved in treating SUDs. Of particular interest to readers of this TIP are the training programs produced as part of the NIDA/SAMHSA-ATTC Blending Initiative:

- Buprenorphine Treatment: Training for Multidisciplinary Addiction Professionals (www.attcnetwork.org/projects/buptx.aspx)
- Buprenorphine Treatment for Young Adults (www.attcnetwork.org/projects/bupyoung.aspx)
- Prescription Opioid Addiction Treatment Study (POATS) (www.attcnetwork.org/projects/poats.aspx)

BupPractice.com Federal Recordkeeping Requirements for Buprenorphine Treatment (www.buppractice.com/node/12246): Provides information about federal recordkeeping requirements.

CDC Smoking & Tobacco Use (www.cdc.gov/tobacco/index.htm): Includes resource links for clinicians on smoking and the treatment of tobacco use.

Centers for Medicare & Medicaid Services (www.cms.gov/Medicare/Medicare-General-Information/Telehealth/index.html): Gives guidance on the delivery of telehealth.

Department of Health and Human Services (HHS):

- Centers for Medicare & Medicaid Services Clinical Laboratory Improvement Amendments Application for Certification (www.cms.gov/Medicare/CMS-Forms/CMS-Forms/downloads/cms116.pdf)
- Medication Assisted Treatment for Opioid Use Disorders: Final Rule (www.federalregister.gov/documents/2016/07/08/2016-16120/medication-assisted-treatment-for-opioid-use-disorders)

Drug Enforcement Administration (DEA):

- DEA Requirements for DATA Waived Physicians (www.deadiversion.usdoj.gov/pubs/docs/dwp_buprenorphine.htm). Lists DEA requirements for Drug Addiction Treatment Act of 2000 (DATA 2000)-waivered healthcare professionals.
- Form DEA-106, Report of Theft or Loss of Controlled Substances (https://apps.deadiversion.usdoj.gov/webforms/dtlLogin.jsp). Provides instructions for completing form DEA-106, which must be filed when stored buprenorphine is lost or stolen.
- *Practitioner's Manual* (www.deadiversion.usdoj.gov/pubs/manuals/pract). Provides guidance on how to comply with federal requirements on recordkeeping for ordering, storing, and dispensing buprenorphine in the office. This manual is from the DEA's Office of Diversion Control.

Drugs.com:
- Buprenorphine Drug Interactions (www.drugs.com/drug-interactions/buprenorphine-index.html?filter=3&generic_only=)
- Drug Interactions Checker (www.drugs.com/drug_interactions.php)

FDA:
- Approved Risk Evaluation and Mitigation Strategy (REMS): Buprenorphine Transmucosal Products for Opioid Dependence (www.accessdata.fda.gov/scripts/cder/rems/index.cfm?event=RemsDetails.page&REMS=9)
- REMS: Probuphine (buprenorphine hydrochloride) (www.accessdata.fda.gov/scripts/cder/rems/index.cfm?event=IndvRemsDetails.page&REMS=356)
- REMS: Sublocade (extended-release injectable buprenorphine) (www.accessdata.fda.gov/scripts/cder/rems/index.cfm?event=IndvRemsDetails.page&REMS=376)
- REMS: Suboxone/Subutex (buprenorphine and naloxone/buprenorphine) (www.accessdata.fda.gov/scripts/cder/rems/index.cfm?event=IndvRemsDetails.page&REMS=352)
- REMS: Vivitrol (extended-release naltrexone [XR-NTX]) (www.vivitrolrems.com)

LAC (https://lac.org): LAC attorneys provide legal advice by phone to service providers and government agencies. They assist dozens of agencies annually with questions about confidentiality of treatment records, discrimination, and other issues. LAC's confidentiality hotline provides information about the federal law protecting the confidentiality of drug and alcohol treatment and prevention records (42 CFR Part 2). The hotline is free to New York treatment providers and government agencies. Outside New York, the hotline is accessible if the state alcohol/drug oversight agency subscribes to LAC's Actionline service. To speak with a hotline attorney, call LAC Monday through Friday 1–5 p.m. (Eastern Time Zone) at 1-212-243-1313, or toll-free at 1-800-223-4044.

National Alliance of Advocates for Buprenorphine Treatment 30–100 Patient Limit (www.naabt.org/30_patient_limit.cfm): Summarizes the DATA 2000 law.

National Association of State Controlled Substances Authorities State Profiles (www.nascsa.org/stateprofiles.htm): Contains a directory of each state's prescription drug monitoring program (PDMP).

National Conference of State Legislatures Drug Overdose Immunity and Good Samaritan Laws (www.ncsl.org/research/civil-and-criminal-justice/drug-overdose-immunity-good-samaritan-laws.aspx): Provides information about naloxone and Good Samaritan immunity.

National Institute on Alcohol Abuse and Alcoholism (NIAAA) Professional Education Materials (www.niaaa.nih.gov/publications/clinical-guides-and-manuals): Provides professional education materials; offers links to screening, treatment planning, and general information for clinicians in outpatient programs.

National Library of Medicine's DailyMed:
- FDA label information for methadone (https://dailymed.nlm.nih.gov/dailymed/search.cfm?labeltype=all&query=METHADONE)
- FDA label information for naltrexone (https://dailymed.nlm.nih.gov/dailymed/drugInfo.cfm?setid=cd11c435-b0f0-4bb9-ae78-60f101f3703f)

NIDA:
- Available Treatments for Marijuana Use Disorders (www.drugabuse.gov/publications/research-reports/marijuana/available-treatments-marijuana-use-disorders). Provides information about treatment options for individuals with marijuana use disorder.
- Opioid Overdose Reversal With Naloxone (Narcan, Evzio) (www.drugabuse.gov/related-topics/opioid-overdose-reversal-naloxone-narcan-evzio). Contains naloxone information for providers.

- NIDAMED, Medical and Health Professionals (www.drugabuse.gov/nidamed-medical-health-professionals). Provides practice-related and professional education-related resources.
- Medications To Treat Opioid Addiction (www.drugabuse.gov/publications/research-reports/medications-to-treat-opioid-addiction/overview). Provides an overview of the need for and efficacy of OUD medications and discusses common misconceptions, impacts on outcome, and use of OUD medications with certain specific populations.
- *Effective Treatments for Opioid Addiction* (https://www.drugabuse.gov/publications/effective-treatments-opioid-addiction/effective-treatments-opioid-addiction).
- Therapeutic Communities (www.drugabuse.gov/publications/research-reports/therapeutic-communities/what-are-therapeutic-communities). Gives a brief overview of OUD medications and links to additional information.
- *Principles of Drug Addiction Treatment: A Research-Based Guide* (www.drugabuse.gov/publications/principles-drug-addiction-treatment-research-based-guide-third-edition/preface). Discusses how OUD affects the brain and covers the state of addiction treatment in the United States, principles of effective treatment, frequently asked questions about OUD medication, evidence-based approaches to treatment, and additional resources.
- *Principles of Adolescent Substance Use Disorder Treatment: A Research-Based Guide* (www.drugabuse.gov/publications/principles-adolescent-substance-use-disorder-treatment-research-based-guide/introduction). Discusses principles of SUDs in adolescents, addresses frequently asked questions, summarizes treatment settings and evidence-based treatment approaches, and provides treatment referral resources.
- *Treating Opioid Use Disorder During Pregnancy* (www.drugabuse.gov/publications/treating-opioid-use-disorder-during-pregnancy/treating-opioid-use-disorder-during-pregnancy). Addresses the risks of OUD to the pregnant woman and the fetus, briefly summarizes OUD pharmacotherapies for use during pregnancy, and provides links to additional information.

North American Syringe Exchange Program (https://nasen.org/directory): Provides a national directory of syringe exchange programs in the United States.

Prescription Drug Abuse Policy System's Naloxone Overdose Prevention Laws (http://pdaps.org/datasets/laws-regulating-administration-of-naloxone-1501695139): Provides a map with a link to each state's naloxone overdose prevention laws, including policies on prescribing, dispensing, and civil and criminal immunity.

Project Lazarus's Naloxone: The Overdose Antidote (www.projectlazarus.org/naloxone): Provides guidance on administering naloxone.

Providers' Clinical Support System's (PCSS's) How To Prepare for a Visit From the Drug Enforcement Agency Regarding Buprenorphine Prescribing (http://pcssmat.org/wp-content/uploads/2014/02/FINAL-How-to-Prepare-for-a-DEA-Inspection.pdf): Provides a description of the DEA inspection process and how to comply with its requirements.

SAMHSA:

- Dear Colleague Letters for Medication-Assisted Treatment Providers (www.samhsa.gov/medication-assisted-treatment/legislation-regulations-guidelines/dear-colleague-letters). Offers regular communications to the opioid treatment community regarding clinical and regulatory issues related to opioid treatment. Regulations, policies, and best practices for OTPs and office-based opioid treatment (OBOT) clinics can change, and Dear Colleague Letters help providers stay up to date.

- Understanding the Final Rule for a Patient Limit of 275 (www.samhsa.gov/sites/default/files/programs_campaigns/medication_assisted/understanding-patient-limit275.pdf). Provides information about the final rule and how to use it to increase patient access to medication for OUD and associated reporting requirements.
- Buprenorphine Waiver Management (www.samhsa.gov/medication-assisted-treatment/buprenorphine-waiver-management). Provides information on the buprenorphine waiver, including links to the buprenorphine waiver application and an explanation of the processes, requirements, and recordkeeping strategies associated with prescribing buprenorphine.
- Qualify for Nurse Practitioners (NPs) and Physician Assistants (PAs) Waiver (www.samhsa.gov/medication-assisted-treatment/qualify-nps-pas-waivers). Provides information for NPs and PAs about the buprenorphine waiver training, with links to trainings and the application process.
- Buprenorphine Training for Physicians (www.samhsa.gov/medication-assisted-treatment/training-resources/buprenorphine-physician-training). Offers links to organizations that provide buprenorphine training for physicians.
- *SAMHSA Opioid Overdose Prevention Toolkit* (https://store.samhsa.gov/product/SAMHSA-Opioid-Overdose-Prevention-Toolkit/SMA16-4742). Prepares healthcare professionals, communities, and local governments with material to develop practices and policies to help prevent opioid-related overdoses and deaths. It addresses issues for healthcare professionals, first responders, treatment providers, and those recovering from opioid overdose.
- *Federal Guidelines for Opioid Treatment Programs* (https://store.samhsa.gov/product/Federal-Guidelines-for-Opioid-Treatment-Programs/PEP15-FEDGUIDEOTP). Provides updated guidelines for how OTPs can satisfy the federal regulations.
- Form SMA-168 Opioid Treatment Exception Request (www.samhsa.gov/medication-assisted-treatment/opioid-treatment-programs/submit-exception-request). Provides instructions for physicians on how to request exceptions to federal standards for opioid treatment.
- Laws and Regulations (www.samhsa.gov/about-us/who-we-are/laws-regulations). Provides an overview and summary of the most frequent questions about disclosure and patient records pertaining to substance use treatment that federal programs maintain.
- *Substance Abuse in Brief Fact Sheet:* Introduction to Mutual-Support Groups for Alcohol and Drug Abuse (https://store.samhsa.gov/shin/content/SMA08-4336/SMA08-4336.pdf). Provides information to help medical and behavioral health service providers understand mutual-help groups and how to make referrals to such groups.
- SAMHSA has developed several resources to guide healthcare professionals in their use of telehealth and telemedicine approaches for OUD:
  - *In Brief:* Rural Behavioral Health: Telehealth Challenges and Opportunities (https://store.samhsa.gov/shin/content/SMA16-4989/SMA16-4989.pdf)
  - Certified Community Behavioral Health Clinics (CCBHCs) Using Telehealth or Telemedicine (www.samhsa.gov/section-223/care-coordination/telehealth-telemedicine)

Practice Guidelines and Decision-Support Tools

ASAM:

- *Appropriate Use of Drug Testing in Clinical Addiction Medicine* (http://download.lww.com/wolterskluwer_vitalstream_com/PermaLink/JAM/A/JAM_11_3_2017_06_02_SAFARIAN_JAM-D-17-00020_SDC1.pdf). Details the ASAM consensus statement on drug testing in addiction treatment.
- The ASAM Criteria (www.asam.org/quality-practice/guidelines-and-consensus-documents/the-asam-criteria). Provides criteria and a comprehensive set of guidelines for placement, continued stay, and transfer/discharge of patients with addiction and co-occurring conditions.
- *The ASAM National Practice Guidelines: For the Use of Medication in the Treatment of Addiction Involving Opioid Use* (www.asam.org/docs/default-source/practice-support/guidelines-and-consensus-docs/asam-national-practice-guideline-supplement.pdf). Provides information on prescribing methadone, buprenorphine, naltrexone, and naloxone. The document also discusses the needs of special populations, including women during pregnancy, patients with chronic pain, adolescents, individuals in the criminal justice system, and patients with co-occurring psychiatric conditions.

CDC:

- CDC Guideline for Prescribing Opioids for Chronic Pain (www.cdc.gov/drugoverdose/prescribing/guideline.html).
- Guideline Resources: Clinical Tools (www.cdc.gov/drugoverdose/prescribing/clinical-tools.html). Provides links and tools to help clinicians prevent opioid overdose deaths.

Credible Meds (www.crediblemeds.org): Maintains a list of medications that may increase QTc intervals. Free registration is required to access the most up-to-date list.

HHS:

- BeTobaccoFree.gov News and Resources (https://betobaccofree.hhs.gov/quit-now/index.html#professionals). Offers links for clinicians that provide guidance on the care for patients with nicotine addiction. The Resources section is at the bottom of the page linked here.
- BeTobaccoFree.gov Nicotine Addiction and Your Health (https://betobaccofree.hhs.gov/health-effects/nicotine-health). Provides information on nicotine addiction and its health effects.

Institute for Research, Evaluation, and Training in Addictions' Management of Benzodiazepines in Medication-Assisted Treatment (http://ireta.org/wp-content/uploads/2014/12/BP_Guidelines_for_Benzodiazepines.pdf): Provides information on managing benzodiazepine use in patients taking medications for OUD.

PCSS for Medication Assisted Treatment (https://pcssmat.org): Provides buprenorphine waiver training for clinicians (physicians, NPs, and PAs).

PCSS Mentoring Program (https://pcssmat.org/mentoring): Gives providers guidance on prescribing OUD medications. This national network of experienced providers is available at no cost. Mentors provide support by telephone, email, or in person if possible.

PCSS Models of Buprenorphine Induction (http://pcssmat.org/wp-content/uploads/2015/02/Buprenorphine-Induction-Online-Module.pdf): Provides information about various buprenorphine induction approaches including in-office, non-OTP, and at-home dosing.

Prescribe To Prevent (http://prescribetoprevent.org): Provides information about naloxone prescribing for overdose prevention, including educational patient handouts and videos.

SAMHSA:

- *MATx Mobile App To Support Medication-Assisted Treatment of Opioid Use Disorder* (https://store.samhsa.gov/apps/mat). Provides information on FDA-approved treatment approaches and medications used to treat OUD. It includes a buprenorphine prescribing guide with information on the DATA 2000 waiver process and patient limits. Clinical support tools (e.g., treatment guidelines; *International Classification of Diseases,* 10th Edition, coding; guidance on working with special populations), help lines, and SAMHSA's treatment locators are also included.
- *Pocket Guide: Medication-Assisted Treatment of Opioid Use Disorder* (https://store.samhsa.gov/shin/content/SMA16-4892PG/SMA16-4892PG.pdf).
- Buprenorphine (www.samhsa.gov/medication-assisted-treatment/treatment/buprenorphine).
- Naltrexone (www.samhsa.gov/medication-assisted-treatment/treatment/naltrexone).
- Decisions in Recovery: Treatment for Opioid Use Disorder (https://media.samhsa.gov/MAT-Decisions-in-Recovery). Provides information on shared decision making in pharmacotherapy for OUD.
- Decisions in Recovery: Treatment for Opioid Use Disorder, Planning for Success (https://media.samhsa.gov/MAT-Decisions-in-Recovery/section/how/planning_for_success.aspx). Provides assistance in developing a recovery plan.
- Bringing Recovery Supports to Scale Technical Assistance Center Strategy (www.samhsa.gov/brss-tacs) and Shared Decision-Making Tools (www.samhsa.gov/brss-tacs/recovery-support-tools/shared-decision-making). Offers training and technical assistance on many topics related to medication for OUD, including recovery-oriented systems of care, mutual-support groups, capacity building, leadership by people in recovery and family members, certification requirements for peer specialists and mutual-support group coaches, and core competencies for recovery-oriented behavioral health workers.
- *Pharmacologic Guidelines for Treating Individuals With Post-Traumatic Stress Disorder and Co-Occurring Opioid Use Disorders* (https://store.samhsa.gov/shin/content/SMA12-4688/SMA12-4688.pdf).
- *General Principles for the Use of Pharmacological Agents To Treat Individuals With Co-Occurring Mental and Substance Use Disorders* (https://store.samhsa.gov/shin/content/SMA12-4689/SMA12-4689.pdf).

Veterans Administration (VA)/Department of Defense (DoD) *Clinical Practice Guideline for the Management of Substance Use Disorders* (www.healthquality.va.gov/guidelines/MH/sud/VADoDSUDCPGRevised22216.pdf): Provides information on screening, assessment, and treatment of OUD as well as other SUDs. It is primarily for VA and DoD healthcare providers and others involved in the care of service members or veterans with an SUD.

Assessment Scales and Screening Tools

AAAP, Education & Training (www.aaap.org/education-training/cme-opportunities): Provides Performance-in-Practice Clinical Modules for alcohol use disorder and tobacco use disorder.

American Psychiatric Nurses Association, Tobacco & Nicotine Use Screening Tools & Assessments (www.apna.org/i4a/pages/index.cfm?pageID=6150): Provides the Fagerström screening tools for nicotine dependence and smokeless tobacco and a screening checklist for adolescent tobacco use.

ASAM *Appropriate Use of Drug Testing in Clinical Addiction Medicine* (www.asam.org/quality-practice/guidelines-and-consensus-documents/drug-testing): Gives information on the appropriate use of drug testing in identifying, diagnosing, and treating people with or at risk for SUDs.

Clinical Institute Narcotic Assessment Scale for Withdrawal Symptoms (www.ncpoep.org/wp-content/uploads/2015/02/Appendix_7_Clinical_Institute_Narcotic_Assessment_CINA_Scale_for_Withdrawal_Symptoms.pdf).

NIDA, Screening, Assessment, and Drug Testing Resources (www.drugabuse.gov/nidamed-medical-health-professionals/tool-resources-your-practice/additional-screening-resources): Gives resources such as an evidence-based screening tool chart for adolescents and adults and drug use screening tool supports; also has a clinician resource and quick reference guide for drug screening in general medical settings.

World Health Organization *Guidelines for the Psychosocially Assisted Pharmacological Treatment of Opioid Dependence* (www.ncbi.nlm.nih.gov/books/NBK143183): Includes links to the Clinical Opiate Withdrawal Scale (www.drugabuse.gov/sites/default/files/files/ClinicalOpiateWithdrawalScale.pdf) and other opioid withdrawal scales from Annex 10 of the guidelines.

Resources for Counselors and Peer Providers

Organizations

Community Care Behavioral Health Organization (www.ccbh.com): A provider network focused on recovery that has published *Supporting Recovery From Opioid Addiction: Community Care Best Practice Guidelines for Recovery-Oriented Methadone Maintenance* (www.ccbh.com/pdfs/providers/healthchoices/bestpractice/MethadoneBestPracticeGuideline.pdf), a set of recovery-oriented practice implementation guidelines for methadone programs.

Faces & Voices of Recovery (https://facesandvoicesofrecovery.org): Dedicated to organizing and mobilizing the millions of Americans in recovery from addiction to alcohol and drugs, their families and friends, and other allies into recovery community organizations and networks. Faces & Voices of Recovery promotes the right resources to recover through advocacy, education, and demonstration of the power and proof of long-term recovery.

International Association of Peer Supporters (https://inaops.org): An organization for mental health and addiction peer recovery support specialists, recovery coaches, recovery educators and trainers, administrators of consumer-operated or peer-run organizations, and others.

Medication-Assisted Recovery Services (MARS) Project (www.marsproject.org): A peer-initiated, peer-based recovery support project sponsored by NAMA Recovery that offers, among other resources, an educational video about the MARS peer support program and an online network for MARS peer support personnel:

- MARS Project Video (www.marsproject.org).
- New York State Peer Recovery Network, Peers Organizing for Results Through Advocacy and Leadership (PORTAL) (http://advocacy.marsproject.org). Created to help peers in recovery more effectively organize their communities, communicate with each other, and create a stronger voice for advocacy efforts.

Pillars of Peer Support Services (www.pillarsofpeersupport.org): Develops and fosters the use of Medicaid funding to support peer recovery services in state mental health systems of care.

Recovery Community Services Program—Statewide Network (www.samhsa.gov/grants/grant-announcements/ti-14-001): A SAMHSA grant program for peer-to-peer recovery support services that help people initiate and sustain recovery from SUDs.

Publications and Other Resources

ATTC's Recovery-Oriented Methadone Maintenance (www.attcnetwork.org/userfiles/file/GreatLakes/5th%20Monograph_RM_Methadone.pdf): This guide is the most thorough document on this topic currently available and is applicable to clients receiving other medications for OUD.

Community Care Behavioral Health Organization: These publications outline phase-specific tasks and accompanying strategies for programs that serve clients who take methadone or buprenorphine:

- *Supporting Recovery From Opioid Addiction: Community Care Best Practice Guidelines for Recovery-Oriented Methadone Maintenance* (www.williamwhitepapers.com/pr/Recovery-oriented%20Methadone%20Maintenance%20Best%20Practice%20Guidelines%202014%20-%20CCBHO.pdf)
- *Supporting Recovery From Opioid Addiction: Community Care Best Practice Guidelines for Buprenorphine and Suboxone* (www.ccbh.com/pdfs/providers/healthchoices/bestpractice/Community_Care_BP_Guidelines_for_Buprenorphine_and_Suboxone.pdf)

Narcotics Anonymous (NA) (www.na.org): The organization's most recent statement on medications for treating OUD—*Narcotics Anonymous and Persons Receiving Medication-Assisted Treatment*—is available online (www.na.org/admin/include/spaw2/uploads/pdf/pr/2306_NA_PRMAT_1021.pdf).

SAMHSA (https://store.samhsa.gov): This agency oversees medications to treat opioid addiction, including methadone, buprenorphine, and naltrexone; sets regulations; guides policy; and offers information and resources for the field. SAMHSA has many recovery-oriented publications for providers:

- *Dear Colleague Letters for Medication-Assisted Treatment Providers* (www.samhsa.gov/medication-assisted-treatment/legislation-regulations-guidelines/dear-colleague-letters). Regulations, policies, and best practices for OTPs can change; these regular communications help providers stay up to date on clinical and regulatory issues related to opioid treatment.
- *Medication-Assisted Recovery: Medication Assisted Peer Recovery Support Services Meeting Report* (www.samhsa.gov/sites/default/files/programs_campaigns/medication_assisted/dear_colleague_letters/2015-prss-summary-report.pdf).
- *Financing Recovery Support Services: Review and Analysis of Funding Recovery Support Services and Policy Recommendations* (www.samhsa.gov/sites/default/files/partnersforrecovery/docs/RSS_financing_report.pdf).
- SAMHSA's *Working Definition of Recovery* (https://store.samhsa.gov/shin/content/PEP12-RECDEF/PEP12-RECDEF.pdf).
- *Access to Recovery Approaches to Recovery-Oriented Systems of Care* (https://store.samhsa.gov/product/Access-to-Recovery-ATR-Approaches-to-Recovery-Oriented-Systems-of-Care/SMA09-4440).
- *Building Bridges—Co-Occurring Mental Illness and Addiction: Consumers and Service Providers, Policymakers, and Researchers in Dialogue* (https://store.samhsa.gov/shin/content//SMA04-3892/SMA04-3892.pdf).

Selected Papers of William L. White (www.williamwhitepapers.com): Contains papers, monographs, and presentations on recovery, including recovery-oriented methadone maintenance, methadone and anti-medication bias, discrimination and methadone, NA and the pharmacotherapeutic treatment of OUD, and co-participation in 12-Step mutual-support groups and methadone maintenance.

Resources for Clients and Families

Organizations

AAOTD (www.aatod.org): Offers a variety of resources, news releases about medication for the treatment of OUD, and information about its national conferences.

Al-Anon Family Groups (www.al-anon.org): Describes group meetings where friends and family members of people with substance use issues share their experiences and learn how to apply the principles of the Al-Anon program to their individual situations. Sponsorship gives members the chance to get personal support from more experienced individuals in the program.

Alcoholics Anonymous (AA) (www.aa.org): Offers group meetings for people who have problems relating to drinking and wish to stop. AA sponsors provide members with more personal support from experienced individuals. Many people who are taking medication to treat OUD find AA increasingly receptive to their decisions about medication, and AA meetings are more widely available to these individuals.

ASAM: Provides patient and family education tools about addiction in general and OUD specifically:

- Patient Resources (www.asam.org/resources/patientresources)
- *Opioid Addiction Treatment: A Guide for Patients, Families, and Friends* (http://eguideline.guidelinecentral.com/i/706017-asam-opioid-patient-piece/0?)

Double Trouble in Recovery (www.hazelden.org/HAZ_MEDIA/3818_doubletroubleinrecovery.pdf): Describes a fellowship of people who support each other in recovering from substance use and mental disorders.

Dual Recovery Anonymous (www.draonline.org): Presents information on mutual-help organization that follows 12-Step principles in supporting people recovering from addiction and emotional or mental illness. Focuses on preventing relapse and actively improving members' quality of life through a community of mutual support.

Faces & Voices of Recovery (https://facesandvoicesofrecovery.org): Offers recovery stories, news, events information, publications, and webinars.

Heroin Anonymous (http://heroinanonymous.org): Describes a nonprofit fellowship of individuals in recovery from heroin addiction committed to helping each other stay sober. This organization holds local support meetings, a directory of which can be found on its website.

LAC (https://lac.org): Offers information about the rights of people with criminal records, HIV/AIDS, and SUDs.

Learn to Cope (www.learn2cope.org): Describes a secular mutual-help group that offers education, resources, and peer support for the families of people with SUDs (although the focus is primarily on OUD). The organization maintains an online forum, but groups are only available in a few states.

NA (www.na.org): Provides a global, community-based organization with a multilingual, multicultural membership that supports addiction recovery via a 12-Step program, including regular group meeting attendance. Members hold nearly 67,000 meetings weekly in 139 countries. NA is an ongoing support network for maintaining a drug-free lifestyle. NA doesn't focus on a particular addictive substance.

NAMA Recovery (www.methadone.org): Offers an education series, provides training and certification for Certified MAT Advocates, and has local chapters and international affiliates that act to advocate for methadone patients. It has a helpful webpage titled FAQs About Advocate Training and Certification (www.methadone.org/certification/faq.html).

Nar-Anon Family Groups (www.nar-anon.org): Provides group meetings where friends and family of people with drug use problems can share their experiences and learn to apply the 12-Step Nar-Anon program to their lives. Nar-Anon groups also offer more individualized support from experienced individuals in the program who act as sponsors.

National Alliance on Mental Illness (NAMI) (www.nami.org): Describes the largest grassroots educational, peer support, and mental health advocacy organization in the United States. Founded in 1979 by a group of family members of people with mental disorders, NAMI has developed into an association of hundreds of local affiliates, state organizations, and volunteers.

Parents of Addicted Loved Ones (https://palgroup.org): Presents a secular support group for parents who have a child with an SUD. The organization has meetings in only some states but also hosts telephone meetings.

Pills Anonymous (www.pillsanonymous.org): Offers a 12-Step mutual-support group that holds regular meetings in which individuals in recovery from addiction to pills share their experiences, build their strengths, and offer hope for recovery to one another.

Secular Organizations for Sobriety (www.sossobriety.org): Describes a nonprofit, nonreligious network of autonomous, nonprofessional local groups that support people in achieving and maintaining abstinence from alcohol and drug addiction.

Self-Management for Addiction Recovery (SMART Recovery) (www.smartrecovery.org): Is a self-empowering addiction recovery support group; participants learn science-based tools for addiction recovery and have access to an international recovery community of mutual-help groups.

Stop Stigma Now (www.stopstigmanow.org): Describes an advocacy organization that works to eradicate prejudice associated with taking medication to treat OUD and offers resources and a media library.

Women for Sobriety (https://womenforsobriety.org/beta2): Offers an abstinence-based mutual-help group that helps women find their individual paths to recovery by acknowledging the unique needs women have in recovery. This organization is not affiliated with any other recovery organization. It offers recovery tools to help women in recovery develop coping skills focused on emotional growth, spiritual growth, self-esteem, and a healthy lifestyle.

Publications and Other Resources

AAAP Patient Resources (www.aaap.org/patient-resources/helpful-links): Offers resources and publications for patients and their families.

Addiction Treatment Forum, *Narcotics Anonymous and the Pharmacotherapeutic Treatment of Opioid Addiction in the United States* (http://atforum.com/documents/2011NAandMedication-assistedTreatment.pdf): Presents William White's publication for people receiving medication for OUD that gives information on the pros and cons of 12-Step groups and how to prepare for meetings.

ASAM, Opioid Addiction Treatment: A Guide for Patients, Families, and Friends (http://eguideline.guidelinecentral.com/i/706017-asam-opioid-patient-piece): Provides a guide about the treatment of OUD for patients, families, and friends.

HHS:

- Smokefree.gov (https://smokefree.gov). Provides useful information that helps individuals in planning and maintaining tobacco cessation.
- BeTobaccoFree.gov (https://betobaccofree.hhs.gov/health-effects/nicotine-health). Provides information for individuals struggling with nicotine addiction and links for clinicians that provide guidance on the care for patients with nicotine addiction.

LAC (https://lac.org/resources/substance-use-resources/medication-assisted-treatment-resources). Maintains a library of documents related to medication for the treatment of OUD and other resources, including an advocacy toolkit, sample support letter form, training materials, and webinars:

- *Driving on Methadone or Buprenorphine (Suboxone): DUI?* (http://lac.org/wp-content/uploads/2014/07/Driving-on-Methadone-or-Suboxone-DUI.pdf) factsheet.
- *Know Your Rights: Employment Discrimination Against People With Alcohol/Drug Histories* (https://lac.org/resources/substance-use-resources/employment-education-housing-resources/webinar-know-rights-employment-discrimination-people-alcoholdrug-histories) webinar.
- *Know Your Rights: Rights for Individuals on Medication-Assisted Treatment* (https://lac.org/wp-content/uploads/2014/12/Know_Your_Rts_-_MAT_final_9.28.10.pdf) publication.
- *Medication-Assisted Treatment for Opioid Addiction: Myths and Facts* (http://lac.org/wp-content/uploads/2016/02/Myth-Fact-for-MAT.pdf) factsheet.

NAMA Recovery (www.methadone.org): Offers many resources and training opportunities to become a certified advocate for pharmacotherapy for OUD and provides links to resources related to medication for the treatment of OUD.

National Council on Alcoholism and Drug Dependence's *Consumer Guide to Medication-Assisted Recovery* (www.ncadd.org/images/stories/PDF/Consumer-Guide-Medication-Assisted-Recovery.pdf).

NIAAA's Rethinking Drinking (www.rethinkingdrinking.niaaa.nih.gov/help-links): Provides links to patient and family education, help lines, and other recovery resources.

SAMHSA (https://store.samhsa.gov): Provides patient and family educational tools about OUD and medication treatment for OUD treatment. The resources below are available in several languages, including Spanish and Russian:

- *Decisions in Recovery: Treatment for Opioid Use Disorders* (https://store.samhsa.gov/product/Decisions-in-Recovery-Treatment-for-Opioid-Use-Disorders/SMA16-4993). Helps clients identify an appropriate path of recovery from OUD.
- *The Facts About Buprenorphine for Treatment of Opioid Addiction* (https://store.samhsa.gov/shin/content//SMA14-4442/SMA14-4442.pdf).
- *The Facts About Naltrexone for Treatment of Opioid Addiction* (https://store.samhsa.gov/shin/content/SMA09-4444/SMA09-4444.pdf).
- *Know Your Rights: Rights for Individuals on Medication-Assisted Treatment* (https://store.samhsa.gov/product/Rights-for-Individuals-on-Medication-Assisted-Treatment/SMA09-4449).
- *Medication-Assisted Treatment for Opioid Addiction: Facts for Families and Friends* (www.ct.gov/dmhas/lib/dmhas/publications/MAT-InfoFamilyFriends.pdf).
- *What Every Individual Needs To Know About Methadone Maintenance* (https://store.samhsa.gov/product/What-Every-Individual-Needs-to-Know-About-Methadone-Maintenance/SMA06-4123).
- *What Is Substance Abuse Treatment? A Booklet for Families* (https://store.samhsa.gov/shin/content/SMA14-4126/SMA14-4126.pdf).

Treatment Locators

Faces & Voices of Recovery Guide to Mutual Aid Resources (http://facesandvoicesof recovery.org/resources/mutual-aid-resources): Offers a comprehensive list of 12-Step and non-12-Step recovery support groups throughout the United States and online.

National Alliance of Advocates for Buprenorphine Treatment (www.treatment match.org/TM_index.php): Offers a free, 24/7 anonymous treatment-matching service for patients and providers.

Probuphine Healthcare Provider Locator (https://probuphinerems.com/probuphine -locator): Offers a list of healthcare professionals who prescribe, insert, and/or remove buprenorphine implants.

SAMHSA:

- Behavioral Health Treatment Services Locator is a directory of inpatient treatment providers (https://findtreatment.samhsa.gov).
- Behavioral Health Treatment Services Locator: Self-Help, Peer Support, and Consumer Groups (Addiction) provides a directory for consumers (https://findtreatment.samhsa.gov /locator/link-focSelfGP).
- Buprenorphine Treatment Practitioner Locator provides an interactive treatment locator of providers who prescribe buprenorphine (www .samhsa.gov/medication-assisted-treatment /physician-program-data/treatment-physician -locator).
- Opioid Treatment Program Directory provides an interactive SAMHSA OTP treatment locator (https://dpt2.samhsa.gov/treatment/directory .aspx).

VA Substance Use Disorder Program Locator (www.va.gov/directory/guide/SUD.asp): Provides an interactive treatment locator for VA SUD treatment programs.

Patient Success Stories

Patients' success stories highlight the powerful ways in which medication for the treatment of OUD can help people achieve remission and recovery. Examples of patient success stories include the following:

- Carol (https://vimeo.com/105287902)
- Brandon (https://vimeo.com/105078010)
- Archie (www.youtube/iHJ6K4VQvrw?list =PLGV_2NAg58zkUOZRupfKc6_Z7jaBf7h-V)
- MARS Project Video (www.marsproject.org)

Online Boards and Chat Rooms

12-Step Forums: A variety of NA and AA meetings are available online, each with its own perspective on medication:

- The AA online intergroup directory lists numerous online AA meetings, which occur at specific times (https://aa-intergroup.org /directory_venue.php?code=CH).
- The NA chatroom asks that participants not talk about medication (www.nachatroom.net).

Facebook Forums and Groups: Many medication-assisted recovery organizations maintain a presence on Facebook because of the ease of creating online mutual-support and chat groups:

- A.T. Watchdog: A Pro Methadone Maintenance Support Group (www.facebook .com/groups/1599996730222196)
- Clean & Sober Today (www.facebook.com /groups/1822841161286327)
- Heroin Anonymous (www.facebook.com /HeroinAnonymous)
- Medication-Assisted Treatment Miracles (www.facebook.com/groups/MATMiracles)
- Methadone Discussion (www.facebook.com /groups/MethadoneSupport)

- NAMA Recovery:
    - NAMA-R (www.facebook.com/groups/NAMARecoveryTN)
    - Boston Methadone & Bupe Patient Discussion (www.facebook.com/groups/833560336673414)
    - NAMA Recovery of Washington (www.facebook.com/groups/398175280306632)
- Secular Organizations for Sobriety (www.facebook.com/groups/251215211975)
- Social Media 4Recovery (www.facebook.com/groups/748016625286020)
- Stop Stigma Now (www.facebook.com/Stop-Stigma-Now-1482990085299885)
- Suboxone/Buprenorphine Treatment and Support—Detox/Maintenance (www.facebook.com/groups/Fightingthestigmaofaddiction)

Heroin Addiction & Recovery Forum (http://killtheheroinepidemicnationwide.org/forum): An online discussion forum for both people who are addicted to heroin and their friends and families.

Moms on Methadone (www.circleofmoms.com/moms-on-methadone): An online support group for pregnant women or women with children who are taking medication to treat OUD.

SMART Recovery Online Forum (www.smartrecovery.org/community/forum.php): An online group that welcomes new members.

We Speak Methadone (and Buprenorphine) (www.methadone.org/wespeakmethadone): A discussion forum for medication-assisted treatment patients, their families, and advocates.

Provider Tools and Sample Forms

Provider Screening and Assessment Tools and Aids

Alcohol Use Disorders Identification Test (AUDIT)

1. How often do you have a drink containing alcohol?
   - (0) Never *[Skip to Questions 9–10]*
   - (1) Monthly or less
   - (2) 2 to 4 times a month
   - (3) 2 to 3 times a week
   - (4) 4 or more times a week

2. How many drinks containing alcohol do you have on a typical day when you are drinking?
   - (0) 1 or 2
   - (1) 3 or 4
   - (2) 5 or 6
   - (3) 7, 8, or 9
   - (4) 10 or more

3. How often do you have six or more drinks on one occasion?
   - (0) Never
   - (1) Less than monthly
   - (2) Monthly
   - (3) Weekly
   - (4) Daily or almost daily

   Skip to Questions 9 and 10 if total score for Questions 2 and 3 = 0

4. How often during the last year have you found that you were not able to stop drinking once you had started?
   - (0) Never
   - (1) Less than monthly
   - (2) Monthly
   - (3) Weekly
   - (4) Daily or almost daily

5. How often during the last year have you failed to do what was normally expected from you because of drinking?
   - (0) Never
   - (1) Less than monthly
   - (2) Monthly
   - (3) Weekly
   - (4) Daily or almost daily

6. How often during the last year have you needed an alcoholic drink first thing in the morning to get yourself going after a night of heavy drinking?
   - (0) Never
   - (1) Less than monthly
   - (2) Monthly
   - (3) Weekly
   - (4) Daily or almost daily

7. How often during the last year have you had a feeling of guilt or remorse after drinking?
   - (0) Never
   - (1) Less than monthly
   - (2) Monthly
   - (3) Weekly
   - (4) Daily or almost daily

8. How often during the last year have you been unable to remember what happened the night before because you had been drinking?
   - (0) Never
   - (1) Less than monthly
   - (2) Monthly
   - (3) Weekly
   - (4) Daily or almost daily

9. Have you or someone else been injured as a result of your drinking?
   - (0) No
   - (2) Yes, but not in the last year
   - (4) Yes, during the last year

10. Has a relative, friend, doctor, or another health professional expressed concern about your drinking or suggested you cut down?
    - (0) No
    - (2) Yes, but not in the last year
    - (4) Yes, during the last year

Note: Add up the points associated with answers. A score of 8 or more is considered a positive test for unhealthy drinking. Adapted from material in the public domain.[3] Available online (http://auditscreen.org).

Stable Resource Toolkit

Audit-C – Overview

The AUDIT-C is a 3-item alcohol screen that can help identify persons who are hazardous drinkers or have active alcohol use disorders (including alcohol abuse or dependence). The AUDIT-C is a modified version of the 10 question AUDIT instrument.

Clinical Utility

The AUDIT-C is a brief alcohol screen that reliably identifies patients who are hazardous drinkers or have active alcohol use disorders.

Scoring

The AUDIT-C is scored on a scale of 0-12.

Each AUDIT-C question has 5 answer choices. Points allotted are:
a = 0 points, **b** = 1 point, **c** = 2 points, **d** = 3 points, **e** = 4 points

- **In men,** a score of 4 or more is considered positive, optimal for identifying hazardous drinking or active alcohol use disorders.
- **In women,** a score of 3 or more is considered positive (same as above).
- However, when the points are all from Question #1 alone (#2 & #3 are zero), it can be assumed that the patient is drinking below recommended limits and it is suggested that the provider review the patient's alcohol intake over the past few months to confirm accuracy.[3]
- Generally, the higher the score, the more likely it is that the patient's drinking is affecting his or her safety.

Psychometric Properties

For identifying patients with heavy/hazardous drinking and/or Active-DSM alcohol abuse or dependence

	MEN[1]	WOMEN[2]
≥3	Sens: 0.95 / Spec. 0.60	Sens: 0.66 / Spec. 0.94
≥4	Sens: 0.86 / Spec. 0.72	Sens: 0.48 / Spec. 0.99

For identifying patients with active alcohol abuse or dependence

	MEN[1]	WOMEN[2]
≥3	Sens: 0.90 / Spec. 0.45	Sens: 0.80 / Spec. 0.87
≥4	Sens: 0.79 / Spec. 0.56	Sens: 0.67 / Spec. 0.94

1. Bush K, Kivlahan DR, McDonell MB, et al. The AUDIT Alcohol Consumption Questions (AUDIT-C): An effective brief screening test for problem drinking. *Arch Internal Med. 1998* (3): 1789-1795.
2. Bradley KA, Bush KR, Epler AJ, et al. Two brief alcohol-screening tests from the Alcohol Use Disorders Identification Test (AUDIT): Validation in a female veterans affairs patient population. *Arch Internal Med Vol 165,* April 2003: 821-829.
3. Frequently Asked Questions guide to using the AUDIT-C can be found via the website:
   https://www.queri.research.va.gov/tools/alcohol-misuse/alcohol-faqs-print.cfm

Continued on next page

AUDIT-C Questionnaire

Patient Name: _____   Dates of Visit: _____

1. **How often do you have a drink containing alcohol?**
   - ☐ a. Never
   - ☐ b. Monthly or less
   - ☐ c. 2-4 times a month
   - ☐ d. 2-3 times a week
   - ☐ e. 4 or more times a week

2. **How many standard drinks containing alcohol do you have on a typical day?**
   - ☐ a. 1 or 2
   - ☐ b. 3 or 4
   - ☐ c. 5 or 6
   - ☐ d. 7 to 9
   - ☐ e. 10 or more

3. **How often do you have six or more drinks on one occasion?**
   - ☐ a. Never
   - ☐ b. Less than monthly
   - ☐ c. Monthly
   - ☐ d. Weekly
   - ☐ e. Daily or almost daily

AUDIT-C is available for use in the public domain.

Reprinted from material in the public domain.[4] Available online (https://www.integration.samhsa.gov/images/res/tool_auditc.pdf).

Drug Abuse Screening Test (DAST-10)

General Instructions

"Drug use" refers to (1) the use of prescribed or over-the-counter drugs in excess of the directions, and (2) any nonmedical use of drugs. The various classes of drugs may include cannabis (i.e., marijuana, hashish), solvents (e.g., paint thinner), tranquilizers (e.g., Valium), barbiturates, cocaine, stimulants (e.g., speed), hallucinogens (e.g., LSD), or narcotics (e.g., heroin). The questions do not include alcoholic beverages.

Please answer every question. If you have trouble with a question, then choose the response that is mostly right.

Segment: _____   Visit Number: _____   Date of Assessment: ____/____/____

These questions refer to drug use in the past 12 months. Please answer No or Yes.

1. Have you used drugs other than those required for medical reasons? ☐ No ☐ Yes
2. Do you use more than one drug at a time? ☐ No ☐ Yes
3. Are you always able to stop using drugs when you want to? ☐ No ☐ Yes
4. Have you had "blackouts" or "flashbacks" as a result of drug use? ☐ No ☐ Yes
5. Do you ever feel bad or guilty about your drug use? ☐ No ☐ Yes
6. Does your spouse (or parents) ever complain about your involvement with drugs? ☐ No ☐ Yes
7. Have you neglected your family because of your use of drugs? ☐ No ☐ Yes
8. Have you engaged in illegal activities to obtain drugs? ☐ No ☐ Yes
9. Have you ever experienced withdrawal symptoms (i.e., felt sick) when you stopped taking drugs? ☐ No ☐ Yes
10. Have you had medical problems as a result of your drug use (e.g., memory loss, hepatitis, convulsions, bleeding)? ☐ No ☐ Yes

Comments:

Scoring
Score 1 point for each "Yes," except for question 3, for which a "No" receives 1 point.

DAST Score: _____

Interpretation of Score:

Score	Degree of Problems Related to Drug Abuse	Suggested Action
0	No problems reported	None at this time
1–2	Low level	Monitor, reassess at a later date
3–5	Moderate level	Further investigation
6–8	Substantial level	Intensive assessment
9–10	Severe level	Intensive assessment

Adapted with permission.[5,6]

Part 5 of 5—Resources Related to Medications for Opioid Use Disorder **TIP 63**

DSM-5 Opioid Use Disorder Checklist[7]

Patient's Name: _____ **Date of Birth:** _____

Worksheet for DSM-5 Criteria for Diagnosis of Opioid Use Disorder

DIAGNOSTIC CRITERIA (Opioid use disorder requires that at least 2 criteria be met within a 12-month period.)	MEETS CRITERIA? Yes OR No	NOTES/SUPPORTING INFORMATION
1. Opioids are often taken in larger amounts or over a longer period of time than intended.		
2. There is a persistent desire or unsuccessful efforts to cut down or control opioid use.		
3. A lot of time is spent in activities necessary to obtain the opioid, use the opioid, or recover from its effects.		
4. Craving, or a strong desire to use opioids.		
5. Recurrent opioid use resulting in failure to fulfill major role obligations at work, school, or home.		
6. Continued opioid use despite having persistent or recurrent social or interpersonal problems caused or exacerbated by the effects of opioids.		
7. Important social, occupational, or recreational activities are given up or reduced because of opioid use.		
8. Recurrent opioid use in situations in which it is physically hazardous.		
9. Continued use despite knowledge of having a persistent or recurrent physical or psychological problem that is likely to have been caused or exacerbated by opioids.		
10. Tolerance,* as defined by either of the following: (a) a need for markedly increased amounts of opioids to achieve intoxication or desired effect (b) markedly diminished effect with continued use of the same amount of an opioid		
11. Withdrawal,* as manifested by either of the following: (a) the characteristic opioid withdrawal syndrome (b) the same (or a closely related) substance is taken to relieve or avoid withdrawal symptoms		

*This criterion is not met for individuals taking opioids solely under appropriate medical supervision.

Severity: mild = 2–3 symptoms; moderate = 4–5 symptoms; severe = 6 or more symptoms

Signed: _____ **Date:** _____

Heaviness of Smoking Index

Ask these two questions of current or recent smokers:

1. How soon after waking do you smoke your first cigarette?
   - Within 5 minutes (3 points)
   - 5–30 minutes (2 points)
   - 31–60 minutes (1 point)
   - 61 or more minutes (no points)

2. How many cigarettes a day do you smoke?
   - 10 or less (no points)
   - 11–20 (1 point)
   - 21–30 (2 points)
   - 31 or more (3 points)

Total score: 1 to 2 points = very low dependence; 3 points = low to moderate dependence; 4 points = moderate dependence; 5 or more points = high dependence

Adapted with permission.[8]

NIAAA Single-Item Screener

How many times in the past year have you had five or more drinks in a day (four drinks for women and all adults older than age 65)?

A response of one or more times is considered a positive screen. Patients who screen positive should have an assessment for alcohol use disorder.

Adapted with permission.[9]

Opioid Overdose: Risk, Prevention, Identification, and Response

Overdose Risk

- Using heroin (possibly mixed with illicitly manufactured fentanyl or fentanyl analogs)
- Using prescription opioids that were not prescribed
- Using prescription opioids more frequently or at higher doses than prescribed
- Using opioids after a period of abstinence or reduced use (e.g., after medically supervised withdrawal or incarceration)
- Using opioids with alcohol, benzodiazepines, or both

Overdose Prevention

- Don't use opioids that were not prescribed.
- Take medications only as prescribed.
- Don't use drugs when you are alone.
- Don't use multiple substances at once.
- Have naloxone available and make sure others know where it is and how to use it.
- Use a small "test dose" if returning to opioid use after a period of abstinence, if the substance appears altered or has been acquired from an unfamiliar source. Beware: This doesn't guarantee safety; illicitly manufactured fentanyl or other substances may be present in the drug, and **any use may be fatal.**

Overdose Identification

- Fingernails or lips are blue or purple.
- Breathing or heartbeat is slow or stopped.
- The person is vomiting or making gurgling noises.
- The person can't be awakened or is unable to speak.

Overdose Response

- Call 9-1-1.
- Administer naloxone (more than one dose may be needed to restore adequate spontaneous breathing).
- Perform rescue breathing. If certified to provide cardiopulmonary resuscitation, perform chest compressions if there is no pulse.
- Put the person in the "recovery position," on his or her side and with the mouth facing to the side to prevent aspiration of vomit, if he or she is breathing independently.
- Stay with the person until emergency services arrive. Naloxone's duration of action is 30–90 minutes. The person should be observed after this time for a return of opioid overdose symptoms.

Adapted from material in the public domain.[10]

Physical Signs of Opioid Withdrawal and Time to Onset

STAGE	GRADE	PHYSICAL SIGNS/SYMPTOMS
Early Withdrawal Short-acting opioids: 8–24 hours after last use Long-acting opioids: Up to 36 hours after last use	Grade 1	Lacrimation, rhinorrhea, or both Diaphoresis Yawning Restlessness Insomnia
Early Withdrawal Short-acting opioids: 8–24 hours after last use Long-acting opioids: Up to 36 hours after last use	Grade 2	Dilated pupils Piloerection Muscle twitching Myalgia Arthralgia Abdominal pain
Fully Developed Withdrawal Short-acting opioids: 1–3 days after last use Long-acting opioids: 72–96 hours after last use	Grade 3	Tachycardia Hypertension Tachypnea Fever Anorexia or nausea Extreme restlessness
Fully Developed Withdrawal Short-acting opioids: 1–3 days after last use Long-acting opioids: 72–96 hours after last use	Grade 4	Diarrhea, vomiting, or both Dehydration Hyperglycemia Hypotension Curled-up position

Total duration of withdrawal:

- Short-acting opioids: 7–10 days.
- Long-acting opioids: 14 days or more.

Signs of Opioid Intoxication

Physical Findings

Drowsy but arousable
Sleeping intermittently ("nodding off")
Constricted pupils

Mental Status Findings

Slurred speech
Impaired memory or concentration
Normal to euphoric mood

Single-Item Drug Screener

How many times in the past year have you used an illegal drug or used a prescription medication for nonmedical reasons?

(A positive screen is 1 or more days.)

Reprinted with permission.[11]

Substance Misuse and SUD Screening

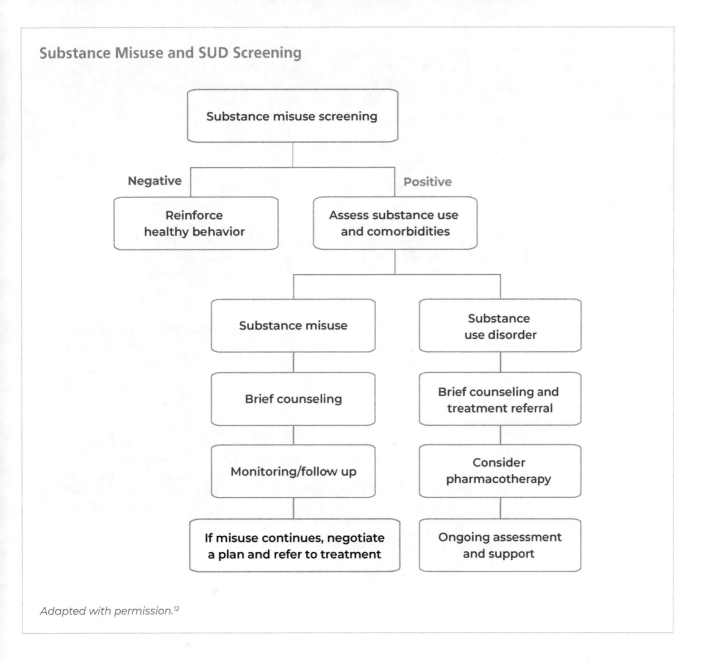

Adapted with permission.[12]

TAPS Tool Part I

Directions: The TAPS Tool Part 1 is a 4-item screening for tobacco use, alcohol use, prescription medication misuse, and illicit substance use in the PAST YEAR. Question 2 should be answered by males, and Question 3 should be answered by females. Each of the four multiple-choice items has five possible responses to choose from. Check the box to select your answer.

In the PAST 12 MONTHS:

1. How often have you used any tobacco product (for example, cigarettes, ecigarettes, cigars, pipes, or smokeless tobacco)?

   ☐ Never   ☐ Less than monthly   ☐ Monthly   ☐ Weekly   ☐ Daily or almost daily

2. How often have you had 5 or more drinks containing alcohol in 1 day? One standard drink is about 1 small glass of wine (5 oz), 1 beer (12 oz), or 1 single shot of liquor. *(Note: This question should only be answered by males.)*

   ☐ Never   ☐ Less than monthly   ☐ Monthly   ☐ Weekly   ☐ Daily or almost daily

3. How often have you had 4 or more drinks containing alcohol in 1 day? One standard drink is about 1 small glass of wine (5 oz), 1 beer (12 oz), or 1 single shot of liquor. *(Note: This question should only be answered by females.)*

   ☐ Never   ☐ Less than monthly   ☐ Monthly   ☐ Weekly   ☐ Daily or almost daily

4. How often have you used any drugs including marijuana, cocaine or crack, heroin, methamphetamine (crystal meth), hallucinogens, or ecstasy/MDMA?

   ☐ Never   ☐ Less than monthly   ☐ Monthly   ☐ Weekly   ☐ Daily or almost daily

5. How often have you used any prescription medications just for the feeling, more than prescribed, or that were not prescribed for you? Prescription medications that may be used this way include opiate pain relievers (for example, OxyContin, Vicodin, Percocet, or methadone), medications for anxiety or sleeping (for example, Xanax, Ativan, or Klonopin), or medications for ADHD (for example, Adderall or Ritalin).

   ☐ Never   ☐ Less than monthly   ☐ Monthly   ☐ Weekly   ☐ Daily or almost daily

Part 5 of 5—Resources Related to Medications for Opioid Use Disorder | TIP 63

TAPS Tool Part 2

Directions: The TAPS Tool Part 2 is a brief assessment for tobacco use, alcohol use, illicit substance use, and prescription medication misuse in the PAST 3 MONTHS ONLY. Each of the following questions and subquestions has two possible answers, yes or no. Check the box to select your answer.

In the PAST 3 MONTHS:

1. **Did you smoke a cigarette containing tobacco?** ☐ Yes ☐ No

   If "Yes," answer the following questions:
   - Did you usually smoke more than 10 cigarettes each day? ☐ Yes ☐ No
   - Did you usually smoke within 30 minutes after waking? ☐ Yes ☐ No

2. **Did you have a drink containing alcohol?** ☐ Yes ☐ No

   If "Yes," answer the following questions:
   - Did you have 4 or more drinks containing alcohol in a day?* ☐ Yes ☐ No
     (Note: This question should only be answered by females.)
   - Did you have 5 or more drinks containing alcohol in a day?* ☐ Yes ☐ No
     (Note: This question should only be answered by males.)
   - Have you tried and failed to control, cut down, or stop drinking? ☐ Yes ☐ No
   - Has anyone expressed concern about your drinking? ☐ Yes ☐ No

3. **Did you use marijuana (hash, weed)?** ☐ Yes ☐ No

   If "Yes," answer the following questions:
   - Have you had a strong desire or urge to use marijuana at least once a week or more often? ☐ Yes ☐ No
   - Has anyone expressed concern about your use of marijuana? ☐ Yes ☐ No

4. **Did you use cocaine, crack, or methamphetamine (crystal meth)?** ☐ Yes ☐ No

   If "Yes," answer the following questions:
   - Did you use cocaine, crack, or methamphetamine (crystal meth) at least once a week or more often? ☐ Yes ☐ No
   - Has anyone expressed concern about your use of cocaine, crack, or methamphetamine (crystal meth)? ☐ Yes ☐ No

5. **Did you use heroin?** ☐ Yes ☐ No

   If "Yes," answer the following questions:
   - Have you tried and failed to control, cut down, or stop using heroin? ☐ Yes ☐ No
   - Has anyone expressed concern about your use of heroin? ☐ Yes ☐ No

6. **Did you use a prescription opiate pain reliever (for example Percocet or Vicodin) not as prescribed or that was not prescribed for you?** ☐ Yes ☐ No

   If "Yes," answer the following questions:
   - Have you tried and failed to control, cut down, or stop using an opiate pain reliever? ☐ Yes ☐ No
   - Has anyone expressed concern about your use of an opiate pain reliever? ☐ Yes ☐ No

*One standard drink is about 1 small glass of wine (5 oz), 1 beer (12 oz), or 1 single shot of liquor.

Continued on next page

7. **Did you use medication for anxiety or sleep (for example, Xanax, Ativan, or Klonopin) not as prescribed or that was not prescribed for you?** ☐ Yes ☐ No

   If "Yes," answer the following questions:
   - Have you had a strong desire or urge to use medications for anxiety or sleep at least once a week or more often? ☐ Yes ☐ No
   - Has anyone expressed concern about your use of medication for anxiety or sleep? ☐ Yes ☐ No

8. **Did you use medication for ADHD (for example, Adderall or Ritalin) not as prescribed or that was not prescribed for you?** ☐ Yes ☐ No

   If "Yes," answer the following questions:
   - Did you use a medication for ADHD (for example, Adderall or Ritalin) at least once a week or more often? ☐ Yes ☐ No
   - Has anyone expressed concern about your use of medication for ADHD (for example, Adderall or Ritalin)? ☐ Yes ☐ No

9. **Did you use any other illegal or recreational drugs (for example, ecstasy, molly, GHB, poppers, LSD, mushrooms, special K, bath salts, synthetic marijuana ["spice"], whip-its)?** ☐ Yes ☐ No

   If "Yes," answer the following question:
   - What were the other drug(s) you used? (write in response)

The complete tool is available online (https://cde.drugabuse.gov/instrument/29b23e2e-e266-f095-e050-bb89ad43472f). Adapted from material in the public domain.[13]

Two-Item Drug Use Disorder Screener for Primary Care Clinics Serving U.S. Veterans

Question 1: How many days in the past 12 months have you used drugs other than alcohol? (A positive screen is 7 or more days.) If <7, proceed with Question 2.

Question 2: How many days in the past 12 months have you used drugs more than you meant to? (A positive screen is 2 or more days.)

Adapted with permission.[14]

Urine Drug Testing Window of Detection[15,16]

DRUG	POSITIVE TEST	WINDOW OF DETECTION*	COMMENTS
Amphetamine; methamphetamine; 3,4-methylenedioxy-methamphetamine	Amphetamine	1–2 days	False positives w/ bupropion, chlorpromazine, desipramine, fluoxetine, labetalol, promethazine, ranitidine, pseudoephedrine, trazadone, and other common medications. Confirm unexpected positive results with the laboratory.
Barbiturates	Barbiturates	Up to 6 weeks	N/A
Benzodiazepines	Benzodiazepines	1–3 days; up to 6 weeks with heavy use of long-acting benzodiazepines	Immunoassays may not be sensitive to therapeutic doses, and most immunoassays have low sensitivity to clonazepam and lorazepam. Check with your laboratory regarding sensitivity and cutoffs. False positives with sertraline or oxaprozin.
Buprenorphine	Buprenorphine	3–4 days	Will screen negative on opiate screen. Tramadol can cause false positives. Can be tested for specifically.
Cocaine	Cocaine, benzoylecgonine	2–4 days; 10–22 days with heavy use	N/A
Codeine	Morphine, codeine, high-dose hydrocodone	1–2 days	Will screen positive on opiate immunoassay.
Fentanyl	Fentanyl	1–2 days	Will screen negative on opiate screen. Can be tested for specifically. May not detect all fentanyl-like substances.[17]
Heroin	Morphine, codeine	1–2 days	Will screen positive on opiate immunoassay. 6-monoacetylmorphine, a unique metabolite of heroin, is present in urine for about 6 hours. Can be tested for specifically to distinguish morphine from heroin, but this is rarely clinically useful.
Hydrocodone	Hydrocodone, hydromorphone	2 days	May screen negative on opiate immunoassay. Can be tested for specifically.
Hydromorphone	May not be detected	1–2 days	May screen negative on opiate immunoassay. Can be tested for specifically.

Continued on next page

Urine Drug Testing Window of Detection (continued)

DRUG	POSITIVE TEST	WINDOW OF DETECTION*	COMMENTS
Marijuana	Tetrahydrocannabinol	Infrequent use of 1–3 days; chronic use of up to 30 days	False positives possible with efavirenz, ibuprofen, and pantoprazole.
Methadone	Methadone	2–11 days	Will screen negative on opiate screen. Can be tested for specifically.
Morphine	Morphine, hydromorphone	1–2 days	Will screen positive on opiate immunoassay. Ingestion of poppy plant/seed may screen positive.
Oxycodone	Oxymorphone	1–1.5 days	Typically screens negative on opiate immunoassay. Can be tested for specifically.

*Detection time may vary depending on the cutoff.

Using Signs and Symptoms To Determine Optimal Methadone Level

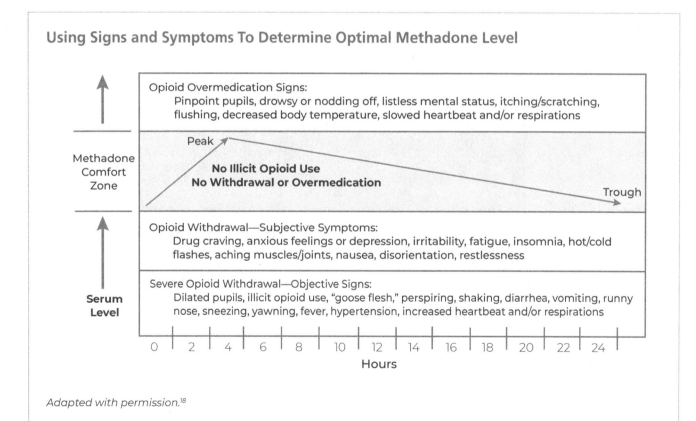

Adapted with permission.[18]

Provider Informational, Educational, and Decision-Making Tools

Key Elements of an OBOT Clinic Diversion Control Plan[19]

New Patients

Check the state's PDMP before admission to determine whether patients are receiving opioids or benzodiazepine prescriptions from other providers.

Ask patients to sign a release of information to speak with the other prescribers. Patients who are unwilling to sign a release of information are poor candidates for outpatient treatment.

Review the clinic diversion control policy with new patients. This should include counseling patients to:

- Keep buprenorphine locked up and out of children's reach.
- Never share medication with anyone.
- Never sell medication to anyone.
- Acknowledge giving or selling medication to others as illegal.
- Take medication only as prescribed.
- Review, understand, and agree to the practice's buprenorphine treatment agreement before they start.

Prescribe buprenorphine/naloxone when possible, rather than monoproduct. Exceptions would include prescribing the monoproduct for pregnant women with OUD.

Prescribe an adequate but not excessive dose. Most patients respond to doses at or below 24 mg per day. Carefully evaluate requests for higher doses and confirm, document, and assess medication adherence continuously.

Ongoing Patients

Periodically check the state's PDMP.

Conduct random urine tests that include a wide spectrum of opioids—including morphine, oxycodone, and buprenorphine—and periodically include buprenorphine metabolites. This will help monitor response to treatment and determine whether patients are taking at least some of their prescribed buprenorphine.

Use **unobserved** specimen collection to preserve patient privacy and dignity:

- Do not let patients bring backpacks, jackets, or other items into the bathroom.
- Do not let others enter bathrooms with patients.
- Temperature test the urine sample.

Use **observed** specimen collection (obtained by a staff member of the same gender) or oral fluid testing if there is reason to suspect tampering or falsification.

Contact patients at random; ask them to bring in their medication within a reasonable period (24 to 48 hours) to count the tablets/films to ensure that all medication is accounted for.

Provide a limited number of days of medication per prescription without refills (e.g., several days or 1 week per prescription) until the patient has demonstrated stability and lowered diversion risk.

Key Points of Patient Education for Buprenorphine

Before starting OUD treatment with buprenorphine, patients should:

- Tell providers the prescribed and over-the-counter medications they take, to allow drug interaction assessment.
- Understand the goal of the first week of treatment: To improve withdrawal symptoms without oversedation.
- Tell providers if they feel sedated or euphoric within 1 to 4 hours after their dose.
- Be given the appropriate buprenorphine medication guide.
- Know possible side effects, including:
  - Headache.
  - Dizziness.
  - Nausea.
  - Vomiting.
  - Sweating.
  - Constipation.
  - Sexual dysfunction.
- Agree to store medication securely and out of the reach of others.
- Alert providers if they discontinue medications, start new ones, or change their medication dose.
- Understand that discontinuing buprenorphine increases risk of overdose death upon return to illicit opioid use.
- Know that use of alcohol or benzodiazepines with buprenorphine increases the risk of overdose and death.
- Understand the importance of informing providers if they become pregnant.
- Tell providers if they are having a procedure that may require pain medication.
- Be aware of resources through which to obtain further education for:
  - Themselves (https://store.samhsa.gov/product/SMA16-4993).
  - Their families and friends (http://www.ct.gov/dmhas/lib/dmhas/publications/MAT-InfoFamilyFriends.pdf).

Key Points of Patient Education for Methadone

Before starting OUD treatment with methadone, patients should:

- Be told that the methadone dose is started low and increased slowly over days and weeks with monitoring, because it takes 4 or more days for the body to adjust to a dose change. This is necessary to avoid the risk of overdose.
- Understand that the goal of the first weeks of treatment is to improve withdrawal symptoms without oversedation. Patients should tell providers if they feel sedated or high within the first 4 hours after their dose.
- Learn the symptoms of methadone intoxication and how to seek emergency care. The first 2 weeks of treatment have the highest risk of overdose.
- Be aware that rescue naloxone does not last very long, so they should remain in emergency care for observation if they are treated for opioid overdose.
- Know that concurrent alcohol, benzodiazepine, or other sedative use with methadone increases the risk of overdose and death.
- Inform OTP nursing/medical staff about prescribed and over-the-counter medications and herbs (e.g., St. John's wort) they are taking, stopping, or changing doses of to allow assessment of potential drug–drug interactions.
- Inform other treating healthcare professionals that they are receiving methadone treatment.
- Plan to avoid driving or operating heavy machinery until their dose is stabilized.
- Learn about other possible side effects of methadone, including dizziness, nausea, vomiting, sweating, constipation, edema, and sexual dysfunction.
- Agree to keep take-home doses locked up and out of the reach of others. Understand that giving methadone, even small amounts, to others may be fatal.
- Inform providers if they become pregnant.
- Understand that stopping methadone increases their risk of overdose death if they return to illicit opioid use.

Key Points of Patient Education for Naltrexone

- Do not use any opioids in the 7 to 10 days (for short acting) or 10 to 14 days (for long acting) before starting XR-NTX, to avoid potentially serious opioid withdrawal symptoms. Opioids include:
  - Heroin.
  - Prescription opioid analgesics (including tramadol).
  - Cough, diarrhea, or other medications that contain codeine or other opioids.
  - Methadone.
  - Buprenorphine.
- Seek immediate medical help if symptoms of allergic reaction or anaphylaxis occur, such as:
  - Itching.
  - Swelling.
  - Hives.
  - Shortness of breath.
  - Throat tightness.
- Do not try to override the opioid blockade with large amounts of opioids, which could result in overdose.
- Understand the risk of overdose from using opioids near the time of the next injection, after missing a dose, or after stopping medications.
- Report injection site reactions including:
  - Pain.
  - Hardening.
  - Lumps.
  - Blisters.
  - Blackening.
  - Scabs.
  - An open wound.

  Some of these reactions could require surgery to repair (rarely).
- Report signs and symptoms of hepatitis.
- Report depression or suicidal thoughts. Seek immediate medical attention if these symptoms appear.
- Seek medical help if symptoms of pneumonia appear (e.g., shortness of breath, fever).
- Tell providers of naltrexone treatment, as treatment differs for various types of pneumonia.
- Inform all healthcare professionals of XR-NTX treatment.
- Report pregnancy.
- Inform providers of any upcoming medical procedures that may require pain medication.
- Understand that taking naltrexone may result in difficulty achieving adequate pain control if acute medical illness or trauma causes severe acute pain.
- Wear medical alert jewelry and carry a medical alert card indicating you are taking XR-NTX. A patient wallet card or medical alert bracelet can be ordered at 1-800-848-4876.

Medication Management for Patients With Respiratory or Hepatic Impairment Who Take Buprenorphine

CONTRAINDICATION/CAUTION	MANAGEMENT
Compromised respiratory function (e.g., chronic obstructive pulmonary disease, decreased respiratory reserve, hypoxia, hypercapnia [abnormally elevated blood levels of carbon dioxide], preexisting respiratory depression).	• Prescribe with caution; monitor closely. • Warn patients about the risk of using benzodiazepines or other depressants while taking buprenorphine.[20] • Support patients in their attempts to discontinue tobacco use.
Hepatic impairment Buprenorphine and naloxone are extensively metabolized by the liver. Moderate to severe impairment results in decreased clearance, increased overall exposure to both medications, and higher risk of buprenorphine toxicity and precipitated withdrawal from naloxone. These effects have not been observed in patients with mild hepatic impairment.[21,22]	• Mild impairment (Child-Pugh score of 5–6):[23] No dose adjustment needed. • Moderate impairment (Child-Pugh score of 7–9):[24] Combination products are not recommended; they may precipitate withdrawal. *Use combination products cautiously for maintenance treatment in patients who've been inducted with a monoproduct;[25,26] monitor for signs and symptoms of buprenorphine toxicity or overdose.[27] Naloxone may interfere with buprenorphine's efficacy.[28,29] • Severe impairment (Child-Pugh score of 10–15):[30] Do not use the combination product.[31] For monoproduct, consider halving the starting and titration doses used in patients with normal liver function; monitor for signs and symptoms of toxicity or overdose caused by increased buprenorphine levels.[32]

*Moderate to severe impairment results in much more reduced clearance of naloxone than of buprenorphine. Nasser et al.[33] found that moderate impairment doubled or tripled exposure (compared with subjects with no or mild impairment) for both medications. In subjects with severe impairment, buprenorphine exposure was two to three times higher; naloxone exposure increased more than tenfold.

Adapted from material in the public domain.[34]

Monitoring Recovery Activities

At medical management visits, do not simply ask about attendance at recovery support meetings; explore the level of participation and engagement in those activities. Some activities include:

- Finding and working closely with a sponsor.
- "Working" the 12 Steps at 12-Step meetings and with a sponsor.
- Doing service at meetings (e.g., setting up chairs, making coffee, going on a "commitment" to speak at a meeting in a jail or an inpatient drug and alcohol program).
- Having and frequently attending a regular "home" group.[35]

Remember this statement from recovery experts A. Thomas McLellan and William White: "Recovery status is best defined by factors other than medication status. Neither medication-assisted treatment of opioid addiction nor the cessation of such treatment by itself constitutes recovery. Recovery status instead hinges on broader achievements in health and social functioning—with or without medication support."[36]

Part 5 of 5—Resources Related to Medications for Opioid Use Disorder

OUD Medications: An Overview[37,38]

CATEGORY	BUPRENORPHINE*	METHADONE	XR-NTX**
Appropriate patients	Typically for patients with OUD who are physiologically dependent on opioids	Typically for patients with OUD who are physiologically dependent on opioids and who meet federal criteria for OTP admission	Typically for patients with OUD who have abstained from short-acting opioids for at least 7–10 days and long-acting opioids for at least 10–14 days
Pharmacology	**Opioid receptor partial agonist** Reduces opioid withdrawal and craving; blunts or blocks euphoric effects of self-administered illicit opioids through cross-tolerance and opioid receptor occupancy.	**Opioid receptor agonist** Reduces opioid withdrawal and craving; blunts or blocks euphoric effects of self-administered illicit opioids through cross-tolerance and opioid receptor occupancy.	**Opioid receptor antagonist** Blocks euphoric effects of self-administered illicit opioids through opioid receptor occupancy. Causes no opioid effects.
Patient Education	**Tell patients:** • That they will need to be in opioid withdrawal to receive their first dose to avoid buprenorphine-precipitated opioid withdrawal. • About the risk of overdose with concurrent benzodiazepine or alcohol use, with injecting buprenorphine, and after stopping the medication.	**Tell patients:** • That their dose will start low and build up slowly to avoid oversedation; it takes several days for a given dose to have its full effect. • About overdose risk in the first 2 weeks of treatment, especially with concurrent benzodiazepine or alcohol use, and after stopping the medication.	**Tell patients:** • That they will need to be opioid free for at least 7–10 days for short-acting and at least 10–14 days for long-acting opioids before their first dose to avoid XR-NTX-precipitated opioid withdrawal (which may require hospitalization). • About the risk of overdose after stopping the medication.
Administration	Daily (or off-label less-than-daily dosing regimens) administration of sublingual or buccal tablet or film. Subdermal implants every 6 months, for up to 1 year, for stable patients. Monthly subcutaneous injection of extended-release formulation in abdominal region for patients treated with transmucosal buprenorphine for at least 1 week.	Daily oral administration as liquid concentrate, tablet, or oral solution from dispersible tablet or powder (unless patients can take some home).	Every 4 weeks or once-per-month intramuscular injection.
Prescribing	Physicians, NPs, and PAs need a waiver to prescribe. Any pharmacy can fill a prescription for sublingual or buccal formulations. OTPs can administer/dispense by OTP physician order without a waiver.	SAMHSA-certified OTPs can provide methadone for daily onsite administration or at-home self-administration for stable patients.	Physicians, NPs, or PAs prescribe or order administration by qualified healthcare professionals.

*Long-acting buprenorphine implants (every 6 months) for patients on a stable dose of buprenorphine are also available through implanters and prescribers with additional training and certification through the Probuphine REMS Program. Extended-release buprenorphine monthly subcutaneous injections are available only through prescribers and pharmacies registered with the Sublocade REMS Program.

**Naltrexone hydrochloride tablets (50 mg each) are also available for daily oral dosing but have not been shown to be more effective than treatment without medication or placebo because of poor patient adherence.

OUD Medications: Comparison To Guide Shared Decision Making

CATEGORY	BUPRENORPHINE	METHADONE	NALTREXONE
Appropriate patients	Typically for patients with OUD who are physiologically dependent on opioids	Typically for patients with OUD who are physiologically dependent on opioids and who meet federal criteria for OTP admission	Typically for patients with OUD who are abstinent from short-acting opioids for 7 days and long-acting opioids for 10–14 days
Outcome: Retention in treatment	Higher than treatment without medication and treatment with placebo[39]	Higher than treatment without OUD medication and treatment with placebo[40]	Treatment retention with oral naltrexone is no better than with placebo or no medication;[41] for XR-NTX, treatment retention is higher than for treatment without OUD medication and treatment with placebo;[42,43] treatment retention is lower than with opioid receptor agonist treatment
Outcome: Suppression of illicit opioid use	Effective	Effective	Effective
Outcome: Overdose mortality	Lower for people in treatment than for those not in it	Lower for people in treatment than for those not in it	Unknown
Location/ frequency of office visits	**Office/clinic:** Begins daily to weekly, then tailored to patient's needs **OTP:** Can treat with buprenorphine 6–7 days/week initially; take-homes are allowed without the time-in-treatment requirements of methadone	**OTP only:** 6–7 days/week initially; take-homes are allowed based on time in treatment and patient progress	**Office/clinic:** Varies from weekly to monthly
Who can prescribe/order?	Physicians, NPs,* and PAs* possessing federal waiver can prescribe and dispense; can be dispensed by a community pharmacy or an OTP	OTP physicians order the medication; nurses and pharmacists administer and dispense it	Physicians, NPs,* and PAs*

*NPs and PAs should check with their state to determine whether prescribing buprenorphine, naltrexone, or both is within their allowable scope of practice.

Continued on next page

OUD Medications: Comparison To Guide Shared Decision Making (continued)

CATEGORY	BUPRENORPHINE	METHADONE	NALTREXONE
Administration	Sublingual/buccal; implant by specially trained provider, and only for stabilized patients	Oral	Oral or intramuscular (Note: Oral naltrexone is less effective than the other OUD medications.)
Misuse/diversion potential	Low in OTPs or other settings with observed dose administration; moderate for take-home doses; risk can be mitigated by providing take-homes to stable patients and a diversion control plan	Low in OTPs with directly observed therapy; moderate for take-home doses; risk can be mitigated by a diversion control plan	None
Sedation	Low unless concurrent substances are present (e.g., alcohol, benzodiazepines)	Low unless dose titration is too quick or dose is not adjusted for the presence of concurrent substances (e.g., alcohol, benzodiazepines)	None
Risk of medication-induced respiratory depression	Very rare; lower than methadone	Rare, although higher than buprenorphine; may be elevated during the first 2 weeks of treatment or in combination with other sedating substances	None
Risk of precipitated withdrawal when starting medication	Can occur if started too prematurely after recent use of other opioids	None	Severe withdrawal is possible if period of abstinence is inadequate before starting medication
Withdrawal symptoms on discontinuation	Present; lower than methadone if abruptly discontinued	Present; higher than buprenorphine if abruptly discontinued	None
Most common side effects	Constipation, vomiting, headache, sweating, insomnia, blurred vision	Constipation, vomiting, sweating, dizziness, sedation	Difficulty sleeping, anxiety, nausea, vomiting, low energy, joint and muscle pain, headache, liver enzyme elevation XR-NTX: Injection site pain, nasopharyngitis, insomnia, toothache

D. Coffa, December 2017 (personal communication). Adapted with permission.

OUD Medications: Formulations[44,45]

GENERIC/ TRADE NAME	FORMULATIONS	ACTION AT THE RECEPTOR	FDA INDICATIONS	DOSING REGIMEN
Methadone (Methadose, Dolophine)	Orally as liquid concentrate, tablet, or oral solution of powder or dispersible tablet	Mu-opioid receptor full agonist	Medically supervised withdrawal and maintenance treatment of opioid dependence; additional formulations FDA-approved for pain are not a focus of this TIP	Once daily (also off-label dosing regimens if appropriate, such as split dose twice daily)
Generic buprenorphine monoproduct	Sublingual tablet	Mu-opioid receptor partial agonist	Treatment of opioid dependence; additional formulations FDA-approved for pain are not a focus of this TIP	Once daily (also alternative off-label regimens)
Generic combination product (buprenorphine/ naloxone)	Sublingual tablet	Mu-opioid receptor partial agonist combined with mu-opioid receptor antagonist; the latter is not absorbed sublingually	Treatment of opioid dependence	Once daily (also alternative off-label regimens)
Buprenorphine/ naloxone (Zubsolv)	Sublingual tablet	Mu-opioid receptor partial agonist combined with mu-opioid receptor antagonist; the latter is not absorbed sublingually	Treatment of opioid dependence	Once daily (also alternative off-label regimens)
Buprenorphine/ naloxone (Bunavail)	Buccal film	Mu-opioid receptor partial agonist combined with mu-opioid receptor antagonist; the latter is not absorbed sublingually	Treatment of opioid dependence	Once daily (also alternative off-label regimens)
Buprenorphine/ naloxone (Suboxone)	Sublingual film; may also be administered buccally	Mu-opioid receptor partial agonist combined with mu-opioid receptor antagonist; the latter is not absorbed sublingually	Treatment of opioid dependence	Once daily (also alternative off-label regimens)

Continued on next page

OUD Medications: Formulations (continued)

GENERIC/ TRADE NAME	FORMULATIONS	ACTION AT THE RECEPTOR	FDA INDICATIONS	DOSING REGIMEN
Buprenorphine (Probuphine)	Implants	Mu-opioid receptor partial agonist	Maintenance treatment of opioid dependence in clinically stable patients taking 8 mg/day or less of Suboxone equivalents	Implants last for 6 months and are then removed, after which a second set can be inserted
Extended-release injection buprenorphine (Sublocade)	Subcutaneous injection in the abdominal region	Mu-opioid receptor partial agonist	Treatment of moderate-to-severe OUD among patients initiated and taking transmucosal buprenorphine for at least 7 days	Monthly
Oral naltrexone (Revia)	Oral tablet	Mu-opioid receptor antagonist	Block the effects of administered opioid agonists	Once daily (also alternative off-label regimens)
XR-NTX (Vivitrol)	Intramuscular injection	Mu-opioid receptor antagonist	Prevent return to opioid dependence after medically supervised opioid withdrawal	Once monthly by injection

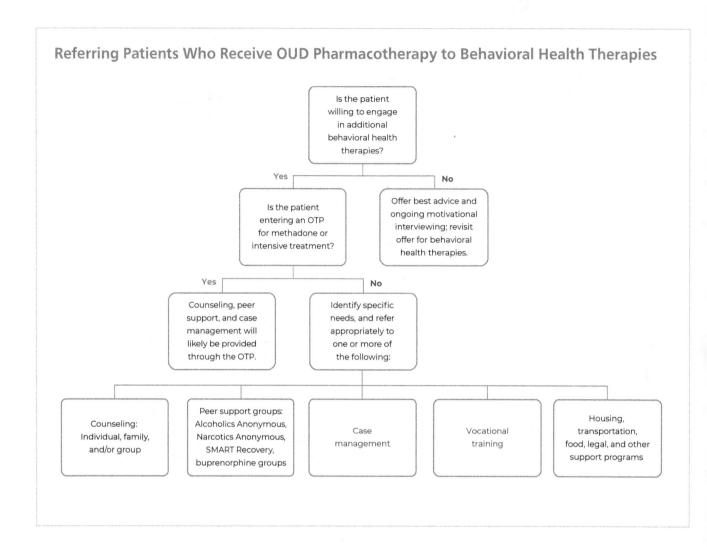

Strategies for Managing Benzodiazepine Use by Patients in OUD Treatment

- **Carefully assess the patient's benzodiazepine use,** including:
  - Intent of use.
  - Source (check the state's PDMP).
  - Amount and route of use.
  - Binge use.
  - Prior overdoses.
  - Harms (e.g., car crashes, criminal acts, sleep trouble).
  - Co-use with other substances that further increase risk for respiratory depression and overdose.
  - Withdrawal history (e.g., seizures, delirium).
- **Also assess the following:**
  - Psychiatric and medical comorbidity
  - Motivation for change
  - Psychosocial support system (obtain history from a significant other if the patient permits)
- **Gauge level of care and setting needed** (e.g., residential, outpatient). Inpatient treatment may be best for patients with poor motivation, limited psychosocial support, serious or complicated comorbidity, or injection or binge use.
- **Coordinate with other prescribers.** Some patients may have taken appropriately prescribed benzodiazepines for years with limited or no evidence of misuse. For such patients, tapering benzodiazepines may be contraindicated and unrealistic.
- **Address comorbid mental disorders (e.g., anxiety, depression)** with other medications or psychosocial treatments, when feasible.
- **Provide medically supervised withdrawal** from benzodiazepines or refer to specialty care for same.
- **Create a treatment plan with built-in conditions** (e.g., urine testing, more frequent visits, short medication supply).
- **Frequently review patient progress and objective outcomes,** such as:
  - Urine drug testing.
  - PDMP reports.
  - Psychosocial functioning.
  - Reports from significant others.
- **Revise treatment plans** as needed, and document the rationale for treatment decisions.

Adapted with permission.[46]

TIP 63 — Medications for Opioid Use Disorder

Sample Provider Forms

General forms

Goal-Setting Form

Patient's Name: _____ **Date:** _____

GOAL CATEGORY	CURRENT SITUATION SCORE 10 = major problems and 0 = no problems	What would need to change to decrease this score?	PRIORITY SCORE 10 = highest priority ("I really want to work on this") and 1 = lowest priority ("I really do not want to work on this")
Opioid use			
Other illicit drug use: _____			
Alcohol use			
Tobacco use			
Physical health			
Mental health			
Legal/court issues			
Finances			
Job/employment			
Hobbies			
Family relations			
Partner relations			
Supportive drug-free network			
Education			
Keeping medication safe (e.g., not giving it away, selling it, having it stolen)			
Other			
Other			

M. Lofwall, February 27, 2017 (personal communication). Adapted with permission.

Goal Sheet and Coping Strategies Form

Goals are things you would like to accomplish.

Patient's Name: _____ **Date:** _____

3-MONTH GOALS
1. _____
2. _____
3. _____

6-MONTH GOALS
1. _____
2. _____
3. _____

1-YEAR GOALS
1. _____
2. _____
3. _____

List of Triggers to Using Drugs

People To Stay Away From

Places To Stay Away From

Ways To Cope or Manage Stress Without Using Drugs

M. Lofwall, February 27, 2017 (personal communication). Adapted with permission.

TIP 63 — Medications for Opioid Use Disorder

Medical Management Visit Form

Patient's Name: _____ **ID#** _____

Date: _____ **Week#:** _____ **Dose:** _____ mg ☐ No Show

Heroin/cocaine or other illicit drug use since last visit?
_____

Symptoms or signs that might indicate return to use (e.g., changes in mood, physical appearance)?
_____

Since the last visit, are there any problems with the following:

If yes, explain

Drug Use	☐ Yes	☐ No	_____
Alcohol Use	☐ Yes	☐ No	_____
Psychiatric	☐ Yes	☐ No	_____
Medical	☐ Yes	☐ No	_____
Employment	☐ Yes	☐ No	_____
Social/Family	☐ Yes	☐ No	_____
Legal	☐ Yes	☐ No	_____

Any new problem to add to Treatment Plan Review?   ☐ Yes   ☐ No

_____

Plan to address any new problem _____

_____

Participation in Narcotics Anonymous or Alcoholics Anonymous since last visit?   ☐ Yes   ☐ No

Length of Session: _____   Healthcare Professional Signature: _____

D. Fiellin, December 3, 2016 (personal communication). Adapted with permission.

Part 5 of 5—Resources Related to Medications for Opioid Use Disorder — TIP 63

Patient Urine Drug Screen and Medication Count Monitoring Form

Patient's Name: _____   **Dates To Be Called:** _____

Called for:
☐ Urine Drug Screen
☐ Medication Count at ☐ Office or ☐ Pharmacy FOR: _____
☐ Buprenorphine/Naloxone
☐ Other (list drug: _____, _____, _____)

Documentation of Phone Call to Patient

Patient was called at _____ (insert phone #) on _____ (date) at ____:____ (time) and informed of monitoring required (described above) within the next _____ hours.

Check One:
☐ I spoke with patient
☐ Message left on answering machine/voicemail
☐ Message left with _____
☐ Other _____

Signature of Staff Member Making Phone Call: _____

M. Lofwall, February 27, 2017 (personal communication). Adapted with permission.

Pharmacy Tablet/Film Count Form

(Note: Before sending this form, discuss with the pharmacist first to explain goals and procedures and to ensure agreement and understanding.)

Date: _____

To: Pharmacists @ _____ Pharmacy

From: Healthcare Provider: _____

Clinic Address: _____

Phone Number: _____

My patient, _____, is starting office-based buprenorphine treatment for opioid dependence.

As part of monitoring this treatment, we ask the patient to do buprenorphine tablet/film counts at random times (we call the patient when it's time for a pill/film count).

The above-named patient lives much closer to your pharmacy than to our treatment clinic. It would be a big help to me and this patient if you would be able to perform periodic tablet/film counts on his/her buprenorphine and then fax this form to us.

On the days we call the patient for a random tablet/film count, the patient would come to your pharmacy with his or her pill bottle. When we call the patient to go for a random tablet/film count, we will fax this form to you. We would appreciate if you could record the tablet/film count results on this form and fax it back to us the same day. This would be a real help to me in monitoring my patient's treatment and also a great service to the patient.

Thank you very much for your help with this! Sincerely,

_____
Signature

Buprenorphine/naloxone formulation: _____

Dose per tablet/film: _____

Total # of tablets/films remaining in bottle: _____   Fill date on bottle: _____

Total # of tablets/films dispensed on fill date: _____   Tablet/film count correct? ☐Yes ☐No

Please fax this back to: _____
Thank You!

M. Lofwall, February 27, 2017 (personal communication). Adapted with permission.

Standard Consent to Opioid Maintenance Treatment Form for OTPs

CONSENT TO PARTICIPATE IN METHADONE OR BUPRENORPHINE TREATMENT

Patient's Name: _____ **Date:** _____

I authorize and give voluntary consent to _____ [insert name of program] to dispense and administer medications—including methadone or buprenorphine—to treat my opioid use disorder. Treatment procedures have been explained to me, and I understand that I should take my medication at the schedule determined by the program physician, or his/her designee, in accordance with federal and state regulations.

I understand that, like all other medications, methadone or buprenorphine can be harmful if not taken as prescribed. It has been explained to me that I must safeguard these medications and not share them with anyone because they can be fatal to children and adults if taken without medical supervision.

I also understand that methadone and buprenorphine produce physical opioid dependence.

Like all medications, they may have side effects. Possible side effects, as well as alternative treatments and their risks and benefits, have been explained to me.

I understand that it is important for me to inform any medical and psychiatric provider who may treat me that I am enrolled in an opioid treatment program. In this way, the provider will be aware of all the medications I am taking, can provide the best possible care, and can avoid prescribing medications that might affect my treatment with methadone or buprenorphine or my recovery.

I understand that I may withdraw voluntarily from this treatment program and discontinue the use of these medications at any time. If I choose this option, I understand I will be offered medically supervised withdrawal.

For women of childbearing age: Pregnant women treated with methadone or buprenorphine have better outcomes than pregnant women not in treatment who continue to use opioid drugs. Newborns of mothers who are receiving methadone or buprenorphine treatment may have opioid withdrawal symptoms (i.e., neonatal abstinence syndrome). The delivery hospital may require babies who are exposed to opioids before birth to spend a number of days in the hospital for monitoring of withdrawal symptoms. Some babies may also need medication to stop withdrawal. If I am or become pregnant, I understand that I should tell the medical staff of the OTP right away so I can receive or be referred to prenatal care. I understand that there are ways to maximize the healthy course of my pregnancy while I am taking methadone or buprenorphine.

Signature of Patient: _____ **Date of Birth:** _____

Date: _____ **Witness:** _____

Adapted from material in the public domain.[47]

Buprenorphine Forms

Buprenorphine Diversion Control Policy

XYZ Medical Practice
Office-Based Opioid Use Disorder Policy and Procedure Manual

Policy Title: Diversion Control for Patients Prescribed Transmucosal (Sublingual) Buprenorphine

Effective Date: _____ (Month, Day, Year)

This Diversion Control Policy is provided for educational and informational purposes only. It is intended to offer healthcare professionals guiding principles and policies regarding best practices in diversion control for patients who are prescribed buprenorphine. This policy is not intended to establish a legal or medical standard of care. Healthcare professionals should use their personal and professional judgment in interpreting these guidelines and applying them to the particular circumstances of their individual patients and practice arrangements. The information provided in this Policy is provided "as is" with no guarantee as to its accuracy or completeness.

Preamble: Healthcare professionals can now treat up to 275 patients with buprenorphine. This increased access may contribute to increased diversion, misuse, and related harms. Signs that a patient is misusing or diverting buprenorphine include (1) missed appointments; (2) requests for early refills because pills were lost, stolen, or other reasons; (3) urine screens negative for buprenorphine, positive for opioids; (4) claims of being allergic or intolerant to naloxone and requesting monotherapy; (5) nonhealing or fresh track marks; or (5) police reports of selling on the streets. Likewise, there are a range of reasons for diversion and misuse (e.g., diverting to family/friends with untreated opioid addiction with the intent of trying to "help" convince them to also get treatment; diverting to family/friends on a treatment waiting list; selling some or all of the medication to pay off old drug debts/purchase preferred opioid of misuse/pay for treatment in places where there are inadequate addiction treatment professionals taking private insurance or Medicaid for such reasons as inadequate reimbursement/no reimbursement/burdensome prior authorization process).

The safety and health of patients and others in the community could be at risk if misuse and diversion are not addressed proactively throughout treatment. The reputation of XYZ Medical Practice may also be put at risk.

Definitions: *Diversion* is defined as the unauthorized rerouting or misappropriation of prescription medication to someone other than for whom it was intended (including sharing or selling a prescribed medication); *misuse* includes taking medication in a manner, by route or by dose, other than prescribed.[48]

Purpose: Misuse and diversion should be defined and discussed with patients at the time of treatment entry; periodically throughout treatment, particularly when there have been returns to illicit drug use; and when suspected (e.g., incorrect buprenorphine pill/film count) or confirmed. These procedures will establish the steps to be taken to prevent, monitor, and respond to misuse and diversion of buprenorphine. The response should be therapeutic and matched to the patients' needs, as untreated opioid use disorder and treatment dropout/administrative discharges may lead to increased patient morbidity and mortality and further use of diverted medications or illicit opioids associated with overdose death.

Procedures for Prevention:

- Use buprenorphine/naloxone combination products when medically indicated and cost is not an issue. Reserve the daily buprenorphine monoproducts for pregnant patients and patients who could not afford treatment if the combination product were required, who have a history of stability in treatment and low diversion risk, or who have arrangements for observed dosing. Buprenorphine monoproducts are recommended for pregnant women.
- Counsel patients on safe storage of, and nonsharing of, medications. Patients must agree to safe storage of their medication. This is even more critical if there are children in the home where the patient lives. Counsel patients about acquiring locked devices and avoiding storage in parts of the home frequented by visitors (e.g., do not recommend storage in the kitchen or common bathrooms). Proactively discuss how medication should be stored and transported when traveling to minimize risk of unintended loss.
- Counsel patients on taking medication as instructed and not sharing medication. Explicitly explain to patients the definitions of diversion and misuse, with examples. Patients are required to take medication as instructed by the healthcare professional; for example, they may not crush or inject the medication.
- Check the prescription drug monitoring program for new patients and check regularly thereafter. Prescription drug monitoring program reports can be a useful resource when there is little history available or when there is a concern based on observation. Check for prescriptions that interact with buprenorphine and for other buprenorphine prescribers.

- Prescribe a therapeutic dose that is tailored to the patient's needs. Do not routinely provide an additional supply "just in case." Question patients who say they need a significantly higher dose, particularly when they are already at 24 mg per day of buprenorphine equivalents.
- Make sure the patient understands the practice's treatment agreement and prescription policies. The XYZ Medical Practice's treatment agreement and other documentation are clear about policies regarding number of doses in each prescription, refills, and rules on "lost" prescriptions. Review the policies in person with the patient. Offer an opportunity for questions. Patient and provider must sign the agreement. Review the policies again with the patient at subsequent appointments. See Sample Buprenorphine Treatment Agreement or Sample XR-NTX Treatment Agreement as needed.

Procedures for Monitoring:
- Request random urine tests. The presence of buprenorphine in the urine indicates that the patient has taken some portion of the prescribed dose. Absence of buprenorphine in the urine supports nonadherence. Testing for buprenorphine metabolites (which are present only if buprenorphine is metabolized) should periodically be included to minimize the possibility that buprenorphine is added directly to the urine sample. Dipstick tests can be subverted or replaced. A range of strategies can be used to minimize falsified urine collections, including (1) observed collection; (2) disallowing carry-in items (e.g., purses, backpacks) in the bathroom; (3) turning off running water and coloring toilet water to eliminate the possibility of dilution; (4) monitoring the bathroom door so that only one person can go in; and (5) testing the temperature of the urine immediately after voiding.
- Schedule unannounced pill/film counts. Periodically ask patients who are at high risk at initial or subsequent appointments to bring in their medication containers for a pill/film count.
- With unannounced monitoring (both pill/film counts and urine tests), the patient is contacted and must appear within a specified time period (e.g., 24 hours) after the phone call. If the patient doesn't show, then the provider should consider this as a positive indicator of misuse or diversion.
- Directly observe ingestion. Patients take medication in front of the healthcare professional or another qualified clinician and are observed until the medication dissolves in the mouth (transmucosal [sublingual or buccal] absorption). Patients who are having difficulty adhering to their buprenorphine can have their medication provided under direct observation in the office for a designated frequency (e.g., three times/week).
- Limit medication supply. When directly observed doses in the office are not practical, short prescription time spans can be used (e.g., weekly, 3 days at a time).

Procedures To Respond to Misuse or Diversion: Misuse or diversion doesn't mean automatic discharge from the practice. However, it will require consideration of one or more of the following procedures:
- Evaluate the misuse and diversion. For instance, describe the incident of misuse (e.g., "the patient took the prescribed dose on three or more occasions by intravenous route immediately after starting treatment, stating that she believed the dose would not be adequate by sublingual route; she has just initiated treatment") or diversion ("the patient gave half of dose to his wife, who is still using heroin and was withdrawing, because he did not want her to have to buy heroin off the street; she is on a waiting list for treatment") and tailor the response to the behavior (e.g., reeducation of the patient on buprenorphine pharmacology in the first example above; assistance with treatment entry for the spouse in the second example). Reassess the treatment plan and patient progress. Strongly consider smaller supplies of medication and supervised dosing for any patient who is taking medication intravenously or intranasally or diverting, regardless of reason. Treatment structure may need to be increased, including more frequent appointments, supervised administration, and increased psychosocial support.
- Intensify treatment or level of care, if needed. Some patients may require an alternative treatment setting or pharmacotherapy such as methadone. The clinician will discuss these alternatives with the patient to ensure optimal patient outcome. This should be discussed at treatment onset so the patient is aware of the consequences of misuse and diversion.
- Document and describe the misuse and diversion incident. Also document the clinical thinking that supports the clinical response, which should be aimed at minimizing risk of diversion and misuse and treating the patient's opioid use disorder at the level of care needed.

Policy adapted from ASAM's *Office-Based Opioid Use Disorder Policy and Procedure Manual*, which is updated periodically; the most current version is available online (https://www.asam.org/docs/default-source/advocacy/sample-diversion-policy.pdf?sfvrsn=6).

Adapted with permission.[49]

Buprenorphine Induction and Maintenance Appropriate Use Checklists

BTOD|REMS

Patient Name: _____

APPROPRIATE USE CHECKLIST:
BUPRENORPHINE-CONTAINING TRANSMUCOSAL PRODUCTS FOR OPIOID DEPENDENCE

This checklist is a useful reminder of the safe use conditions and monitoring requirements for prescribing buprenorphine-containing transmucosal products for opioid dependence.

Requirements to address during each patient's appointment include:
- understanding and reinforcement of safe use conditions
- the importance of psychosocial counseling
- screening and monitoring patients to determine progress towards treatment goals

If a patient continues to abuse various drugs or is unresponsive to treatment, including psychosocial intervention, it is important that you assess the need to refer the patient to a specialist and/or a more intensive behavioral treatment environment.

Additional resource: Physician Clinical Support System: http://pcssb.org/

This checklist may be used during the induction period and filed in patient's medical record to document safe use conditions. Once a maintenance dose has been established, use the maintenance checklist.

MEASUREMENT TO ENSURE APPROPRIATE USE	NOTES
Date:	
INDUCTION	
☐ Verified patient meets appropriate diagnostic criteria for opioid dependence	
☐ Discussed risks described in professional labeling and Medication Guide with patient	
☐ Explained or reviewed conditions of safe storage of medication, including keeping it out of the sight and reach of children	
☐ Provided induction doses under appropriate supervision	
☐ Prescribed limited amount of medication at first visit	
☐ Scheduled next visit at interval commensurate with patient stability • Weekly, or more frequent visits recommended for the first month	

Continued on next page

Part 5 of 5—Resources Related to Medications for Opioid Use Disorder

Patient Name: _____

APPROPRIATE USE CHECKLIST:
BUPRENORPHINE-CONTAINING TRANSMUCOSAL PRODUCTS FOR OPIOID DEPENDENCE

This checklist may be used for visits following the induction period and filed in patient's medical record to document safe use conditions.

MEASUREMENT TO ENSURE APPROPRIATE USE	NOTES
Date: Visit #	
MAINTENANCE	
☐ Assessed and encouraged patient to take medication as prescribed • Consider pill/film count/dose reconciliation	
☐ Assessed appropriateness of dosage • Buprenorphine combined with naloxone is recommended for maintenance: 　• Buprenorphine/Naloxone SL tablet and film (Suboxone®): doses ranging from 12 mg to 16 mg of buprenorphine are recommended for maintenance 　• Buprenorphine/Naloxone SL tablet (Zubsolv®): a target dose of 11.4 mg buprenorphine is recommended for maintenance 　• Buprenorphine/Naloxone Buccal Film (Bunavail®): a target dose of 8.4 mg of buprenorphine is recommended for maintenance • Doses higher than this should be an exception • The need for higher dose should be carefully evaluated	
☐ Conduct urine drug screens as appropriate to assess use of illicit substances	
☐ Assessed participation in professional counseling and support services	
☐ Assessed whether benefits of treatment with buprenorphine-containing products outweigh risks associated with buprenorphine-containing products	
☐ Assessed whether patient is making adequate progress toward treatment goals • Considered results of urine drug screens as part of the evidence of the patient complying with the treatment program • Consider referral to more intensive forms of treatment for patients not making progress	
☐ Scheduled next visit at interval commensurate with patient stability • Weekly, or more frequent visits are recommended for the first month	

Available online (www.accessdata.fda.gov/drugsatfda_docs/rems/BTOD_2017-01-23_Appropriate_Use_Checklist.pdf).
Reprinted from material in the public domain.[50]

Buprenorphine Treatment Agreement

This form is for educational/informational purposes only. It doesn't establish a legal or medical standard of care. Healthcare professionals should use their judgment in interpreting this form and applying it in the circumstances of their individual patients and practice arrangements. The information provided in this form is provided "as is" with no guarantee as to its accuracy or completeness.

TREATMENT AGREEMENT

I agree to accept the following treatment contract for buprenorphine office-based opioid addiction treatment:

1. The risks and benefits of buprenorphine treatment have been explained to me.
2. The risks and benefits of other treatment for opioid use disorder (including methadone, naltrexone, and nonmedication treatments) have been explained to me.
3. I will keep my medication in a safe, secure place away from children (for example, in a lockbox). My plan is to store it [describe where and how _____].
4. I will take the medication exactly as my healthcare provider prescribes. If I want to change my medication dose, I will speak with my healthcare provider first. Taking more medication than my healthcare provider prescribes or taking it more than once daily as my healthcare provider prescribes is medication misuse and may result in supervised dosing at the clinic. Taking the medication by snorting or by injection is also medication misuse and may result in supervised dosing at the clinic, referral to a higher level of care, or change in medication based on my healthcare provider's evaluation.
5. I will be on time to my appointments and respectful to the office staff and other patients.
6. I will keep my healthcare provider informed of all my medications (including herbs and vitamins) and medical problems.
7. I agree not to obtain or take prescription opioid medications prescribed by any other healthcare provider without consulting my buprenorphine prescriber.
8. If I am going to have a medical procedure that will cause pain, I will let my healthcare provider know in advance so that my pain will be adequately treated.
9. If I miss an appointment or lose my medication, I understand that I will not get more medication until my next office visit. I may also have to start having supervised buprenorphine dosing.
10. If I come to the office intoxicated, I understand that my healthcare provider will not see me, and I will not receive more medication until the next office visit. I may also have to start having supervised buprenorphine dosing.
11. I understand that it's illegal to give away or sell my medication; this is diversion. If I do this, my treatment will no longer include unsupervised buprenorphine dosing and may require referral to a higher level of care, supervised dosing at the clinic, and/or a change in medication based on my healthcare provider's evaluation.
12. Violence, threatening language or behavior, or participation in any illegal activity at the office will result in treatment termination from the clinic.
13. I understand that random urine drug testing is a treatment requirement. If I do not provide a urine sample, it will count as a positive drug test.
14. I understand that I will be called at random times to bring my medication container into the office for a pill or film count. Missing medication doses could result in supervised dosing or referral to a higher level of care at this clinic or potentially at another treatment provider based on my individual needs.
15. I understand that initially I will have weekly office visits until I am stable. I will get a prescription for 7 days of medication at each visit.
16. I can be seen every 2 weeks in the office starting the second month of treatment if I have two negative urine drug tests in a row. I will then get a prescription for 14 days of medication at each visit.
17. I will go back to weekly visits if I have a positive drug test. I can go back to visits every 2 weeks when I have two negative drug tests in a row again.
18. I may be seen less than every 2 weeks based on goals made by my healthcare provider and me.
19. I understand that people have died by mixing buprenorphine with alcohol and other drugs like benzodiazepines (drugs like Valium, Klonopin, and Xanax).

Continued on next page

20. I understand that treatment of opioid use disorder involves more than just taking medication. I agree to comply with my healthcare provider's recommendations for additional counseling and/or for help with other problems.
21. I understand that there is no fixed time for being on buprenorphine and that the goal of treatment is for me to stop using all illicit drugs and become successful in all aspects of my life.
22. I understand that I may experience opioid withdrawal symptoms when I stop taking buprenorphine.
23. I have been educated about the other two FDA-approved medications used for opioid dependence treatment, methadone and naltrexone.
24. I have been educated about the increased chance of pregnancy when stopping illicit opioid use and starting buprenorphine treatment and been informed about methods for preventing pregnancy.

Other specific items unique to my treatment include:

Patient's Name (print): _____

Patient's Signature: _____ Date: _____

This form is adapted from the American Society of Addiction Medicine's Sample Treatment Agreement, which is updated periodically; the most current version of the agreement is available online (https://www.asam.org/docs/default-source/advocacy/sample-treatment-agreement30fa159472bc604ca5b7ff000030b21a.pdf?sfvrsn=bd4675c2_0).

Adapted with permission.[51]

Naltrexone forms

Key Techniques for Reducing Injection Site Reactions[52]

To reduce severe injection site reactions when administering XR-NTX via intramuscular injection, use the following techniques:

- **Use one of the administration needles provided with the XR-NTX kit to ensure that the injection reaches the gluteal muscle.** Use the 2-inch needle for patients who have more subcutaneous adipose tissue. Use the 1.5-inch needle for patients with less subcutaneous adipose tissue. Either needle is appropriate for use with patients who have average amounts of subcutaneous adipose tissue.
- **Use aseptic technique when administering intramuscularly.** Using a circular motion, clean the injection site with an alcohol swab. Let the area dry before administering the injection. Do not touch this area again before administration.
- **Use proper deep intramuscular injection technique into the gluteal muscle.** XR-NTX must not be injected intravenously, subcutaneously, or into adipose tissue. Accidental subcutaneous injection may increase the risk of severe injection site reactions.
  - **Administer the suspension by deep intramuscular injection into the upper outer quadrant of gluteal muscle,** alternating buttocks per monthly injection.
  - **Remember to aspirate for blood before injection.** If blood aspirates or the needle clogs, do not inject. Change to the spare needle provided in the package and administer into an adjacent site in the same gluteal region, again aspirating for blood before injection.
  - **Inject the suspension in a smooth, continuous motion.**

A patient counseling tool is available to help you counsel your patients before administration about the serious risks associated with XR-NTX.

The above information is a selection of key safety information about the XR-NTX injection. For complete safety information, refer to the directions for use and the prescribing information provided in the medication kit. You can also obtain this information online (www.vivitrolrems.com) or by calling 1-800-VIVITROL.

Available online (www.vivitrolrems.com/content/pdf/patinfo-injection-poster.pdf).

Part 5 of 5—Resources Related to Medications for Opioid Use Disorder

Patient Counseling Tool for XR-NTX

Patient Counseling Tool
VIVITROL® (naltrexone for extended-release injectable suspension)

Risk of sudden opioid withdrawal during initiation and re-initiation of VIVITROL
Using any type of opioid including street drugs, prescription pain medicines, cough, cold or diarrhea medicines that contain opioids, or opioid dependence treatments buprenorphine or methadone, in the 7 to 14 days before starting VIVITROL may cause severe and potentially dangerous sudden opioid withdrawal.

Risk of opioid overdose
Patients may be more sensitive to the effects of lower amounts of opioids:

- After stopping opioids (detoxification)
- When the next VIVITROL dose is due
- If a dose of VIVITROL is missed
- After VIVITROL treatment stops

Patients should tell their family and people close to them about the increased sensitivity to opioids and the risk of overdose even when using lower doses of opioids or amounts that they used before treatment. Using large amounts of opioids, such as prescription pain pills or heroin, to overcome effects of VIVITROL can lead to serious injury, coma, and death.

Risk of severe reactions at the injection site
Remind patients of these **possible** symptoms at the **injection site:**

- Intense pain
- The area feels hard
- Large areas of swelling
- Lumps
- Blisters
- Open wound
- Dark scab

Some of these injection site reactions have required surgery.
Tell your patients to contact a healthcare provider if they have any reactions at the injection site.

Risk of liver injury, including liver damage or hepatitis
Remind patients of the possible symptoms of liver damage or hepatitis.

- Stomach area pain lasting more than a few days
- Dark urine
- Yellowing of the whites of eyes
- Tiredness

Patients may not feel the therapeutic effects of opioid-containing medicines for pain, cough or cold, or diarrhea while taking VIVITROL.

> Patients should carry written information with them at all times to alert healthcare providers that they are taking VIVITROL, so they can be treated properly in an emergency.
>
> A Patient Wallet Card or Medical Alert Bracelet can be ordered from: 1-800-848-4876, Option #1.

PLEASE SEE PRESCRIBING INFORMATION AND MEDICATION GUIDE.

Alkermes®
Alkermes® and VIVITROL® are registered trademarks of Alkermes, Inc.
©2013 Alkermes, Inc.
All rights reserved VIV-001317 Printed in U.S.A
www.vivitrol.com

Vivitrol®
(naltrexone for extended-release injectable suspension)

Available online (www.vivitrolrems.com/content/pdf/patinfo-counseling-tool.pdf).
Reprinted with permission.[53]

Sample XR-NTX Treatment Agreement

This form is for educational/informational purposes only. It doesn't establish a legal or medical standard of care. Healthcare professionals should use their judgment in interpreting this form and applying it in the circumstances of their individual patients and practice arrangements. The information provided in this form is provided "as is" with no guarantee as to its accuracy or completeness.

TREATMENT AGREEMENT

I agree to accept the following treatment agreement for extended-release injectable naltrexone office-based opioid use disorder treatment:

1. The risks and benefits of extended-release injectable naltrexone treatment have been explained to me.
2. The risks and benefits of other treatment for opioid use disorder (including methadone, buprenorphine, and nonmedication treatments) have been explained to me.
3. I will be on time to my appointments and respectful to the office staff and other patients.
4. I will keep my healthcare provider informed of all my medications (including herbs and vitamins) and medical problems.
5. I agree not to obtain or take prescription opioid medications prescribed by any other healthcare provider.
6. If I am going to have a medical procedure that will cause pain, I will let my healthcare provider know in advance so that my pain will be adequately treated.
7. If I miss a scheduled appointment for my next extended-release naltrexone injection, I understand that I should reschedule the appointment as soon as possible because it is important to receive the medication on time to reduce the risk of opioid overdose should I return to use.
8. If I come to the office intoxicated, I understand that my healthcare provider will not see me.
9. Violence, threatening language or behavior, or participation in any illegal activity at the office will result in treatment termination from the clinic.
10. I understand that random urine drug testing is a treatment requirement. If I do not provide a urine sample, it will count as a positive drug test.
11. I understand that initially I will have weekly office visits until my condition is stable.
12. I can be seen every 2 weeks in the office starting the second month of treatment if I have two negative urine drug tests in a row.
13. I may be seen less than every 2 weeks based on goals made by my healthcare provider and me.
14. I understand that people have died trying to overcome the opioid blockade by taking large amounts of opioids.
15. I understand that treatment of opioid use disorder involves more than just taking medication. I agree to follow my healthcare provider's recommendations for additional counseling and/or for help with other problems.
16. I understand that there is no fixed time for being on naltrexone and that the goal of treatment is for me to stop using all illicit drugs and become successful in all aspects of my life.
17. I understand that my risk of overdose increases if I go back to using opioids after stopping naltrexone.
18. I have been educated about the other two FDA-approved medications used to treat opioid use disorder, methadone and buprenorphine, and I prefer to receive treatment with naltrexone.
19. I have been educated about the increased chance of pregnancy when stopping illicit opioid use and starting naltrexone treatment and have been informed about methods for preventing pregnancy.
20. I have been informed that if I become pregnant during naltrexone treatment, I should inform my provider and have a discussion about the risks and benefits of continuing to take naltrexone.

Other specific items unique to my treatment include:

Patient Name (print): _____

Patient Signature: _____ Date: _____

This form is adapted from ASAM's Sample Treatment Agreement, which is updated periodically; the most current version of the agreement is available online (www.asam.org/docs/default-source/advocacy/sample-treatment-agreement30fa159472bc604ca5b7ff000030b21a.pdf?sfvrsn=0).

Adapted with permission.[54]

Glossary of TIP Terminology

Abuse liability: The likelihood that a medication with central nervous system activity will cause desirable psychological effects, such as euphoria or mood changes, that promote the medication's misuse.

Addiction: As defined by ASAM,[55] "a primary, chronic disease of brain reward, motivation, memory, and related circuitry." It is characterized by inability to consistently abstain, impairment in behavioral control, craving, diminished recognition of significant problems with one's behaviors and interpersonal relationships, and a dysfunctional emotional response. Like other chronic diseases, addiction often involves cycles of **relapse** and **remission**. The *Diagnostic and Statistical Manual of Mental Disorders*, Fifth Edition[56] (DSM-5), does not use the term for diagnostic purposes, but it commonly describes the more severe forms of opioid use disorder.

Bioavailability: Proportion of medication administered that reaches the bloodstream.

Care provider: Encompasses both **healthcare professionals** and other professionals who do not provide medical services, such as counselors or providers of supportive services. Often shortened to "provider."

Cross-tolerance: Potential for people tolerant to one opioid (e.g., heroin) to be tolerant to another (e.g., methadone).

Dissociation: Rate at which a drug uncouples from the receptor. A drug with a longer dissociation rate will have a longer duration of action than a drug with a shorter dissociation rate.

Half-life: Rate of removal of a drug from the body. One half-life removes 50 percent from the plasma. After a drug is stopped, it takes five half-lives to remove about 95 percent from the plasma. If a drug is continued at the same dose, its plasma level will continue to rise until it reaches steady state concentrations after about five half-lives.

Healthcare professionals: Physicians, nurse practitioners, physician assistants, and other medical service professionals who are eligible to prescribe medications for and treat patients with OUD. The term "**prescribers**" also refers to these healthcare professionals.

Induction: Process of initial dosing with medication for OUD treatment until the patient reaches a state of stability; also called initiation.

Intrinsic activity: The degree of receptor activation attributable to drug binding. **Full agonist, partial agonist**, and **antagonist** are terms that describe the intrinsic activity of a drug.

Maintenance treatment: Providing medications to achieve and sustain clinical remission of signs and symptoms of OUD and support the individual process of recovery without a specific endpoint (as with the typical standard of care in medical and psychiatric treatment of other chronic illnesses).

Medically supervised withdrawal (formerly called detoxification): Using an opioid agonist (or an alpha-2 adrenergic agonist if opioid agonist is not available) in tapering doses or other medications to help a patient discontinue illicit or prescription opioids.

Medical management: Process whereby healthcare professionals provide medication, basic brief supportive counseling, monitoring of drug use and medication adherence, and referrals, when necessary, to addiction counseling and other services to address the patient's medical, mental health, comorbid addiction, and psychosocial needs.

Mutual-help groups: Groups of people who work together on obtaining and maintaining recovery. Unlike peer support (e.g., the use of recovery coaches), mutual-help groups consist entirely of people who volunteer their time and typically have no official connection to treatment programs. Most are self-supporting. Although 12-Step groups such as AA and NA are the most widespread and well-researched type of mutual-help groups, other groups may be available in some areas. They range from groups affiliated with a religion or church (e.g., Celebrate Recovery, Millati Islami) to purely secular groups (e.g., SMART Recovery, Women for Sobriety).

Office-based opioid treatment (OBOT): Providing medication for OUD in settings other than certified OTPs.

Opiates: A subclass of opioids derived from opium (e.g., morphine, codeine, thebaine).

Opioid misuse: The use of prescription opioids in any way other than as directed by a prescriber; the use of any opioid in a manner, situation, amount, or frequency that can cause harm to self or others.[57]

Opioid receptor agonist: A substance that has an affinity for and stimulates physiological activity at cell receptors in the central nervous system that are normally stimulated by opioids. **Mu-opioid receptor full agonists** (e.g., methadone) bind to the mu-opioid receptor and produce actions similar to those produced by the endogenous opioid beta-endorphin. Increasing the dose increases the effect. **Mu-opioid receptor partial agonists** (e.g., buprenorphine) bind to the mu-opioid receptor. Unlike with full agonists, increasing their dose may not produce additional effects once they have reached their maximal effect. At low doses, partial agonists may produce effects similar to those of full agonists.

Opioid receptor antagonist: A substance that has an affinity for opioid receptors in the central nervous system without producing the physiological effects of opioid agonists. Mu-opioid receptor antagonists (e.g., naltrexone) can block the effects of exogenously administered opioids.

Opioid receptor blockade: Blunting or blocking of the euphoric effects of an opioid through opioid receptor occupancy by an opioid agonist (e.g., methadone, buprenorphine) or antagonist (e.g., naltrexone).

Opioids: All natural, synthetic, and semisynthetic substances that have effects similar to morphine. They can be used as medications having such effects (e.g., methadone, buprenorphine, oxycodone).

Opioid treatment program (OTP): An accredited treatment program with SAMHSA certification and DEA registration to administer and dispense opioid agonist medications that are approved by FDA to treat opioid addiction. Currently, these include methadone and buprenorphine products. Other pharmacotherapies, such as naltrexone, may be provided but are not subject to these regulations. OTPs must provide adequate medical, counseling, vocational, educational, and other assessment and treatment services either onsite or by referral to an outside agency or practitioner through a formal agreement.[58]

Opioid use disorder (OUD): Per DSM-5,[59] a disorder characterized by loss of control of opioid use, risky opioid use, impaired social functioning, tolerance, and withdrawal. Tolerance and withdrawal do not count toward the diagnosis in people experiencing these symptoms when using opioids under appropriate medical supervision. OUD covers a range of severity and replaces what the DSM-IV termed "opioid abuse" and "opioid dependence." An OUD diagnosis is applicable to a person who uses opioids and experiences at least 2 of the 11 symptoms in a 12-month period. (See Exhibit 2.11 in Part 2 for full DSM-5 diagnostic criteria for OUD.)

Peer support: The use of peer support specialists in recovery to provide nonclinical (i.e., not requiring training in diagnosis or treatment) recovery support services to individuals in recovery from addiction and to their families.

Peer support specialist: Someone in recovery who has lived experience in addiction plus skills learned in formal training. Peer support specialists may be paid professionals or volunteers. They are distinguished from members of mutual-help groups because they maintain contact with treatment staff. They offer experiential knowledge that treatment staff often lack.

Prescribers: Healthcare professionals who are eligible to prescribe medications for OUD.

Psychosocial support: Ancillary services to enhance a patient's overall functioning and well-being, including recovery support services, case management, housing, employment, and educational services.

Psychosocial treatment: Interventions that seek to enhance a patient's social and mental functioning, including addiction counseling, contingency management, and mental health services.

Receptor affinity: Strength of the bond between a medication and its receptor. A medication with high mu-opioid receptor affinity requires lower concentrations to occupy the same number of mu-opioid receptors as a drug with lower mu-opioid receptor affinity. Drugs with high mu-opioid receptor affinity may displace drugs with lower affinity.

Recovery: A process of change through which individuals improve their health and wellness, live a self-directed life, and strive to reach their full potential. Even individuals with severe and chronic SUDs can, with help, overcome their SUDs and regain health and social function. Although abstinence from all substance misuse is a cardinal feature of a recovery lifestyle, it is not the only healthy, prosocial feature. Patients taking FDA-approved medication to treat OUD can be considered in recovery.

Recovery capital: The sum of the internal (e.g., motivation, self-efficacy, spirituality) and external (e.g., access to health care, employment, family support) resources that an individual can draw on to begin and sustain recovery from SUDs.

Recovery-oriented care: A service orientation that supports individuals with behavioral health conditions in a process of change through which they can improve their health and wellness, live self-directed lives, and strive to reach their full potential.

Relapse: A process in which a person with OUD who has been in **remission** experiences a return of symptoms or loss of remission. A relapse is different from a **return to opioid use** in that it involves more than a single incident of use. Relapses occur over a period of time and can be interrupted. Relapse need not be long lasting. The TIP uses relapse to describe relapse prevention, a common treatment modality.

Remission: A medical term meaning a disappearance of signs and symptoms of the disease.[60] DSM-5 defines remission as present in people who previously met OUD criteria but no longer meet any OUD criteria (with the possible exception of craving).[61] Remission is an essential element of **recovery**.

Return to opioid use: One or more instances of **opioid misuse** without a return of symptoms of OUD. A return to opioid use may lead to **relapse**.

Tolerance: Alteration of the body's responsiveness to alcohol or other drugs (including opioids) such that higher doses are required to produce the same effect achieved during initial use. See also **medically supervised withdrawal**.

Notes

1. Centers for Disease Control and Prevention. (2017). *Drug overdose death data.* Retrieved January 9, 2018, from www.cdc.gov/drugoverdose/data/statedeaths.html

2. National Safety Council. (2017). *NSC motor vehicle fatality estimates.* Retrieved October 31, 2017, from www.nsc.org/NewsDocuments/2017/12-month-estimates.pdf

3. Babor, T. F., Higgins-Biddle, J. C., Saunders, J. B., & Monteiro, M. G. (2001). *The Alcohol Use Disorders Identification Test. Guidelines for use in primary care* (2nd ed.). Geneva, Switzerland: The World Health Organization.

4. Bush, K., Kivlahan, D. R., McDonell, M. B., Fihn, S. D., & Bradley, K. A. (1998). The AUDIT alcohol consumption questions (AUDIT-C): An effective brief screening test for problem drinking. Ambulatory Care Quality Improvement Project (ACQUIP). Alcohol Use Disorders Identification Test. *Archives of Internal Medicine, 158*(16), 1789–1795.

5. Skinner, H. A. (1982). The Drug Abuse Screening Test. *Addictive Behavior, 7*(4), 363–371.

6. Yudko, E., Lozhkina, O., & Fouts, A. (2007). A comprehensive review of the psychometric properties of the Drug Abuse Screening Test. *Journal of Substance Abuse Treatment, 32,* 189–198.

7. American Psychiatric Association. (2013). *Diagnostic and statistical manual of mental disorders* (5th ed., p. 541). Arlington, VA: American Psychiatric Publishing.

8. Heatherton, T. F., Kozlowski, L. T., Frecker, R. C., Rickert, W., & Robinson, J. (1989). Measuring the heaviness of smoking: Using self-reported time to the first cigarette of the day and number of cigarettes smoked per day. *British Journal of Addiction, 84*(7), 791–799.

9. Smith, P. C., Schmidt, S. M., Allensworth-Davies, D., & Saitz, R. (2009). Primary care validation of a single-question alcohol screening test. *Journal of General Internal Medicine, 24*(7), 783–788. doi:10.1007/s11606-009-0928-6

10. Substance Abuse and Mental Health Services Administration. (2016). *SAMHSA opioid overdose prevention toolkit.* HHS Publication No. (SMA) 16-4742. Rockville, MD: Substance Abuse and Mental Health Services Administration.

11. Smith, P. C., Schmidt, S. M., Allensworth-Davies, D., & Saitz, R. (2010). A single-question screening test for drug use in primary care. *Archives of Internal Medicine, 170*(13), 1155–1160.

12. Shapiro, B., Coffa, D., & McCance-Katz, E. F. (2013). A primary care approach to substance misuse. *American Family Physician, 88*(2), 113–121.

13. McNeely, J., Wu, L. T., Subramaniam, G., Sharma, G., Cathers, L. A., Svikis, D., … Schwartz, R. P. (2016). Performance of the Tobacco, Alcohol, Prescription Medication, and Other Substance Use (TAPS) Tool for substance use screening in primary care patients. *Annals of Internal Medicine, 165*(10), 690–699.

14. Tiet, Q. Q., Leyva, Y. E., Moos, R. H., Frayne, S. M., Osterberg, L., & Smith, B. (2015). Screen of drug use: Diagnostic accuracy of a new brief tool for primary care. *JAMA Internal Medicine, 175*(8), 1371–1377.

15. Lynch, K. (2014). *San Francisco General Hospital laboratory protocol.* San Francisco, CA: San Francisco General Hospital.

16. Warner, E., & Lorch, E. (2014). Laboratory diagnosis. In R. K. Ries, D. A. Fiellin, S. C. Miller, & R. Saitz (Eds.), *Principles of addiction medicine* (5th ed., pp. 332–343). Philadelphia, PA: Wolters Kluwer.

17. Milone, M. C. (2012). Laboratory testing for prescription opioids. *Journal of Medical Toxicology, 8*(4), 408–416. doi:10.1007/s13181-012-0274-7

18. Leavitt, S. B., Shinderman, M., Maxwell, S., Eap, C. B., & Paris, P. (2000). When "enough" is not enough: New perspectives on optimal methadone maintenance dose. *Mount Sinai Journal of Medicine, 67*(5–6), 404–411.

19. American Society of Addiction Medicine. (2016). *Sample office-based opioid use disorder policy and procedure manual.* Retrieved October 19, 2017, from www.asam.org/docs/default-source/advocacy/sample-diversion-policy.pdf?sfvrsn=0

20. Roxane Laboratories. (2015). *Buprenorphine HCl sublingual tablets: Full prescribing information.* Retrieved October 16, 2017, from http://dailymed.nlm.nih.gov/dailymed/drugInfo.cfm?setid=1bf8b35a-b769-465c-a2f8-099868dfcd2f

21. Roxane Laboratories. (2015). *Buprenorphine HCl sublingual tablets: Full prescribing information.* Retrieved October 16, 2017, from http://dailymed.nlm.nih.gov/dailymed/drugInfo.cfm?setid=1bf8b35a-b769-465c-a2f8-099868dfcd2f

22. Nasser, A. F., Heidbreder, C., Liu, Y., & Fudala, P. J. (2015). Pharmacokinetics of sublingual buprenorphine and naloxone in subjects with mild to severe hepatic impairment (Child-Pugh classes A, B, and C), in hepatitis C virus-seropositive subjects, and in healthy volunteers. *Clinical Pharmacokinetics, 54*(8), 837–849.

23. Durand, F., & Valla, D. (2008). Assessment of prognosis of cirrhosis. *Seminars in Liver Disease, 28*(1), 110–122.

24. Durand, F., & Valla, D. (2008). Assessment of prognosis of cirrhosis. *Seminars in Liver Disease, 28*(1), 110–122.

25. Indivior. (2015). *Suboxone (buprenorphine and naloxone) sublingual film: Full prescribing information.* Retrieved October 16, 2017, from www.suboxone.com/content/pdfs/prescribing-information.pdf

26. Nasser, A. F., Heidbreder, C., Liu, Y., & Fudala, P. J. (2015). Pharmacokinetics of sublingual buprenorphine and naloxone in subjects with mild to severe hepatic impairment (Child-Pugh classes A, B, and C), in hepatitis C virus-seropositive subjects, and in healthy volunteers. *Clinical Pharmacokinetics, 54*(8), 837–849.

27. Roxane Laboratories. (2015). *Buprenorphine HCl sublingual tablets: Full prescribing information.* Retrieved October 16, 2017, from http://dailymed.nlm.nih.gov/dailymed/drugInfo.cfm?setid=1bf8b35a-b769-465c-a2f8-099868dfcd2f

28. Indivior. (2015). *Suboxone (buprenorphine and naloxone) sublingual film: Full prescribing information.* Retrieved October 16, 2017, from www.suboxone.com/content/pdfs/prescribing-information.pdf

29. Nasser, A. F., Heidbreder, C., Liu, Y., & Fudala, P. J. (2015). Pharmacokinetics of sublingual buprenorphine and naloxone in subjects with mild to severe hepatic impairment (Child-Pugh classes A, B, and C), in hepatitis C virus-seropositive subjects, and in healthy volunteers. *Clinical Pharmacokinetics, 54*(8), 837–849.

30. Durand, F., & Valla, D. (2008). Assessment of prognosis of cirrhosis. *Seminars in Liver Disease, 28*(1), 110–122.

31. Nasser, A. F., Heidbreder, C., Liu, Y., & Fudala, P. J. (2015). Pharmacokinetics of sublingual buprenorphine and naloxone in subjects with mild to severe hepatic impairment (Child-Pugh classes A, B, and C), in hepatitis C virus-seropositive subjects, and in healthy volunteers. *Clinical Pharmacokinetics, 54*(8), 837–849.

32. Roxane Laboratories. (2015). *Buprenorphine HCl sublingual tablets: Full prescribing information.* Retrieved October 16, 2017, from http://dailymed.nlm.nih.gov/dailymed/drugInfo.cfm?setid=1bf8b35a-b769-465c-a2f8-099868dfcd2f

33. Nasser, A. F., Heidbreder, C., Liu, Y., & Fudala, P. J. (2015). Pharmacokinetics of sublingual buprenorphine and naloxone in subjects with mild to severe hepatic impairment (Child-Pugh classes A, B, and C), in hepatitis C virus-seropositive subjects, and in healthy volunteers. *Clinical Pharmacokinetic, 54*(8), 837–849.

34. Substance Abuse and Mental Health Services Administration. (2016). Sublingual and transmucosal buprenorphine for opioid use disorder: Review and update. *Advisory*, Vol. 15, Issue 1. Rockville, MD: Substance Abuse and Mental Health Services Administration.

35. Donovan, D. M., Ingalsbe, M. H., Benbow, J., & Daley, D. C. (2013). 12-step interventions and mutual support programs for substance use disorders: An overview. *Social Work in Public Health, 28*(3–4), 313–332.

36. McLellan, A. T., & White, W. (2012). *Opioid maintenance and recovery-oriented systems of care: It is time to integrate* (p. 2). London, England: National Treatment Agency for Substance Misuse.

37. Substance Abuse and Mental Health Services Administration. (2016). *Pocket guide: Medication-assisted treatment of opioid use disorder.* HHS Publication No. (SMA) 16-4892PG. Rockville, MD: Substance Abuse and Mental Health Services Administration.

38. Substance Abuse and Mental Health Services Administration. (2015). *Clinical use of extended-release injectable naltrexone in the treatment of opioid use disorder: A brief guide.* HHS Publication No. (SMA) 14-4892R. Rockville, MD: Substance Abuse and Mental Health Services Administration.

39. Mattick, R. P., Breen, C., Kimber, J., & Davoli, M. (2014). Buprenorphine maintenance versus placebo or methadone maintenance for opioid dependence. *Cochrane Database of Systematic Reviews, 2014*(2), 1–84.

40. Mattick, R. P., Breen, C., Kimber, J., & Davoli, M. (2009). Methadone maintenance therapy versus no opioid replacement therapy for opioid dependence. *Cochrane Database of Systematic Reviews, 2009*(3), 1–19.

41. Minozzi, S., Amato, L., Vecchi, S., Davoli, M., Kirchmayer, U., & Verster, A. (2011). Oral naltrexone maintenance treatment for opioid dependence. *Cochrane Database Systems Review, 4*, CD001333.

42. Krupitsky, E., Zvartau, E., Blokhina, E., Verbitskaya, E., Wahlgren, V., Tsoy-Podosenin, M., ... Woody, G. E. (2012.) Randomized trial of long-acting sustained-release naltrexone implant vs oral naltrexone or placebo for preventing relapse to opioid dependence. *Archives of General Psychiatry, 69*(9), 973–981.

43. Lee, J. D., Friedmann, P. D., Kinlock, T. W., Nunes, E. V., Boney, T. Y., Hoskinson, R. A., Jr., ... O'Brien, C. P. (2016). Extended-release naltrexone to prevent opioid relapse in criminal justice offenders. *New England Journal of Medicine, 374*(13), 1232–1242.

44. Minozzi, S., Amato, L., Vecchi, S., Davoli, M., Kirchmayer, U., & Verster, A. (2011). Oral naltrexone maintenance treatment for opioid dependence. *Cochrane Database of Systematic Reviews, 2*, CD001333.

45. Substance Abuse and Mental Health Services Administration. (2016). Sublingual and transmucosal buprenorphine for opioid use disorder: Review and update. *Advisory*, Vol. 15, Issue 1. Rockville, MD: Substance Abuse and Mental Health Services Administration.

46 Lintzeris, N., & Nielsen, S. (2010). Benzodiazepines, methadone and buprenorphine: Interactions and clinical management. *American Journal on Addictions, 19*(1), 59–72.

47 Substance Abuse and Mental Health Services Administration. (2015). *Federal guidelines for opioid treatment programs.* HHS Publication No. (SMA) PEP15-FEDGUIDEOTP. Rockville, MD: Substance Abuse and Mental Health Services Administration.

48 Lofwall, M. & Walsh, S. (2014). A review of buprenorphine diversion and misuse: The current evidence base and experiences from around the world (p. 316). *Journal of Addiction Medicine, 8*(5), 315–326.

49 American Society of Addiction Medicine. (2016). *Sample office-based opioid use disorder policy and procedure manual.* Retrieved October 19, 2017, from www.asam.org/docs/default-source/advocacy/sample-diversion-policy.pdf?sfvrsn=0

50 Food and Drug Administration (2017, May). *Appropriate use checklist: Buprenorphine-containing transmucosal products for opioid dependence.* Silver Spring, MD: Food and Drug Administration.

51 American Society of Addiction Medicine. (2017). *Sample treatment agreement.* Retrieved October 19, 2017, from www.asam.org/docs/default-source/advocacy/sample-treatment-agreement30fa159472bc604ca5b7ff000030b21a.pdf?sfvrsn=0

52 Alkermes. (2015). *Key techniques to reduce severe injection site reactions: VIVITROL (naltrexone for extended release injectable suspension) intramuscular injection.* Retrieved January 9, 2018, from www.vivitrolrems.com/content/pdf/patinfo-injection-poster.pdf

53 Alkermes. (2013). *Patient counseling tool: VIVITROL (naltrexone for extended-release injectable suspension).* Retrieved January 9, 2018, from www.vivitrolrems.com/content/pdf/patinfo-counseling-tool.pdf

54 American Society of Addiction Medicine. (2017). *Sample treatment agreement.* Retrieved October 19, 2017, from www.asam.org/docs/default-source/advocacy/sample-treatment-agreement30fa159472bc604ca5b7ff000030b21a.pdf?sfvrsn=0

55 American Society of Addiction Medicine. (2011). Definition of addiction. Retrieved October 30, 2017, from www.asam.org/resources/definition-of-addiction

56 American Psychiatric Association. (2013). *Diagnostic and statistical manual of mental disorders* (5th ed.). Arlington, VA: American Psychiatric Publishing.

57 Department of Health and Human Services, Office of the Surgeon General. (2016). *Facing addiction in America: The Surgeon General's report on alcohol, drugs, and health.* Washington, DC: Department of Health and Human Services.

58 Substance Abuse and Mental Health Services Administration. (2015). *Federal guidelines for opioid treatment programs.* HHS Publication No. (SMA) PEP15-FEDGUIDEOTP. Rockville, MD: Substance Abuse and Mental Health Services Administration.

59 American Psychiatric Association. (2013). *Diagnostic and statistical manual of mental disorders* (5th ed.). Arlington, VA: American Psychiatric Publishing.

60 National Cancer Institute. (n.d.). *NCI dictionary of cancer terms: Remission.* Retrieved November 22, 2017, from www.cancer.gov/publications/dictionaries/cancer-terms?cdrid=45867

61 American Psychiatric Association. (2013). *Diagnostic and statistical manual of mental disorders* (5th ed.). Arlington, VA: American Psychiatric Publishing.

Available TIPs

TIPs may be ordered or downloaded for free from SAMHSA's Publications Ordering webpage at https://store.samhsa.gov. Or, please call SAMHSA at 1-877-SAMHSA-7 (1-877-726-4727) (English and Español).

TIP 21	Combining Alcohol and Other Drug Abuse Treatment With Diversion for Juveniles in the Justice System
TIP 24	A Guide to Substance Abuse Services for Primary Care Clinicians
TIP 27	Comprehensive Case Management for Substance Abuse Treatment
TIP 29	Substance Use Disorder Treatment for People With Physical and Cognitive Disabilities
TIP 30	Continuity of Offender Treatment for Substance Use Disorders From Institution to Community
TIP 31	Screening and Assessing Adolescents for Substance Use Disorders
TIP 32	Treatment of Adolescents With Substance Use Disorders
TIP 33	Treatment for Stimulant Use Disorders
TIP 34	Brief Interventions and Brief Therapies for Substance Abuse
TIP 35	Enhancing Motivation for Change in Substance Abuse Treatment
TIP 36	Substance Abuse Treatment for Persons With Child Abuse and Neglect Issues
TIP 37	Substance Abuse Treatment for Persons With HIV/AIDS
TIP 38	Integrating Substance Abuse Treatment and Vocational Services
TIP 39	Substance Abuse Treatment and Family Therapy
TIP 41	Substance Abuse Treatment: Group Therapy
TIP 42	Substance Abuse Treatment for Persons With Co-Occurring Disorders
TIP 44	Substance Abuse Treatment for Adults in the Criminal Justice System
TIP 45	Detoxification and Substance Abuse Treatment
TIP 46	Substance Abuse: Administrative Issues in Outpatient Treatment
TIP 47	Substance Abuse: Clinical Issues in Intensive Outpatient Treatment
TIP 48	Managing Depressive Symptoms in Substance Abuse Clients During Early Recovery
TIP 49	Incorporating Alcohol Pharmacotherapies Into Medical Practice
TIP 50	Addressing Suicidal Thoughts and Behaviors in Substance Abuse Treatment
TIP 51	Substance Abuse Treatment: Addressing the Specific Needs of Women
TIP 52	Clinical Supervision and Professional Development of the Substance Abuse Counselor
TIP 53	Addressing Viral Hepatitis in People With Substance Use Disorders
TIP 54	Managing Chronic Pain in Adults With or in Recovery From Substance Use Disorders
TIP 55	Behavioral Health Services for People Who Are Homeless
TIP 56	Addressing the Specific Behavioral Health Needs of Men
TIP 57	Trauma-Informed Care in Behavioral Health Services
TIP 58	Addressing Fetal Alcohol Spectrum Disorders (FASD)
TIP 59	Improving Cultural Competence
TIP 60	Using Technology-Based Therapeutic Tools in Behavioral Health Services
TIP 63	Medications for Opioid Use Disorder

Upcoming TIPs

TIP 61	Behavioral Health Services for American Indians and Alaska Natives
TIP 62	Relapse Prevention and Recovery Promotion in Behavioral Health Services

CPSIA information can be obtained
at www.ICGtesting.com
Printed in the USA
BVHW012158161020
591030BV00015B/1121